D0713508

CALGARY PUBLIC LIBRARY

JAN - - 2009

SHAKESPEARE'S WOMEN

David Mann examines the influence of the Elizabethan cross-dressed tradition on the performance and conception of Shakespeare's female roles through an analysis of all 205 extant plays written for the adult theatre. The study provides both a historical context, showing how performance practice developed in the era before Shakespeare, and a comparative one, in revealing how dramatists in general treated their female characters and the influence their characterisation had upon Shakespeare's writing. The book challenges current views of the sexual ethos of Elizabethan theatre, offering instead a picture of Shakespeare which pays less attention to his supposed gender politics and more to his ability to exploit the cross-dressed convention as a dramatic medium. The late-adolescent performer identified here, more capable of empathy, perhaps, than the received version of the 'boy actress' but often mockingly satirical, was ultimately, Mann argues, disengaged from the roles he played and a spokesman for the male point of view.

DAVID MANN has directed, designed and acted in many theatrical productions and was in charge of Drama and Theatre Studies at Huddersfield University. He is the author of *The Elizabethan Player: Contemporary Stage Representations* (1991) and has also published several articles and reviews.

Placed In Memory Of

Elizabeth Heimbecker

CALGARY PUBLIC LIBRARY
FOUNDATION

SHAKESPEARE'S WOMEN

Performance and Conception

DAVID MANN

CAMBRIDGE
UNIVERSITY PRESS

CAMBRIDGE UNIVERSITY PRESS
Cambridge, New York, Melbourne, Madrid, Cape Town, Singapore, São Paulo

Cambridge University Press
The Edinburgh Building, Cambridge CB2 8RU, UK

Published in the United States of America by Cambridge University Press, New York

www.cambridge.org
Information on this title: www.cambridge.org/9780521882132

© David Mann 2008

This publication is in copyright. Subject to statutory exception
and to the provisions of relevant collective licensing agreements,
no reproduction of any part may take place without
the written permission of Cambridge University Press.

First published 2008

Printed in the United Kingdom at the University Press, Cambridge

A catalogue record for this publication is available from the British Library

ISBN 978-0-521-88213-2 hardback

Cambridge University Press has no responsibility for
the persistence or accuracy of URLs for external or
third-party internet websites referred to in this book,
and does not guarantee that any content on such
websites is, or will remain, accurate or appropriate.

To my wife Carole and daughters Miranda and Eleanor

Contents

Tables and illustrations

(Figures 3–8 and 11 by Inigo Jones from the Devonshire Collection, Chatsworth, reproduced by permission of the Duke of Devonshire and the Trustees of the Chatsworth Settlement. Photographs: Photographic Survey, Courtauld Institute of Art. Figures 1 and 2, 9 and 10 by Carole Mann)

Preliminary: the persistence of all-male theatre

Why were there no women on the Elizabethan public stage? This book is about the original performers of Shakespeare's female roles and how they, and the possibilities and limitations of the representational tradition in which they worked, may have influenced his conception. We do not know for certain any of the individuals concerned but we do know they were all male. To our society it seems odd if not perverse to have excluded women from playing their own gender. It is appropriate, therefore, to begin by considering why, in England at least, it was not acceptable for women to appear on the public stage until after the Restoration in 1660.

There is evidence of their widespread use in the earlier periods of theatre in other European countries, although mainly in non-speaking roles. The silent figure of the 'very beautiful girl who looks after Zeus's thunderbolts for him' in Aristophanes' *The Birds*, and becomes Peisthetaerus's prize at the end of the play, may well have been played by a woman. Women were prominent in the Roman *Mime* tradition. In the princely Renaissance spectacles women danced, sang, and posed naked. On the Continent it seems to have become acceptable for women to perform in religious plays by the thirteenth century, as well as in aristocratic imitations of New Comedy by the early sixteenth. The first professional actress recorded in France appears to have been in 1545.[1] Italian actresses performed before Henry II and Catherine de' Medici at Lyons in 1548, and at about the same time they seem to have become established in their native country when the first permanent theatres housing regular companies were opened. Spain eventually followed suit by the end of the century. Actresses appeared on the Dutch stage at its inception in 1655. Only the Papal States resisted the spread of women longer than England, and cross-dressing was still in operation in Rome when Goethe visited in 1788.

In England the evidence of women performing in public before 1660 is uncertain. Robert Busse, Abbot-elect of Tavistock, was accused in 1324 of giving away valuable trinkets 'to actors, *actresses*, whores and other loose

and disreputable persons' (my emphasis).[2] There is some debate as to
whether the Wives of Chester performed or merely organised the
Assumption of the Virgin in the town's Corpus Christi Cycle. In respect of
the Elizabethan and Jacobean public stage most of the recent evidence of
female performance offered by scholars refers to activities other than acting
(such as singing, dancing, or posing), and these outside conventional
theatre; or it relates to amateur, mostly courtly, activities where the propri-
eties depended not only on the extent to which they were private but also
whether they took place in Whitehall or in the provinces, along with some
greater freedom for younger performers; or it relates to foreign touring
companies, as may be the case in Thomas Coryat's reference to female
performance, 'I have heard that it hath been sometimes used in London.'[3]
Only a single reference by Richard Madox in 1583 seems to offer the
possibility of direct evidence:

> went to the theater to see a scurvie play set out al by one virgin, which there proved
> a fyemarten without voice, so that we stayed not the matter.

Mrs Colman in *The Siege of Rhodes* in 1656 is generally cited as the first
British actress, but it was not until 1660 that women began to appear
regularly, a practice formalised by Charles II in his patent of two years later,
and much encouraged by him; as Cibber put it so delicately of the new
recruits to the stage, 'more than one of them had charms sufficient at their
leisure hours to mollify the cares of Empire'. It is fair to say, however, that
by 1660 attitudes to gender and its representation as well as the content of
plays had changed and the English practice of all-male performance was
widely seen to be anachronistic. Charles had visited George Jolly's English
touring company in Frankfurt in 1655 which incorporated actresses, probably German ones, and the Court in exile had plenty of opportunity during
the Interregnum to become familiar with the practice in France, and
included at different times both Killigrew and Davenant, the two subsequent Restoration managers. There was briefly some resistance in England
from the established actors, hurrying to re-form for the King's return
and recruiting new male actors to play the female roles, but this was soon
overcome, although for a short period both men and women played
female roles.

Madox says of the woman he saw on the stage that she lacked a 'voice'.
This might mean her voice did not carry in an open amphitheatre. Certain
registers are more difficult to hear out-of-doors. On the other hand, it
might mean her voice was untrained. One reason adduced for using boys
rather than women was because boys had opportunities to be trained in

singing and oratory that women lacked, and dramatic verse, far from being everyday speech, was a highly wrought form deemed to require such training.[4] Related to this was widespread illiteracy amongst women, which would make learning parts more difficult; less than 10 per cent of women could read, and most could not even write their names.[5] It did not, however, prevent, for instance, a young woman playing the title role in the *Mystère de St Catherine* at Metz in 1468, and it scarcely explains the variation of practice between the different countries.[6]

One factor that might have some bearing on the absence of women from the Elizabethan stage was the acknowledged quality of English male performance, developed over a period of a hundred years of professional playing. Visitors to Europe comment unfavourably not only on the morals but also on the standard of acting they found there, as Thomas Nashe:

Our Players are not as the players beyond Sea, a sort of squirting bawdie Comedians, that haue whores and common Curtizens to playe womens partes, and forbeare no immodest speech or vnchaste action that may procure laughter . . .

Thomas Coryat is surprised at the quality of Italian actresses when he visits Venice in 1608, that 'they performed . . . with as good a grace, action, gesture, and whatsoever convenient for a Player, as ever I saw any masculine Actor'. Not only does Nashe contrast the quality of the performers between the two countries but also their dramatic fare:

our Sceane more statelye furnisht than euer it was in the time of *Roscius*, our representations honourable, and full of gallant resolution, not consisting like theirs of a Pantaloun, a Whore, and a Zanie, but of Emperours, Kings and Princes; whose true Tragedies (*Sophocleo cothurno*) they do vaunt.

Michael Shapiro offers a series of practical reasons for continuing to use male performers to represent women on the English as distinct from the Continental stage: 'such factors as protection of male employment, the maintenance of recruitment and training systems already in place, the lack of a pool of potential actresses, and the relative advantages and disadvantages of touring with women'.[7] Another reason may well have been the developing role of theatre in a distinctive Protestant bourgeois culture. The Tudor moralities of the early itinerant professional troupes, influenced by the Medieval mystery cycles of the proto-bourgeois city guilds, developed an aesthetic of profit and pleasure in which didacticism was conceived as an inherent part and the drama's chief social justification (and in this context it is particularly unhelpful to apply the term 'Renaissance' to a drama that has its roots so firmly in the Middle Ages.) It was not a long step from generating plays to lecture one social group, the young, in the late hybrid educational moralities, to the targeting of another, the female spectator.

Shorn of traditional certainties and in a society experiencing rapid social and economic change, this developing culture shows evidence of considerable anxiety about the emerging 'problem' of women. Jean Howard stresses the extent to which the sixteenth century was concerned with controlling women because of the destructive consequences of their sexual appetites.[8] 'The disciplining and restraint of women increased during this period', she says, 'particularly where economic change was most rapid and changes in family form most pronounced.' Furthermore, there was an 'outpouring of books on housewifery and female piety after the 1580s', and it is arguable that, at least in the hands of some dramatists, theatre became an extension of that process. Puritanism was a broad movement and whilst it is often associated with the anti-theatricalists, it also embraced, as Margot Heinemann has shown, many of the theatre practitioners too.[9] Although Howard later argues that the theatre was often a site for challenges to hegemonic attitudes rather than merely a means of disseminating them,[10] nonetheless an inspection of the surviving canon of plays reveals just how far the theatre of the late 1590s and the early years of the seventeenth century was hijacked by Heywood, Dekker, and their considerable penumbra to serve the ends of the bourgeois culture's anxiety about women, and chapter 4 below shows the extent of this movement. With female characters carefully crafted to show models of good behaviour and the dangers of sexual transgression, it might well have been assumed that the cross-dressed tradition was essential for their effective transmission. Only an experienced male actor, it might be argued, could adequately portray the impossible virtue of a Patient Griselda or the monstrous concupiscence of a Lucretia Borgia. An actress, as now, could only have humanised them, and that would have taken away from their didactic intent.

As well as practical reasons for the continuance of all-male playing, there also appears to have been a series of rooted objections to the concept of female performance.

'PLAYING THE WOMAN'S PART'

There is a complex web of meanings around this single phrase. Not all the uses of the term are hostile. Some in Shakespeare are merely descriptive. In *The Two Gentlemen of Verona*, IV.iv.158f., Julia, pretending to be a page, tells her new mistress that she as a youth once played 'the woman's part' in a play as Ariadne lamenting her abandonment by Theseus so that it reduced her former mistress to tears, perhaps with some suggestion of it being a woman's natural place to grieve. Similarly in *Twelfth Night*, I.iv, Orsino urges Viola's youth, 'all semblative of a woman's part', as making Cesario a suitable messenger, whose smooth lip and light voice Olivia will find persuasive, but in combination with the masculine boldness that Orsino requires in representing his unrequited love: 'Be clamorous and leap all civil bounds.'

More significantly, however, in terms of its range of meaning, Posthumus in *Cymbeline*, believing his wife to be unfaithful, uses the same phrase to assert the definitive woman's role as dissembling whore:

> It is the woman's part: be it lying, note it,
> The woman's; flattering, hers; deceiving, hers;
> Lust and rank thoughts, hers; hers revenges, hers;
> Ambitions, covetings, change of prides, disdain,
> Nice longing, slanders, mutability . . .   (II.v.22–6)[11]

Women in this vision are not divided into chaste and lascivious, but either are frank in their lasciviousness or use a show of virtue to conceal it, and this seems to have been the assumption behind much male stage representation of the female from the earliest times. A ninth-century epitaph thought to be to the mime Vitalis, and put into his mouth, in celebrating his versatility draws attention to his imitation of the mask of female modesty:

> How oft did they laugh to see, as I mimicked a dainty wife,
> My gestures so womanly quaint, the shy blush done to the life![12]

Thomas Godwin in *Romanae Historiae Anthologiae*, 1606, compares the Roman mime to the clowns of his own day who 'go a tip-toe in derision of the mincing dames'.[13] *King Lear* provides a third version of the same topos:

> Behold yond simp'ring dame,
> Whose face between her forks presages snow;
> That minces virtue, and does shake the head
> To hear of pleasure's name –

Her virtue is pretence. Only her face announces chastity. Beneath the waist:

> is all the fiends': there's hell, there's darkness,
> There's the sulphurous pit, burning, scalding,
> Stench, consumption.   (IV.vi.118f.)

Both 'playing' and 'part' could, of course, be given even more overtly sexual meanings. It is from the period immediately before the closure of the theatres in 1642, when direct comparisons with established theatres using actresses in France, Italy, and Spain generated an increasing awareness of what the English theatre was being denied, and moreover whilst such change was still being resisted, that the most deeply held prejudices against female performers emerged. In a poem published by Randolph in 1638, the poet, seeking to answer why the elderly Lesbia should so indulge her lover, the play-boy Histrio, concludes:

> Then this I can no better reason tell;
> 'Tis 'cause he playes the womans part so well.[14]

Randolph goes on to describe what hard work it is to satisfy her sexual demands. Hence 'Playing the woman's part' now combines a pun on the young man's profession with a third sense, the stimulation of the female genitalia. This then is the undertow of two other references in the 1630s to female actresses. Brome's *Court Beggar* performed in 1632 contains the passage (v.ii): 'the boy's a pretty Actor; and his mother can play her part; women-Actors now grow in request'; and in Shirley's *The Ball*, also 1632, a foolish character describing the French theatre says: 'Yet the women are the best actors, they play / Their own parts, a thing much desir'd in England by some ladies, Inns-o'-Court gentlemen and others.' This sentiment, Elizabeth Howe suggests, put into the mouth of a buffoon, is Shirley's way of 'mocking those who favour the idea of actresses and inviting his audience to join him'.[15]

Thus for a woman to 'play' her own 'part' means that she achieves her climax by herself, and in doing so annexes what is by right the male prerogative. A 'woman-actor' is a contradiction, a cross-gender enormity, for a woman does not *act*, she is *acted upon* and for her to 'act', either by taking the sexual initiative or by performing on the stage, is to transgress her assigned role in the scheme of things, hence the association with the prostitute who presumes to take charge of her own sexuality and dispose of it as she chooses.

The association of actresses and prostitution goes back as far as actresses can be traced. In ancient China they were officially classed as courtesans. In ancient Rome, until the *mima* Theodora married the Emperor Justinian c. AD 521, the *mimae* were forced to strip and perform naked at the Florialia, and could not renounce their profession, a fate passed on to their children. There was plenty of gossip in the sixteenth century to support Nashe's gibes at Continental actresses. Talleman des Reaux said of the early French companies: 'They were nearly all rascals and their women lived with great licentiousness', and 'were common property . . . amongst the members of the company'. Lupercio reported to Philip of Spain in 1598 that the actress currently playing the Virgin in Madrid was living as the mistress of St Joseph, which apparently caused some mirth during the performance of the *Annunciation*. The Spanish seemed to have found it particularly difficult to adjust to the use of women onstage. A Jesuit writing in 1589, shortly after their first introduction, notes:

> The low women who ordinarily act are beautiful, lewd, and have bartered their virtue, and with gestures and movements of the whole body, and with voices bland and suave, with beautiful costumes, like sirens they charm and transform men into beasts to lure them the more easily to destruction as they themselves are the more wicked and lost to every sense of virtue.[16]

Women were found so disturbing that they were banned again in 1596 and replaced by boys, but reintroduced in 1600. Madox in the sole testimony to a woman on the Elizabethan stage describes her as a 'virgin' and a 'fye-marten', both cant terms for prostitute.[17] Did she perform because she was a prostitute or was she deemed so because she performed?

The repulsion as well as the fascination expressed in Elizabethan plays towards the loose woman's sexual aggressiveness (discussed in chapter 5) lies in her putting the man into the passive position. Meretrix in *Cambises*, 1561, demonstrates this when she offers herself for auction to the highest bidder:

HUF: But hear'st thou, Meretrix? With who this night wilt thou lie?
MERETRIX: With him that giveth the most money.
RUF: . . . I will give thee sixpence to lie one night with thee.
MERETRIX: Gog's heart, slave, dost thou think I am a sixpenny jug?
            No, 'wis, ye jack, I look a little more smug.
SNUF: I will give her eighteen pence to serve me first.
MERETRIX: Gramercy, Snuf, thou are not the worst.   (lines 2445–55)

This sets the three soldiers into a quarrel over her, which she resolves by belabouring them with her staff. The others run away and eventually only Ruf is left: '*He falleth down; she falleth upon him, and beats him, and taketh away his weapon.*' She then completes his humiliation by making him go before her as her usher. Her pugnacity is of a piece with her promiscuity. Such behaviour is seen as unnatural, a reversal of roles; hence the recurring motif of the she-wolves and adulteresses who attempt to force men, always unsuccessfully in these plays, to have sex with them. It falls appropriately to Thomas Heywood to provide the definitive rebuke to the woman who takes the sexual initiative: 'men couet not / These proffered pleasures; but loue-sweets deny'd' – so Adonis replies to the forwardness of Venus in

The Brazen Age, part of Heywood's bourgeoisification of classical myth, when she attempts to reverse conventional roles:

VENUS: Why doth *Adonis* flye the Queene of loue? . . .
         Come, let vs tumble on this violet banke:
         Pre'thee be wanton; let vs toy and play,
         Thy icy fingers warme betweene my breasts . . .
ADONIS: This loosenesse makes you foul in *Adons* eye . . .   (II.ii)

Heywood, however, is not being entirely frank. 'Looseness' could on occasion be highly attractive. As Simone de Beauvoir says: 'Man does not devote himself wholly to the Good . . . he retains shameful lines of communication with the Bad'.[18] Despite the widespread determination to make Elizabethan plays improving experiences for the female spectators, the presentation of whores in these plays matches in frequency that of the Good Woman and provides a compensatory erotic interest for the inevitable tedium involved in the presentation of female purity.

Before leaving the 'woman's part', it has one further set of important associations. While in its first use by Posthumus quoted above it carried the sense of 'role', it is also perceived in his misogynist raving in the same passage, like Jung's concept of *anima*, as part of the male psyche, the feminine element in man, which presumably Posthumus would like to expunge:

> Could I find out
> The woman's part in me – for there's no motion
> That tends to vice in man, but I affirm
> It is the woman's part . . .   (*Cymbeline*, II.v.19–22)

This may go some way towards explaining the extreme ambivalence with which the male performer treats, and the male spectator receives, the female role: part condemnation and part fascination; part self-display, perhaps, but also part self-exorcism?

Introduction: the significance of the performer

At the end of *The Taming of the Shrew* Petruchio commands Katherine to tell the other wives what duty they owe their husbands. This prompts a forty-four line speech stressing the need for women to accept their husbands as lords and masters:

> Such a duty as the subject owes the prince,
> Even such a woman oweth to her husband;
> And when she is froward, peevish, sullen, sour,
> And not obedient to his honest will,
> What is she but a foul contending rebel,
> And graceless traitor to her loving lord?   (v.ii. 155–60)

It ends with Kate offering to put her hand beneath her husband's foot. Few dramatic moments have received so much attention, or led to so many interpretations.

Most modern critics find the notion of Kate's submission unacceptable, especially by so obsequious a gesture, and tend to suggest instead some sense of playfulness in which Kate delivers the speech in an ironic tone. Some argue that Kate is being insincere in order to deceive Petruchio. Harold Goddard suggests it is a case of 'What Every Woman Knows', namely that a wife gains her supremacy in marriage by making the man think that he is in charge.[1] According to Coppélia Kahn, Kate protects her 'intellectual freedom' by 'deluding' her husband.[2] Other critics take the view that it is Shakespeare who does not mean it, either because he is satirising the patriarchy, Petruchio's taming being a mockery of male prejudice and wish-fulfilment,[3] or because the convention in which he wrote by its nature releases the author from meaning what he says. H. J. Oliver would have it that:

9

The lecture by Kate on the wife's duty to submit is the only fitting climax *to the farce* – and for that very reason it cannot logically be taken seriously, orthodox though the views expressed may be.[4]

He takes the view that Shakespeare was in the process of remoulding the wife-beating tradition to make it more sympathetic to women. Similarly, to John Bean the play constitutes 'the emergence of a humanised heroine against a background of depersonalized farce unassimilated from the play's fabliau sources'.[5]

The most popular view, however, amongst those critics who take an optimistic view of the play is that Petruchio does not believe in wifely submission either.[6] Margaret Ranald claims that:

Shakespeare has skilfully remoulded his material to portray an atypical Elizabethan attitude towards marriage through the development of a matrimonial relationship in which mutuality, trust, and love are guiding forces.[7]

It is a shared burlesque of inequality by two equals. Petruchio, having guided his new wife to an understanding of mutuality, is thus no longer a male chauvinist breaking her will, but a benevolent psychiatrist who has brought his wife to sanity using, says Ranald, 'subtlety, art, reason, and love'. According to Hugh Richmond:

[Kate's] beating of the bound Bianca (II.i.21) is obviously pathological; and even her wit has a strain of physical violence (II.i.220f.) which implies a mind close to breakdown. Thus ... her disintegrating personality seems to justify almost any kind of shock therapy ...[8]

Bean regards the process of Petruchio's taming as containing:

a consistent pattern of romantic elements ... that show Kate's discovery of her inward self through her discovery first of play and then of love. ... Thus Kate is tamed not by Petruchio's whip but by the discovery of her own imagination ... the liberating power of laughter and play.

By the end, according to Richmond, 'Katharina ... displays all the signs of recovered mental health', and the ultimate indication that Kate is fully 'cured' is that she is able to laugh at herself.

Why critics should want to reach these conclusions is all too obvious. They are determined to save the play from attacks such as those of the theatre critics Michael Billington, who argues that such a 'totally offensive' work 'should be put back firmly and squarely on the shelf', and Harold Hobson, who described the play as 'dull, brutal, ill-written, and indecent'.[9] Only by making the play and its author conform with modern views about gender relations will they preserve it for performance and enable its continued use as a prescribed text for study. It is not so easy, however, to see *how* they could have reached such conclusions, in despite of what the play so obviously says about Petruchio's mercenary motives and his violent methods, combining associations of breaking the will of an animal with what are for us the sensory deprivations of mind-bending, such that finally Kate will agree that the sun is the moon if that is what he demands of her.

In order to prove that Kate's final speech does not mean what it so evidently says, the optimistic critics have to show some evidence of a process of gradual yielding, and some sort of growing rapport between the two. Even her speech of acquiescence in their penultimate scene (IV.v.17–22), however, directly before the sequence under discussion, in suggesting Petruchio is insane, still has more than a hint of truculence: 'And the moon changes even as your mind.' Hence it remains difficult to plot any clear path to her obedience or enlightenment, and critics who elsewhere would assert the primacy of the text in determining meaning are reduced to introducing a non-authorial quizzicalness, as Ranald:

All she need do is indicate by a question in her voice her mischievous doubt as to which, sun or moon, is shining. Now Kate has outsmarted Petruchio, but her method shows her advancement in civilized subtlety by her use of the private joke they share.

'Subtlety' is perhaps the last thing to be expected from this play. In the same way, Kahn, in the absence of anything more direct, says Shakespeare 'just makes it clear to us, through the contextual irony of Kate's last speech, that his mastery is an illusion'. Shakespeare thus exposes the male 'wish for dominance', she says, 'as an idle dream'. More than one kind of irony, however, is possible here.

All these interpretations purport to explain the original play, rather than merely putting a modern gloss on it, but even where they rely on gesture or intonation to counter what the words themselves actually say, i.e. on the performer, *none of them takes cognizance of the original performance context*. Once this is factored in, it becomes very questionable whether an *all-male* company would favour a sympathetic feminist heroine, especially at the expense of upstaging the leading player. With nearly three times as many lines as Katherine, it is extremely unlikely the performance ambience would allow Petruchio to be relegated to the supporting 'stereotype' that Kahn envisages, 'animated', she suggests, 'like a puppet by the *idée fixe* of male dominance'. It is surely much more likely that performer-irony, had it existed, communicated not a recognition of an underlying mutuality between Petruchio and Kate, nor a lambasting of the patriarchy, but a rueful recognition that the conclusion of the play *was* indeed a fantasy of male wish-fulfilment, but one that was not 'childish' or despicable but highly desirable: if only women could be tamed so in real life and male dominance assured! This is certainly the import of all the numerous plays derived from it, and in particular John Fletcher's sequel, *The Woman's Prize, or the Tamer Tam'd*, 1611, in which Petruchio marries again and the tables are turned on him. In that play Kate and Petruchio's subsequent married life, imagined to have taken place between the two plays, is described as having been one of her constant rebellion, scolding, and violence. In Lacy's version, *Sauny the Scott*, 1667, the Petruchio-figure threatens to flog his wife and completes her cure by pretending she is dead and tying her to a bier. She sounds to have been a fairly unsympathetic character, announcing that, 'I have a good mind to marry him to try if he can tame me.' Garrick's influential version published in 1756 has her finally submit in a speech which leaves little scope for irony even when delivered by an actress:

> Nay, then I am all unworthy of thy Love,
> And look with Blushes on my former self.

If the anonymous *Taming of a Shrew* is a redaction or Bad Quarto of Shakespeare's play, then it too assumes the same moral and has Sly go home to practise it on his wife. While critics can argue that Shakespeare modified or even challenged the crudities of earlier taming plays, it is much more difficult to resist the testimonies of *subsequent* versions without somehow suggesting Shakespeare's plays are coded messages that have baffled intervening centuries and have been waiting for the present day to be unravelled.

The suppression of the performer

How could it be that the original performers of the roles could have disappeared so completely from critical awareness as to produce interpretations of Shakespeare's plays so clearly at variance with their existence? Some of the reasons are obviously historical. The cross-dressed tradition survived Shakespeare effectively for only twenty-six years. Since actresses were introduced almost immediately after the Interregnum and have played his roles ever since, inevitably the theatre-based associations of the women's roles are more or less exclusively female. While actresses began as creatures of a salacious Court and in a theatre that openly exploited their sexuality, it was not long before, in a politer society, an altogether different set of associations emerged. Mary Hamer charts the development from the middle of the eighteenth century of a way of playing Rosalind, for instance, that involved 'the idealisation of the feminine' as an exemplum of 'bright, tender, loyal womanhood', which stressed the character's 'tenderness', 'charm' and 'enchantment', but rested on the actress's 'willingness to display her femininity in a particularly appealing and unthreatening way' so that it became 'the seduction of the audience'.[10] By 1832 Shakespeare's women were being taken as accurate depictions, indeed vindications, of the female sex, as Anna Jameson presented them in her immensely popular *Shakespeare's Heroines: Characteristics of Women, Moral, Political and Historical*, which, aided by expurgated editions of his plays following on from Henrietta Maria Bowdler's 'Family' Shakespeare (first published in 1807 under her brother's name), led the Victorians to offer his characters as models of female behaviour. Mary Cowden Clarke, author of *The Girlhood of Shakespeare's Heroines* (1851), tells the reader of *Girls Own Paper* (1887) that from Shakespeare's 'youthful women' she can:

gain lessons in artlessness, guilelessness, modesty, sweetness, ingenuousness and the most winning candour; from his wives and matrons she can derive instructions in moral courage, meekness, magnanimity, firmness, devoted tenderness, high principle, noble conduct, loftiest speech and sentiment.[11]

The only exception to the playing of Shakespeare's female roles by actresses, apart from the experiments of William Poel between 1881 and 1905, has been in their late nineteenth- and early twentieth-century amateur performance in schools. This has led to a sub-stratum of criticism which in the process of safeguarding morality and propriety and aided by the writings of Mrs Jameson and others stresses the asexual purity of both female role and juvenile performer. Inevitably this became a model for how the Elizabethan cross-dressed tradition is supposed to have operated which survived unchallenged until more recent developments in the sexual politics of criticism and still has its adherents.[12] One consequence of the critical popularity of the 'boy actress' perhaps was that by 1910 there was a growing consciousness amongst thinking women of the female characters as male constructs. To Dorothy Richardson, 'There was no reality in any of Shakespeare's women. They please men because they show women as men see them', whilst Virginia Woolf in 1920 opined, 'it is daily more evident that Lady Macbeth, Cordelia, Ophelia ... and the rest are by no means what they pretend to be. Some are plainly men in disguise; others represent what men would like to be, or are conscious of not being.' In envisioning a vehicle for the poetry which involves no interposing of personality between the words and their reception, Granville Barker's 'boy actress' provided critics with a valuable tool by which to separate off play-text from performance, but with the unfortunate consequence that, as well as lambasting contemporary actresses and falsifying the nature of Elizabethan theatre, it has radically lowered estimates of its general effectiveness. Sidney Lee in 1906 observed: 'it seems almost sacrilegious to submit Cleopatra's sublimity of passion to interpretation by an unfledged representative of the other sex.' Thus for many Shakespearean scholars too much attention to the all-male performance tradition would jeopardise the seriousness of their enterprise.

There were further reasons too for reticence in this quarter. At the end of the nineteenth century, as the passive purity of Shakespeare's women was being extolled by critics and artfully represented by schoolboys and actresses alike, a new pseudo-science was emerging, 'Sexology', in which deviancy was being identified and classified, and some might say invented. Although as part of this process, 'Eonism', as transvestitism was then called, was explained as a 'sexual–aesthetic *inversion*' of heterosexuality,[13] nonetheless in the popular imagination all such 'perversions' were lumped together under the same general heading and associated with homosexuality, which now came under sustained and increasingly open attack. The *North London Press* referred to it in 1889 as 'indescribably loathsome'.[14] When Robertson Davies attempted the first full-length account of Shakespeare's cross-dressed performers in 1939, it contained a severe attack on homosexuals in the theatre of his own time together with a fulsome account of William Prynne's charges against the Elizabethans which Davies in large part accepts. As late as 1955 Lord Hailsham was still warning that homosexuality was 'as much a moral and social issue as heroin addiction'.

Nonetheless, from being an aberration, homosexuality had by now become all but a separate gender, and the long-term consequences had to be the repeal of laws against it, its increasing prominence in society, and the acceptance of legal equality. In 1958 the Lord Chamberlain allowed its discussion on the stage.[15] New York State followed suit in 1965. In 1967 British law permitted homosexual relations between consenting adults in private, and in the following year formal censorship ceased.

Paradoxically, despite an apparent increase in general permissiveness in this period, reaction against this change in the sexual map, especially as Alfred Kinsey's claims with respect to its widespread occurrence filtered into the popular consciousness, brought with it ever more prescriptive gender roles within mainstream heterosexuality. This is very evident, for instance, in the abandonment of the experiment in male narcissism which had followed on from the Beatles and the Rolling Stones, Carnaby Street and King's Road, when long hair and bright colours, high heels and flowered shirts, kipper ties and tight pants, had swept the entire nation's youth, and then disappeared just as abruptly into the present unkempt and monochrome fashions of male attire with their self-consciously gender-specific associations of brutality and laddishness. At the same time, partly because of confusions between transvestitism and homosexuality, an undertow of suspicion grew towards any kind of male gender ambiguity, especially cross-dressing. As early as 1948, the year of the Kinsey Report, all-male school performances had ceased at Stephen Orgel's school in New York because, as his teacher later explained, they were thought to make boys into 'pansies'.[16] In a social climate in the 1960s in which American boys as young as three years old suspected of 'effeminacy' were being sent to gender re-orientation clinics,[17] whilst British youths were being subjected to aversion therapy, and an increasing number of plays on both sides of the Atlantic turned on the revelation or imputation of homosexuality,[18] any genuinely honest critical discussion of Elizabethan cross-dressing would have been regarded as teetering on the edge of condoning a dangerous, possibly contagious, immorality, a brush that would all too easily tar the critic himself. Nor was the problem eased by the tendency amongst more extreme feminist writers to label the patriarchy and all its transactions as 'homosexual' or at the very least 'homosocial'.[19] 'For us today', says Alan Sinfield, writing in 1996: 'homosexuality polices the entire boundaries of gender and social organisation . . . . Male–male relations, and hence male–female relations, are held in place by fear of homosexuality . . . Fear even of thinking homosexually serves to hold it all in place . . .'[20] Hence the academic vacuum thus created in respect of the implications of the original performance of the female roles has been left for hostile feminist and then gay and homophilic critics to fill, with the, perhaps inevitable, conse-quence, explored below in chapter 2, that Elizabethan theatre has come to be found gay and homophilic too.[21] It is perhaps not surprising, there-fore, that literary criticism in general has continued instead to operate within the theatre-of-the-mind, peopled by more elevated female charac-ters than such performance circumstances might allow.

Female characters and gender politics

Thus it was that when feminist critics turned to Shakespeare, the gains that had been made by Richardson and Woolf were thrown aside and many chose to ignore the earlier insights into Shakespeare's women as the artificial products of an all-male theatre in favour of taking the female characters as real people capable of psychological analysis and, above all, in need of defence.

The collection of feminist essays on Shakespeare, *The Woman's Part*, 1983, clearly preferred its female characters to be 'real' because, as its Introduction makes clear, its intentions were to pursue 'the struggle for women to be human in a world which declares them only female'. Gayle Greene exonerates Cressida, who 'reminds us of the effects of capitalism on women',[22] and in a widespread misunderstanding about the nature of stage dialogue, Rebecca Smith would have Gertrude as other than Hamlet and the Ghost describe her, as if the characters could somehow have an existence separate from what was said about them.[23] The book's contributors set out to liberate imaginary characters not only from critical misinterpretations but also from Shakespeare too, as Paula Berggren, talking of Imogen, Viola, and Rosalind:

When the disguises donned for protection expose them instead to unexpected danger, the heroines stand their ground as males despite the onrush of that stereotype 'feminine' apprehension with which Shakespeare seems to signal their forthcoming return to their true selves.[24]

Quite how Rosalind's fainting could be called 'standing her ground' is difficult to see; nor Viola, who, aware of the 'little thing' she lacks, prays for God to defend her. Berggren takes no account of the male performers, whose 'maleness', of course, as these examples show, is precisely what they would hope to conceal by exaggerating their character's femininity *especially* when in breeches.

The Woman's Part is only one of many such exercises in which even the she-wolves have their crimes shuffled off. Irene Dash dismisses the unnatural crimes of Queen Margaret in *Henry VI* with scarcely more than a tinge of censure: 'Unfortunately Margaret has assimilated patriarchal values.' To Paula Berggren, 'Lady Macbeth . . . is caught in a web that crippled women in a paternalistic society', which seems a strange defence for a woman who so much takes the initiative; whilst Coppélia Kahn argues Macbeth's wife attempts to mould him because, like Volumnia, it is 'the only power their cultures allow them'. Only finally does such defence become self-evidently unsupportable when it reaches *King Lear*. 'Are there any women in *King Lear*?' asks Ann Thompson. The unspoken answer is surely, 'No', and she cites Kathleen McLuskie: 'Feminism cannot simply take the "woman's part" when that part has been so morally loaded and theatrically circumscribed',[25] a judgement that applies equally, one would have thought, to all the aforementioned characters.

Much of the problem, however, lies in the double bind that whilst a female character may be highly individualised, often so as to make a general defence seem from the point, her token position as the only woman in the scene, sometimes perhaps in the entire play, always leaves open the possibility of her being interpreted as representative of her sex. It is the nature of prejudice to generalise from the particular, so that whilst Gertrude may not have all the virtues that Smith and others ascribe to her, she has to be defended because Shakespeare, homing in once again on that central issue of the male inability to determine how women dispose of their sexuality, has Hamlet leap from her individual shortcomings to brand the whole of her sex: 'Frailty, thy name is woman.' Penny Gay may be right to counsel the 'determined actress' to fight to make her role 'the embodiment of a *particular* woman enclosed in a narrative that pretends to be universal', but nonetheless when Barrie Kyle attempts the same defence of his 1982 production of *The Taming of the Shrew*, appealing to its title, Gay will have none of his 'specious nonsense', as she puts it, sensing that, underneath, 'shrewishness' is a male charge against all her sex.[26]

It also needs to be recognised that such studies have to be set against several hundred years of male criticism in which the tone taken towards the female characters has sometimes been more negative even than that of the Elizabethans themselves. Cleopatra was a particular victim of this process. In a society increasingly dependent on the fruits of imperialism, and determined to maintain its veneer of moral probity, scholars were often less than sympathetic towards those who threatened either. Thus both English and American nineteenth-century productions of *Othello*, for instance, cast around for alternatives to presenting their hero as a blackamoor in favour of models that did not invoke the associations of the unenfranchised descendants of the slave trade. Salvini played him moustachioed and turbaned, Forbes-Robertson as an aquiline Moor, whilst Daniel Bandmann modelled his performance on a Hindu he had met with a 'slightly olive complexion' and 'noble bearing'.[27] Thus when critics turned to *Antony and Cleopatra* they too automatically identified with Antony as the sole protagonist, endorsing the Roman view of the play that it showed the corruption of an imperial ruler, 'the triple pillar of the world transform'd / Into a strumpet's fool', and great efforts were made to marginalise its heroine. Ignoring the evidence that Shakespeare had gone out of his way to amend Plutarch's unfavourable portrait of Cleopatra, critics attempted to discount the whole of the last act devoted to her noble death;[28] Robert E. Fitch had it that Act V is 'given over to the stark confrontation of pleasure and power . . .'. Others went further and, with evident distaste for the eroticised female, on Antony's death replaced him as the central focus of the conclusion with the next available male character. According to Daniel Stempel, 'the play ends, as it should, with the defeat and death of the rebel against order', and the final act, he says, 'shows us that Octavius is proof against the temptress'. The most popular view amongst critics, however, unwilling to let Antony go, was that he continues to be the rightful focus of attention even after his death. Julian Markels argued that Cleopatra 'now learns the lessons of Antony's life ... and by her loyalty to him confirms Antony's achieved balance of public and private values', and John Middleton Murry similarly talked of 'the mysterious transfusion of his royal spirit into the mind and heart of his fickle queen', whilst Peter Alexander saw the purpose of her suicide as enabling Cleopatra 'to vindicate her right to his devotion'. It is left to E. A. J. Honigmann, however, to transform the dramatic effects that had been created by Shakespeare in an all-male theatre as a positive tribute to womanhood and heterosexuality into a virtual diatribe of misogyny:

Showmanship, we quickly learn, means as much to Cleopatra as love. We often wonder whether she is interested in love for its own sake, or whether she merely needs it as a pretext for posing in amusing new attitudes.[29]

It suits neither side in the application of sexual politics to Shakespeare's female characters to treat them as anything less than real three-dimensional people, and hence in need of condemnation or defence, but in the process their purpose as dramatic constructs disappears from view, as do the circumstances of performance which might reasonably be said to have a bearing on what the plays originally communicated. Some recent schools of criticism do promise a more historical approach, but often one that is heavily circumscribed, as with that of Lisa Jardine, for instance, who talks approvingly of 'Feminist Critique's insistence that its politics precede the encounter with the text – is part of the way of addressing the text.'[30] Jean Howard prefaces her study by announcing a Marxist, feminist, materialist credo, dismissing those who attempt objectivity as mere mouthpieces of the ruling hegemony. Unfortunately, the results of adopting an ideological position in advance can be extremely dull because however meticulously researched or strongly argued, it is so easy to anticipate their conclusions. 'Hegemony', of course, is rapidly becoming a charge that can be levelled at the new schools of criticism themselves, excellent at handing out negative criticism but noticeably less tolerant at receiving it.[31]

There is a strong sense too that all such studies that seek to apply the texts of the plays to some external end are from the point. 'The desire to give theatre a purpose', says David Cole, 'is a refusal of what theatre gives – of the theatrical event itself':

> Theatre does not *serve* a purpose; it *has* a purpose; to bring us into the presence of imaginative events … If someone does attempt to make theatre serve an extraneous purpose, theatre initiates a subtle resistance. It offers no overt opposition, but instead sets about re-channelling the energies and resources that are being siphoned off from it back to its own use.[32]

Hence the inherent paradox in all studies which attempt to attach serious arguments to a phenomenon as playful, childish, and self-absorbed as Theatre, trivial even in its most sensitive, thought-provoking paradigms of human experience, and which betrays all that it touches. However grand, tragic, and cathartic the events of an Elizabethan play, it is ephemeral; it only 'seems', and the afternoon's performance invariably ended with a bawdy jig.[33] To ignore theatre's often transgressive playfulness, with its roots in carnival release and the ritual temporary inversion of values, leads all too easily to solecisms like Coppélia Kahn's humourless judgement on the dialogue of the servants who open *Romeo and Juliet*, which, she says, 'links sexual intercourse with aggression and violence against women, rather than with pleasure and love', and claims to be representative of the ethos of the play.[34] She can only reach this conclusion by ignoring the earthy priapic quality of the servants' bawdy jests in a tradition in which clowns boast and urge others to copulate without doing so themselves, are very circumspect in actually fighting and pretend to do so only when they see their masters coming, and in both activities are meant to be contrasted with the virtue and sophistication of their social betters in the play. Locker-room talk apart, we see only one actual male–female relationship in the play, and that is one in which sexual intercourse is certainly not linked with aggression or violence.

Speaking to our own age

A modern production has a different set of responsibilities from those of the scholar. It has to speak directly to its audience in terms that it will understand, but also ones hopefully that will relate the past to the present, whilst remaining faithful to the received text. Hence when theatre directors turn to *The Taming of the Shrew* they are obliged to take account of current gender attitudes. In 1908 Margaret Anglin delivered Kate's final speech 'as if it were mere mockery – implying that it is hypocritical, a jest, secretly understood between Petruchio and his wife'.[35] In Mary Pickford's 1929 film with Douglas Fairbanks, a contemporary notice reports:

In the scene when Petruchio soliloquizes on how he is going to break Katherina's spirit and make her a dutiful wife, we see Mary eavesdropping. Audiences realize then that Mary is in complete control of the situation, and, just in case we miss the point, she gives us a big wink in the closing scene.[36]

The film included lots of comic and farcical business in a tradition much developed in the 1935 Broadway production with Alfred Lunt and Lynn Fontanne, which involved a 'band, a troupe of tumblers, a cluster of midgets, a pair of comic horses, and some fine songs set to good beer-garden music', a style somewhat reprised in Zeffirelli's 1966 film with Elizabeth Taylor and Richard Burton. At Stratford in 1953 with Yvonne Mitchell, and again in 1960 with Peggy Ashcroft, the taming was made acceptable by having Kate and Petruchio fall in love at first sight,[37] and as late as 1969 Janet Suzman interpreted the final speech as 'a paean to the secretiveness of real passion'.[38] Other techniques at this period to avoid its unpalatable message included setting the play in a nostalgic past as in John Barton's 1960 production, augmenting the Induction with material borrowed from the anonymous *Taming of A Shrew*, and making the whole thing into a comic dream. When in more recent productions the real nature of Petruchio's wooing became more evident, a darker tone prevailed, and with it, inevitably, new strains began to appear in attempts to harmonise the parts. In Bogdanov's 1978 production at Stratford, although Paola Dionisotti maintained the tradition of falling in love at the beginning, the final oration, according to a review in the *Times Literary Supplement* was 'delivered in a spiritless, unreal voice and received without appreciation by the men, and with smouldering resentment by the women'.[39] Meanwhile a 1974 Hungarian production ended with Kate broken and submissive, whilst a Turkish one in 1988 revealed that under her shawl in the final scene she had cut her veins.[40] All no doubt said something significant to their own societies at that moment in time.

Certainly old plays serve no function unless they speak to us, and in some sense in our own language, but must they always agree with us? Why do so many scholars still try to prove that Shakespeare held the same views as they do? It is a solecism that has grown to monstrous proportions since Coleridge first saw in Hamlet 'great, enormous, intellectual activity, and a consequent proportionate aversion to real action'. Radicals find Shakespeare challenging the *status quo*, pinning much on a few Roman mechanicals, gay critics find him debauching apprentices, others find him sympathetic to lesbian love or to chastity, to have a 'powerful matriarchal vision',[41] or a 'man–womanly mind'.[42] Even Juliet Dusinberre's misapprehension that 'the drama from 1590 to 1625 is feminist in sympathy' continues to find echoes in recent criticism; Alison Findlay, for instance, perceives the 'stirrings of a feminist consciousness in Renaissance England',[43] whilst to Irene Dash Juliet as written by Shakespeare seems 'to illustrate' (sic) Simone de Beauvoir; and indeed the frequency with which Dash cites Virginia Woolf and J. S. Mill rather suggests she thinks Shakespeare found them congenial reading too. The process is extending beyond Shakespeare so that Simon Shepherd for instance finds a quite remarkable correlation between his own views and those of a Marlowe who uses *Tamburlaine*, we are told, to 'problematize the male and masculinity'.[44] As Ann Thompson implies in discussing the need to continue to deal with 'what we do not like but recognise as nonetheless valuable, serious, good', it ought to be possible to accept differing views from our own as a valid contribution to what ought to be a genuine dialogue.[45]

Shakespeare and character sympathy

Critics who acknowledge this dialogue have no difficulty in identifying the basic orthodoxy which underlies Shakespeare's presentation of sexual conflict in *The Taming of the Shrew*.[46] It is perfectly true as the optimistic school points out that there was a new emphasis in humanist writing on a husband's responsibility to treat his wife well, but largely in his own interests and by way of ameliorating rather than abandoning her subordination, and the play makes no bones about using force to obtain that. In *The Comedy of Errors*, the Abbess, with the authority both of being a Good Wife and of resolving the plots, rebukes Adriana at some length for making her husband 'mad':

> The venom clamours of a jealous woman
> Poisons more deadly than a mad dog's tooth . . .   (v.i.69f.)

As it turns out, it is not Adriana but the plot that has confused her husband, but the condemnation is allowed to stand. Shakespeare reflects a society that regards shrewishness more severely than we do. That is why, despite all the animal imagery of taming which has so caught the imagination of some recent critics who make Kate the victim of barbarous cruelty, Petruchio's chief method, as Shakespeare clearly signals in Peter his servant's aside, is to copy the destructive characteristics of Kate's own shrewishness: 'He kills her in her own humor' (IV.i.180). By contradicting, jangling, stopping the partner from sleeping, and withdrawing creature comforts, including matrimonial ones, Petruchio shows how unacceptable such behaviour is. Erika

Gottlieb argues that a number of Shakespeare's plays, after some initial sympathy for those who challenge the accepted order of things, show that:

rebellion is shortsighted . . . equality may have disastrous consequences, destroying the security of order and harmony in the family circle, in the body politic, indeed in the whole cosmos . . . challenging . . . the ordering Intelligence beyond it all.[59]

Shakespeare's orthodoxy ought not, however, to be pressed too far. As chapter 4 will show, there was a broad consensus in Elizabethan dramaturgy on the dangers of assertive women and the need to warn others not to imitate them, which is in considerable measure reflected in Shakespeare's work. However, it is not clear when such sentiments are expressed in his plays how far they indicate an authorial point of view rather than being merely the assumptions that underlie the received material that Shakespeare is using, and, with his focus more on the theatrical than the political, he is perhaps less concerned to challenge than many of his supporters would wish him to be.

The optimistic interpretation of *The Taming of the Shrew*, that neither character really means Kate's final speech to be taken at its face value as an act of submission, is often justified as the only option which will make the play consistent with the rest of his canon, which critics see as being sympathetic to women. In fact, of course, similar views in favour of female submissiveness are to be found in *The Comedy of Errors* (II.i.15f.), and *The Merchant of Venice* (III.ii.157f.), and sympathy for women in his plays is a highly variable factor. Kate, far from being an exception in terms of Shakespeare's lack of concern, is by no means untypical. At the beginning of *Titus Andronicus* Lavinia is swapped between Saturninus and Bassianus with scant concern for her preferences. In *Measure for Measure* the Duke manipulates Isabella so that she is left mourning for the death of her brother even though he is still alive, and is then carried off to prison as a false accuser merely to give the denunciation of Angelo an edge and 'To make her heavenly comforts of despair, / When it is least expected'. In *A Midsummer Night's Dream* Hippolyta is wooed with a sword, and has apparently no complaints, whilst Titania, having been drugged into wooing and possibly being penetrated by an ass, when awakened is immediately reconciled to Oberon. At the end of *Much Ado* Hero accepts Claudio after all his cruelty, and without comment. At the end of *The Two Gentlemen of Verona* Silvia's willingness to marry Valentine is no whit impaired by his offering her to his friend who has just attempted to rape her. Play after play involves manipulating the female characters with scant concern for their feelings.

Such a recital could, of course, be matched by another revealing Shakespeare as insightful, libertarian, and sympathetic to many of his other young women. Why should one play, say *As You Like It*, seem so sensitive to the minutiae of a woman's feelings, and yet another, say *Julius Caesar*, be so cursory in its treatment? The answer surely is that it depends entirely on the focus of the play, which, with the exception of a small group of romantic comedies, is generally on the male characters, and always reflects the male point of view. Why, for instance, does Lady Anne succumb to Gloucester in *Richard III*? Logically there are very many reasons why she should not, given that he has just killed her husband and her father-in-law. In her defence she may be said to be particularly vulnerable and in a state of shock. But the principal level of concern is theatrical, and she constitutes little more than a property by which Gloucester's cleverness is demonstrated, as pointed in his intimate soliloquies with the audience which frame the scene. The extent to which she is vulnerable to flattery at once designates her as the unknowable other and places her and her sex on an inferior moral plane. As he says of Queen Elizabeth in the parallel scene in Act IV: 'Relenting fool, and shallow, changing woman!' (IV.iv.431).

Structurally important roles are often remarkably brief. Anne Page, the focus of three quite separate marriage plots in addition to her own elopement in *The Merry Wives of Windsor*, has just thirty-one lines. Juliet, for whose impregnation Claudio is condemned to death in *Measure for Measure*, receives even shorter shrift. Made to parade her advanced state of pregnancy in I.ii, she is said in II.ii to be in prison 'groaning', and in II.iii, told by the Duke that she is more to blame than Claudio, she spends the only ten lines she has in repentance. We never learn whether she had her child, though she may of course be holding it in the final scene.

Shakespeare is justly celebrated for his 'negative capability', what Norman Holland has called 'his astonishing power to understand the "other" and imagine stage characters at once like and unlike his real self'.[47] As Hazlitt observed, Shakespeare 'had only to think of anything in order to become that thing, with all the circumstances belonging to it'. Whereas this is often interpreted as evidence of Shakespeare's broad humanity, there is a case for seeing it rather merely in terms of its being part of his extraordinary dramatic technique. Empathy does not necessarily imply sympathy – as in the classic example of the snail. We may conceive of what it is like to slither along the ground, carrying a shell on our backs, withdrawing antennae at the sense of danger, but we may still feel no pity when we see it smashed upon a rock by a thrush. The amazing particularity with which Shakespeare invests his, broadly stereotypical, individuals by means of a remarkably sustained imaginative involvement with the minutiae of their thoughts and feelings is perhaps sometimes no more than his way of being theatrically exciting. It is technique, rather as Diderot says of the actor: 'He feels neither trouble, nor sorrow, nor depression, nor weariness of soul. All these emotions he has given to you'; hence the unevenness of Shakespeare's sympathies, called into play where the dramatic focus is appropriate, often at the promptings of his source, but equally absent where the character or the dramatic moment is subordinate to something else.

Even if Shakespeare had held and wished to express more radical views about gender equality, it is not at all clear that his plays would have provided the means to do so. For Madelaine Gohlke to argue that Shakespeare's tragedies are a 'vast commentary on the absurdity and destructiveness' of the 'structures of male dominance', or Penny Gay to claim that *As You Like It* effects a 'thorough deconstruction of patriarchy and its gender roles', takes no account of the circumstances in which the plays were written and performed. The dramatist was an employee of the company, and Shakespeare almost certainly writing his earliest plays as a hired man. The plays were the company's assets and were not written for anything other than performance. In general they were only printed when a company was in difficulties, or, since no adequate copyright laws existed to prevent rival performance, when the particular play had ceased to be part of the company's repertoire. Thus the option of addressing another – perhaps more discriminating – public of readers was not open to a company playwright. The normal procedure, as G. E. Bentley demonstrates, was for the senior members of the company to monitor closely the development of the scripts on which so much of their livelihood depended. In particular there was close state censorship and a business-orientated company would want to avoid the delays involved in giving offence.[48] Is it really likely then that such circumstances would be receptive to a 'vast commentary on the absurdity and destructiveness' of the 'structures of male dominance'? The whole Shakespeare-as-feminist project is predicated on an autonomous creative process that never existed.

SHAKESPEARE AND THE PERFORMERS

'Most writers on Shakespeare', Guy Boas observed, reflecting the earlier reticence on this topic, 'have noted the original playing of his female characters by boys as an historical fact and have left it at that.' 'The measure of a convention', said Michael Jamieson, 'is that it goes unquestioned.' Both critics in their studies of the 'boy actress' were concerned to minimise the possible imputations of impropriety and in doing so shared the inhibitions of the critical tradition in which they wrote. It will not do, however, to ignore what must have been the considerable and far-reaching consequences of the cross-dressed tradition, in terms both of the performance of the roles and more particularly of their conception which so much depended upon it.

It is strange that the various modern challenges to conventional theatre have not done more to alert students of Elizabethan theatre to their implications in its own performance aesthetic.[49] If more attention in Elizabethan studies were given to the relation of playwright to company, to the stylising, distancing elements likely in cross-dressed performance, and to the general male assumptions about women brought to it, not to mention itinerancy, doubling, and the broad generic tradition of playing, perhaps less would be heard about Shakespeare's women as psychological studies of real people and more about them as (often incidental) male dramatic constructs. In particular the age and status of the Elizabethan performers of the female roles is vital to an understanding both of the sort of collaborative input they might have made to the roles' conception, and of the ethos in which they were played. Such considerations therefore inform the structure of this book and provide the focus of its first chapters.

The external evidence of Shakespeare's working practices and his relations with his colleagues is very sparse. For the key period 1579–92, between his leaving school and establishing himself as a playwright in London, at the age of twenty-eight prominent enough to draw Greene's malicious attention in his pamphlet, *A Groatsworth of Wit*, and only two years before becoming a leading member of the finest company in the land, not a shred of evidence survives. Two contrasting hypotheses are offered by scholars to account for these 'Lost Years', both of which have implications for his subsequent relations with the company and the nature of their collaboration.[50]

Did he join them as a relatively 'hands-off' dramatist, if perhaps beginning humbly as a tutor and having written for a number of companies, protected by his aristocratic connections from the worst vicissitudes of the plague periods, still to jaunt off regularly to Stratford where his fortune lay, and contemptuous of the 'dyer's hand', chafing at company restraint, as is supposed in the *Troilus and Cressida* dedication? His aristocratic connections have to be taken seriously.[51] There is clear evidence of close early association with the Stanleys, the Earls of Derby (whose heir-presumptive took the title of Lord Strange), then Southampton, dedicatee of the poems published at the time of the founding of the company and perhaps a statement of Shakespeare's relative independence, and then the company patrons, the two Lord Hunsdons, successively Lord Chamberlain, at the very centre of the aristocracy, linked by marriage with the Stanleys and by birth with the Queen herself. Not only did Shakespeare have a direct association with a Court at which it is estimated there were 187 performances of his plays during his lifetime, but the plays themselves, it can be argued, reveal a sympathy with aristocratic values and the nuances of Court life.

Or was his association with the London theatre earlier, more immediate, and more direct? John Aubrey, who obtained the material in his *Brief Lives* from William, son of Christopher Beeston, Shakespeare's fellow, says that Shakespeare had been a schoolmaster in his younger years (i.e. immediately after leaving school), which seems to have gained general acceptance, but that he came to London at the age of eighteen (i.e. in 1584). This is not the place to enter into the wrangle over the possible earlier dating of some of the plays, but the sooner he started writing clearly the more feasible becomes his considerable output as well as his other duties both professional and domestic. Aubrey says Shakespeare went home every year and the evidence of a commuter playwright, such that the Ogburns can argue quite cogently for two entirely separate people, is just one of the enigmas of the man.[52]

If only more were know of these early relations . . . Andrew Gurr argues for such companies as constructed, even head-hunted, by their powerful patrons, ever jockeying for position at Court, who closely supervised them thereafter, so that conjunctions were forced, and possibly sometimes uncongenial.[53] Many of the original sharers were old clowns and tumblers who could entertain touring in countries where no English was spoken. Where did Shakespeare fit in? Did his acting talents, for instance, allow him to be integrated as a full member of the playing company, or did his writing skills take precedence? The tradition of Shakespeare's limited thespian talent is still widely disseminated, but based perhaps on no more than a piece of post-Restoration gossip, passed on from one writer to another, all concerned to establish their superiority to the former age. The author of *Historia Histrionica* [1699], perhaps James Wright, observed that 'Shakespeare (. . . as I have heard, was a much better Poet than a Player)'; Rowe [1709], on the basis of information from Betterton and D'Avenant, neither his contemporary, reported that 'the top of his Performance was the Ghost in his own *Hamlet*'; and Capell [1780] citing

Thomas Jones, a Warwickshire resident, tells the story of his playing Adam in *As You Like It.*

Testimonies of actual contemporaries give a more favourable view. Chettle (though ostensibly under pressure to apologise) describes Shakespeare as 'excellent in the quality he professes', whilst Aubrey (who got his material from the Beestons) contrasts him with Jonson, who was better as an instructor, and says Shakespeare 'did act exceedingly well'. Shakespeare is known to have continued as a jobbing actor at least until 1605, playing in *Sejanus*, heading the cast-list of *Every Man in His Humour*, and being remembered in Augustine Phillips' will as, 'my fellow', like the others. He may be the 'old Player', W. S. mentioned by Willobie and referred to as 'the man, Shakespeare' by Lady Herbert at Wilton in 1603.[54]

John Southworth makes an excellent case for seeing Shakespeare's writing, staging, and playing as an integrated and continuous whole.[55] He believes the Bard to have been a gifted actor and a leading member of his company and regards it as a literary-critical conspiracy to denigrate his ability, as well as to try to make his entry into playing as late and his exit as early as possible. There is no doubt that the strongest argument for a 'hands-on' dramatist are the play-texts themselves, redolent with theatrical practicality and a more lively apprehension of the process of performance certainly than anyone before him and probably anyone since, and it makes considerable sense to see this as the product of an active involvement onstage and in rehearsal. However, Southworth's enthusiasm in tracing the roles Shakespeare is supposed to have played (and written for himself) leads him, alas, into ever more extravagant claims, and whilst some of his supporting arguments are intriguing – Shakespeare, he says, favoured slightly disengaged characters, with not too much to say, but who could be onstage at the beginning and end to supervise things – the result is to leave the reader increasingly uneasy as to how Shakespeare, whilst playing parts like Iago and Menenius, ever found time to write as many plays as he did.

Although the specifics of role assignment cannot be proven, what of the more general issue of Shakespeare tailoring his work for the company of players with whom he spent so many profitable years? When young Richard Burbage, immensely talented, joined the Chamberlain's Men, his father with a theatre, his brother handling the business, the family soon dominated the company with a web of interconnecting friendships, dependencies, and marriages. Clearly Shakespeare had a rapport with Burbage that created so much of his, perhaps we should say 'their', best work. Hamlet's instruction that the clowns 'speak no more than is set down for them' seems to chime in with some sort of discord that sent Kemp packing, with or without the leave of his lord, and the arrival of Armin seems to have led to a change not only in the sort of clown-role but its degree of integration into the rest of the play as a whole. Beyond this, evidence of collaboration is tantalisingly fragmentary. Gurr provides a detailed profile of a whole series of parts apparently especially written for John Sincler. Does this suggest a wider practice involving more of Shakespeare's colleagues, or merely the exploitation of his extreme thinness? Kemp's name survives in transmitted versions of the scripts as Peter in *Romeo and Juliet* and Dogberry in *Much Ado About Nothing*. There is evidence in *Twelfth Night* and *Love's Labours Lost* of parts having been emended to take account of their performers (see below pp. 35 and 36), but the much bigger issue is not what Shakespeare forgot but what he kept in mind about the anticipated performers in conceiving of their roles.

The topic is still haunted by T. W. Baldwin's book which purported to assign all Shakespeare's roles to known players. He proposed a system of what he called 'lines', similar to the nineteenth-century stock company, types of character which each sharer always played, which were apparently written into each play, and when the player died or left the company were inherited by his successor. Baldwin derived his 'lines' from the surviving King's Men cast lists of the 1620s and 30s, long after Shakespeare's death, mostly from the relatively formulaic plays of Massinger, and then projected them backwards, largely ignoring his own evidence of changing performance circumstances.[56] Influenced by the theories of Stanislavski, Baldwin argued that, 'the actor did not strive to be a fictitious person; he strove rather to be himself under fictitious circumstances', and ransacked Shakespeare's plays for what he regarded as personal descriptions of the performers, not only their appearance even down to the colour of their eyes, but also their temperament. Moral virtue, for instance, was seen as a 'line' in itself. He took no account of doubling, revivals, or even cross-dressing. Hired men had to be dismissed, as in some more recent attempts at casting, because the exercise demanded a finite number of performers. 'Our record' of the performers of the plays, he says, with quite staggering confidence, 'is almost certainly complete'.

Notwithstanding the flaws in its application, however, Baldwin's initial thesis, that 'Shakespeare's plays represent not only his own individual invention but also the collective invention of his company', remains unassailable. It is inconceivable that Shakespeare did not have individuals in mind when he wrote roles as demanding as Cleopatra, Juliet, and Rosalind, or that he did not take a personal hand in directing them. As Peter Thomson argues, talking of the construction of *Richard III*: 'Shakespeare observed his fellow actors . . . at work and created characters for them through his perception of the histrionic temperament in action.'[57] Beyond that, however, the concept of the 'line' does not take account of the Elizabethan tradition of versatility or the relatively impersonal style brought about by more formal acting techniques. Perhaps Lowin did take over from Pope as *miles gloriosus*, but he would have had to play many other kinds of parts as well. As Bernard Beckerman shows, using the comparison of Molière's practice in which the number and distribution of roles are constant, it is difficult, if not impossible, to find any similar consistency in the work of Shakespeare and his immediate contemporaries that would clearly indicate a significant number of specialist performers.[58]

Baldwin has to be a warning to all scholars of the dangers of incorporating contemporary assumptions from their own period into reconstructions of the past, and of providing definitive answers to impossible questions simply because there is a hunger for them. Unfortunately it has not always been heeded. Perhaps the most extreme of his modern disciples is David Grote[59], who, to make his project of casting every play and even revivals possible, has to insist that all the sharers appeared in every play and between them undertook all of what he calls the 'significant' roles, and that they could only play roles of exactly the same age as themselves, a view also adopted by Southworth. Apprentices, we are told, only acted with their own masters. Juliet was thus the apprentice of the player of Romeo, Perdita that of Florizel, and so on. 'It would have been awkward and inconvenient, ' he claims, 'for an adult to find the time to work alone with the apprentice of another master'. This theory required Burbage 'to have been a most remarkable talent-spotter to so consistently identify such potential in boys of ten with no stage experience'. For Grote, the female characters must be played with complete verisimilitude. The breeches convention, for instance, he considers principally as a stratagem for coping with young men who are really too old to be playing female roles. To be really successful, he says, a boy should have a 'physical femininity' with 'a different sense of movement' and be able to wear nightgowns 'convincingly'.

The biggest obstacle to all of these elaborate casting theories is the actual nature of Elizabethan stage practice, especially the tradition of doubling. 'Significant roles', according to Grote, could not be doubled because:

If an actor playing a significant character reappears in a different costume, audiences will assume it is the earlier character . . . rather than a new character, and be confused . . .

Performance circumstances, he argues, precluded the level of facial concealment he thinks necessary for doubling. 'The Elizabethan theatre', he

claims, 'had no make-up as we understand the term.' Wigs would have
been too expensive, and it would have taken too long to change. So often
such assertions rely on the validity of the author's own more recent
practical experience, with no perspective beyond Shakespeare, and little
by way of historical context. In reality Shakespeare's theatre grew out of an
itinerant performance tradition honed over a century of professional playing, and one to which he and his fellows regularly returned. Most travelling
actors in Tudor times were young men, and they played kings, old men,
viragoes and whores, and any ethnic type, and were especially skilled at
alternating virtuous and vicious characters in equal measure. The first
professional companies were necessarily small, usually four or five, and
for them to undertake the elaborate demands of the early morality required
most actors to undertake several roles.[60] Even when a more economic
dramatic structure evolved, the practice of extensive doubling continued,
evidently because it brought its own incidental pleasures in the display of
skill and versatility. Playing a series of easily recognisable generic roles, the
Tudor actor did not 'identify' in the modern sense with the character he
was playing, but drew it in a series of broad strokes for a generally
unlettered audience, before passing on to his next role and its all-important
entry. Clown and young woman to some extent apart, he did not specialise
and the broad tradition remained down almost to our own day that any
actor could play virtually any part; for the audience did not look for
physical resemblance but mimetic skill. Thus J. K. Jerome, writing in the
1880s, recalls his first experience of a stock company with 'an old queer-
looking little lady, who walked with a stick, and complained of rheuma-
tism', and 'did the doting old mothers and comic old maids', but who, he
said, 'could play anything': 'She would have been ten minutes making up
for Juliet, and then, sitting in the middle of the pit, you would have put her
down for twenty.'[61] Companies may have grown slightly bigger by
Shakespeare's time (though seven will comfortably perform *The Jew of
Malta*), but the practice of strolling continued, and between 1603 and 1611
it is estimated that the King's Men spent as much as two-thirds of their
time on the road. Hence doubling, versatility, and improvisation all still
continued to flourish throughout his working lifetime, and with them a
consciousness of performer in contradistinction to role; as much storyteller
as actor.

CHAPTER I

Age and status

Analysis of the statistics gathered from the 205 surviving plays written for the adult professional stage between 1500 and 1614 (and summarised in the Appendix) provides two striking conclusions apparently at variance with one another. The numbers of players required for the performance of the female roles is remarkably constant, suggesting the fairly rapid development after 1560 of a specialist cadre of performers, and yet the wide divergences in the size of the leading female role during the main part of this period, from a few lines to several hundred, and from leading characters to parts so brief they scarcely register, seems to cast doubt on this assumption. Why have specialists, if you do not use them? The following discussion attempts to explore and reconcile this apparent inconsistency.

Leaving aside for the moment the earlier material before 1589, of the 161 extant play-texts from the adult repertory contemporary with Shakespeare's career as a playwright some 70 per cent have either four female speaking roles or fewer (see table 1), and in almost all of the remainder the extra roles could be doubled by the original four performers. In only a handful of plays do the female roles require more than four performers and in all such cases there appear to be special circumstances related to them.[1]

The disposition of non-speaking female roles, in contrast, is often much less restrained. Sometimes they are clearly numerous, especially where as in *Satiromastix* dancing partners are needed to match the male principals. Often they are brought on for their musical talent, as in *Alphonsus, Emperor of Germany* with 'a train of ladies following with music' or the country wenches singing a harvest song in *The Silver Age*. Frequently there are dumb shows with silent female characters in splendid costumes, usually from classical myth, the best known being Helen of Troy in *Dr Faustus* with two cupids and Alexander's paramour. Where there are no indications of attendant women in the text in situations where they might be expected, as with Bel-Imperia in *The Spanish Tragedy*, their presence may well have been assumed.

Table 1. *Numbers of female speaking roles*

Roles	Adult plays 1589–1614		Children 1599–1611		Restoration 1660–1700	
	Plays	%	Plays	%	Plays	%
0	0	0	0	0	0	0
1	3	2	0	0	1	2
2	16	10	0	0	2	4
3	39	24	7	22	11	21
4	54	34	5	16	13	25
5	14	9	9	28	6	11
6	13	8	3	9	9	17
7	8	5	6	19	5	9
8	9	6	2	6	1	2
9	0	0	0	0	4	8
10	1	1	0	0	1	2
11	1	1	0	0	0	0
12	1	1	0	0	0	0
13	0	0	0	0	0	0
14	1	1	0	0	0	0
15	0	0	0	0	0	0
16	0	0	0	0	0	0
17	0	0	0	0	0	0
18	1	1	0	0	0	0
	161		32		53	

Why then should the number of female speaking roles be so restricted? The evidence suggests there was no shortage of younger players. In the Admiral's 'plats' around 1597, which list entrances and exits, almost every sharer is credited with a 'boy', whilst of the Chamberlain's Men, Burbage, Phillips, Heminges, Pope, Shank, Kemp, and Robinson are all recorded as having apprentices, boys, or servants, a number of them two or more.[2] In the Admiral's lists of c.1602, five of the fourteen boys mentioned do not play female parts. There were after all many other tasks in the playhouse, and any apprentice genuinely following in his master's footsteps would presumably *not* be playing a female part. Pollard, for instance, trained as a clown under Shank.

If such large numbers of performers could be used to represent non-speaking female roles, this suggests that the exclusiveness of the core group who spoke did not depend simply on a propensity for physical likeness or necessarily extreme youthfulness. Granville Barker suggests persuasively 'at its best the mere speaking of the plays was a very brilliant thing, comparable to *bel canto*'.[3] Was it then the level of appropriate vocal skill that limited the number of female speaking roles? It must have been a significant factor, but evidence from outside the adult theatre suggests it was not the determining one. As table I shows, a random sample of Jacobean Children's plays, in which virtually the entire company would by conventional standards have been suitable for female roles, indicates very little increase in their numbers. Even in Restoration plays, for which actual women were available, although the average female role is larger the numbers in the table show very little increase. A survey of modern drama would probably reveal, with some notable exceptions, very little advance in the male/female ratio; certainly not overall. The initial reason for the limit of numbers, therefore, must be sought not in the practical circumstances of cross-dressing, where no doubt it eventually became a determinant, but in the relatively marginal place of women in the fables used, written predominantly by men, and with female characters organised mainly around a series of polarities, as rewards, possessions to be exchanged, betrayers, and so on. Jacqueline Pearson shows how women dramatists in the Restoration were 'forced to compromise in order to succeed', and found themselves progressively reducing the proportion of female lines to do so.[4] Susanna Centlivre's plays, she suggests, 'succeeded almost exactly in inverse proportion to their emphasis on women'.

Such a remarkable conformity in terms of numbers of roles and the manpower required suggests a fixed group of specialists in each company for whom the female parts were written. Who were they, and what was their status in the companies?

THE ARGUMENT FOR JUVENILE PERFORMERS

Most writers on Elizabethan theatre have long accepted that the performers of the female roles, ever a marginal topic, were what we would now call 'boys', i.e. in pre-puberty. Granville Barker's 'boy actress' has had a new lease of life in recent gay criticism, albeit not in a form of which he would have approved, and most other studies still accept the implied age-range and performer limitations elaborated in late nineteenth- and early twentieth-century criticism.

The theory of their pre-pubescence is based mainly on references to 'boy players' in Elizabethan 'inner plays', episodes in the plays where the players represent their own profession.[5] In *Hamlet* concern is expressed lest the boy player grow too tall or lose his treble voice. Sir Bounteous in Middleton's *A Mad World, My Masters* [1606], performed by the Children of Paul's, looks in vain for 'boys' amongst the counterfeit travelling company, evidently to be recognised by their stature, and is told they come with the waggon. The eponymous hero of *Sir Thomas More* [c.1595] associates female parts exclusively with boys: 'How many are ye?' 'Four men and a boy, sir.' 'But one boy? then I see / There's but few women in the play', a comment which suggests a very limited historical perspective.[6]

The application of the term 'boy' in this context is, however, problematical. Technically boyhood ended at puberty, legally in England recognised as fourteen for boys (and twelve for girls), when boys became 'youths'. Steve Brown argues that in Elizabethan usage the term 'boy' was applied well beyond puberty and until social and economic manhood, often not achieved until the late twenties.[7] There is a good deal of evidence to suggest that 'player-boy' became a technical term for players of female roles and could similarly be applied to members of the Children's groups whatever their age. Philip Gaudy, writing about 1602, records that the Dowager Countess of Leicester had married 'one of the playing boys of the chapel'. Not surprisingly those trained to perform in the monarch's service were reluctant to give up its benefits and so the average age of the Children was ever upwards. At his death Sebastian Westcott, Master of Paul's and semi-official theatrical impresario, had seven ex-choristers in his company and living in his house, three between sixteen and twenty-one, and the eldest probably thirty[8]. In 1606, 'the Youthes of Paules, commonly cald', an informant complains, 'the Children of Paules', played before James and his guest Christian of Denmark.[9] Similarly ex-choristers of their rivals the Chapel Royal went on tour using the royal cachet and regularly calling themselves 'Children'. Nor are contemporaries consistent in their use of terminology. Thomas Heywood's *Apology*, 1612, talks of 'youths' playing the female roles, Lady Mary Wroth in 1626 of 'a boy', whilst *Pathomacia*, 1630, uses the term 'men'. Cross-dressed heroines, who presumably looked much the same age as their performers, are generally called 'youths', although Bellario in *Philaster* is described as 'a boy about 18'. Pepys in his diary entry for 7 January 1660–1 likewise refers to 'Kinaston, the boy', then aged eighteen, although Cibber, writing a little later, describes pre-Restoration performers of female roles as 'Boys or young men' . Hence the term 'boy' used of players of female parts cannot with any certainty be take as evidence of pre-pubescence.

'Pray God your voice', says Hamlet, '. . . be not crack'd within the ring.' Supporters of juniority point to the need for treble voices. *The Actor's Remonstrance* of 1643 complains, 'Our boys, ere we shall have liberty to act again, will be grown out of use, like cracked organ pipes and have faces as old as our flags.' Orsino's description of Viola in breeches as being a youth appropriate for a 'woman's part' emphasises her voice as 'shrill and sound'. Pepys praises Kynaston's appearance but complains: 'her voice not very good'. Robertson Davies, however, provides evidence that the speaking voice with skill can be kept unchanged until aged seventeen or even as late as twenty, whilst there is evidence that puberty arrived later in the sixteenth century than it does today.[10] Bottom is certainly prepared to play the Lady, presumably in falsetto, 'a monstrouse little voice', and it may be something similar that Cleopatra has in mind when she talks of her imagined imitator 'squeaking'.

Davies, however, distinguishes between the singing and the spoken voice; the former, in his view, cannot remain unbroken beyond sixteen. If such performers were in their later teens, as increasingly seems more likely, this may well account for the especial care with which Shakespeare treats the expected association of heroine and singing in his plays. Desdemona and Ophelia both have prominent songs, which contribute to their pathos and impression of vulnerability. In other cases, however, the association is retained but the performer himself excused. The most obvious example is Viola in *Twelfth Night*. When she first plans to go into Orsino's service, she resolves to be presented as a eunuch, because, she says: 'I can sing / And speak to him in many sorts of music' (I.ii.57–8). However, we hear no more of this. When the Duke asks for music at the beginning of II.iv it looks very like he intends Viola/Cesario to sing for him, but then some business is invented to fetch Olivia's clown, Feste. Singers are evidently in such short supply in Illyria that two noble households scarcely on speaking terms have to share one between them. Clearly Shakespeare intended Viola to sing and the change was made fairly clumsily at rehearsal. Rosalind is excused altogether and nameless pages brought in to do the honours. Mariana in *Measure for Measure* IV.i enters accompanied by a 'boy singing'. Marina in *Pericles* V.i likewise brings with her a maid to serenade her father, and although there are references to her singing, it is more likely that the actual singing was carried out by the accompanying boy. When Imogen in *Cymbeline* is said to sing like an angel she is offstage, and it could well have been someone else singing on the actor's behalf. Her brothers have a strange conversation in IV.ii in which it is decided they will 'say' and not sing their funeral song, because, 'our voices / Have got the mannish crack'. This seems indicative of a growing inhibition. *Cymbeline*, like *Pericles*, was presumably written with an eye to performance at the newly acquired Blackfriars. Andrew Gurr suggests the King's Men absorbed the musicians who had played for its previous occupants the Children, celebrated for their pre-performance music.

Perhaps as well as indicating older performers of the female roles, this new circumspection towards vocal performance, into which the rougher and readier itinerant had been prepared so confidently to plunge, indicates a taste for what F. W. Sternfeld called 'art' songs rather than theatrical ones, and a greater specialisation, culminating, of course, in its physical manifestation in the cult of the castrato by 1700.

Hamlet's second and lesser concern is the height of the player boy, who has grown 'by the altitude of a chopine'. William Ringler Jr points to a passage in *Love's Labours Lost* in which the height and girth of the Princess is made an object of mockery;[11] and it is difficult not to accept, as with T. W. Baldwin's much more extensive conjectures, some element of individually tailored excuse here, together with the inference that female characters, especially those in amorous exchanges, would normally be expected to be realistically more fragile than their partners. Height and age, however, are not necessarily concomitant, and one would expect any older juveniles chosen for female roles to be slighter than average, although not necessarily, as Cibber would have it, 'of the most effeminate Aspect'.[12] Beauty need not be even skin deep when it was applied so liberally in the tiring house.

The main argument against pre-pubescence, however, is less one of historical detail than of the sort of special allowances that generations of scholars have thought it necessary to build into the supposed performer practices and dramaturgy to accommodate them.

The 'boy actress'

Before the advent of Jardine's 'potentially rapeable boy', which gave tongue to gay and homophilic convictions, earlier generations of critics had seen the player's juniority as a protection against unwanted lasciviousness in the female roles. Granville Barker warned his contemporaries in 1930:

Let the usurping actress remember that her sex is a liability, not an asset.

Sir Walter Raleigh writing in 1901 doubted:

whether Shakespeare has not suffered more than he has gained by the genius of latter-day actresses, who bring into the plays a realism and a robust emotion which sometimes obscure the sheer poetic value of the author's conception.

Instead of Cibber's sceptical Restoration view of 'ungain Hoydens' seen as a 'Defect' and written down for, these critics embraced the concept of the young boy as the perfect vehicle for their idealised conception of Shakespearian womanhood, based on the tradition from Anna Jameson and Mary Clarke, and for the idealised poetic language in which it was rendered. Their preference for boys over actresses rested on a cultural construction of juvenile purity from Rousseau, as expressed in Wordsworth's 'Intimations of Immortality':

> Heaven lies about us in our infancy!
> Shades of the prison house begin to close
> Upon the growing Boy . . .

Performer and role were thus perceived to be bonded by what Guy Boas, Headmaster of Sloane School, taking his cue from his mentor Granville Barker's references to a higher 'spiritual' plane, called Shakespeare's 'etherealised goal'. They saw no incongruity in projecting this back onto the Elizabethans. 'The nature of boys', observed Sir Sidney Lee in 1906, 'is a pretty permanent factor in human society.' 'Common sense', says Alfred Harbage 'dictates that Elizabethan boys were no different in essentials from boys today'.[13] The gender characteristics these school performers were alleged to possess in themselves, together with those they might acceptably simulate in the roles they played, were incorporated *in combination* into the critics' conception of Shakespeare's female characters. Critics persuaded themselves that in his invention of a race of spiritualised elfin females Shakespeare was merely drawing on what Michael Jamieson describes as 'the boy's natural qualities' of 'gaiety and impudence . . . innocence, openness of disposition, and an elusive selflessness'.[14] They were insulated from impropriety by a continual awareness of their boyishness. Boas recalls how his Desdemona:

Possessed of the healthiest masculine temperament . . . would be found cheerfully fighting the guards behind the scenes with Othello's sword . . . thus proving that for the acting of Shakespeare's women there is nothing like a real boy for the job.

The genteel purlieus of Sloane School, however, were a far cry from the realities of the sixteenth-century playhouse. Elizabethan boys were breeched at the age of seven, after which they were in training to be men, as contemporary portraits such as that of Sir Walter Raleigh and his son avouch. There was no indulgent concept of extended childhood. Pupils, apprentices, undergraduates even, were flogged if they stepped out of line, and indeed to encourage them in their studies. The ancient Shepherd in *The Winter's Tale* sees youth as a continuous process from the age of ten:

I would there were no age between ten and three-and-twenty, or that youth would sleep out the rest; for there is nothing in between but getting wenches with child,wronging the ancientry, stealing, fighting . . . (III.iii.59–63)

And Shakespeare should know. He was married and a father by the time he was eighteen. Edward Alleyn was a sharer by the age of seventeen, as was Ezekiel Fenn, still playing female parts and important enough to be summoned with four other leading players before the Privy Council to answer for their profession, whilst Richard Burbage was a player perhaps by the time he was sixteen, a sturdy youth able to defend his father's takings with a broom handle. Their anonymous predecessors toured at the head of itinerant companies whilst still young enough to double female roles with the leads, as in *Horestes*, 1567, and *The Longer Thou Livest*, 1559.

Literary criticism and the boy player

As well as depending on a historically specific, some might say highly artificial, version of pre-pubescence as conceived in the Edwardian prep school, the concept of the 'boy actress' has also encouraged a view of theatre that subordinates everything else to the text. Not only did the 'boy actress' and Mrs Jameson's ethereal female fuse together so as to be almost indistinguishable, but, drawing much on Ariel and his spirit servers, the former became all but invisible too. Raleigh talks of the boy actors providing '*a transparent medium* for the author's wit and pathos', and Barker requires of them a '*self-forgetful clarity of perception*, and … a sensitive, spirited, athletic beauty of speech and conduct'. This view still persists. Using the boy actor, according to Juliet Dusinberre, means that, 'The personality and the image of the actor does not interpose itself between the playwright and his conception of character.' 'The psychological action', says Robertson Davies, 'is implicit in the verse, and if this is spoken intelligently and appropriately … with suitable accompanying physical action, the necessary effect is achieved completely.' In this he anticipates Raymond Williams' dictum on poetic drama that: 'when, in the known conditions of performance, the words are enacted, the whole of the drama is thereby communicated'.[15]

Neither Davies' 'physical action' nor Williams' concept of what constitutes 'enactment' seem to carry much weight in their scheme of things, and both seem to be trying to steer clear of a more full-blooded recognition of the player's role in interacting with the text, and its consequence in performance. The meeting on the open stage was one between players and spectators even before the issue of character or fable came into play, let alone text. It was *players* the audience came to see and it was their 'performance' that took precedence, involving improvisation, gagging, and ad-libbing as well as fighting, dancing, and singing. An audience responds to the physical presence of the actor, his sense of danger, charisma and charm, sweat and tears, the roughness of the performance and the occasional failures and consequent unevenness, none of which is accommodated on the 'celibate' – and, in the hands of these critics, increasingly cerebral – stage. Doubling, clowning, cross-dressing, and the more general actor/role disparities, together with the acknowledged conventions of staging, and more particularly of dramatic writing with its stress on moral context, all served to set the character at a distance and invite continuous awareness of the artifice of performance. Acting is always a lot more than merely 'speaking' the words or even accompanying them with gestures. To concentrate so exclusively on the words spoken with purity is to invent a sort of half-theatre only a step from closet drama and another kind of incipient anti-theatricalism. It is regrettable that in many modern editions of play-texts where the performance context is mentioned at all it tends to be in an addendum at the back of the book or at the tail-end of the introduction, a mere quirk of history mentioned for the sake of completeness rather than being apprehended as the driving force that gave the text its purpose and fulfilment.

Performer inadequacies

The consensus on the juniority of the players of female roles has also led to a general unease as to their adequacy, and one that continues to be expressed. Michael Jamieson sub-titles his essay on the subject, 'The Problem of Accommodating to the Boy Actors', which, given an extended playing tradition of nearly a century before Shakespeare began to write, is strangely anachronistic. A. F. Kinney observes, 'Boy players must have brought their own limitations to the stage.' H. J. Oliver, editing *As You Like It*, remarks Shakespeare 'would not ask too much of the boy apprentices who had to play the female roles, capable as these boys must have been' – which seems a strange comment to make on one of the longest roles in the canon. Jan Kott discusses how the major female roles were 'curtailed to suit a boy actor's scope', whilst H. M. Richmond suggests 'Limitations in the boys' technical skill seem to have required women roles to be adjusted in each Shakespeare play'.[16] Strangely enough, such supposed limitations have rarely been recognised as an argument *against* the theory itself. Instead, critics insist that Shakespeare was hampered, as James Hill puts it, by 'the capacities and limitations of his boy actors', which had to be borne constantly in mind as he wrote.[17] Female roles had to be made easier, shorter, and able to be performed in a more formal style than the rest of the play to meet the young boy's limitations of skill and understanding. Robertson Davies, setting out to show how all the female roles were kept simple, says of Juliet, for instance, that it is easier to play than the breeches roles because it does not require 'charm', only 'enthusiasm'. He considers that the part of Cressida 'presents no difficulties because of its remarkable consistency'. He says that throughout the play she 'has been shown as a foolish and shallow girl, and every appearance and speech of hers is designed to further this end'.

The theory of pre-pubescent purity performing etherealised womanhood is based on a very selective treatment of Shakespeare's plays, concentrating on a handful of young heroines and ignoring a lot of important Shakespearian female roles. When he pauses to consider this, Davies' solution is to incorporate grown men into his theory, working alongside the boys, and he offers a whole series of criteria to determine when their services would be required: if the characters had to speak vigorously, for instance, or stand up to male characters, be malignant, possess an 'Amazonian physique', a depth of humour, or an experience of the 'sordid side of life'.[18] James Hill even seems to think that it was easier for the boys when they had the stage to themselves.

Furthermore, to concentrate so exclusively on Shakespeare's plays is to ignore the sort of performance demands made by the plays of other contemporary dramatists, many of them by the nature of things performed by the very same players in tandem with Shakespeare's two or three plays each year. The very first recorded youthful specialist in female roles – in *Cambises* in 1561 – plays, amongst other parts, a virtuous young lady forced to marry the tyrant king, displaying all the qualities this theory associates with the 'boy actress', but then in the opening lines of his first assumption, Meretrix, the camp whore, invokes all of Davies' criteria for *adult* playing:

> What, is there no lads here that hath a lust
> To have a passing trull to help at their need?   (lines 221–2)

Since the performer is also called upon to play the roles of a young man old enough to be a judge, a weeping mother, and a country virago, his assignments show this distinction between juvenile and adult roles to be unworkable, and their range suggests instead that this proto-performer of female roles was a young adult.

Too many of the assumptions about the ages of the players have made a false dichotomy between what William Ringler Jnr envisages as he tries to cast Shakespeare's plays as 'large lumbering adult actors' on the one hand, and 'small, graceful' boys on the other, without giving sufficient attention to those in between, who must have comprised a substantial proportion of the regular playing forces.[19] Indeed, given the stress on non-verbal accomplishments in the company which Shakespeare joined in 1594, it is unlikely that many of the older players would have been 'large' and certainly not 'lumbering'.

Nevertheless, the theory of mature players in leading female roles, as the only alternative to children, continues to be promulgated. 'It's laughable', declared Declan Donnellan in an interview defending his decision to cast a six-foot man as Rosalind, 'to think pre-pubescent boys played Lady Macbeth and Cleopatra. They were obviously grown men.' 'The weight of maturity and power in a woman of Gertrude's age', says Peter Hyland, '. . . is surely beyond the capacities of an adolescent boy', and he suggests the Japanese *onnagata* as a possible model for adult involvement.[20] In such a fluid medium as theatre there is no reason to expect complete uniformity of practice. It was no doubt always possible for players who had graduated from female roles to return to them if the circumstances demanded, but as a regular practice it comes into conflict with the very considerable evidence in the corpus of plays showing fixed numbers of performers of female roles.

There are some possible exceptions to this generalisation, but even they raise further problems in respect of the general reluctance of adult players to assume serious female roles.

Adult-player inhibitions

Of the earliest itinerant plays in our survey, eleven, most of them shortly after 1500, contain no female roles at all, and there is evidence too to suggest some playwrights at this time even adapted their sources to avoid them.[21] When female roles do emerge, they are largely restricted to burlesque portrayals of shrews, whores, and viragoes, which, as ritual folk comedy developed into social satire, are used to police the gender boundary, pillorying women who transgress accepted norms. Such portrayals seem to have become popular during the middle of the sixteenth century as amusing cameos like the whore Abominable Living in *Lusty Juventus*, 1550, who says of the hero, 'If it lie in me to do him pleasure, / He shall have it, you may ye [be?] sure', and Mother Coote in *All For Money*, 1577, a hundred years old, blind, with a nose and chin that almost meet, but still lascivious and determined to suborn a witness to reclaim a lost husband.[22] It was not until a different and presumably slightly younger player emerged in the 1560s in response to changing tastes in the drama and the inclusion of romance – and perhaps initially only a single talented individual – that nubile, virtuous female roles were attempted.

Although the adult players continued to include their burlesque cameo roles alongside the new specialism – a couple of them in *Cambises*, 1561, and again in *Horestes*, 1567 – it is significant that even as late as 1581 the two specialists in *The Three Ladies of London* who play nubile young women get no help from the rest of the company of eight in presenting the three title roles. This poses major problems: the three Ladies can never meet onstage and the third, Love, has to be shared between the performers of the other two, using the clumsy device of a mask.

The convention, therefore, seems to have been that players other than specialists could occasionally continue to take female roles, providing they were not meant to be young and attractive, and where they could be burlesqued. This is borne out by cross-gender doubling in itinerant plays such as *Cambises*, *Horestes*, and *The Longer Thou Livest*, and in the Admiral's *plats*, in all of which male roles are doubled either with nurses, old women, servants, or viragoes. Comic serving-women may well have been one area in which this tradition survived into Shakespeare's period and beyond.[23] The popular attribution of Petella the waiting-woman in *The Wild Goose Chase*, 1621, to John Shank is not altogether secure. A more reliable piece of evidence seems to be Anthony Turner's kitchenmaid in *The Fair Maid of the West*, c.1630. He had been a sharer since 1622, specialising in old men, but was probably still quite young since he went on acting until at least 1659. James Horne, a hired man who had married thirteen years previously, probably played Kala, a servant in *Lover's Melancholy* in 1628. All three would fit into a longer tradition already apparent in Ambidexter's assumption (i.e. in his Vice's *persona*) of the Maid attendant on the Lady in *Cambises*, and brought to a specialism by James (Nurse) Nokes after the Restoration.

Juliet's Nurse is an inspired but extraneous insertion into the play, presumably for a particular performer, and party to a double act with Will Kemp as Peter in II.iv. Almost always played, arguably as written, as an old crone with her aches and pains – Juliet calls her 'Ancient damnation', II.v.235 – nonetheless she must actually be of a similar age to Lady Capulet, since she was Juliet's wet nurse, with her own child, the casualty of Lady Capulet's purchase of private health care for her daughter.

Some insight into the relish with which young adults undertook female burlesque is to be found in the brief fortunes of Lady Elizabeth's Men. Their *A Chaste Maid in Cheapside* is unique in having no fewer than eighteen female roles, but the circumstances of its performance are highly untypical.

The company was mainly recruited from the increasingly less-juvenile Children of the Queen's Revels and included a number of players who had appeared in Jonson's *Epicoene*. Middleton himself had honed his brittle, lively, satirical style on a series of city comedies written for their likewise ageing rivals the Children of Paul's. Hence *Chaste Maid* is conceived for a company of confident experienced young men, possibly reinforced for the occasion by Rosseter's Blackfriars Boys, including Nathan Field. In one scene, eleven female characters are onstage together: gossips, nurses, and elderly Puritan women at a christening feast, getting drunk and urinating on the floor.

Bartholomew Fair, performed by the same company, takes such portrayals to new heights of social realism and comic grotesquerie in Dame Purecraft and the remarkable Ursula, the pig woman. In place of the conventional stage beauties, Ursula 'is too fat to be a fury, sure some walking sow of tallow', a whore whose pleasure, 'he that would venture for't, I assure him, might sink into her, and be drown'd for a week, ere any friend he has could find where he were'; and one who, let it be said, gives as good as she gets.

Lady Elizabeth's also had a line in bravura representation of gender complexities, as in Veramour in *Honest Man's Fortune* and Mrs Low-Water in *No Wit, No Help like a Woman's* (both discussed below). Their early members chopped and changed, and eventually a number of them rejoined the King's Men and erstwhile colleagues who had come there straight from the Queen's Revels. This may account for the tendency towards the end of our period for an increasing number of female roles in King's Men plays, like *The Woman's Prize* and *Two Noble Kinsmen*. These, however, are exceptional and in the bulk of plays under consideration from Shakespeare's writing lifetime very few require the female roles to be shared beyond the standard four – presumably regular – players of such roles.

THE ARGUMENT FOR YOUNG ADULTS

Performer competence

The strongest argument for older juveniles is that only they could have done the major female roles justice. The creation of the pre-pubescent 'boy actress' as a solution to Victorian propriety, which is then made into an impediment to be overcome, has similar flaws to Bernard Beckerman's views on how the players compensated for the supposed shortcomings of the Globe's sightlines, a surely fictitious problem created by an over-zealous fidelity to the enormous pillars supporting the stage heavens that the visitor De Witt drew in his sketch of the Swan in a letter to a friend in Holland. 'Essentially [the sightlines] were poor', Beckerman says, and, dismissing at a stroke three-quarters of the stage's potential, 'We are dealing with an aural theatre, not a visual one.' With an extensive itinerant tradition of over a century, using halls, churches, market squares, and of late the great inn yards to the east of London now no longer needed by the wool trade, the players had long identified the most effective performance configurations and when they came to build their own theatres would scarcely have hampered themselves in this fashion.

In precisely the same way, by the 1590s it is extremely unlikely that the companies would have used juvenile performers in the manner of the sneering, genteel, amateur apprentice-presenters of *The Hog Hath Lost His Pearl*, dismissing the common player with, 'We'll give him a speech he understands not', rather than relying on their own experienced younger fellows for the major female roles. It may be that for minor parts the advice in *The Wise Woman of Hogden* (II.i) would suffice: 'Thou shalt be tyred like a woman; can you make curtsie, take small strides, and seem modest?', to which the breeched Luce replies, 'Doubt not me, I'll act them naturally', but it is scarcely adequate for the performers entrusted with the principal role in *As You Like It*, say, or for the whole of the final act of *Antony and Cleopatra*.

The statistics alone suggest a level of importance for the performers of female roles in the 205 plays under analysis, sharing an average of one-fifth of the play's lines between them, that would make tolerance of the sort of constraints envisaged by the pre-pubescent argument most unlikely. The average leading female role has 10 per cent of the total lines, and many, of course, have more. The relative importance of its performer in the company would depend upon the number of players, but if Ringler is correct in his estimate of sixteen players then he rates quite highly. Of the six leading roles in *The Merry Wives of Windsor* three are women, including the second and third largest after Falstaff. In *Romeo and Juliet* there are three female characters amongst the top eight, as is true, perhaps surprisingly, in *Richard III*. La Pucelle is the second largest part in *1 Henry VI*, and Adriana joint-largest in *The Comedy of Errors* – and this is before mentioning any of the later great roles like Portia (571 lines), Beatrice (308), Rosalind (736), Viola (339), Helena (448), Cressida (348), Isabella (390), Desdemona (352), Lady Macbeth (255), Cleopatra (591), Volumnia (298), Imogen (529), Hermione (294), and Queen Katherine (346). And in a number of these plays there are substantial secondary roles too.

One of the strongest arguments for the relative maturity of the main players of female roles lies again in the statistics. In contrast to the consistency in the numbers of roles, rarely going above four and suggesting that the playwright kept in mind a regular group of players, the *size* of individual roles, on the other hand (as shown in the Appendix), varies enormously. Although the general trend is upward, beginning hesitantly after 1500 and a number of plays without female characters, and developing through the century so that by 1600 a large proportion of plays have important female roles, some their central characters, nonetheless their use is uneven throughout. Even alongside Shakespeare's most demanding female roles such as Rosalind, Viola, and Cleopatra there are plays like *Julius Caesar* and *Timon of Athens* in which female roles are minuscule and perfunctory.

What, then, did the female specialists do when there were no roles, or they were very brief? The options are few. If they played nothing else, then talent that could create a Juliet, a Beatrice, or a Lady Macbeth would lie idle for long periods of the repertory, and there is no precedent for such profligacy. Where the mechanics of dramaturgy are clearly visible, as in the plays 'offered for acting', all the evidence points to the sort of detailed planning to keep each performer fully employed that one would expect from a cost-conscious professional industry in which every player was a mouth to feed, and in which each company employed its own playwrights in order to best maximise its playing potential.[24] The 1620s/30s cast lists likewise show that as long as the players of female roles were active, their employment seems to have been continuous.

The inevitable conclusion has to be that, in Shakespeare's time, when they were not playing female roles the leading such players played male ones. There are a few obvious roles that would be a natural extension, such as Ariel in *The Tempest*, himself a player of female roles, Veramour in *Honest Man's Fortune*, or the Good Angel, perhaps, in *Dr Faustus,* together with boys and servants for the junior players. They will not, however, fully serve to make up the difference, and the logic ever presses towards the likelihood that a wider range of characters was appropriate for them, and that the dividing line between the ages and physical attributes of players of male and female roles was a relatively fine one, especially given the emphasis on the youth of so many of the juvenile-leads like Troilus, Orlando, and Bertram. Sebastian, of course, raises the most speculation, since he is to be indistinguishable, except in his behaviour, from his twin sister; whilst the lusty Jove can convincingly cross-dress in *The Golden Age*. Where the gender line was perceived to be under threat, as in the 'tall' and 'thick' Princess in *Love's Labours Lost*, then it had to be excused, and the inference must be that there was a fairly fixed conception of what was appropriate for a player of female roles, which in turn meant that it was a one-way process that did not normally allow male-character players to undertake female roles.

Biographical evidence

What evidence there is about the players of female roles later in the seventeenth century after Shakespeare's death confirms this interpretation of the statistics. Recent research by David Kathman has greatly added to the number of performers whose ages we know, or about whom it is reasonable to speculate. Such an exercise is not without its problems. Parish registers are not entirely reliable when the more popular names regularly recur, and in assembling the existing evidence in table 2, I have not included anyone about whom there is serious disagreement. There is also circumstantial evidence for several other players in the 1620s and 30s which suggests some degree of maturity. John Barret, who played the title role in *Messalina*, probably in 1634, had children christened in 1637 and 1638, and John Thompson had certainly conceived his first daughter whilst he was still playing female parts in 1631. Hugh Clark married in 1627 after playing Gratiana in *The Wedding* in 1626, and probably before playing the lead, Bess Bridges, in the revival of *Fair Maid of the West*, c.1630. Notwithstanding individual uncertainties, the cumulative effect of all of this information is to confirm the proposition that major roles were played mainly after the age of fifteen and up to the early twenties.

This is further confirmed by the surviving evidence of the ages of performers of female roles in the brief period between the re-opening of the theatres in 1660 and the introduction of women to the stage. William Betterton (born 1644) and Edward Kynaston (born 1643) were youths of sixteen and seventeen respectively when they began to perform in 1660. Betterton died the following year, and Kynaston, as women took over the female roles, was probably acting male parts by the time he was twenty. Cardell Goodman was nineteen when he played a female role in the burlesque of *The Empress of Morocco* in 1673.[25] James Nokes went on for a time to make a specialism of elderly comic females, as did his contemporary, Hubert, in Molière's company, but he began in straight female roles before graduating to male ones and his death in 1696 suggests he was of the same generation as the others.

Hamlet is unspecific about the age of the boy player who arrives at Elsinore, though his concern suggests he too is not getting any younger, but in a much less-often quoted passage in *Coriolanus*, Shakespeare gives us an

Table 2. *Ages of known performers of female roles, 1625–47*

Name	Born	Role	Play	Date	Age
Richard Sharpe	1601	Duchess	*The Duchess of Malfi*	1620–3	19/22
Robert Pallant	1605	Cariola	*The Duchess of Malfi*	1620–3	15/18
Timothy Reade	1606	Cardona	*The Wedding*	c.1626	19/20
Theophilus Bird	1608	Paulina	*The Renegado*	1624–30	16–22
		Tota	*2 Fair Maid of the West*	1626–30	18–22
William Trigg	1612	Julia	*The Roman Actor*	1626	14
		Rosalura	*The Wild Goose Chase*	1632	20
John Honeyman	1613	Domitilla	*The Roman Actor*	1626	13
		Sophia	*The Picture*	1629	16/17
		Carinda	*The Deserving Favourite*	1627–9	14/17
Alexander Gough	1614	Caenis	*The Roman Actor*	1626	12
		Acanthe	*The Picture*	1629	15
		Eurinia	*The Swisser*	1631	17
		Lillia Bianca	*The Wild Goose Chase*	1632	18
John Wright	c.1615	Millicent	*Hollands Leaguer*	1631	c16
John Page	1615	Jane	*The Wedding*	1626	11
Arthur Savill	1617	Quartilla	*Hollands Leaguer*	1631	14
Thomas Jordan	c1617	Lepida	*Messalina*	1634	c17
Robert Stratford	1618	Triphoena	*Hollands Leaguer*	1631	13
Ezekiel Fenn	1620	Sophonisba	*Hannibal and Scipio*	1635	15
		Winifred	*The Witch of Edmonton*	1635/7	15/17
Charles Hart	1625	Duchess	*The Cardinal*	1641/2	16/17
Edmund Kynaston	1643	Epicoene	*Epicoene*	1661	18
William Betterton	1644	Aminta	*Maid of the Mill*	1660	16
Cardell Goodman	1654	Mariamne	*Empress of Morocco –* *Burlesque*	1673	19

actual age for the leading player of female roles. Cominius, urging Coriolanus' suitability to be consul, contrasts his earlier deeds with his youth (my italics):

> *At sixteen years,*
> When Tarquin made a head for Rome, he fought
> Beyond the mark of others . . .
> . . .In that day's feats,
> *When he might act the woman in the scene,*
> He prov'd best man i' th' field, and for his meed
> Was brow-bound with the oak.   (II.ii.87–98)

This observation, written in 1608, might be seen to confirm the continuity of the proposed age range for leading players of female roles back to Shakespeare.

David Kathman's research into the extent and significance of apprenticeship in the Elizabethan theatre corrects a number of common misapprehensions.[26] While certain of the sharers, like Armin, did practise the craft in which they had the 'freedom' alongside playing, many did not, and their principal reason for obtaining, or sustaining an inherited, membership of the liveried company was the opportunity it provided in the absence of a players' guild for 'binding' apprentices, thus ensuring their continued service for a period of seven years, and preventing them from marrying or being poached by other companies. Although not universal, mastership seems to have been extremely common amongst the sharers, as a way of housing, supervising, and training young players.[27] Occasionally the master of an apprentice player was not himself a performer and then he rented his apprentice out. Since the guild regulations stipulated fourteen as the minimum age for an apprenticeship and seven years as its minimum, this broadly supports the age-range proposed here, and certainly makes any theory of pre-pubescence more difficult to sustain.

The concept of 'apprentice', borrowed from other sorts of craft, however, still remains problematical. In the typical trade the apprentice was not paid because in theory he was not a producer of value. He would be given lots of menial tasks, and little by little would learn the skills of his trade, as did his theatrical equivalent; but the latter, if chosen for playing female roles, was immediately engaged in a specialism quite different from that of his master, and fairly soon working at a level far superior in skill and importance in his profession relative to that of any conventional trade apprentice.

The status of the players of female roles

An attractively simple schema of company organisation has been handed down, virtually unquestioned, in which the Chamberlain's Men, somehow *both* democratic *and* hierarchical, maintained a clear artistic split, exactly mirroring the financial one, between sharers who played the male roles, apprentices who played the women, and hired men who walked on and did the backstage tasks.

Democratic it was not. The Burbages and their closest associates kept a firm grip on the company through a network of marriages, friendship, and dependency, and the housekeeping indicates an internal hierarchy deliberately constructed and selectively maintained thereafter. The older sharers clung onto power and whenever possible bought up shares, and had eventually to be forced to redistribute them. They brought in other sharers when they needed capital, but also the sharer system, as Henslowe's documents make clear, was primarily a means of maintaining discipline and preventing companies from breaking.[28]

Roles in this received notion are restricted to a fixed set of sharers who are conceived as dividing all the major roles between them, and scholars argue about the company numbers available for this, and whether there were twelve or sixteen players. This makes it more feasible to cast the plays, but reduces the activity to the level of a parlour game. In reality the extant cast lists show that every sharer did not play a major role in every production. We know of some business duties, and there must have been many tasks other than performance. Henslowe's papers suggest that individual sharers may have taken responsibility for the wherewithal of particular productions.[29] They also reveal a much less clear artistic distinction between sharers and hired men.

The witty byplay in the Induction for the King's Men's revival of *The Malcontent* in 1604, in which five of the leading players are introduced in their own persons, is written for three sharers and two hired men without distinction. One of the latter, Lowin, was shortly to be made a sharer, and it looks very much like accelerated promotion on account of his talent. Something similar may have occurred with both Armin and Taylor. Talent itself was a marketable commodity and there were obvious benefits in knitting any talented player into the mesh of interconnecting obligations and rewards. Versatile the tradition may have been, but a company could not do without a clown or a juvenile lead. Richard Allen played Prologue, Epilogue, and Frederick in *Frederick and Basilea* in 1597 whilst still a hired man, and appears to have been similarly rewarded. The considerable imbalance in Jonson's 1616 *Works* between his lists of sharer–players involved in the productions and their *dramatis personae* suggests the presence of very considerable numbers of hired men, as in say *Volpone*, with thirteen-plus roles and only six sharers credited. We know, for instance, that hired men went on tour with Alleyn, who would not have carried supernumeraries. Heywood, and probably Shakespeare and Jonson, were hired men when they started writing plays.[30]

Hugh Clark became a sharer whilst still playing female roles, as did Ezekiel Fenn. Distinctions of grade were probably financial rather than artistic. John Rice, recorded in two civic pageants whilst with the King's Men, in 1607 as a 'very proper Child' and in 1610 as a nymph, the very next year became a sharer in Lady Elizabeth's. Older hired men certainly played burlesque females, and William Bird and Edward Collins may have continued to play female roles after they became hired men.[31] Hence female

roles were certainly not restricted to apprentices, and were sometimes
played by young men of substance and importance in their companies.
R. M. in his character of 'A Player' in *Micrologia*, 1629, confirms the
impression that it was a young profession:

He is one seldom takes care for old age ... and he scarcely survives to his natural
period of days.

The performance of mature and ageing women

One early solution to the difficulties of representing mature women in the
plays is to make the female characters either young or very old and thus
bring them within the scope of a youthful player, as suggested by the
doubling of Boy and Old Woman in *Mucedorus*. Not all ageing women,
however, were played as caricatures. Perhaps the most remarkable is the
Countess in *All's Well That Ends Well* who has a wisdom, tolerance, and
broad humanity quite beyond the narrow stereotype of Old Crone. The
insistence on moral placing is in a sense axiomatic in cross-dressed performance and rarely does it seem to have been possible to present women as
rounded human beings on their own account without exaggeration or
polemic. Only the Countess' extreme age, given Bertram's immaturity,
seems an accommodation of young male performance.

   The sprawling time-span of some plays, in which young women such as
Grissil and Bethsabe become mothers, who, as their children grow up, pass
into middle age and must presumably be played throughout by youths, also
suggests fairly rudimentary distinctions of age (as in the passage in *The
Winter's Tale* (v.iii.227f.) in which the sculptor is said to have added
wrinkles to the 'statue' Hermione pretends to be, indicating precisely
that elision from youth to age and the simple means by which it was
achieved). Such may account too for the inconsistencies of Lady Capulet,
who in i.ii says to fourteen-year-old Juliet, 'I was your mother much upon
these years / That you are now a maid', which would make her twenty-
eight, but by v.iii, perhaps worn down by the cares of a teenage daughter,
declares, 'O me, this sight of death is as a bell / That warns my old age to a
sepulcre.' Capulet's indication that Juliet is the sole survivor of a larger
family (i.ii.14) is also a reminder of the toll which constant childbirth took
on women's health. Simone de Beauvoir's remark about conditions for the
rural poor in the earlier twentieth century would be at least as apposite to
the sixteenth: 'if the woman is not strong, if hygienic precautions are not
taken, repeated child-bearing will make her prematurely old and

misshapen'. Lisa Jardine gives an account of one fifteenth-century Florentine who wore out three wives. The first bore him eight children, the second eleven, and the third, who must have been something of a disappointment, only six. Fit, healthy, sexually attractive middle-aged women could not have existed in any numbers before the advent of modern birth control.

In fact, however, despite a widely held critical prejudice to the contrary, mature as distinct from aged females – mothers, say, with teenage children – are quite common in the plays, occurring in half of Shakespeare's and a third of those of his contemporaries.[32] Shakespeare's *King John*, for instance, has three mature-to-elderly females and only one young one, whilst *The Merry Wives of Windsor* has a similar pattern, with its two leading female roles, Mistress Page and Mistress Ford, in precisely that most difficult category of the mature and sexually attractive. Hence, it can be argued, such characters occurred too often for them not to be considered well within the scope of the regular players of female roles, and further indication that such were in their late teens.

Representing innocence

Lisa Jardine argues for an equivalence between female-character subordination and boy-actor dependency, and hence his juniority. Certainly there is strong evidence of female subordination in the character representation in the plays but, as the succeeding chapters will show, it is polemical rather than performer-orientated, focusing on male concerns and male versions of how women should or should not behave such that any performer of whatever age or gender is likely to be required to present women within its parameters.

The issue crystallises around a role like that of Ophelia: quiescent, subordinate, opaque in motive, and with a stylised mad scene. Is it written thus to allow for the limitations of the juvenile performer, as James Hill argues, or are the qualities there for other reasons, and capable of being represented by a more seasoned player? The contrived artificial nature of Ophelia's mad scene is in contrast to the more psychological representation of Hamlet's own mental disturbance. As with Gertrude's choric description of Ophelia's flower-laden death, it is, it could be argued, the means both to generate the secondary incidental pleasures of female pathos, and to keep the subordinate female character at a suitable distance that will augment rather than compete with Hamlet's own central tragedy. Maturing adolescents would be able to reproduce the effect of innocence, but they would also be able to put it into a more sophisticated, artful context, as perhaps suggested by the Bad Quarto (with some claims to authenticity as a record of performance) in which Ophelia enters her mad scene, '*playing on a Lute*'. If the feelings and reactions of female characters often appear naive or unworldly that is perhaps not because playwrights thought this was all the performers were capable of representing but because it reflected society's views of women.

Because a female character is presented as naive and malleable, or even beautiful and sexy, does not necessarily tell us anything about the performer, other than perhaps the level of skill demanded. An Elizabethan character, however modest or retiring, had to have that modesty projected, enlarged, displayed – on a thrust stage with an encircling audience. This must often have involved some consciousness of the disparities, skills, and artfulness inherent in such an overt act of communication such as to set the performer apart and invite an attitude towards the opposite-sex character being represented which he himself in his playing suggests.

'Of Miranda', writes Coleridge, 'we may say that she possesses in herself all the ideal beauties that could be imagined'; to which Mrs Jameson adds, 'so perfectly unsophisticated, so delicately refined, that she is all but ethereal'. But the text itself carries quite other implications for its performance:

FERDINAND: Wherefore weep you?
MIRANDA: At mine unworthiness, that dare not offer
   What I desire to give: and much less take
   What I shall die to want. But this is trifling,
   And all the more it seeks to hide itself,
   The bigger bulk it shows. Hence, bashful cunning,
   And prompt me, plain and holy innocence!
   I am your wife, if you will marry me . . .   (*The Tempest*, III.i.76–83)

Shakespeare is straining for a sensuous love without sexuality, a maiden sheltered from the corrupting power of her own sex, and so protected by 'plain and holy innocence' as to be unaware of the sexual puns about 'dying' and pregnancy that come without her conscious aid. Thus idealism is blended with male fantasies of sexual innocence and availability. Her representation is at least in part a male joke if a relatively benign one and surely incorporating the performer and his delivery of it. Note also the naivety of her final speech:

                O wonder!
   How many goodly creatures are there here!
   How beauteous mankind is! O brave new world
   That has such people in't!   (v.i.181–4)

Given that the stage is presently occupied, Ferdinand apart, by the 'three men of sin' (III.iii.53) and their attendants, it is difficult to avoid the possibility of irony here also. Richard Robinson appears to have been the chief player of female roles in the period 1611/12 when Miranda was first performed. He may, of course, have played Ariel, but in either event some reference to the likely range of his parts sets the representation of maidenly innocence into context, for he is recorded as playing the ice-cold Lady (or her Ghost) in the *The Second Maiden's Tragedy* of that year, and almost certainly the lascivious Fulvia in *Catiline*, alternately defend-ing herself with a knife from rape and seducing her lover Curius with kisses, finally to lead him off to congress. If as Alfred Harbage suggests the King's Men may have shared in the production of *The Brazen Age*, he could also have played Venus, inviting Adonis to warm his hands in her bosom, and, in a later sequence, ending naked and *in flagrante* with Mars in Vulcan's net to the amusement of the assembled gods.[33] This ought to be a timely reminder of the sort of repertory circumstances in which *all* of Shakespeare's roles were conceived and, whatever the nature of the character, were performed to the hilt by the same small group of seasoned performers.

The demands of the breeches role

Edwardian critics greeted the breeches-role convention with relief as easier for the young male to play. Granville Barker suggests of Rosalind: 'through three parts of the play a boy has the best of it', being 'unhampered', as Davies puts it, 'by the necessity to pretend that he is a woman'. This is, of course, not so. Far from being easier, breeches roles are more difficult, requiring the performer to communicate a continuous sense of femaleness underneath his male appearance without any of the usual aids but merely through inflection and gesture.

A useful comparison is with the modern television impressionist who may use elaborate make-up, prosthesis, and costume to imitate the appear-ance of his target, but may instead dispense with all of these and bring him to life merely with intonation and gesture. Contrived verisimilitude risks the distaste described by Max Beerbohm of cross-dressing:

The greater the aesthetic illusion, the more strongly does our natural sense of fitness rebel against the travesty of nature.[34]

The impressionist in his ordinary clothes, on the other hand, like the Elizabethan youth in breeches, is free of the temptations of making verisimilitude an end in itself. Both aim rather than merely to reproduce the *appearance* of their subject to capture instead their very *essence*, and at one stage removed – for our contemplation. The process is also an ethical and political one. It invites and demands an attitude towards the object of portrayal. The earliest female stage portrayals, like those of the mime Vitalis, for instance, assert of the *genus* that female modesty is a cover for lustfulness. If, as seems likely, the performers of the breeches roles did not indicate by any adjustments in their appearance that they were girls whilst they were dressed as boys, then the imitation of female embarrassment at, for instance, showing their legs in 'long hose and short coat', is reduced to a humorous and probably salacious male mime. Cheek by Jowl's all-male production of *As You Like It* demonstrated that the key moment for Rosalind, bringing greatest attention to the male actor's assumed femininity, was her first appearance in boy's clothes. It was not so much that the actor needed the audience's imaginative help, as the opportunity it provided to amuse by exaggerating and pointing the sudden exposure of the lower limbs hitherto shrouded in skirts. The breeches role as interpreted by Shakespeare was a humorous display of the male point of view towards sexual difference and further opportunity for the display of skill.

The character of Mistress Low-Water in *No Wit, No Help like a Woman's*, 1613, shows the direction in which this convention was moving by the end of Shakespeare's career. Probably writing for Lady Elizabeth's Men, Middleton has coarsened the 'female character *en travestie*' convention to provide a bravura role for an experienced if still relatively youthful performer. Unlike the earlier heroines, forced hesitantly by circumstances into breeches, continuously aware of their dangers and impropriety, and acutely conscious of their own inadequacy to sustain the disguise, Mistress Low-Water, setting out to court the rich widow Lady Goldenfleece in her male disguise and thus repair her husband's fortunes, deliberately puts herself into the sort of situation which earlier heroines had tried to avoid:

Come, make but short service, widow, a kiss and to bed . . . (II.iii.129–30)

She goes on to marry the widow and thus regain her husband's lost fortune and then faces the problem of sustaining the impersonation on her wedding night, with the lusty widow urging consummation and the plot teetering, as so often in Middleton, on the very edge of grossness. She saves herself from displaying her (supposed) genital inadequacy only at the very last moment by picking a quarrel over the source of her new-found wealth. And then the playwright provides her with the means of release from her bigamy, whilst keeping the money, in the shape of a long-lost brother to take her place.

There are strong parallels between Middleton's clearly circumscribed play-world and that which had existed a generation earlier in John Lyly's plays for the Paul's choristers, in which the decorative aesthetics of their fanciful storylines took priority over characterisation, so that costume, identity, gender could be exchanged at will, cross-dressing was innocent of street-life associations, and even sex-change, as in the ending of *Gallathea*, no more than a mildly amusing plot resolution; for as Dionysus shows in *Bartholomew Fair*, the actor–puppets have nothing beneath their shifts. Many things have changed, however, since the 1580s, and Middleton's comic theatre is ever more confident and ever more insulated from reality in its fictions, with ample opportunities for even more distasteful exploitation of the breeches role, as in the pregnant-page plot in *The Widow* (1616) and the threatened body-search in *More Dissemblers Besides Women* (1619?). That sense of the theatre being the crucible of the nation's concerns, so prominent in the intervening years, is now dissipated in catering for separate class-interests and jaded palates. The success and invulnerability of Mistress Low-Water's assumption is anticipated in another of Middleton's plays, *A Mad World, My Masters*, 1606, in which Follywit's disguise as Sir Bountiful's mistress so easily fools the old codger, (and is undertaken by a character who is a young man rather than a boy). The cost in both plays of their hero/ heroine's level of resourcefulness is a loss of any serious fidelity to the representation of sexual difference, so that instead of the triumphant success of Mistress Low-Water reflecting any confidence in what real women might achieve, it becomes no more than a series of contrivances to show off the skill of the male performer in something approaching burlesque. The seeds of this ultimately imaginatively sterile imperturbability can of course be seen in Rosalind in *As You Like It*, who is never wrong-footed nor short of a witty reply and by the end of the play is in total command of everyone's fortunes.

Did the ages vary between 1500 and 1660?

All the direct evidence of player ages relates to the half-century after Shakespeare's death and the key question has to be how far it can be taken to reflect his period and that which preceded it. Are there factors that would account for variations in the average age of players of female roles during the sixteenth century and perhaps a rise in their average age in Shakespeare's later period, and from then onward?

There is a case for suggesting that Shakespeare, through showing areas of male/female interaction not hitherto attempted in theatre, and by some of the presentational techniques he developed through his dramaturgy (to be discussed in the later chapters), did much to establish a more sophisticated performance style for major female roles played by a new cadre of young adults that lasted until the closure of the theatres in 1642. There is no doubt that in the later period, players became more established, more confident, and more professional, and that the formulaic plays of the Caroline period offered more opportunity for performer specialism. If this is so, then the corollary might well be that this new, more sophisticated tradition was created out of a more primitive convention that Shakespeare inherited and which was in some respects quite different, and perhaps sustained by younger players. Shakespeare might, therefore, constitute a transition between one performance tradition and another. This would explain why the characteristics ascribed to the touring companies in the inner plays, as they relate to the young performers, are perhaps inconsistent with current practice in Shakespeare's mature theatre. They reflect a sometimes poorly focused nostalgia for an earlier, simpler life of strolling, before the establishment of larger companies in the wake of the Queen's Men (1583), and evident by the mid-1590s in larger touring ensembles.[35]

One factor that has to be taken into account in considering age-patterns in players of female roles before women came on the scene is the post-Restoration assertions that fully grown men made such roles ridiculous, and the implication, therefore, of a further increase in age at least during the later Caroline period. In his 'Prologue to the King' of 16 August 1660, Thomas Jordan, himself a former player of female roles, claimed:

> We curse the Misery in which our Trade is,
> And are imprison'd, but our large siz'd Ladies
> (Thinking to 'scape them) are torn by the throats
> And like Wine Porters put in Petty-coats)
> Dragg't to the *Muse* for Plotters . . .

He repeated his charge the following December in the prologue to Killigrew's revival of *Othello*, which, in presenting itself as the first to introduce women to the stage, claimed of their predecessors:

> Our women are so defective, and so siz'd
> You'd think they were some of the guard disguis'd:
> For to speak truth, men act, that are between
> Forty and Fifty, wenches of fifteen;
> With bone so large, and nerve so incompliant,
> When you call Desdemona, enter Giant.

Clearly Jordan has ulterior motives for his charges. In the first passage he is urging royal blessing for the introduction of actresses. Killigrew's production, already in preparation, was riding on royal favour. In the second passage Jordan is concerned to disparage what went before in order to raise support for the innovation, not yet altogether welcome:

> The woman plays today; mistake me not,
> No man in gown, nor page in petticoat . . .

However, he is not alone. Cibber's *Apology* contains a second-hand anecdote about a performance being delayed whilst Desdemona shaved, and Shadwell's prologue to his *The Tempest*, 1674, asserts that but for the ingenuity of the company, 'some with grizl'd beards had acted Women still' (although his motives may be similar to Jordan's).

Is there any more objective evidence that things had changed by the Restoration, and that grown men had come to specialise in female roles? Could any have survived since the closure of the theatres in 1642? One slight piece of evidence is James Wright's remark in his *Historia Histrionica*, 1699, concerning the surreptitious performances during the Interregnum, that under Oliver Cromwell:

Alexander Goffe, the woman-actor at Blackfriars (who had made himself known to persons of quality), used to be the jackal and give notice of time and place.

Cromwell was Protector from 1653–8, playing finally stopped at Blackfriars in 1653, and it was pulled down in 1655. Gough, born in 1614, is known to have played female roles between 1626 and 1632 (i.e. until eighteen), perhaps coached by his father Robert, who himself had played female roles before graduating to male ones. There are no male roles assigned to Alexander, but he never became a sharer, so they may not have been recorded. If Wright's description of Gough relates to the period immediately before 1653, then Gough would have been thirty-nine in that year. On the other hand, acting as 'Jackal' suggests he may by then have been part of the management, perhaps as a minor functionary, and that the description 'Woman Actor' referred back to when he had been celebrated as a youth. This is no direct help in identifying Jordan's alleged adults, who are referred to in the present tense, since there is no evidence that Gough performed after 1660 or even after 1632. None of the former boy players who did re-emerge as actors at the Restoration – Bird, Hart, Clun, and Burt – returned to female roles, and none of the known actors of female parts after 1660 indicate any pre-Restoration history in the theatre. Downes supplies the names of six actors;[37] nothing is known of Angel, 'Mosley and Floid commonly Acted the Part of Bawd and Whore', and Nokes apparently played the female lead in *The Maid of the Inn*, and although nothing is known directly about their ages, they all appear to have been youths recruited freshly for that purpose; whilst the remaining two, Betterton and Kynaston, whose ages we do know, confirm the continuance of the tradition of performing the female roles in their late teens. Furthermore, the lavish praise of Downes and Pepys concerning Kynaston's effectiveness as a female character is in sharp contrast to the jibes being made at exactly the same time about incongruous maturity. On 18 August 1660, for instance, only two days after Jordan's charge of 'our large siz'd Ladies . . . like Wine Porters put in Petty-Coates' is spoken onstage, Pepys describes the seventeen-year-old Kynaston as Olympia in *The Loyal Subject* as making 'the loveliest lady I ever saw in my life'.[38] With no firm evidence to counter this, and despite Jordan's detail, it seems likely that he was exaggerating for his own purposes. After all, the incongruities by which he seeks to deride what he alleges to have been men of forty and fifty cross-dressing to play teenage girls are precisely those we have seen earlier generations of players taking such care to avoid.

CONCLUSION

The evidence both of the plays themselves and of the biographical material associated with the players suggests that mid-to-late teens, say fifteen to eighteen, could be seen as the optimum age for playing leading female roles, towards which any cross-dressed performance tradition might naturally gravitate; a compromise between on the one hand the benefits of the freshness and energy of youth, together with the slightness of frame which is the *sine qua non* for the male construction of femininity, and the advantages on the other of experience and acquired skill that enabled the performer to take a full and cognisant part in ensemble playing.

The issue is not whether there were young boys on the Elizabethan stage. It is manifest that there must have been. Whatever the delaying techniques favoured by Robertson Davies, or for that matter the gin and late nights recommended in another context by Mr Vincent Crummles, there is no way of halting the ageing process. 'Youth's a stuff will not endure.' Boys will still 'wear out'. Hence new recruits for the female roles must have regularly been taken up and received their training in minor parts. What is at issue are the general characteristics of the performers of the *leading* roles and the theatrical and erotic culture they are supposed to have sustained.

CHAPTER 2

Erotic ambience

There has been an increasing tendency in modern criticism to assume an ever closer association between Elizabethan theatre and homosexuality. Jan Kott in 1967 linked the attractions of sexual indeterminacy in Shakespeare's plays with Leonardo and Italian neo-platonic pederasty, whilst Lesley Fiedler in 1973 imagined 'mincing little queens' behind the scenes performing 'blatant homosexual travesties' of Shakespeare's heroines.[1] It was left to Lisa Jardine, however, in 1983 to put it more bluntly:

male prostitution and perverted sexual activity is the inevitable accompaniment of female impersonation.[2]

Even she, however, took care to ascribe these sentiments to the Elizabethan anti-theatrical scholar, John Rainolds, but though she makes a token gesture of distancing herself from his tone, it is clear from what follows that his views form the basis of her subsequent argument.

Other critics were quick to follow suit. According to Jonathan Goldberg, the Elizabethan 'theatrical milieu' was 'as hospitable to homosexuality as any institution in the period'. He adds, 'boy actors were regularly suspected of being what they counterfeited' (though that would mean, of course, that at least 50 per cent of them must have been extremely virtuous).[3] By 1992, Susan Zimmerman could talk of 'audience participation' through having its attention drawn to the real identities of the performers 'in the erotic transgression' of what she calls 'culturally inscribed categories', and could assert that the adult actors in their relations with the female characters likewise 'put a pederastic gloss on the homosexual valances of cross-dressing'.[4] In short, 'desire on the Renaissance stage', the sub-title of the collection of essays she edited, was taken to be more or less exclusively homoerotic.

Analysis of the nature of eroticism in Elizabethan plays, after being suppressed for so long, is certainly overdue. Kott's allusive chapter on homoeroticism, for instance, was omitted as recently as 1964 from the first English edition of his book. From being a possible, perhaps unavoidable, element in Elizabethan theatre, however, homoeroticism has rapidly come to be seen as its *raison d'être*, addressed, according to the critics who now find it so widespread in text and performance, to a fundamental homosexual propensity in the Elizabethan male. Both the major studies of cross-dressed performers in recent times *Gender in Play on the Shakespearean Stage* by Michael Shapiro, 1994, and *Impersonations* by Stephen Orgel, 1996, are made to turn on this theme. 'The love of men for boys', according to Stephen Orgel in an earlier essay, 'is all but axiomatic in the period',[5] and this view has become so widely accepted that Zimmerman can assert, 'Male spectators not only lusted for the woman in drama, but', and she quotes Orgel,' "after the boy beneath the woman's costume, thereby playing the woman's role themselves"'. Although Michael Shapiro finds no evidence of this supposed spectator impropriety, he focuses his attention instead on allegations of abuse of young apprentices by their masters. That 'the boy actors served as catamites', he says, 'was widely perceived as the common treatment of apprentices in all-male theatrical troupes', and he brings this charge into the discussion of practically every play with which he deals.[6] Dympna Callaghan in 2000 talks of 'Theatre as an institution . . . based on the forced expropriation of child labor and the threat of sexual victimization', which 'molded the boys, aesthetically, if not surgically, into the shape of eunuchs.'[7] Thus by 2001, theatrical pederasty had become a historical fact, and Sarah Werner could talk of 'the sexual relations that historically pertained to boy actors and adult males', and conclude: 'Shakespeare and his contemporaries were indeed queer by modern standards.'[8] The enthusiasm and conviction of these critics has been emboldened by Alan Bray's historical study for the Gay Men's Press which unambiguously asserts:

Given the prevalence of homosexuality in the theatrical milieu and the importance of prostitution in London generally, it is understandable that homosexual prostitution should have taken root in a distinctive way in the theatres.[9]

Despite its wide citation, this view is based on very limited evidence, all of it open to doubt. It is to Bray's credit that he acknowledges so, but all the more unfortunate that this does not prevent him from basing his subsequent generalisations upon it. The evidence offered to underpin his assertions in respect of homosexuality in Elizabethan and contemporary European society more generally will be dealt with later. The immediate concentration below is on its supposed occurrence in the theatre.

Analysis of the historical evidence offered

This takes three forms:

(i) Poetical satire

Firstly there are allegations of theatrical homosexuality in contemporary satires, but all derived directly from Roman models. Jonson and Marston in particular, with what they saw as the licence of Juvenal, highly fashionable in the 1590s, attempted to demean and sully as many targets as possible. It is for this reason that their satires were eventually banned. With Roman models came Roman vices. It is this genre of vitriolic, intentionally offensive satire that introduced the terms for pederasty into the English language: 'ganymede' (1591), 'ingle' (1592), and 'catamite' (1593).[10] Their purpose was to shock with ever more dangerous and depraved vices, hence the repeated declension of whore, catamite, *and goat*, as for instance John Donne in 'Satyr IV', 1597, and Jonson in his poem 'Sir Voluptuous Beast':

> Telling the motions of each petticoat
> And how his Ganymede moved, and how his goat.

Notwithstanding Orgel's evidence that between 1553 and 1602 indictments for bestiality in the Home Counties outnumbered indictments for sodomy six to one (although neither was very common), critics have not been inclined to apply the perhaps less sympathetic charge of bestiality to the Elizabethan theatre.

Bray himself recognises 'how little (these satires) are the stuff of social life and how much the product of purely political and literary influences', and yet this does not prevent him from using them in the absence of anything more reliable as corroboration for his generalisations about the alleged popularity of homosexuality in the theatre.

One supposed piece of evidence regularly cited, which gives some indication of the parlous nature of such garnering, is Middleton's reference in his satirical work *Father Hubbard's Tale* to the children's company at Blackfriars as a 'nest of boys able to ravish a man'. While 'ravish' may refer to physical assault, it might equally well be a reference to the children's acting *giving delight*, i.e. by 'ravishing' *the senses*, a meaning then also current (see *OED* for examples as far back as 1087).

(ii) Theatre controversy

Secondly, charges of homosexuality were thrown at the players as part of the 'flyting' of theatre controversies. Jonson, ever quarrelsome, ever changing the company he wrote for, uses the charge of pederasty along with much else in his attacks on his erstwhile colleagues in the adult theatre in *The Poetaster*, written for the Children, and, no doubt in order to be able to use the authority of Juvenal, set in Rome. His purpose, as part of the so-called 'War of the Theatres', is as much to stimulate controversy and bring people into the theatre to see his plays as anything else.[11] Both sides used whatever ammunition they could find, and it bears little value as historical evidence.

On the face of it the most serious charge is that of J. Cocke in one of a series of 'characters' (itself often a satirical form), entitled *A common Player*:

If hee marries, hee mistakes the Woman for the Boy in Womans attire, by not respecting a difference in the mischiefe: But so long as he lives unmarried, hee mistakes the Boy, or a Whore for the Woman; by courting the first on the stage, or visiting the second at her devotions.

Although this is precisely the burden of the homophilic case, it has to be noted that it is but a small part of a much longer almost unremittingly satirical attack on the common player by a member of the Inns of Court as part of a dialogue for and against playing. It is a reply to Webster's defence of it and evidently a feeling retort to 'a certain number of saucy rude jests against the common lawyer'. In other words Cocke is meeting like with like. Furthermore, in its nicely cautious conclusion he covers himself by claiming he is attacking only 'the base artless *appendants* of our city companies' and not the 'many' that 'may deserve a wise man's commendation' (presumably the sharers). It should be obvious too that the central charge is more a bawdy joke than a literal truth. Regular entries of new-born infants in the parish registers make it clear that the players were perfectly capable of heterosexual activity; a point that would scarcely need making were it not that such satirical jibes are now so solemnly recounted as evidence of actual social *mores*.

In addition, there are a few allegations of homosexual activity made during the Interregnum in political attacks on Hugh Peters, and one or two oblique and passing slurs after the Restoration, but again these are part of discrediting the former tradition in favour of the introduction of actresses, which itself had little to do with improving morality.

(iii) The anti-theatricalists

The main source of evidence relied upon to support the widespread allegations of homosexuality in the Elizabethan theatre are the accusations from amongst those writers who, from the 1580s, latched onto the prohibition against cross-dressing in Deuteronomy as a means of banning theatrical activity altogether. Their evidence is in no sense objective or informed, much of it unadapted traditional patristic diatribe against the obscenities of the Roman theatre, repeatedly copied during the Dark Ages long after playing of any kind had ceased. Elizabethan anti-theatricalists furthermore borrow copiously from one another.

Nor was cross-dressing a significant target in the original attacks upon theatre. William Ringler Snr long ago put forward a compelling case to show that opposition to the commercial theatre began as a direct consequence of James Burbage's construction of the first two playhouses, the Theater and the Curtain, in the fields outside London.[12] This, he suggests, was the cause of, rather than a response to, citizen hostility (the original motive for location being the opportunity to exploit cheaper land). The initial attacks from 1577 were not predominantly theological, and certainly not psychological, but immediate and practical and more concerned with the threats to commerce by distracting employees during the working day, with the emptying of churches on the sabbath, and with the increased opportunities for crime and civil disorder. Burbage's commercial enterprise showed a ready market and several of the larger inns immediately followed suit, so that it has been estimated that with eight playing-venues by 1578 there were as many as half a million visits to the theatre in that year. This is an enormous increase, and since mainly amongst new theatregoers from the lower classes, was perceived as a major challenge to the existing cultural and social order, and there is plenty of evidence that it did attract prostitution, petty thieving and affrays.

It is not surprising, therefore, that, without a police force and conscious of royal and noble patronage for the players, it appears to have been civic leaders, citizens and guildsmen, who commissioned hack writers like Gosson and Munday to stir up opposition on their behalf, whilst almost all the sermons from clergy attacking theatres were likewise commissioned by and preached before these very same people, the Mayor, aldermen and members of the livery companies at Paul's Cross, with the preachers often having their subjects chosen for them. Furthermore, the particular focus of all this ire is not the players or the plays, but the *spectators* and *their* behaviour.

The key figure who provides the transition from these early, essentially practical, objections to commercial theatre to the later fundamentally unbalanced diatribes about 'transforming' men into women and so on, which have provided such a rich hunting ground for the homophilic argument, is Stephen Gosson. An Oxford man, failed playwright, unsuccessful player and self-publicist, his three mischievous attacks on his erstwhile colleagues have much the smack of the incestuous theatre controversies touched on above, in that he seeks to draw out his opponents to reply in order to keep the quarrel going and to benefit thereby. It is only in his third attempt, *Plays Confuted*, 1582, that he hits upon the argument that cross-dressing offends against Deuteronomy (previously mentioned briefly by Calvin and Northbrooke), but as simply one of a whole series of random charges.

The most frequently cited opponent of theatre in modern criticism, however, is John Rainolds, who according to Susan Zimmerman, brushing aside Lisa Jardine's earlier more scrupulous circumspection, gives an insight into how the generality of audiences approached theatre, providing what she describes as 'an incisive sensitive account of the psychodynamics of male spectatorship'. What is generally overlooked, however, is the relatively exceptional and highly personal nature of his charges.

Rainolds was a considerable scholar, Greek Reader, and eventual President of Corpus Christi College, Oxford. His lectures on Aristotle were several times reprinted after his death, he was a prominent translator of the Authorised Version, and J. W. Binns suggests his theological writings did more than those of any other to justify the English schism.[13] However, given that his voluminous correspondence on Deuteronomy and the sins of cross-dressing was occasioned by an innocent and fraternal invitation in 1591/2 to watch a student performance of another Oxford academic's work, an activity given the blessing of the authorities and described by the Chancellor of the University, the Earl of Leicester, as 'commendable and great furtherances of Learning', as well as his subsequent repeated and lengthy refusals of further invitations such as drew even the Queen's ire,[14] it is extremely unlikely that Rainolds ever went to the public theatre at all.

His only documented contact with drama was as a performer, playing the female role Hippolyta in *Palamon and Arcite* in 1566 as an undergraduate, and perhaps under duress.[15] It seems to have been an unfortunate experience. 'A woman's garment being put upon a man', he observes, 'doth vehemently touch and move him with rememberance and imagination of a woman; and the imagination of a thing desirable doth stir up the desire.' Elsewhere he writes, 'what sparkles of lust the putting of women's attire on men may kindle in unclean affections', and although he goes on to cite the cross-dressing of Heliogabalus as his example, the reader is left with the strong impression that Rainolds himself had experienced, perhaps involuntarily, a 'stirring of desire' leading to a 'sparkle of lust' during his own brief transformation, and that it is this personal element that sustains his rage over such a long and obsessive campaign, as well as keeping him away from the scene of his self-humiliation. Beyond this unfortunate experience it is fair to assume, and especially as his illustrations are drawn so exclusively from antiquity, that of the reverse side of the coin, of Zimmerman's so-called 'psychodynamics of spectatorship', male or otherwise, he had no experience whatsoever. It should be added too, that whilst his observations have been applied very freely to the professional theatre of his day and the supposed young boys in it, his controversy with Gager, and later with Gentili, was about *students* performing. He seems to have had no connection at all with London or its theatre.

In respect of the allegation that cross-dressing in Elizabethan theatre encouraged homosexuality, although Rainolds does link wearing female attire with male prostitution, his examples are drawn exclusively from antiquity and in non-theatrical contexts, and, alongside its stimulation of self-abuse in the performer, the *main* thrust of his objections to theatrical cross-dressing is what we would describe as 'heterosexual', in its recreation of the temptations of womankind, which evidently haunted him with their forbidden power. Somewhat incongruously he cites the Roman elegiac poet Propertius to testify to the erotic qualities of the female:

more fullie by his own experience; affirming that hee was not ravished so much with his mistresses face though marvellous faire and beautifull, *nor with her heare hanging down loose after the facion about her smooth necke*, nor *with her radiant eyes, like starres*; nor *with her silkes*, and outlandish braverie; as hee was with her *galant dancing*.

Not only the female in motion but any figural representation of her is liable to cause sinful desire. So powerful were female charms, Rainolds says, citing the myth of Pygmalion, that 'men may be ravished with love of stones, of dead stuff, framed by cunning gravers to beautiful women's likeness'. How much greater temptation then is 'the cladding of youths in such attire' and allowing them to dance on the stage, which he says, 'is an occasion of drawing and provoking corruptly-minded men to most heinous wickedness'. His is a world of constant temptation and denial, obsessed with sex, and unrealistic about the levels of eroticism that exist and are contained within a civilised society.

It is not until William Prynne's exhaustive compendium of insults, *Histrio-Mastix*, 1633, a generation and more later (and amply answered by Sir Richard Baker's *Theatrum Redivivum*, 1662),[16] that a sustained link between cross-dressing and homosexuality is attempted. Prynne writes of 'how a male might be effeminated into a female, how their sex might be changed by Art', so that, we are told, 'men rush on men with outrageous lusts', and society then wreaked a very public vengeance using the supposed attack on the Queen's theatricals as its provocation.

In contrast, the general tenor of anti-theatrical criticism was to attack the stage representation of female wantonness for stimulating not homosexual but *heterosexual* misbehaviour amongst spectators. Modern critics are too inclined to follow Prynne in seizing on Philip Stubbes' reference in *The Anatomy of Abuses* to 'playing the Sodomites' to support their case:

> Then, these goodly pageants being done, euery mate sorts to his mate, euery one brings another homeward of their way verye freendly, and in secret conclaues (couertly) play the *Sodomits*, or worse. [17]

Though much cited, this passage cannot be made to support the homophilic case once it has been put into context, since Stubbes' preceding paragraphs make it clear that his principal focus is on the plays as 'devourers of maidenly [i.e. *female*] virtue and chastity'. Hence the term 'Sodomy' here, as in much of the corpus of this material, means not anal sex but the much larger category of illicit fornication, i.e. all sexual activity not directed towards procreation within marriage. In Bale's *Three Laws*, for instance, the term includes nuns having illegitimate children. [18] Only Stubbes' rhetorical flourish, 'or worse', is perhaps a passing reference to sodomy. Thus what he goes on to describe after the passage quoted above are spectators stimulated by the heterosexual lasciviousness represented onstage finding partners and going home or to a nearby inn to practise it. Gosson elaborates on their techniques:

> it is the fashion of youthes to go first into the yarde, and carry theire eye through euery gallery then like vnto rauens where they spye the carion thither they flye, and presse as nere to ye fairest as they can ... They giue them pippines, they dally with their garments to passe ye time, they minister talke vpon al occasions, & eyther bring them home to their houses on small acquaintance, or slip into tauerns when ye plaies are done.

Anthony Munday, likewise in turn both playwright and anti-theatrical hack, indicates the sort of chat-line such youths would employ. Referring to a character onstage, the aspiring seducer asks:

> is it not pittie this passioned lover should be so martyred? And if he find her inclined to foolish pittie, as commonlie such women are, then he applies the matter to himself and saies that he is likewise carried awaie with the liking of her.

Reprehensible such tactics may be, but there could hardly be any clearer testimony not only to the 'heterosexual' uses to which plays were put, but, more centrally, subsuming performers and performance, to the 'hetero-sexual' reception of the play itself.

The treatment of homosexuality in the plays

Homosexuality is not often mentioned in the plays, but where it occurs it is unequivocally condemned. In *The Atheist's Tragedy* the ridiculous Chaplain Snuff, seeking his quarry in the dark, mistakenly embraces a dead man: 'Now purity defend me from the Sin of Sodom.' In *Honest Man's Fortune*, Laverdine fears hanging. Whatever the truth of Marlowe's alleged procliv-ities detailed in the testimonies of Baines, a Government informer, and Kyd, his friend, under torture (and after Marlowe's death), *Edward II* provides an uncompromising moral on the dangers of sodomy, brought to its climax in the hero's death, anally penetrated with a red-hot poker.[19]

Shakespeare's only sustained reference to homosexuality is in the alle-gations made by Thersites against Patroclus and Achilles in *Troilus and Cressida*, especially in v.i where he calls Patroclus a 'masculine whore'. It is difficult to know how far to accept Thersites' evaluation. His mordant wit debases everything in the play; to him 'the argument' of the war 'is a whore and a cuckold', the generals are windbags and the heroes fools to serve as their instruments; though arguably he is never far wrong. On the other hand, Patroclus appears to have a taste for heterosexual encounters (v.ii.192–3). In either event, Shakespeare provides a less than attractive account of the consequences of male-on-male congress. According to Thersites it causes:

the rotten diseases of the south, the guts-griping, ruptures, [catarrhs,] loads a' gravel in the back, lethargies, cold palsies, raw eyes, dirt-rotten livers, whissing lungs, bladders full of impostume, sciaticas, lime-kills i' th' palm, incurable bone-ache, and the rivell'd fee-simple of the tetter . . . (*Troilus and Cressida*, v.i.17–23)

In John Bale's Protestant polemic, *Three Laws*, Sodomy is inevitably associated with Catholicism and appears dressed 'like a monk of all sects', a consequence of Idolatry, and an offence against the law of Nature. Papists are really unbelievers, 'For God they have no fear', and Pope Julius II is impugned with homosexual rape:

> Which sought to have, in his fury,
> Two lads, and to use them beastly . . . (Act II)

A similar theme is treated in more detail in *The Devil's Charter*, 1607, by Barnaby Barnes. Astor Manfredi and his brother Phillipo are wards of court of the Borgia pope, Alexander, who proposes to make them his 'concubines'. They are in no two minds about the merits of this plan:

PHILLIPO: I rather choose within the riuer *Tiber*
                To drowne my selfe, or from the *Tarpeyan* hill,
                My vexed body to precipitate,
                Then to subject my body to the shame
                Of such vild brutish and vnkindely lust.
ASTOR: He that with fire and Brimstone did consume
                Sodome and other Citties round about,
                Deliuer vs from this soule-slaying sinne,
                To which our bodies are made prostitute.   (II.i.1163–71)

It is an account of pederasty scarcely consonant with Stephen Orgel's view that 'the love of men for men in this culture appears less threatening than the love of men for women', or that it raised 'surprisingly little anxiety'.

Finding homosexuals in the plays

Rather than addressing these concrete examples of sodomy in the plays, critics prefer to shift their ground to the more attractive possibilities of subjective inference. Simon Shepherd points to the many ways that 'Homos have been spotted' in recent Shakespearian studies, and how that condition has been used to explain 'mysterious melancholies', 'inexplicable villainies', and why characters 'make a muck of their countries', and in turn offers, 'warrior camaraderie, male friendship, ruler's favourites, and ladies tailor'.[20] Most of these are beyond the scope of the present study, but it is necessary to look again at Sebastian and Antonio in *Twelfth Night*, because Orgel argues, leaping effortlessly from relations between characters to ones between the performers, that as an 'overt homosexual couple', they somehow signal by analogy that the central relationship of Viola and Orsino is one of a 'man wooing a man'.

One way of charging the plays with homoeroticism is to refuse to accept the traditional distinction between Love and Friendship; and to insist that 'male bonding' is no more than sublimated homosexuality, even when plays clearly say the contrary as in the anonymous Paul's *Maid's Metamorphosis*, 1600, when the transformed heroine, Eurymine, now a man, offers to be a friend in place of a wife, but promises not intimacies but only the masculine virtues of courage and loyalty: 'whose dearest blood and life / Shall be as ready as thine own for thee' (V.i.47–9). Her husband specifically rejects the possibility of loving her as a boy, which he says would lead him to be, 'haunted with . . . lunacy'.

Antonio in *Twelfth Night* is obviously infatuated with the much younger, more high-ranking, and as the likeness to Viola requires, more beautiful Sebastian, offering his service, his money, his protection, and his love; offering in fact rather too much. When we first meet them, Sebastian is trying to extricate himself from the association, made more difficult because Antonio has saved his life, but there is no evidence in the text that he in any way returns Antonio's great affection. Such ideals of service are commonplace in the plays. Orgel himself, citing Bray, points out that 'the rhetoric of patronage, gratitude and male friendship in this period is precisely the language of love'.

When young women in male disguise woo their prospective husbands, arguments that impute homoeroticism, as Shapiro repeatedly does of *Twelfth Night*, and Jardine, Callaghan, and Orgel of *As You Like It*, the latter referring several times to 'Rosalind the catamite', depend upon a deliberate misreading of the plays, or rather two contradictory misreadings:

(a) Male heroes, we are told, develop a homoerotic interest in the cross-dressed heroines because they accept them at face-value as boys. In fact, of course, none of these critics provides evidence that any of the heroes ever goes beyond the sort of affection appropriate to be shown to a page. To do so would not only transgress propriety, but more importantly ruin the plot, which depends for its effect on our accepting, within certain bounds, that the figure is a girl disguised as a boy and thereby a person entitled to precisely the sort of marks of erotic attraction that, with amusing frustration, disguise hinders. The more complex the disguise, as when the breeched heroine who is pretending to be a boy pretends to be a boy-pretending-to-be-a-girl, the more all concerned have to keep their minds on the plot. There continued to be in the Elizabethan reception of the drama an awareness of and an admiration for the cleverness of the performer, but to suggest, as Susan Zimmerman does, the establishment onstage of a homoerotic level between adult and juvenile male performers is to risk just that elision of levels of identity that would destroy the whole structure. To maintain this view, as for instance Sue-Ellen Case's assertion of the cross-dressed theatre that 'The fictional "norm" . . . simply mediates and enhances the homoerotic flirtation between two males',[21] is as anti-theatrical as Prynne and Rainolds in denying or ignoring the nature of stage fiction and of mimesis. No hero ever admits to a homosexual attraction towards what he thinks is a boy, nor is there a shred of objective evidence to convict either playgoer or adult player of the same offence. What we would regard as homoerotic feelings may well have been stimulated by youths in drag, but they cannot be adduced from the calumnies of a handful of vengeful satirists and a few unbalanced Puritans.

Typically critics now base their interpretations not on the text but on what the current sexual–political orthodoxy in this field conditions them to find. Thus:

Rosalind's refusal of what she desires, out of modesty or fear of discovery, disguises a much deeper fear that "she" may not be what Orlando wants, that he may want to kiss a boy.[22]

This exposition by Alison Findlay finds not the slightest echo in the play and is surely an example of an entirely extraneous layer of meaning having been grafted onto the original.

Granville Barker and Robertson Davies, in a more innocent age, argued that the female parts were easier to play when the young women adopted breeches because the players could then return to their own clothes, and this view has been taken up again more recently by Michael Shapiro, but whereas Davies assumed that an apparent boy wooing a man did not involve any 'sexual irregularity', invoking instead neo-platonic 'emotional friendships . . . without having any smack of sin', Shapiro suggests that for the young actor to resume breeches was by its nature self-referential and therefore, he claims, invoked the by now common assumption amongst Elizabethan audiences of player/apprentice pederasty. He bases this on the argument that when the actor returned to his own costume he returned to his own personality as well:

For a play-boy of Shakespeare's day, however talented and experienced, to present a woman in the process of impersonating a man would have been extremely difficult and would probably have produced either a very broad farcical effect or a muddle. The simpler, more effective solution was a clear stylistic differentiation of the two genders, playing the female role in the usual style and making the male disguise seem like a version of himself, as if the performer were stepping out of character.

To argue so, in my view, involves a serious failure of imagination, comparable to Beckerman's insistence that because of the size of De Witt's pillars the Elizabethan theatre was aural and not visual, or the widespread view that older players had to be brought in because certain parts were too difficult for the regular performers of female roles, or the even more extraordinary claim that some of the major roles in the canon were so difficult that they were in advance of their time and as a consequence scarcely performed. All such arguments fail to acknowledge that this was a continuous performance tradition, honed over a hundred years of professional playing, in which many of the writers were themselves actively involved in the production of their plays and learned by trial and error and repeated practice. The heroine pretending to be a youth was not a 'problem' requiring a 'solution', but an added sophistication, equivalent perhaps to the tumbler's triple somersault, and would surely not have been attempted if it could not have been achieved satisfactorily. There is some justice in supposing a simultaneous appreciation of different 'layers', but it can also be misleading in suggesting some sense of a permanent equivalence between those layers, or that performer awareness with its supposed erotic distractions was continuous. The imputations of satirist and anti-theatricalist were sufficiently pervasive, whatever the realities of relations in the tiring house, or society's attitude to them, to have made the breeches role virtually unperformable unless the primary focus had been on creating a female personality so convincing that her characteristics would be carried over even when she disguised herself. Any close reading of *Twelfth Night* or *As You Like It* will show that their texts are studded with references, not to the 'self' of the actor – that only emerges in the latter's Epilogue, and then in the form of an assumed *persona* rather than the real identity of the performer – but, in order to maintain the primacy of the narrative, to the 'self' of the underlying girl character.[23] As soon as Rosalind, for instance, appears in male disguise, its strain and inappropriateness are established in the text:

I could find in my heart to disgrace my man's apparel and to cry like a woman, but I must comfort the weaker vessel, as doublet and hose ought to show itself courageous to petticoat ... (II.iv.4–7)

Furthermore, for much of the time that Rosalind is in breeches she is in dialogue with Celia/Aliena and they simply continue to talk as two girls. In III.ii, her very next scene, when she first hears of Orlando's presence in the forest, she refers to her female personality beneath the disguise four times in seventy lines:

Alas the day, what shall I do with my doublet and hose? (219–20);

But doth he know that I am in this forest and in man's apparel? (229–30);

Do you not know I am a woman? when I think, I must speak. (249–50);

I will speak to him like a saucy lackey, and under that habit play the knave with him. (295–7)

And if that were not sufficient to establish a continuous sense of female identity beneath the male attire, she goes on to keep it prominent in her 'wooing' scenes with Orlando:

ORLANDO: But will my Rosalind do so?
ROSALIND: By my life, she will do as I do.   (IV.i.157–8)

Fainting at the sight of Orlando's blood in IV.iii, her dialogue once again reinforces both her disguise and its inappropriateness to her character and inclinations:

OLIVER: Be of good cheer, youth. You a man?
   You lack a man's heart.
ROSALIND. I do so, I confess it . . .
OLIVER: Well then, take a good heart and counterfeit to be a man.
ROSALIND: So I do; but 'i faith, I should have been a woman by right. (164–76)

The dialogue also makes clear the nature of her male impersonation as a 'saucy lackey', and it is this, perhaps, rather than in the establishment of the female identity, in which Shapiro's 'very broad farcical effect' *might* come into play. Again, at the risk of wearying the reader with the obvious, the texts of the plays provide broad hints (perhaps, indeed, broader than their eventual performance) as to the sort of stratagems involved. Rosalind is to play her saucy lackey, cousin of Portia's 'bragging youth' (*Merchant of Venice*, III.iv.62–78), with a 'swashing and a martial outside' (I.iii.120) in order to hide her 'woman's fear'.

However the '*travestie*' role is played, it is surely likely to have been quite different from the actor's own person, and a return to the text itself is a reminder, if one is needed, of its good humour and lack of the sort of salaciousness that recent critics have been so industrious to invent and project upon it. Shapiro is right to point to the multiple dimensions of such performances in which an awareness of the performer must always have been an element – here for instance the reference to women being unable to hold their tongues is the sort of gibe that offers momentarily to separate performer and role – but there is simply no evidence to support his insistence that each play in turn led towards a revelation of homosexual abuse in the tiring house, and that, not unlike the denouement of a number of the plays of the 1950s, it provides the climax of every Shakespearean breeches comedy.

(b) Critics searching for evidence of lesbian affections, on the other hand, argue instead that the female characters love the breeched heroines as *women* and can discern their underlying femininity, (even though they are being played by youths, and dressed as youths). Men are stupid and can be fooled by such disguise, whereas women are more discerning. This may well be true in real life, but it is the direct opposite of what the plays actually say. There is no simple symmetry of 'mistakings', as Howard would have it, 'that temporarily allow man to love man, woman to love woman'.[24] Instead, it is the male lovers who respond intuitively to the underlying femininity of the heroines which is kept fresh in the spectator's mind by regular references and allusions in the text; just as other lovers can sense, as Florizel, that their peasant maid is really a princess. (Arviragus in *Cymbeline* even senses that the wandering page is actually kin to him.) Women, on the other hand, the chauvinist convention of this genre says, are easily fooled, programmed in their sheltered innocence to fall in love with the first apparently eligible young man to ride by and pay them attention; a fact Viola regrets when the infatuated Olivia, after their first meeting, sends a messenger with a ring:

> How easy is it for the proper-false
> In women's waxen hearts to set their forms!
> Alas (our) frailty is the cause, not we,
> For such as we are made (of), such we be.
>
> (*Twelfth Night*, II.ii.29–32)

Once, however, a female character realises that the object of her infatuation is also female, as Lady Anderson does in *James IV* (V.v.48), like the husband of the boy-bride she is instantly discomfited: 'Beauty bred love, and love hath bred my shame.' Olivia has no difficulty in accepting Sebastian as a replacement for Viola, for he is the *man* she always wanted, and not, as in some wayward modern versions, a sort of punishment.[25] Brown and Parolin claim that the Italian *commedie erudite* have lesbian love plots 'performing homoerotic desire', when in fact, as in their English derivatives, same-sex attraction is merely a temporary and farcical side-effect of disguise in plots which are firmly heterosexual in tone and celebrations of natural couplings. Similarly, in French literature, the Queen in the prose romance *Amadis de Gaule* cannot understand why she is so strongly attracted to another woman: '(Elle) ne pouvoit comprendre ceste violance d'Amour de fille a fille.' The reader can, of course, since it is an amorous man in disguise.

Valerie Traub asks, 'To whom is same-sex love between women funny?'[26]. The answer has to be, alas, to men in general and to Elizabethan men in particular. She puts forward an elaborate argument to make the affection shown between votaries of chastity, Diana's nymphs in Heywood's *The Golden Age*, 1610, who are 'twinned in love', into a lesbian one. Given the breadth of activities comprehended for instance under Adrienne Rich's 'lesbian continuum', it might well qualify,[27] but the important point is that it was not perceived as such by an Elizabethan dramatist and his audience, and the proof of this lies in the detail of the lines. Jupiter, disguised as a nymph, attempts Callisto, arguing for ever great intimacy on the grounds of what girls do together. Traub's quotations stop just short of the key line: 'We maids', says the disguised Jupiter, 'may wish much, but can nothing do'; 'we might love', as Aphra Behn says, 'and yet be innocent'. In a phallocentric culture only penetration followed by ejaculation constitutes satisfaction, or shame. Women, the plays say, lack the essential equipment to give satisfaction. 'As well a woman with a eunuch play'd', says Cleopatra, 'As with a woman' (II.v.56). Only when women attempted to usurp the male function, either as supposed *tribades* with enlarged clitorises, or by artificial means, were their activities noted, and then severely punished (but according to Judith Brown there are no examples in England).[28]

The pleasures of impossible desire

A closer look at the main plot of *Twelfth Night*, so often taken as *paean* to homoeroticism, shows how the cross-dressing of the heroine is used to explore the nature of *heterosexual* love and, by means of the confusions brought about by disguise, to prolong the prelude to coupling, as well as to illustrate the pain of unrequited love. Viola, though, is no Rosalind. Far from managing her lover as she pleases as a proxy mistress, Viola finds her breeches a danger, as well as a hindrance in attaining her desires.

In the early modern period, in contrast to the consumption-driven values of our own society, there were considerable disincentives to sexual activity: no effective birth control, a lack of personal hygiene, the prevalence of illness and disease particularly of the disfiguring kind, a fear of venereal disease (much of it incurable), sickness, malnutrition and exhaustion amongst the poor, the practice of late marriage and the Church's stress on matrimonial chastity.[29] The Elizabethans, therefore, were much more inclined to accept lack of consummation of their desires than we are, devoting themselves instead to God, or admiring their mistresses at a distance. John Bean, discussing the views of Andreas Cappelanus, says, 'the purest form of romantic love . . . is highly sexual but never consummated, for passion to him seems to depend on intense, prolonged, unsatisfied desire'.[30] They took pleasure in sadness and the unattainable; hence the frequency of sad, often singing pages in the plays, and the wealth of beautiful melancholic songs like Dowland's 'I saw my lady weep', 'In darkness let me dwell', and most famously, *Lacrimae*, 'Flow my tears'; or Wyatt's sonnet sequence bewailing the cruelty of his mistress, imagining her as a deer he hunts unsuccessfully, with the motto around her neck, *Noli me tangere*, linking the chastity of courtly love with the celibacy of Christ to produce a pleasing, agonising, stasis:

> I fede me in sorrowe, and laugh in all my pain.
> Likewise displeaseth me boeth deth and lyffe,
> And my delite is causer of this stryff.   (Egerton MS 26)

They built a culture around sexual sublimation. 'All desire', according to Christian Metz, 'depends on the infinite pursuit of its absent object'.[31] 'You must have a maximum of ardour', says Wilson Knight of the artist, 'with a minimum of possible accomplishment, so that desire is forced into eye and mind to create'. [32]

One of the best examples of a culture built around impossible desire is Olivia's wooing of the cross-dressed Viola. It does, of course, depend on the lack of ambiguity in the heterosexuality of both characters' sex-drives. Believing Viola to be a youth, Olivia attempts to woo her, first sending a ring, 'After the last enchantment you did here', and then attempting in III.i to intimate her love more directly and prompt some reciprocation:

OLIVIA: To one of your receiving
    Enough is shown . . . .
                              . . . So let me hear you speak.
VIOLA: I pity you.
OLIVIA: That's a degree to love.
VIOLA: Not, not a grize [= *step*]; for 'tis a vulgar proof
    That very oft we pity enemies.
OLIVIA: Why then methinks 'tis time to smile again . . .
    The clock upbraids me with the waste of time.
    Be not afraid, good youth, I will not have you . . .
    There lies your way, due west.   (III.i.120–34)

In Olivia's responses propriety jostles with desire, and the player must register the mingling regret, hope, sympathy, fear, longing, and the final effort to pretend these things were never said. These characters are entered into more deeply than almost any that preceded them. They are not merely romantic or comic ciphers, nor indiscriminate scatterers of wit, and, in contrast say to Rosalind, who tends to be so much wittier and more aware than any of the other characters and the auditor the only person with whom she can fully engage, they genuinely interact with one another.

Olivia knows by now that her love is hopeless, but she cannot bring herself to let it go. Once the 'youth's perfections / With an invisible and subtle stealth' have crept into her eyes, she is like Plato's lover, in a 'state of mingled pleasure and pain', struggling helplessly, driven to do anything that may give sight of the beloved. As she says later:

> There's something in me that reproves my fault;
> But such a headstrong potent fault it is
> That it but mocks reproof. (III.iv.203–5)

And so, drawn by Viola's attractiveness, she abandons her attempts to disavow the injudiciousness of her previous proposal:

OLIVIA: Stay!
    I prithee tell me what thou think'st of me.
VIOLA: That you do think you are not what you are.
OLIVIA: If I think so, I think the same of you.
VIOLA: Then you are right: I am not what I am ... (III.i.137–41)

Olivia, in despite of her good sense, breaks into a direct confession of her love. Viola replies by saying she loves no woman. And they part – Olivia reduced to a direct lie, that she might yield to Orsino, in order to continue seeing Viola:

> Yet come again; for thou perhaps mayst move
> That heart that now abhors, to like his love.

When they reappear in III.iv, Olivia has evidently made further fruitless efforts to win Viola, and her only recourse is to repeat this insistence that the youth come again tomorrow. That it is a woman wooing another woman, traditionally the material of farce, has tended to obscure the central human pathos of this exchange, further distanced by being played by male performers. Yet Olivia expresses real anguish and humiliation, even in this relatively civilised exchange. It is a play about the heartbreak of unreciprocated love – Olivia, Malvolio, Antonio ... Even though set in the sunlit alleys of a formal garden, its characters still plumb the very depths of despair. In that sense it is the first of the problem comedies rather than the last of the romantic ones.

THE SOCIAL CONSTRUCTION OF EROTICISM

Alan Bray's project is, of course, much larger than the theatre, and in no sense a piece of unbiased scholarship. He sets out to prove the existence of homosexuality in Elizabethan England 'on a massive and ineradicable scale'. 'Most if not all' Elizabethans, he claims, 'would have had actual experience of homosexuality.' Ralph Trumbach similarly asserts that 'in traditional European societies, men who did not restrict their sexual experience to marriage usually had sex with both adolescent boys and female whores'.[33] Perhaps inevitably their evidence involves, as with James Saslow, ever arguing from the particular to the general:

Sodomy was practiced across the entire spectrum of middle- and lower-class occupations: London merchants and actors, Venetian barber-surgeons and *gondolieri*, Genevan printers, labourers, and servants, and the navy.[34]

With this kind of logic, there need only be one isolated example, and a whole class then labours under the imputation. When such arguments descend to individuals, it is often apparent that they are wildly untypical, as with Castlehaven (see below p. 97), Bluebeard, who sexually abused and murdered over a hundred children, and Rochester. Before 1700, so the argument goes, bisexuality was acceptable and boys and women interchangeable as sexual objects. Rochester's 'The Maimed Debauchee' is widely cited as typical:

> Nor shall our love-fight Chloris be forgot,
> When each the well-looked Link-boy strove to enjoy
> And the best kiss was the deciding lot,
> Whether the boy fucked you or I the boy.

Rochester, however, made his life into a piece of extraordinary performance art. Too young to have been in France with the Court, he spent the Interregnum receiving a strict upbringing, against which at the Restoration he rebelled with all his might, creating a rake-hell *persona* so striking precisely because of his upbringing and moral sensitivity that it became the epitome of vice for the returning Court, the model not only for Dorimant in *The Man of Mode* but during the rest of his short life a whole genre of similar theatrical rakes. He disappeared in disguise for weeks on end, once playing an Italian mountebank, claimed to have been continuously drunk for five years, killed a man in a drunken brawl, and died in syphilitic agony 'pissing matter'.[35] His bisexual references may well indicate his own sexual tastes, but like those of Marston and Jonson they are also meant to shock, and in doing so they reveal a society that found such behaviour unacceptable. As charges of sodomy were linked with atheism and sedition in the previous century, marking their unnatural rarity, so here they are associated with debauchery on an almost superhuman scale. He certainly cannot be used as an example of any kind of general trend.

'*Eros socraticus*' in Elizabethan society, says Kott, by which he means pederasty, voicing what is now a general presumption, was 'a more or less tolerated practice'. This view rests, however, on a rather convoluted interpretation of the two facts we have: that punishments were severe, and that prosecutions were very rare. The Act of 1533 prescribed death and remained in force until 1772. In France as late as 1760 convicted sodomites were being burned to death. According to Bray, 'for the 66-year period 1559–1625, for the whole of the counties of Kent, Sussex, Herefordshire, and Essex there are only four indictments for sodomy'. Michel Foucault seems to have originated the ingenious paradox that extreme reticence on the subject of sodomy enabled severe punishments on the one hand and widespread tolerance on the other – hence the confidence with which gay polemicists join the dots of actual cases to produce a picture of widespread homosexual activity.[36] Orgel argues, citing Bruce Smith in support, that only coercive sex against minors was recognised as sodomy, but then the evidence suggests that pederasty was the only kind of homosexuality that took place, and it is likely that the law would take the view than any sex with minors was coercive. 'Boy-love', says Robin Morgan, 'is a euphemism for rape regardless of whether or not the victim is likely to invite it'.[37]

An alternative and more likely interpretation of the evidence is that severe punishment discouraged such activities. And punishment was not to be restricted to this world. Critics are inclined to ignore the importance of religious conditioning on Elizabethan England. God saw everything. Although once again Bray inverts the equation so that 'sodomite' becomes just another epithet to throw at heretics, the simpler truth is that only those rare individuals who did not believe in God would dare commit sodomy. Such was William Payne, arraigned in Connecticut in 1646, who in answer 'to some who questioned the lawfulness of such filthy practice' in corrupting the town's youths, 'did insinuate seeds of atheism, questioning whether there was a God'. 'An Atheist', said Nicholas Breton, 'is a figure of desperation, who dares do anything even to his soul's damnation.' In a society conditioned to belief by the powers of Church and State, and maintained by extreme cruelty, very few would adopt so dangerous a course. For Stephen Greenblatt to suggest that because women were regarded as inferior, men would 'naturally be drawn to love other men', that the Elizabethans found this practice easier to justify than heterosexual love, and that in the process the prohibitions of religion and the law could somehow be set aside, seems anachronistic in the extreme.[38] Nor is it possible to accept Jean Howard's claim that homosexual practices only became 'deviant' with 'the full emergence of the bourgeois culture' and its '"elevation" of heterosexual passion', since the severest punishments had long been on the statute book.

Beyond the specifics of faith, there were wider social pressures that would have discouraged the practice of homosexuality. Ed Cohen argues that the new Protestant Church lacked the ubiquitous control of the Catholic confessional, but ignores the fact that it had its own means in what Kathleen McLuskie calls the 'shaming rituals which enforced community norms'. It was arguably the first society to take Christianity seriously, replacing a veneer of faith, covering a still basically rural pagan medieval peasant society in which genuine belief was concentrated mainly in enclosed orders, with one which stressed individual commitment to God and an increasing obsession with morals and behaviour, and one that led to many punitive excesses.[39] It was also a society with very little privacy to facilitate sexual transgression:

The church courts as social institutions could not have functioned without the willingness of members of the rural community to spy and investigate and follow those thought to be involved in illicit sex.[40]

Steve Brown argues that late marriages led to sodomy as the only alternative sexual satisfaction, whilst Bray suggests it was tolerated by society to encourage 'capital accumulation'. However, there were other safer alternatives, as the frequency of cases of bastardy amongst servant girls testifies. One of the most striking features of Lawrence Stone's fascinating study of Pepys' sex life is the relative infrequency with which he proceeds to intercourse, even in a much more libertarian age, and the pleasure he takes in other activities. Among the young and unmarried full intercourse was probably a comparative rarity, and for cost-conscious married couples possible for limited periods only.

The essentialist nature of the argument

To Bray, 'the ways of love do not change over the centuries'. At the heart of the debate over the prevalence or otherwise of homosexuality in Shakespeare's time, and therefore its likely impact on the theatre, lies the issue of whether sexual practice is trans-historic and unchanging, or historically specific and the result of particular cultural pressures. Diana Fuss defines the difference as:

whilst the essentialist holds that the natural is *repressed* by the social, the constructionist maintains that the natural is *produced* by the social.[41]

After generations of shameful persecution, it is hardly surprising that modern homosexuals should want to strengthen their position by showing that it has a long history and distinguished forebears, but the argument for cultural specificity is difficult to resist. All the evidence points to the restriction of same-sex activity to pederasty before 1700, notwithstanding the recent attempts to challenge this, and whilst there is some debate as to the precise point at which homosexuality was formulated, to use Foucault's terminology, as a 'species' rather than a 'temporary aberration', it is generally agreed to be fairly recent. Most historians of homosexuality, however, remain at heart essentialists and attempt to compromise with constructivism. Bray, for instance, argues that homosexuality is 'a plastic element in human life susceptible to historical and social moulding to an extreme degree'; it is, as Valerie Traub puts it, only the 'conceptual framework' articulating desire that differs; whilst Trumbach suggests 'two worldwide human patterns' that will account for differences.

Another strategy has been to suggest that homosexuality is the root phenomenon: present, according to Stephen Greenblatt, 'in all sexuality'; 'implicit', says Traub, 'within all psyches'; 'the precondition', says Fuss, of heterosexuality, 'since all identity is based on exclusion'. 'Heterosexuality', says Jane Gallop, 'once it is exposed as an exchange of women between men . . . reveals itself as a mediated form of homosexuality'.[42]

The struggle to give one sexual preference greater status than the other seems increasingly from the point. Heterosexuality has hitherto been privileged as the means of procreation, but that has long since ceased to be its major function and need not be so in the future. The only biological 'givens' are a particular set of genitalia and the urge to seek satisfaction from them; as Mercutio puts it so inelegantly, 'this drivelling love is like a great natural that runs lolling up and down to hide his ba[u]ble in a hole' (*Romeo and Juliet* II.iv.91–3). Freud suggests: 'It seems probable that the sexual instinct is in the first instance independent of its object . . . the sexual instinct and the sexual object are merely soldered together . . .' Cultural pressures determine the nature of the 'sexual object' and the values associated with it. Elizabeth Wilson argues:

The rigid sexual identities we cultivate, and which are popularly experienced as 'natural' and given at birth, are really fictions elaborated by the nineteenth-century sexologists; they merely imprison the waywardness of lust, constraining us in sexual and social roles.

However, 'even if our sexual identities are socially constructed', as the editors of Duberman *et al.* point out, 'they cannot readily be changed'. Indeed, the fierceness with which they are defended and transgressions from them punished is perhaps a tacit admission of their arbitrariness.

There is no doubt that homosexuality has been deliberately and systematically 'Hidden from History'. The question is, how far was such censorship itself deterministic? How far did it shape behaviour in the process of shaping expectations? In short, how much homosexuality was there to hide? Clearly there have always been exceptions, individuals with strong sexual urges who stood out from the crowd and did what they felt was right for them, just as there have always been others unable to meet society's gender expectations, and no model of sexuality can afford to ignore either extreme. For the overwhelming mass of people, however, with middling sexual appetites, sexuality is seen as the most signifying element in their *social* identity from which they derive their sense of *amour propre*. The blind fury they experience is more than anything else a desire to conform, especially when they are young; thus allowing their sexual behaviour to be adapted to meet the needs of any current socio-political system. The Spartans appear to have encouraged homosexuality as a spur to martial bravery;[43] whilst the nunnery has long been an economic solution for unwanted daughters. Modern lesbianism, it has been argued, is often less an erotic preference than a political reaction against the status of women.[44]

The admiration of male beauty

In modern Western society, as John Boswell points out, no distinction is permitted between male beauty and male erotic attractiveness, as it is in Hellenistic and Islamic societies.[45] This is one area in which a lack of awareness of historical change and the importation of modern attitudes seriously impedes an understanding of relations between Elizabethan aesthetics and eroticism. Critics assume that any acknowledgement of male attractiveness is tantamount to a statement of homoeroticism. Jardine regards the reference to Jessica dressed in the 'lovely garnish of a boy' in *The Merchant of Venice* as indicating an 'unhealthy' interest in the performer, whilst Fiedler says, 'the literary tradition of praise of lovely boys' had a 'homosexual basis', and Saslow assumes the portrayal of male beauty by Renaissance artists to be symptomatic of homoeroticism.

Camille Paglia, whose very considerable energies are devoted to 'outing' sexual deviancy from 'Nefertiti to Emily Dickinson', is typical in associating the cult of the beautiful Greek youth with a homosexually dominated society in which women had no place.[46] The evidence, however, does not entirely bear this out. In Xenophon's less well-known *Symposium*, the chief guest, the youth Autolycus, has been sent on ahead to the banqueting room. When the other guests arrive:

The whole company became immediately sensible of the power of beauty ... the effect which the sight of so lovely a person produced was to attract the eyes of the whole company to him ... All hearts surrendered to his power and paid homage to the sweet and noble mien and features of his countenance and the manly gracefulness of his shape.[47]

The subsequent talk is of male love, in which Socrates goes on to prove that the love of the soul is incomparably superior to the love of the body. The ending of the banquet is thereby something of a surprise. The male and female entertainers return in the habits of Bacchus and Ariadne and so stimulate the company with the vividness of their love-play that it 'occasioned both married guests, and some that were not, to take horse immediately and ride back full speed to Athens with the briskest resolutions imaginable'. Their intention, it is implied, is of engaging in heterosexual intercourse. Socrates and some of the others stay behind to walk with their host and his *enamoratus*. This episode seems to suggest that male beauty could be admired by a broad cross-section of society and was not merely limited to a homosexual coterie. 'The Greek concept of beauty', says Rita Freedman, 'encompassed the whole person, outer form as well as inner qualities.' Early Christian teachings, she says, challenged the idea of beauty as a mind–body composite and 'set Beauty adrift – as an alienated, arbitrary, superficial enchantment';[48] hence sentiments in plays that it was a curse to the possessor and a means of male entrapment.

It may no longer be possible to determine with any conviction the relation of Xenophon's writings, along with those of Plato on which so much current theory is based, to the more general attitudes of their society, but in respect of the early modern period it is evident from the fashion of the time that from the mid-fourteenth century admiration of the young male figure was acceptable throughout society in a way which it no longer is today. Much had depended on the introduction of the button about 1360, producing a closer fit, and accompanied by a shortening of the upper garment to the fork (figure 1). Moralists inveighed, and satirists like Chaucer in the person of the virtuous Parson drew amusement:

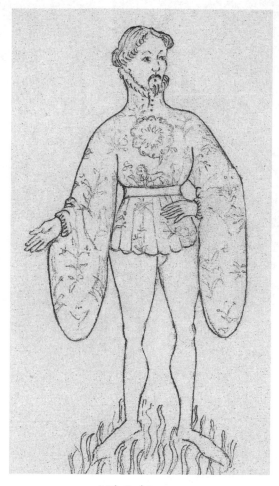

1 Male Fashion c.1410

The horrible discordinat scantness of clothyng as been these cutted sloppes . . . that thurgh hire shortnesses ne covere nat the shameful membres of man, to wikked entente . . . and eek the buttokes of hem farren as it were the hyndre part of a she ape in the full of the moone. (*The Canterbury Tales*, lines 420f.)

Fashion was not abashed. By 1440 the shortened tunic was discarded to reveal the even closer-fitting doublet and hose, formerly undergarments, a combination of short waistcoat to which were tied long stockings (figure 2). As a result, the genitalia hitherto lurking under the hem of the tunic became fully exposed and were capped with a codpiece variously fashioned as modest or boastful.

2 Fashion c.1470

And so the basic fashion remained, with various additions, inviting admiration for male beauty until into the seventeenth century. It is not to be confused with the effeminisation of later periods but hammers home with glaring obviousness the male shape and male potency. J. C. Flugel points out that whereas female sexuality is diffuse, and in our society all parts of the female anatomy can be erotic, hence the alternating fashions of exposure and concealment, decoration and modesty, and what James Laver called 'shifting erogenous zones', male sexuality by contrast is concentrated around the genitalia.[49] Hence even when they were themselves concealed emphasis was nearly always on the thighs adjacent to them.

Valerie Traub, searching for signs of an awareness of women-to-women eroticism in Shakespeare, sees in Phoebe's description of Rosalind as Ganymede (III.v.113–23) what she describes as an underlying (female) eroticism:

During the first half of her recollection, as she measures Ganymede against the standard common male attributes – height, leg – Phoebe fights her attraction, syntactically oscillating between affirmation and denial: he is, he is not. In the last four lines, as she 'feminises' Ganymede's lip and cheek, she capitulates to her desire altogether.

This is to make the sort of anachronistic gender distinctions which elsewhere Traub would eschew and criticise in others. Phoebe is not responding to Ganymede as a girl but as a youth, attractive by the standards of the time. As she says: 'He'll make a proper man' (line 115). In Shirley's *The Cardinal*, 1641, the ladies are discussing who is the most handsome man at court:

VALERIA: Were I a princess, I should think Count D'Alvarez
   Had sweetness to deserve me from the world . . . .
   He's young and active, and composed most sweetly.
DUCHESS: I have seen a face more tempting.
VALERIA: It had then
   Too much of women in't.   (I.ii.34–9)

The line is evidently a very thin one. The third lady, Celinda, admits D'Alvarez to be the most handsome, but prefers the more soldierly qualities of Columbo. At its revival in 1662, Kynaston played D'Alvarez, and Pepys' heterosexual credentials are extensive and unimpeachable and yet he had no difficulty in recognising and praising his beauty. Viola and Sebastian in *Twelfth Night* are identical twins. They are identical in appearance and both very attractive (to Olivia). What clearly distinguishes them is Sebastian's martial bravery. The Elizabethans liked their young men pretty *and* spunky. Just so the Greeks, whatever their sexual proclivities; it is the 'manly gracefulness' of Autolycus that takes the guests at Xenophon's *Symposium*, whilst Plato in *Phaedrus* describes the natural qualities of toughness, bred in the clear sunshine through manly toil and honest sweat, as the philosophical ideal of male attractiveness, and contrasts them with those of the pampered catamite of the sensual lover.

Male beauty in courtly entertainments

Gaveston's vision of how he will entertain the homosexual Edward II, dramatising Ovid's *Metamorphoses*, is widely taken as firm evidence of the visibility of homoeroticism in Elizabethan public theatre:

Like *Sylvian* Nimphes my pages shall be clad;
My men like Satyres grazing on the lawnes
Shall with their Goate feete daunce an antick hay.
Sometime a lovelie boye in *Dians* shape,
With haire that gilds the water as it glides,
Crownets of pearle about his naked armes,
And in his sportfull hands an Olive tree
To hide those parts which men delight to see,
Shall bathe him in a spring; and there hard by,
One like *Actaeon* peeping through the grove,
Shall by the angrie goddess be transformde,
And running in the likenes of an Hart,
By yelping hounds puld downe, and seeme to die.
Such things as these best please his majestie   (1.1.58–71)

Catherine Belsey suggests a close relationship between Gaveston's intended masque and the public stage because both are supposed to entertain the monarch and both deal with illicit forms of desire not sanctioned in official culture; whilst Bruce Smith repeats the same mistake: 'Gaveston's idea of theatre sounds very much like the Italian entertainments that Nashe, Coryat, and Sandys saw and scorned'.[50] Nothing could be further from the truth. These travellers are describing visits to the *public* theatres where the standard fare remained the *Commedia dell'arte*, indicated in some detail in Nashe's account of 'a Pantaloon, a Whore, and a Zanni', whereas the model on which Marlowe draws is the aristocratic *Intermezzo* and more particularly the casual glimpses of simulated classical myth which were strewn regularly by competing courtiers before European princes on their garden strolls.

Jonson's 'Highgate Entertainment' (*The Penates*), 1603, includes a long speech from Maia, Goddess of the Earth, together with Aurora and Flora in song, all of them played by male performers. James I may be thought to have been particularly susceptible to such private displays, but the practice had already been well established under Elizabeth. Although Gascoigne's forest play with Diana and her nymphs never achieved performance at Kenilworth in 1575, the Queen did chance upon a Sybil in an arbour, as well as receive a water visit from the Lady of the Lake and her nymphs; whilst at Woodstock later in the same year she was attended by a Fairy Queen who led her through a singing grove. At Sudeley in 1592, Lord Chandos had his professional company stage an *al fresco* entertainment in which, after Apollo had changed the unwilling Daphne into a laurel, '*the tree rived, and Daphne issued out ... running to her Majesty*'. The player knelt before Elizabeth with a pretty compliment: 'I stay, for whither should Chastity fly for succour, but to the Queen of Chastity.' Again, at Althorpe in *The Satyre*, 1603, Queen Mab appeared with a host of fairies before the newly arrived Queen Anne and Prince Henry. To any royal tourist, the countryside must have seemed positively bursting with young men in simulated female semi-nudity behind every bush and brake; lovely boys 'in Dian's shape', or something similar, were, in short, commonplace.[51]

How far did the interest of the spectator lie in the youths for themselves and how far in the ideals of female beauty which they essayed to represent? In short, whose 'parts which men delight to see' in Gaveston's vision are to be hidden by the olive tree – the lovely boy's or Diana's? To the modern observer seeking for evidence of homosexuality, attention is likely to be conceived as on the youth himself; for the pronouns 'his' and 'him' refer to the performer and not the role. Gaveston's eye, however, is on the means by which the Entertainment will be staged: Actaeon is not to be destroyed by the hounds, as in the story, but only 'seem to die', as in its stage management. Also the homophilic view ignores the novel quality of what was being represented. In our society images of naked or scantily clad women are commonplace on billboards, and in films, magazines, advertisements and art galleries, none of which were available to the Elizabethans. Even many features of modern fashion are revealing or suggestive, from the bikini to the leotard. From the invention of the lithograph in 1796 onwards, printing has enabled the widespread acquisition and consumption of the sort of images of female beauty which before that time had been the exclusive possession of the rich. Charles V, for instance, commissioned Correggio to paint a set of four of Jupiter's 'seductions' in 1534 for his private collection. Just so Jonson's Sir Epicure Mammon envisions:

> mine oval roome,
> Fill'd with such pictures, as TIBERIUS tooke
> From ELEPHANTIS: and dull ARETINE
> But coldly imitated . . .   (*The Alchemist*, II.ii.42–5)

As private erotica, such images would have been screened from the view of lesser mortals by a curtain that only the owner would draw. Hence the primary function of these dramatisations of classical myth would be, I suggest, the images they provide of female sexual attractiveness, much as John Rainolds notes the power of cross-dressing to 'ravish' men with the remembrance of 'wanton thought(s) stirred up . . . by looking on a beautiful Woman' and compares it with that of erotic statues in aristocratic collections.

Another cognate form of courtly entertainment offers more clear evidence to determine the focus of its sexuality and that of the cross-dressed performances that supported it. Critics are fond of making what Peter Erickson calls the 'self-sufficient' all-male theatre into an excluding homosocial conspiracy, which embodies, according to Stephen Greenblatt, giving emphasis to the post-Galen theory of biology at the expense of the more usual post-Aristotelian version, 'a conception of gender that is teleologically male'.[52] The Stuart Masque, however, paradoxically, brings this supposedly closed circle into question, since whilst it incorporates these very same youthful players from the adult companies, particularly the King's Men, giving a special emphasis in their professional roles of presenter and anti-masquer to juvenile and female characters, and, judging by the surviving designs and descriptions, dressing them in scanty and erotic costumes, it does so in a context the principal focus of which is unquestionably heterosexual (see chapter 3). These players sustained the narrative context, undertook the actual speeches, and often provided a visual antithesis to the royal and noble, but silent, masquers, of either sex, whose entries and dances formed the central activity of this court ritual.

From their very beginning there were complaints about the erotic and scandalous quality of the costumes worn by the ladies of the Court, and although the dusky make-up in *The Masque of Blackness* was not repeated, having so much discomfited the ambassadors when, as custom demanded, they kissed the Queen's hand, Inigo Jones' designs for subsequent masques make it very clear that the 'curtizan-like' diaphanous fabrics and revealing designs continued; even their mock armour displays the female form. And whilst bared breasts were nothing special, Orazio Busino observing of the 1618 Masque audience, 'the plump and buxom display their bosoms very liberally', Jones' masque designs went much further.[53] From the source material that Orgel and Strong so usefully provide it is evident that Inigo Jones added the appearance of naked breasts to clothed originals both for the cross-dressed presenters/anti-masque characters and for the noble lady masquers themselves. This presumably indicates the wishes of his young patroness, the twenty-two year-old Henrietta Maria, and the multitude of sketches for the Queen's costume for *Chloridia* seem to turn on how much breast she should show. In the end, modesty seems to have drawn a line just above the nipple (figure 3), but an alternative final design reveals the whole breast (figure 4). Moreover, the exposed forearms, feet, and ankles of the dancing costumes also had all the sexual excitement of the transgression of sartorial codes. Nor were these scantily clad young women a mere brief vision of delight high upon the stage in their *machina versatilis*, but having posed and then danced before the

3 Final designs for Queen's costume for *Chloridia*

spectators, they came out of the 'scene' and danced *with* them. For all Jonson's insistence on serving 'nourishing and sound meats' in the elevated poetry that accompanies this display of scantily clad nubility, suffering, as he claims in the Preface to *Hymenaei*, 'no object of delight to pass

4 Final designs for Queen's costume for *Chloridia*

without his mixture of profit, and example', the masques had a more fleshly undercurrent and at least one young woman was found *in flagrante delicto* amongst the scenery.[54]

The youths from the King's Men who undertook the speaking roles, together with the choristers and musicians from the Chapels Royal who sang and danced as nymphs and naiads, cupids and satyrs, were merely part of the packaging for this erotic if not lascivious and essentially participatory Court event.

Lust's Dominion, 1600, used to be ascribed to Marlowe and it is not difficult to see why. In the opening scene the Queen Mother's attempt to refresh Eleazar's waning love has strong echoes of Gaveston:

> Smile on me, and these two wanton boys,
> These pretty lads that do attend on me,
> Shall call thee Jove, shall wait upon thy cup,
> And fill thee nectar; their enticing eyes
> Shall serve as crystal, wherein thou may'st see
> To dress thyself, if thou wilt smile on me.
> Smile on me, and with coronets of pearl
> And bells of gold, circling their pretty arms,
> In a round ivory fount these two shall swim,
> And dive to make thee sport . . . (I.i)

The associations may at first seem to be pederastic, but what the Queen is offering is *herself*:

> Bestow one smile, one little, little smile,
> And in a net of twisted silk and gold
> In my all-naked arms thyself shall lie.

Her pages are to be *amoretti*, cupids, a lascivious setting for her ageing charms, not unlike the youths described as attending on Cleopatra at Cydnus, 'pretty dimpled boys, like smiling cupids', again as part of the trappings for a heterosexual seduction in 'pursing up' Antony's heart (II.ii.186f.). They owe their inspiration to the *putti* and cherubs that decorate Baroque depictions of amorous heterosexual encounters on ceilings, frescoes and arrases, where 'love is' – as it were – 'in the air . . .'

NEO-PLATONISM

The Socratic dialogues seem to be a mixture of biography and fiction, but principally a medium for Plato to express his own ideas. He wrote extensively about the love of boys and individual of his writings, particularly

The Symposium, are often taken to be representative of Greek attitudes towards the unproblematic acceptability of homosexuality. Scattered through his dialogues, however, are plenty of references that make it clear firstly, that pederasty was frowned upon by society at large;[55] and secondly, that it was practised by enough high-ranking, probably military, personnel, to make it difficult for Plato to dismiss it out of hand. He seems to have managed to do so only finally in *The Laws*.[56] These factors seem to have led him to try to hammer out a justification for boy-love that gave particular emphasis to a spiritual relationship that ennobled the lover and was closely related to a moral/aesthetic concept of knowledge, which he calls 'philosophy', that satisfied his own higher aspirations, but which did not totally preclude a physical, lower level, variously hedged about, towards which his works show some ambiguity and variation. Probably the most indicative and relevant treatment, however, lies in the allegory of the Charioteer in *Phaedrus*, which describes the libido. The chariot is drawn by one good, spiritual horse, and one bad, lecherous horse, which constantly threatens to turn platonic affection into physical assault, and is only restrained by considerable force. The charioteer

with a still more violent backward pull jerks the bit from between the teeth of the lustful horse, drenches his abusive tongue and jaws with blood, and forcing his legs and haunches against the ground reduces him to torment.

Hence, for the platonic lover of boys, Plato seems to be saying, the process involves severe self-restraint against natural inclination. So far, few modern commentators would disagree. However, where our post-Freudian society parts company with Plato, Shakespeare, and the rest, is in its attitude to self-restraint. We are conditioned to believe that if the libido is frustrated in its 'natural' inclinations, being as it is the central dynamo of our nervous system, it will compensate, unhealthily, by other means; they believed in self-restraint. In fact there is a good deal of confusion in our view; for every day brings temptations that we must resist; otherwise no pretty girl could ever get into a lift.

To the older cynicism that neo-platonism was no more than a cloak for pederasty has recently been added the view that boys and women were treated by the Elizabethans in exactly the same way as erotic objects and that as a universally accepted principle they owed sexual submission to those above them.[57] The evidence to support this assertion is fragmentary and anecdotal, and it goes against the assumptions that underlie so much fiction and social practice. Heroines dress in breeches, as Julia says, precisely to avoid, 'the loose encounters of lascivious men' (*Two Gentlemen of Verona*, II.vii), whilst Rosalind indicates the considerations that drive her to disguise:

> Alas, what danger will it be to us,
> Maids as we are, to travel forth so far!
> Beauty provoketh thieves sooner than gold.   (I.iii.108–10)

Donne, humorously discouraging his wife from following him abroad as a page in the Romance tradition, says the French, with their familiarity with theatre, will know she is a woman and debauch her, whilst the Italians will debauch her as a boy, a common prejudice which Aretino confirms, and adds a third danger, the attentions of other women.[58] Such foreigners, however, are generally denigrated. In the wider picture, women were considered safer in male disguise, as a number of real-life examples indicate. Notwithstanding Rosalind's famous assertion that boys and women are cattle of the same colour (said in a specific context when it is her intention to insinuate herself into Orlando's company as Ganymede playing a substitute-Rosalind), the sexes are not simply interchangeable, for the admiration of the male, as has been demonstrated, involved his masculine qualities as well as his beauty.

Pages are several times exchanged as objects of value in Shakespeare. The fairies quarrel over the Indian Boy in *A Midsummer Night's Dream*. Falstaff's page in *The Merry Wives of Windsor* is used as a go-between, and at one point Mistress Quickly brings a message that Mistress Page would like to have him sent to her: 'Her husband has a marvellous infection [= *affection*] to the little page; and truly Master Page is an honest man.' One searches in vain for any more specific indication of impropriety, and likewise in *Cymbeline* the dealings of Lucius and her father for the cross-dressed Imogen suggest an untroubled and unsalacious admiration:

CYMBELINE: Boy,
  Thou hast look'd thyself into my grace,
  And art mine own   (v.v.93–5)

The duties of a page could cross boundaries that we might observe, but they were well within the chivalrous code of traditional service and platonic affection:

LUCIUS: Never master had
  A page so kind, so duteous, diligent,
  So tender over his occasions, true,
  So feat, so nurse-like.   (v.v.85–8)

Such tribute is, of course, conditioned by our knowledge that the page is a girl in disguise.

Few things show more clearly the failure of critics to adjust to different historical values than the widespread assumption that for people of the same sex to sleep in the same bed automatically meant homosexual inter-course. 'The childhood liaison of Rosalind and Celia', according to Camille Paglia, is 'homoerotic . . . *even sleeping together*'. The German director Peter Stein apparently built an entire production around this view, with the couple pursuing 'their amorous game', Kott reports, 'in the thickets of the Forest of Arden most to the very end of the comedy'.[59] Within living memory, however, there have been practical reasons for the multiple occupation of beds: poverty, lack of space, and particularly for warmth. Servants were sent to bed early to warm them. Probably few people before the twentieth century slept alone. Mixed couples were a different thing. Traditionally the sword divides the bed. Hermia has Lysander lie further off in the forest, and Rose in *The Recruiting Officer* is disappointed to have slept with Sylvia *en travestie* as a soldier and to have had an untroubled night. Amongst those of the same sex, notwithstanding Clunch's joke in *The Old Wives' Tale*, 'Come on my lad, thou shalt take thy unnatural rest with me' (lines 102–3), it is commonplace that friends, such as Beatrice and Hero in *Much Ado*, or Arden and Franklin in *Arden of Faversham*, kinsmen, like Richard and Edward in *Alphonsus, Emperor of Germany*, mistress and maid, as in *The Duchess of Malfi*, master and page, in *Honest Man's Fortune*, *Four Prentices*, and *Look About You*, even perfect strangers, like Eusanius and Ragadon in *The Thracian Wonder*, shall share beds without impropriety. Iago uses this accepted custom to frame his lie about Cassio's lascivious dream of Desdemona. Nobody asks what *they* were doing in bed together.

This then is the context in which girls can follow their lovers to the wars disguised as pages and lie undiscovered beside them, like Neronis in *Clyomon and Clamydes*, and as the French Lady does in *Four Prentices* for a whole year, and not necessarily 'amounting to a *reductio ad absurdum*', as the sceptical Freeburg suggests.[60] Similarly, when Celinda in the later, more fleshly, world of *The Cardinal*, muses on the possibility of taking service with the manly Columbo, and asks, 'Do not such men / Lie with their pages?', she is not imputing pederasty but considering whether this common-place activity, innocent of sex, might provide her with a pretext which she can turn to her own carnal advantage.

John Fletcher's *Honest Man's Fortune*, 1613, articulates clearly and sympathetically the nature of the received neo-platonic tradition, as well as satirising its use in contemporary drama. Veramour (True-Love), the page, describes what he would do for love of his master, Montague, the hero:

> I will follow you through all countries;
> I'll run (as fast as I can) by your horse-side,
> I'll hold your stirrup when you do alight,
> And without grudging wait till you return:
> I'll quit assur'd means, and expose myself
> To cold and hunger, still to be with you;
> Fearless I'll travel through a wilderness;
> And when you are weary, I will lay me down,
> That in my bosom you may rest your head;
> Where, whilst you sleep, I'll watch, that no wild beast
> Shall hurt or trouble you: and thus we'll breed
> A story to make every hearer weep,
> When they discourse our fortunes and our loves. (IV.i)

Girls in breeches may be capable of a gesture, even of the supreme sacrifice of their lives for their loved one, but there is more in the day-to-day privations Veramour will suffer than would suit a Julia with her hair knit up in silver threads.

Montague's response to this protestation of love is to exclaim: 'Oh what a scoff might men of women make, / If they did know this boy!' It is not, however, an observation he applies to himself, for he has liaisons with all three women in the play, one of whom immediately appears:

CHARLOTTE: ... Good Veramour, leave thy master and me; I have earnest business with him.
VERAMOUR: Pray, do you leave my master and me; we were very merry before you came: he does not covet women's company; what have you to do with him? – Come, sir, will you go? and I'll sing to you again. – I' faith, his mind is stronger than to credit women's vows, and too pure to be capable of their loves.
CHARLOTTE: The boy is jealous ... (IV.i)

Montague says nothing all this whilst, but a little later signals Veramour to withdraw, and Charlotte then sets about persuading him to marry her. Veramour neither offers a physical relationship, nor does Montague respond in that kind. Veramour seems to think, in his immaturity, that is it satisfying to them both to be suspended in a golden world of platonic androgyny, symbolised by the songs, which merely lengthen out the present and leave the situation as they found it. He is unaware of the urges of the flesh that so evidently affect his master whenever a woman is on the horizon. To Veramour, as yet, women are merely the targets of generalised misogyny. It is a well-observed study of a certain phase of adolescence; perhaps what Peter Blos calls the 'transitory narcissistic stage', which precedes the search for a heterosexual partner, and is often characterised, according to Coppélia Kahn, by leading to 'a same-sex object choice based on an ego ideal'.[61]

The corrupt courtier, Laverdine, takes a fancy to Veramour, half-believing him to be a whore in disguise. Charlotte too had wondered if he were a wench. Finally, tired of Laverdine's attentions, Veramour as a joke pretends he *is* a lady and is brought on at the end in skirts, to Laverdine's ultimate discomfiture. When quizzed by his master and the others, he satirises the current theatrical vogue by pretending to have been a lady in disguise following him for love, and not to have realised his own identity until Laverdine kindly pointed it out to him.

When Laverdine first approaches Veramour, he offers to take him into his service and dress him in fine clothes:

LAVERDINE: and thy lodging –
VERAMOUR: Should be in a brothel.
LAVERDINE: No; but in mine arms.
VERAMOUR: That may be the circle of a bawdy house, or worse.
LAVERDINE: I mean thou shouldst lie with me.
VERAMOUR: Lie with you! I had rather lie with my lady's monkey; 'twas never a good world since our French lords learned of the Neapolitans to make their pages their bedfellows; it doth more hurt to the suburb ladies than twenty dead vacations. (III.iii)

Veramour cannot mean here that the practice of sharing beds is new, since he himself sleeps with his master, and as we later learn, innocently so. What he must mean is that the Neapolitans have passed on the practice of pederasty to some of the French (the play being set in France). Laverdine, however, is making a distinction between what he would do with a woman and what with a page – something that would not involve being hanged for sodomy; hence his excitement when Veramour pretends to be a woman:

A woman! how happy am I! now we may lawfully come together, without fear of hanging ... (IV.i.)

Montague is surprised when he thinks his page is a woman:

> It may be so; and yet we have lain together,
> But, by my troth, I never found her lady. (v.iii)

How far did he look? And what is it that Laverdine proposes to do when he thinks Veramour is a page?

The great sodomy scandal of the period came to trial in 1631. It was a complex and murky affair.[62] The Earl of Castlehaven had taken a second wife, a widow older than himself, and reputed to be sexually insatiable. The Earl assisted in her rape by Broadway, one of his servants, and she subsequently took lovers from the household, including Skipwith, 'the special favourite of the Lord'. Although the couple had betrothed together their eldest children from their previous marriages, the Earl insisted Skipwith had intercourse with his daughter-in-law in preference to his own twelve year-old son. He was fond of watching such acts, and of making others do so, and there is some suggestion of sadism with a whore, Blandina, kept in the house. The chief indictment of the Earl, however, was for sodomy with his male servants. The truth of this is lost to history, but what is of concern here is the defence he chose to offer.

Two of the servants, Broadway and Fitzpatrick, were suborned by the State to testify that Castlehaven had, 'spent his seed' between their thighs. Nothing further was alleged and on this alone Castlehaven was condemned to death and subsequently executed, as were the informers, with an awesome logic – if he was liable to death for the same activity, then so were they – despite having been promised immunity. At first the two servants had refused to co-operate, admitting only to lying with their lord, an admission also made by Skipwith, in reality probably the most culpable.

Castlehaven's final argument in his defence, therefore, was that external emission did not constitute sodomy, but the Lord Chief Justice ruled that *emissio semenis* was sufficient proof. It is significant that the assize did not entirely support this view. While his twenty-seven peers agreed unanimously on the charge of rape, they split, fifteen for and twelve against, on the charge of sodomy. This suggests that although it did not save Castlehaven on this occasion, since his various other crimes probably disposed his peers towards a harsher verdict, it was a defence with considerable chance of success elsewhere. In other words, the current *mores* did distinguish between penetration and what Castlehaven in his defence called 'pollution man with man'.[63]

Hence there could indeed be smoke without fire: the concomitants to intercourse, so gleefully discovered and elaborated in modern studies, are no certain evidence of the thing itself; which makes questionable the construction so often placed on Francis Osborne's description of James I and his favourites:

the love the King shewed was as amourously conveyed as if he had mistaken their sex, and thought them ladies; which I have seene Sommerset and Buckingham labour to resemble in the effeminateness of their dressings . . . (James) kissing them after so lascivious a mode in publicke, and upon the theatre, as it were, of the world . . . prompted many to imagine some things done in the tyring house that exceed my expressions . . .

The normally sagacious Kathleen McLuskie leaps upon this as evidence of both royal and player impropriety,[64] but it need indicate neither, and is surely a variation of the schoolboy howler, 'the violence in the Greek theatre took place offstage', instead of in what Celia Daileader calls the 'diegetic space'; i.e. that 'referred to by characters'.[65] James' show of affection in public is likened to the lascivious stage business of lovers in the drama which arouses the spectator to imagine consummation as the actors go off, when *he* knows, and we know, they change their costumes and go for a beer. If there is any impropriety here, it is the structural and emotional weight which Shakespeare's eschewing of sexual activity between the characters during the course of the play puts on that imagined conclusion.

The exact nature of James' sexuality remains a mystery.[66] He gave his wife eight children. In 1607, after the last two died in infancy, Sophie after a day and Mary in her second year, he and Anne appear to have given up conjugal relations. Earlier he had had an extra-marital affair with Anne Murray of Tullibardine and written poems to her and to her sister-in-law. Insecure and devoid of parental love – he was one year old when his mother was made to abdicate in his favour, subsequently to be imprisoned and eventually executed in England, and his minority, under the tutelage of the uncompromising George Buchanan ('*Ye may kiss his arse, madam, but I ha'e skelped it*') was a contest between the Scottish nobles, with assassination attempts and kidnappings – he responded strongly to any mark of affection. Kings cannot have equals as friends; they are always lonely and susceptible to flattery. 'They . . . told me I had white hairs in my beard', says King Lear, 'ere the black ones were there.' The classic pattern is a succession of favourites until one achieves dominance. For such men it is an opportunity for advancement, as Buckingham openly admitted in his Masque at Burley-on-the-Hill, presenting himself as a stealing gypsy. Favourites have lives and lovers of their own, as had Gaveston, and being a favourite becomes a job, with calculated favours. James was a scrupulous man. In *Basilikon Doron*, his manual on kingship, which continued to be prized by his son Charles after his death, James says there are 'some horrible crimes that ye are bound in conscience never to forgive: such as witchcraft, wilful murder, sodomy'. It may be that he thought as issues of sedition they did not apply to him, but it may be that he salved his conscience by acts short of penetration.

The frequent term 'ingle', so often glossed as 'catamite', may in fact be an acknowledgement of same-sex intimacies without intercourse accepted by this society. The dominant association of 'ingle' is surely the 'inglenook', a corner in the old-style fireplace for lovers to kiss and court.[67]

The picture that seems to emerge of Elizabethan sexual attitudes as they relate to the theatre and its cross-dressed performers is one in which the open admiration of male beauty and the expression of same-sex affection were consistent with a taboo on its physical, or at least penetrative, expression, as articulated in Shakespeare's Sonnet 20:

> A woman's face with Nature's own hand painted
> Has thou, the master mistress of my passion;
> A woman's gentle heart but not acquainted
> With shifting change as is false woman's fashion;
> An eye more bright than theirs, less false in rolling,
> Gilding the object whereupon it gazeth;
> A man in hue all hues in his controlling,
> Which steals men's eyes and women's souls amazeth.
> And for a woman wert thou first created,
> Till Nature as she wrought thee fell a-doting,
> And by addition me of thee defeated,
> By adding one thing to my purpose nothing.
> But since she prick'd thee out for women's pleasure,
> Mine be thy love, and thy love's use their treasure.

It expresses sensuous male friendship and the admiration of an epicene standard of male beauty but one virile enough to give women physical pleasure and render the male relationship a platonic one. Only if this distinction is understood, arbitrary though it may now seem, between the acceptability of sensuous platonism and the prohibition of sodomy, will the eroticism of the plays make sense.

Thus it is that in contrast to the revulsion with which sodomy is treated within the drama, there is a confident, apparently unproblematic attitude towards sexual ambiguity, sometimes at the very centre of the play's interest, as in *Cymbeline* and *Philaster*, and for which a character in *Honest Man's Fortune* coins the term 'liquid epicene'. Young males in the plays frequently dress as women and flirt with men, as the young Robin Hood, disguised as Lady Faulconbridge, does in *Look About You* with Prince Richard, or Snip the cheats' boy dressed as a wench in *The Blind Beggar of Bethnal Green*. In both versions of the *Shrew*, boys simulate genteel sexual starvation and then when Sly is sufficiently aroused either disappear or find ways of keeping him at bay. The confidence with which they do so, given the seriousness of the punishments for sodomy, suggests these sequences rest on an absolute distinction drawn between the sexes, in life and onstage, and a consensus concerning the naturalness of heterosexuality and hence the ineligibility of boys as sexual partners, which underpins the whole cross-dressed tradition, together with some acknowledgement of the special nature of its theatrical use. Thus when Veramour, who has dressed as a woman to humour Laverdine, shows his breeches beneath his dress, the latter's hopes are completely dashed and he becomes the butt of general ridicule.

Situations in which a man is tricked into taking a boy as his bride, as in the Wily plot in *George a Green* or in the multiple deception at the end of *The Merry Wives of Windsor*, turn on the fact that the man can do nothing (and indeed has done nothing), but accept communal mockery. Men who chance on cross-dressed lovers, like the usurer Pisaro in *An Englishman for my Money*, or the Sultan in the prose romance *Amadis de Gaule*, and mistaking them for women attempt to woo them, are always old, impotent, or foolish.[68] Even Jonson, who virtually single-handed promulgates the slur against his quality, is obliged to follow this convention at the end of *Epicoene*, where not only is Morose the unwitting husband mocked, but so are two fools who have boasted of carnal knowledge of the bride. It is not that they have groped in the wrong place, but that they have not groped at all. The distinction is absolute, and the flirtation with androgyny and gender-bending is able to take place precisely because society is confident in its distinctions, and not because it is uncertain of them.[69]

Critics have noted what they take to be a deliberate trailing of sexual ambiguity through Shakespeare's names for the breeches roles. Imogen's 'Fidele' is, of course, unexceptionable, and Viola's 'Cesario' is presumably a reference to her original disguise as a eunuch before casting precluded her singing. Only Rosalind's 'Ganymede' may carry associations of pederasty, but it is received from Shakespeare's source in Lodge's novel. Even then it is probably a kind of *sprezzatura*, a slight scathing sideswipe at the shadowy pederastic sub-culture from which their professional status distinguishes them. An analogous sort of confidence also underlies the warrior-fighting and camaraderie references that use images of female emotions, such as a 'woman's longing' in *Troilus and Cressida* and others in *Coriolanus*. They are striking precisely because of the acknowledged gender differences; not homoerotic but merely hyperbolic.

CHAPTER 3

Stage costume and performer ethos

Pederasty or prosthesis?

Peter Stallybrass, seeking to establish that scenes of undressing on the Elizabethan stage concentrated on the titillating anticipation of glimpses of the 'boy' beneath, argues against any kind of prosthesis in the representation of female breasts. Instead, he suggests they were simulated by tight-lacing, or simply not attempted at all, in order to create an indeterminacy charged with considerable excitement:

If Renaissance theatre constructs an eroticism that depends upon a play of differences (the boy's breast / the woman's breast), it also equally conjures up an eroticism which depends upon the total absorption of male into female, female into male.[1]

The second proposition has been dealt with above. In respect of the first, no such conclusion could be reached from the wealth of evidence available to the contrary, which points quite clearly to considerable and routine prosthesis, whilst giving no indication of any excitement in the process itself.

Stallybrass acknowledges cases where breasts are apparently toyed with, but insists that, as when Cleopatra puts the asp to her bosom, it is the 'boy's' breast that is revealed. In a similar episode in Peele's *Edward I*, however, not included in his survey, the dialogue makes it clear that prosthesis *was* used:

ELINOR: ... Katherina binde her in the chair and let me see how sheele become a Nurse, so now Katherina draw forth her brest and let the Serpent sucke his fil ...

This is not an action merely threatened, but one quite evidently carried out:

ELINOR: ... why so now shee is a Nurse, suck on, sweet Babe.
MAYORESS OF LONDON: Ah Queene, sweet Queene, seeke not my bloud to spill:
    For I shal die before this Adder haue his fil.   (lines 2328–34)

And the Mayoress is left to die upon the stage. It may be possible to substitute a male breast for many of the actions described in the plays – kissing, groping, stabbing, and so forth – but one thing that cannot be done is to 'draw' one 'forth'. The Elizabethans liked their violence bloody and they liked it realistic; even the itinerants in *Cambises* carried with them a complete skin to allow someone to be flayed alive, along with the more routine bladders filled with vinegar, and a trick sword. It seems unlikely, therefore, that Fidelia in *The Rare Triumphs of Love and Fortune*, for instance, who has to bare her breast and prick it in order to restore speech to her brother, was not provided with a property one for the purpose. 'The displayed breast', as Stallybrass rightly says, 'is a metonym for woman', and the insistence with which it is featured in the canon surely argues for its representation. The heroine in *Mary Magdalene* in her moral descent changes into an indecent costume that either reveals her breasts or can be adjusted by Pride to do so:

> Your garments must be worn alway
> That your white pappes may be seen if you may.   (lines 58–9)

Isabella in *The Spanish Tragedy* plunges a knife into 'this hapless breast that gave Horatio suck'. The dying Sulla in *The Wounds of Civil War* asks to put his hands on his daughter's breasts. In *The Devil's Charter* Lucretia Borgia parades between two mirrors held by pages, praising her own beauty:

> A chin the matchless fabric of fair nature,
> A neck, two breasts upon whose cherry nipples
> So many sweet solicitious Cupid(s) sucked . . .

Jupiter in *The Golden Age* groping Calisto says:

> Thy bosom lend
> And by thy soft paps let my hand descend.

Venus in *The Brazen Age* invites Adonis to 'tumble' and 'toy and play, / Thy icy fingers warm between my breasts'. The disguised Mistress Low-Water revealing her true identity at the end of *No Wit, No Help Like a Woman's* in order to get out of her marriage contract, points to her breasts, anticipating the classic denouement so favoured of Restoration actresses and their audiences:

> And I've got my neck verse perfect, here and here.   (v.i.344)

Arguably, as Stallybrass claims, many of these moments could be mimed to male bodies, but such concentration on the female breast, the softness of their paps, their nipples, and their nourishing functions, would make it more than reasonable to suppose they were catered for by prosthesis, a conclusion clearly supported by the surviving visual evidence.

In defending his recipe for paedophilic voyeurism Stallybrass argues that the illustrations on some published quarto title pages, 'draw attention to the specifications of women's bodies in ways which would be extremely difficult (if not impossible) to represent upon the stage', and he dismisses these woodcuts on the grounds that they were merely for readers. But this is to ignore exactly contemporary surviving costume designs by Inigo Jones for non-masquer roles in the Stuart Masque, performed either by these very same players, their colleagues in the Chapel Royal, or in some later cases other subordinate gentlemen in the royal service. These indicate even franker representations of the female anatomy. Those for *Chloridia*, 1631, especially of the anti-masque dancers, Jealousy, Disdain, etc. (figures 5 and 6) show female figures stripped to the waist with prominent bare breasts.

Such female torsos were presumably moulded in papier maché or leather, their edges concealed by heavy necklaces and puffed sleeves. Without the aid of modern materials, such simulations are unlikely to have been of a very high level of realism, which is perhaps why, when the same techniques were applied to aristocratic male and female masquer costumes, they represented military corselets cut close to the body rather than naked torsos. Thus, where an awareness of male performer obtruded, it would more likely lead to humorous incongruity rather than homoerotic desire.

Perhaps the most telling piece of evidence, because it relates to everyday fashion, is Jones' design for the wife of an 'old-fashioned gentleman' (catalogue no. 424) for an anti-masque entry in *Salmacida Spolia*, 1641, which Orgel and Strong describe as 'A woman wearing Jacobean bourgeoise dress of the period' (figure 7). Between her large ruff and low-cut bodice are clearly sketched a substantial pair of naked breasts. The costume was designed for William Murray, Gentleman of the Bedchamber, later the first Earl of Dysart. Murray is recorded as already being in post with the then Prince of Wales in 1625, so it is likely that he would have been at least thirty by the time of the Masque in 1641, and a man of some influence.[2]

Although male-performer nudity may have existed in similar court entertainments in Italy and France,[3] there is no evidence for it in England and much to the contrary. The cupids in Francis Beaumont's *Inns of Court Masque* were 'attired in flame-coloured taffeta close to their bodies like naked boys'; whilst Cupid 'the naked boy' in *Love Freed From Ignorance and Folly*, 1611, wore 'a suit of flesh-coloured satin decorated with lace and

5 Jealousy from *Chloridia*

6 Disdain from *Chloridia*

7 The wife of an old-fashioned gentleman from *Salmacida Spolia*

8 Cupid from *Chloridia*

puffs', similar presumably to the one illustrated for *Chloridia* (figure 8).
Following the same convention, the 'twelve wild men wildly habited' in *The
Triumph of the Prince d'Amour* wore 'waistcoats of flesh colour', which 'made
them show naked to the middle'. It is much more likely, therefore, that
female characters so presented relied on costume and prosthesis, as is also
suggested in an item in Henslowe's costume list, 'Eves bodeyes' (bodice?),
rather than on revealing the inappropriate torsos of the presenters.

As has already been shown, naked breasts onstage caused no great excitement. They were commonplace, real or simulated, in royal shows and popular entertainments in Paris, Florence, and Venice, as well as London. The whole thing was much more matter-of-fact. Several adult-player texts, such as 'Bethsabe Bathing' and a number of incidents in Heywood's *Ages* plays, threaten to show a good deal more than naked breasts, whilst there are some remarkable scenes of pregnancy with vivid detail of its discomfort, tetchiness, and longings, and with both Jane Seymour in *When You See Me You Know Me* and the heroine of *The Duchess of Malfi* going into labour onstage, even to miming contractions. There are scenes of the childbed in *Edward I*, with a well-observed episode of post-natal depression, and another more riotous episode in *A Chaste Maid in Cheapside* where the presence of a wet-nurse suggests the possibility of further business. Indeed, references to lactation are not infrequent. The heroine of *Patient Grissil* presents her breasts to the creature sent to take her babies away:

> heer's a fountaine,
> Which heauen into theis Alablaster bowles,
> Instil'd to nourish them; man theyle crie,
> And blame thee that this ronnes so lauishly,
> Heres milk for both my babes, two brests for two.   (IV.i.124–8)

And the watching Marquis says in an aside, 'Poore babes I weep to see what wrong I doe.' There is no satire here, no misogyny. Grissil's misery is heartfelt and shared by her observers onstage and off. And there is no suggestion of erotic frisson. If we find so much of it in these representations of the female body, then perhaps the problem is ours.

Proving the existence of false breasts may seem a peculiar endeavour, but their very evident presence counters the paedophilic argument by suggesting that spectator attention was on the fables, and where it took in the performer, on his telling of them.

A more legitimate object for investigation perhaps is the attention given to the female garments worn on the stage.

The significance of women's clothes on the Elizabethan stage

It was in many ways the costume as much as the player wearing it that proceeded across the Elizabethan stage and was the focus of attention. Perhaps the costumes of the time would not actually have stood up on their own, but they often look in illustrations as though they have an independent life that dwarfs the wearer. The finest women, says the courtesan in

Michaelmas Term, 'are but deluding shadows, begot between tirewomen and tailors' (III.i.4–5). Philip Stubbes observed:

when they have all these goodly robes upon them, women seem to be the smallest part of themselves, not natural women, but artificial women, not women of flesh and blood, but rather Puppets, or Mammets, consisting of rags and clouts compact together . . .

Fashionable costumes, alternating constraint and exposure and often with considerable appendages to be managed, determined to a very large extent the posture and mobility of the wearer, emphasising, as Sandra Clark says, 'modesty and constraint of movement'.[4] Such would be represented in the frequent formal dances that punctuate the plays, reflecting their importance in Court social life. Sir Thomas Elyot in *The Governour* describes how dancing reinforces gender stereotypes: 'for the man expressing in his motion and countenance fortitude and magnanimity . . . the maiden moderation and shamefastness'; whilst Sir John Davies in *Orchestra*, 1596, stresses the more obvious uses of dancing for sexual display, the male 'like a reveller in rich array, / Doth dance his galliard in his leman's sight'.

The stage paraded the panoply of State, reproducing its principal females in great detail, as for instance in the stage directions to *Henry VIII*: '*The Queen in her robe, in her hair, richly adorned with pearl, crowned . . . The old Duchess of Norfolk, in a coronal of gold, wrought with flowers, bearing the Queen's train . . .*' and so on. 'Show me like a queen', says Cleopatra, preparing for her suicide, 'go fetch my best attires', and her women dress her onstage, satisfying a voyeuristic spectator thirst for closer views of high-born ladies, normally seen only at a distance, and here revealed in distress, undress, even intimacy; and, in some instances, indeed, in the very garments of actual court ladies. Even Henrietta Maria's costumes for *The Shepherd's Paradise* were worn in 1634 by professional players. Sir Simonds D'Ewes 'purposely avoided' a Latin Comedy at Trinity College in the following year, 'because of the women's apparel worn in it by boys and youths'. It is the costumes themselves apparently, before the wearing of them, that he fears will inappropriately excite him.

Not only gender identity, but beauty too is created by costume. 'Dress yourself', says the Lord to the Player Boy in the anonymous *Taming of a Shrew*, 'like some lovely lady', and the joke of the impersonation, as in Shakespeare's version, is that Sly is turned on not by the boy beneath the disguise, but by the disguise itself. In Lodge's novel, *Rosalind*, as though anticipating the ambiguities of the cross-dressed stage the Celia-character attempts to put down the heroine in breeches:

He hath answered you Ganymede (quoth Aliena) it is enough for pages to waite on beautifull Ladies, and not to be beautiful themselves. Oh Mistres (quoth Ganimede) hold you your peace, for you are partiall: Who knowes not, but that all women have desire to tie soverein to their peticoats, and ascribe beautie to themselves, where if boyes might put on their garments, perhaps they would proove as comely. . .[5]

Aliena's criterion is a good example of the cultural construction of beauty in the making, determining by social fiat what is and is not be to be admired, whilst Ganymede's reply asserts the Elizabethan reality that beauty is transferable with the clothes.

If beauty and status lie in richness of attire, then it is hardly surprising that in a flourishing and increasingly commercially driven economy the upwardly mobile should have aped their betters; so much so that the sumptuary laws designed to prevent this were increasingly seen as ineffectual as well as superfluous (and bad for trade), and were repealed in 1604.[6] 'What base birth', says the courtesan in *Michaelmas Term* the following year, 'does not raiment make glorious?' (III.i.1–2). It seems at first a strange inconsistency that the *Homily Against Excess of Apparel* should regard 'fine bravery' as an inducement to 'wanton, lewd and unchaste behaviour' amongst the lower orders and yet accept it as appropriate for what Thomas Puttenham in *The Arte of English Poesie*, using dress as a metaphor to justify poetic ornament, describes as 'great Madams of honour' who wear the 'courtly habillements . . . as custom and civility have ordained'. The clue, however, lies in the description of what 'great Madams' wear. They:

think themselves more amiable in every man's eye when they be in their richest attire, suppose of silks of tissues and costly embroideries, than when they go in cloth or in any other plain and simple apparel

'Tissue' was light and gauzy, interwoven with threads of gold or silver. Thus the material for courtly wear was, literally, 'fine' compared with the coarser hand-woven fabric in ordinary use. This is the implication of the criticism of the sort of materials used for *The Masque of Blackness* as being 'too light and Courtesan-like'. Lear's comment on Regan's costume testifies not only that similar styles and materials, with their erotic implications for aristocratic women as objects of desire, were incorporated into day wear, but also that they were imitated onstage:

> Thou art a lady;
> If only to go warm were gorgeous,

> Why, nature needs not what thou gorgeous wear'st,
> Which scarcely keeps thee warm.   (*King Lear*, II.iv.267–70)

The humiliation of a fashionable or high-born female character being stripped of her finery upon the stage, as in *'Larum for London*, *The Miseries of an Enforced Marriage*, *The Fair Maid of Bristow*, *Patient Grissil*, and *2 Honest Whore*, is less erotic than a loss of status. As the rich outer garments and fine jewellery are taken from her, she is left, like any peasant woman, in her smock. Removing such garments deprives a woman too of the fashionable female shape. 'Cut my lace', says Paulina *in extremis*, referring to the tight-fitting outer layer of clothing, the bodice. The simple smock carried none of the tactile or revealing associations of modern women's underwear, themselves very recent. Thus, at a stroke, many of the presumed analogies between Elizabethan theatrical cross-dressing and modern transvestitism disappear. Except for such scenes of undressing, the Elizabethan player very evidently wore breeches beneath his gowns, as revealed in *Honest Man's Fortune*. 'I saw his legs, h'as boots on like a player, under his wenches clothes', a servant observes of the cross-dressed hero in *Monsieur Thomas*. Robes anyway were commonplace garments for both sexes, and, of course, all males spent their first seven years in skirts.

'The girl I'll call my own', says a modern popular song, 'Will wear velvet and satin, and smell of cologne.' These sorts of gender distinctions simply did not apply in the sixteenth century. Silks, satins, velvet, and lace were all commonplace in male aristocratic garments, whilst John Donne, creeping into her father's house to sleep with his mistress in 'Elegie IV', although evading the nosy mother, cruel father, and 'eight-foot-high iron-bound serving-man', is finally betrayed by his own 'loud perfume'. The cut and shape of gender-specific garments, on the other hand, was perceived as absolute.

The fashionable garments of the Elizabethan era were padded, tailored, wired, and laced, some of them, like the women's coffee-table farthingale and the male Mr Punch peascod belly, grotesquely so, to produce a series of gender-specific costume shapes that bore little resemblance to the natural figures of either sex and drew their strength as icons of gender (figures 9 and 10).

An incredible amount of fuss was made about women borrowing male styles of doublet and headgear, with an absolute prohibition on women wearing breeches, for their all-too phallic associations; so much so that when Henrietta Maria and her ladies performed *The Shepherd's Paradise* at Court in 1633, all the male costumes had skirts (figure 11).

9 The farthingale

Likewise, although men dyed their beards and sometimes plucked their eyebrows, make-up was a highly sex-specific phenomenon in Elizabethan society indicating and constructing female beauty. Those men that did wear make-up, said Castiglione, 'should be treated ... as public harlots, and driven ... from the society of all noble men'. Benedick's temporary assumption is meant to indicate he is madly in love. Shirley Garner quotes

10 The peascod belly

Balsam and Sagarin on the materials used: the foundation was 'white lead, occasionally mixed with sublimate of mercury and ground orris; rouge was red ocher, vermillion, or cochineal', and the result was 'a highly artificial mask-like appearance'.[7] Thus when Hamlet commands that my lady 'paint an inch thick' his exaggeration is only relative. Women wore make-up, says Garner, to cover the results of small-pox, but mainly to embody 'the ideal beauty that their culture fostered ... lily-white skin, rosy cheeks, cherry lips, and teeth of pearl'. Coupled with this was the widespread practice amongst fashionable women of wearing wigs. 'Elizabeth', says Garner, 'supposedly had eighty at one time.'[8]

  Hence the result of assembling all of this in the tiring house: the fashionable, exaggeratedly gender-specific, generally aristocratic costumes,

11 Male costume design from *The Shepherd's Paradise*

on which the largest sums of the players were expended – twice, Andrew Gurr has calculated, what was paid for the scripts – and which determined the player's posture, movement, and outline on the stage, together with prosthesis, wigs, and the thick doll-like make-up, must have been not merely disguise or impersonation, but in the case at least of the aristocratic female, complete transformation to give the appearance of the thing itself, of archetypal, erotic womanhood, and not so very different from the cross-dressed conventions of *Kabuki* and Chinese Opera. Even the gaze of the most dedicated paedophile would find the process of disentangling the physical person of the performer from the formally constructed stage female a difficult one. Compared say with the figure-hugging garments of the fifteenth century or the softer flowing ones that followed later in the seventeenth century, there can have been few periods in which fashion concentrated more on surface appearance and paid less attention, aside from the areas of exposed flesh simulated on the Elizabethan stage by rough-and-ready prosthesis, to the body beneath.

The effect, however, did not stop here. Appearance is one thing; behaviour quite another. The moral and intellectual context within the drama always placed its 'women' within quotation marks whilst at the same time acknowledging the artifice involved in their creation. Far from any 'absorption of male into female' as Stallybrass envisions, the performance, as this study has made clear, often stressed the aesthetic distance between performer and role. This, in combination with the elaborately constructed and highly gender-specific appearance, must from time to time have offered some of the immanence so celebrated in the combination of stillness and movement in the masked dancer; not creating man as woman, but celebrating 'woman-ness'.[9]

Distinguishing performer from part

Critics resisting the imputation of homoeroticism in the performances have sometimes taken refuge in what they see as the supremacy of theatrical illusion. Ejner Jensen insisted that 'the use of boy actors in female roles was a practice audiences accepted without confusion or feelings of sexual ambivalence' because the drama presented a 'convincing illusion'.[10] 'The tendency of Elizabethan dramatic technique, and particularly in the plays of Shakespeare', said Robertson Davies, 'is to take great pains to present a boy actor as a woman and not to disturb the illusion when it has been established.' Much of the foregoing has demonstrated that neither of these statements can be wholly justified.

Elizabethan dramaturgy incorporated a whole series of pressures towards disengagement from the character. Framing devices such as prologues and self-reference drew attention to the actor, and to the differences rather than the similarities between him and his role, and encouraged the appreciation of acting as a skill, as a piece of artifice. Such remarks as, 'Our wooing doth not end like an old play' (*Love's Labours Lost*, V.ii.874), and 'Nay, then, God buy you, and you talk in blank verse' (*As You Like It*, IV.i.31–2) suggest the potential for some kind of dual- or multi-consciousness, especially character-istic of entertainments for a popular audience, which involve an awareness of the artifice of performance. Nothing impeded the spectator's involvement with the unfolding events on the stage, which is self-willed and inexhaustible, but many things punctuated or delayed that process, and whetted his appetite, including recognition of and interaction with the player. This factor is apparent from the very earliest plays for the professional theatre, as in *Mankind* (c.1465–70), where the players exploit this audience predis-position by letting the play start and then, once they are involved, halting proceedings and making them pay before they can see the Devil Titivillus.

Robert Kimbrough argues that 'a speech assigned by Shakespeare to a woman in disguise as a boy can work in the theatre *only* if the audience knows and accepts that the speaker is a woman'.[11] His rhetoric, however, carries him to over-statement. Yes, it does depend upon the audience '*accepting*' the speaker as a woman, but at the same time it '*knows*' that it is a male. Kathleen McLuskie, resisting what she rightly sees as Jardine's simple concentration on performer at the expense of fable, observes, 'The fictions of Elizabethan drama would have been rendered nonsensical if at every appearance of a female character ... their gender were called into question'.[12] Interruptions are thus seen as destructive to illusion or to concentration. However, it is not at all clear, firstly, whether the act of *accepting* the speaker as female alternates with that of *knowing* that he is male, or coexists with it. In either event, the 'illusion' is not necessarily weakened by acknowledgement that it is a performance, since the spec-tator's involvement is consciously willed and not merely the result of trickery imposed upon him. Secondly, there is always a judgemental element, responding to events placed in a moral context, and this is often sharpened by cross-dressing; that is to say, the audience is involved in the story and its implications and not merely in the fortunes of the characters.

The process of involvement appears to be one in which the early stages require a greater imaginative input by the spectator, so that the regular breaking and re-establishing of the fiction, it can be argued, by repeatedly calling on that imaginative input to 'kick-start' commitment to it, strengthens rather than weakens his involvement. Furthermore, complicity in the mechanics of performance seems to serve to reinforce the spectator's commitment to the success of the enterprise by engaging his loyalty, and thus preventing any negative reactions that might otherwise be brought about by a sudden inadvertent consciousness of falseness quite likely in the rough conditions of a touring performance. No-one can see a live performance by modern itinerants, like *7:84* for instance, without being reminded how little it takes to produce a consciousness of spectator-as-collaborator; the performers come into 'your' hall or 'your' school, and being asked to clear a space, or hold a property, or – to revert to Panto – shout out when the Indians appear, makes you *part* of the performance and committed to its success. On each new entry the actor may momentarily appear to be someone else, some new character in the fable, often by an only perfunctory change in his appearance, so that the audience will laugh in humorous recognition whilst at the same time accepting the new character with pleasure; thus illustrating how the mixture of responses towards a performance includes simultaneously an awareness of contrivance along with, arguably, an increased involvement in the fable and its outcome.

In a widely misunderstood passage in *Antony and Cleopatra*, Cleopatra anticipates her own mockery on the Roman mimic stage:

> Antony
> Shall be brought drunken forth, and I shall see
> Some squeaking Cleopatra boy my greatness
> I' th' posture of a whore   (V.ii.218–21)

It does not imply, as some critics suggest, the inadequacy of what is being shown, or suspend the question of gender, or celebrate 'the credible and life-like Cleopatra they were beholding', nor even the transforming power of the audience's imagination.[13] Instead, it is a tribute to the effectiveness of the convention being used that made no bones about admitting the means of performance: i.e. the cross-dressing, the open stage, the dramatic poetry. These things allowed the spectator to concentrate on the events of the stage fiction and their outcome rather than being distracted by mere verisimilitude.[14]

Rosalind and the male actor

The cult of the *ephebos*, the beautiful youth, described by Camille Paglia as 'sexually self-complete ... sealed in silence, behind a wall of aristo-cratic disdain', has its origins in myth: Narcissus who, scorning Echo, was cursed to be consumed by self-love, and Hermaphroditus who rejected Salmacis until she so clung to him they merged into one. Such a figure is popular in the Ovid-fixated poetry of the late sixteenth century, such as Golding's *Hermaphroditus*, and echoed in Leander, the passive object of Neptune's desire in Marlowe's poem. Undoubtedly Shakespeare was much taken with the *ephebos* in his own life. His early sonnets urge a beautiful, self-contained young nobleman to procreate and not become 'the tomb / Of his self-love', as Venus similarly warns Adonis in his poem.

But the languid aristocratic recipient of the sonnets must not be confused with the busy plebeian collaborators who created the female roles. Shakespeare's 'Unthrifty loveliness', who spends upon himself his 'beauty's legacy' in the retreats of his London house or Hampshire estate, ever absent – 'the pleasure of the fleeting year', the poet calls him, the passive, silent object of a hundred and more sonnets – is a thousand miles from the active theatrical energy of a Rosalind. Her delight at attracting Phoebe, in whose 'pageant' she becomes a 'busy actor', shows her origins in the shape-stealer and plot-motivator of Lesley Soule's vision of 'Cocky Ros' as the performer of Ganymede, a sinewy, resilient, mocking, male *persona*, descendant of the Aristophanic *eiron* and the Medieval vice.[15] Although Viola and Imogen may not quite share her relish, their relative passivity too is stirred into actions that go out to meet their heart's desire. Even though at times Soule's Cocky Ros model threatens to create too much tension between *persona* and fable, it is a good deal nearer the likely reality than is the pre-pubescent hothouse flower of much recent specula-tion. At 736 lines, it is an enormous role, longer than Macbeth or Falstaff, only 16 lines short of Lear, and much the longest female part in the period. It is incredible that anyone should think it was played by a 'simpering' young boy, as Lisa Jardine would have it, 'mincing and lisping his way through his "woman's part"'.

The Epilogue to *As You Like It* has long been used as a peg on which to hang disquisitions such as that of Valerie Traub on 'the constructedness of gender and the flexibility of erotic attraction': Fiedler thinks it sets homo-sexual hearts a-throbbing, Jardine that Rosalind 'is ... saucily provoking the male members of the audience with her problematic sex', whilst Orgel suggests it 'may be a way of offering Orlando (or any number of spectators of either sex) what he "really" wants'. Far from doing any of these things, this study suggests, it begins by celebrating the naturalness of heterosexual attraction:

I charge you, O women, for the love you bear to men, to like as much of this play as please you; and I charge you, O men, for the love you bear to women . . .
(lines 12–15)

The function of the Epilogue is to return the spectators from the imaginary world of Arden to the reality of their own via an acknowl-edgement of the falseness of the playhouse and their superiority to it. The player is not, he says, 'furnish'd like a beggar' (of their applause), because he still wears the wedding outfit in which he came on with Hymen. By the time he steps forward to the conclusion, however, I suggest, he has removed part of his costume, opened perhaps the gown to reveal his breeches beneath, or even half-wiped the make-up from his face.

If I were a woman I would kiss as many of you as had beards that pleas'd me, complexions that lik'd me, and breaths that I defied not . . . (lines 18–20)

He is now an incongruously half-cross-dressed creature, upsetting rather than alluring, and, with a final gender-twist, threatening the men in the audience.[16] If he really were a woman, he says, which he is not, he would take the initiative and kiss whom he chose, out-Rosalinding Rosalind for nerve. He is forward on the stage surveying the male spectators' faces, pretending to choose. Perhaps he takes a half-step towards them, contem-plating reviving the terms of the fiction which he has just revoked and taking it into the auditorium; a monster in their midst:

. . . and I am sure, as many as have good beards, or good faces, or sweet breaths, will for my kind offer, when I make curtsy, bid me farewell (lines 20–3)

Indeed they will! And as quickly as possible. By applauding him, they will give him, like Prospero, his release from the 'bare island' of the stage, 'bare' because now stripped of any illusion, and then he will go, the comedy will be ended – and they will be safe from all such 'kind offers'. The curtsy when it comes will be a particularly masterful one.

The cross-dressed convention is never far from collapse, particularly in a tradition in which its principal motive is the containment, through mock-ery as well as example, of the other sex. The 'girl' has only to wink at the audience inappropriately, reveal to it the secrets of her lust – any woman's lust – beneath her demure exterior, and it is reminded that she too is not what she seems:

people clapped their hands in merry spirits to the young man, rejoicing that he knew so well the dangerous qualities of the loved sex, and that by a happy imitation of their behaviour he revenged us, as it were, on the fair ones for all the ills of that kind we had suffered at their hands.[17]

CHAPTER 4

Male didacticism and female stereotyping

Literary critics frequently acknowledge unease with the presence of stereo-typical elements in Shakespeare's female characters, and more especially when, after a more individual treatment, there is a return to stereotyping at the end of the play, and they are right to do so.[1]

Scholars concerned with plays as theatre as distinct from literature, on the other hand, and who regard characters as raw material for actors rather than as rounded personalities in their own right and available for psychological analysis, are more inclined to see stereotyping as a positive benefit, even a necessity. Edward Burns argues that a simple stereotype such as that of the courtesan actually offers greater scope to the player as the basis for elaboration than the more specific golden-hearted whore, which he says, 'closes off possibilities of further ... development'; whilst Michael Goldman regards stereotypes as 'not so much reductions of the real world as vividly simplified expressions of the actor's power' and argues that, 'each forcefully projects some motif of the actor's repertory of emo-tional aggression'. Stereotypes, he says, 'heighten the actor's uncanniness. Being a "type" gives him that inanimate freeze which renders his high vitality and animation more terrific.'[2] For the dramatist the use of the stereotype can be creative, offering the combined possibilities of tradi-tional iteration with development and surprise. A good example is the virago. When Shakespeare first takes up this stereotype it still bears clear evidence of its folk-play origins with mannish women beating their hus-bands or other male characters and breaking things over their heads, as in *Johan Johan* [1520], *Cambises* [1561], *Horestes* [1567], *The Famous Victories of Henry V* [1586], *The Old Wives' Tale* [1590], and *Locrine* [1591]. The joke is an enduring one and the performer is able clearly (and safely) to distinguish himself from the part. Shakespeare retains many of these elements in his early viragoes in the *Henry VI* plays and *The Shrew*, but the theatre is clearly tired of such simplicities, and 'mannishness' from being a misogynist calumny against the shrew becomes a more subtle characteristic of the 'womanly' woman – perhaps pioneered in Doll Williamson in *Sir Thomas More*, at its most distinctive in Cleopatra, but also significant in the development and celebration of quasi-historical personages who are both erotic and courageous like Moll Frith and Bess Bridges.

Stereotyping aids narrative compression and allows instant character recognition, for a performance, especially a humorous one, is a joint enterprise in which the audience and its reactions play an important part in its success. The main characters in the Tudor itinerant doubling tradition would have been cast according to the appropriateness of the performers available, but the chief qualification for undertaking the bulk of the secondary and minor roles was simply that of not otherwise being on the stage at the time. Hence stereotyping, in reflecting commonly held assumptions and expectations, enabled relatively unsuitable performers to play a wider range of roles successfully.

THE NEGATIVE CONSEQUENCES OF STEREOTYPING

Despite the positive and necessary functions of dramatic stereotyping, however, its overall consequence in Elizabethan theatre so far as female characters were concerned was to demean and arguably misrepresent them. An interview in 1992 with three of the actors who played the female roles in Cheek by Jowl's adult all-male *As You Like It* explored the difficulties cross-dressed performers had in trying to avoid gender stereotypes. Initially they insisted they had built their characters 'from the inside out'; Adrian Lester (Rosalind) said, 'we just looked at the feminine side of ourselves and exposed that'. Inevitably, however, they found themselves observing women and drawing generalisations. Even though they knew that, as Tom Hollander (Celia) put it, 'the notion of all girls doing the same thing is a dodgy one', nevertheless they found themselves repeatedly using words like 'protective', 'defensive', and 'yielding'. In rehearsal they had considered how Celia would respond to being grabbed by another character. A man, Tom thought, would have pushed him away, but playing a woman, 'was just as much a question of saying "I am a woman because *I do not* behave like a man". . . within the kind of theatrical generalised world that we're operating in, you're probably onto a winner if you yield rather than have a fist fight'.[3]

Gender stereotypes thus emerge, however hard they are resisted, above all because every actor wants to be 'onto a winner'. Furthermore, Tom, by identifying behaviour in terms of complementary opposites, was adapting the classic technique of gender stereotyping as used by Sir Thomas Elyot in *The Governour* :

A man in his natural perfection is fierce, hardy, strong in opinion, covetous of glory, desirous of knowledge, appetiting by generation to bring forth his semblance. The good nature of women is to be mild, timorous, tractable, benign, of sure rememberance, and shamefast.

Narrative subordination

Above all, the main function of stereotyping is to provide easily recognisable subordinate characters to support the narrative around the more three-dimensional main characters. In Elizabethan plays, whilst female characters are often the fulcrum of the action in some moral crisis or transgression, it is almost always one which relates to *male* sexuality, and the actual focus of their contribution to the plot; hence their frequent relationship to the principal male character as wife, mother, or daughter. This accounts both for female prominence in the fables enacted, most frequently at the point of marriage, and also in most cases for their ultimate dramatic subordination. What most usually gives shape, where it exists, to an Elizabethan play is the focus on a single central figure, which is very rarely female. 'If you are playing one of Shakespeare's women', says Juliet Stevenson, acknowledging a few exceptions such as Rosalind, 'you are by definition in a supporting role.' Even Kate in *The Taming of the Shrew* has no soliloquies. The actress Fiona Shaw, drawing on her own experience, acknowledges, 'There are moments when Kate's story simply isn't tenable, because she doesn't have the lines'.[4] 'In the purest feminist literary criticism', says Elaine Showalter, 'we are ... presented with .... a demand that we see meaning in what has previously been an empty space'.[5] Kate's defenders, therefore, are reduced to interpreting her silence. When Petruchio arrives late at the wedding, Kate, according to Margaret Ranald, 'is so glad he has come that she does and says nothing'. On the other hand, it could be argued that she is given nothing to say because at this moment she is little more than a property in the leading actor's bravura. Gertrude in *Hamlet* similarly illustrates the dangers of allowing the critical attention given to female characters to outstrip their significance in the play. According to Carolyn Heilbrun she is 'intelligent, penetrating, and gifted with remarkable talent for concise and pithy speech'.[6] Concise Gertrude certainly is. Her only two speeches of more than four lines are choric descriptions of other characters.

Although often associated with the basic rhythms of love comedy as symbols of fertility or re-birth, nonetheless most young women, outside Shakespeare at least, remain largely passive, and arguably under-written. Moll Yellowhammer, for instance, whose fortunes provide the main plot of *A Chaste Maid in Cheapside*, has just seven lines in her very brief love scene, and only a single line after her resurrection from the coffin at the end; and one which speaks volumes for the character convention:

I am silent with delight. (v.iv.51)

Among other romantic heroines, Infelice at the end of *1 Honest Whore* has one line, and Mary in the closing moments of *The Roaring Girl* only two. Female silence, of course, had a social dimension. Contemporary marriage manuals advised women to be sparing in their speech. In the anonymous *Edmund Ironside*, young Egina is brought into the feast by her father, apologising for her youth. Canute insists she sits with them and, pleased with her reply to his single question, invites her to marry him. She replies:

I say a woman's silence is consent. (line 452)

And so it would appear to be the case in much Elizabethan drama. Modern directors and performers often prefer to use a female character's reticence in, say, *Measure for Measure*, *The Comedy of Errors*, or *All's Well that Ends Well* to suggest otherwise, but in line with the prejudice in favour of the married state over chastity, the Elizabethan convention seems to have been that heroines accepted their suitors in silence at the end of plays.[7] Likewise it must be assumed in those difficult moments for a modern production where heroines are propositioned or threatened with rape, as in *Women Beware Women* and *The Changeling*, but denied the sort of lines we might expect by way of response, their silence also constitutes acquiescence.[8]

Polarisation

Whether plots are driven by the desire for true love to triumph or the achievement of revenge for some terrible wrong, or whether they relate back to the older struggle of the *psychomachia*, what they all have in common is a central conflict, what the Greeks called *agon*, usually between opposing sets of values and loyalties but expressed through individual characters. Personalised conflict is at once the great strength of theatre, in creating a formal dynamic structure for the play, and its greatest weakness as a medium for ideas.

Although dualism as a technique of categorisation has many uses, bringing us for instance to the point of choice, as a principle of thought it has serious limitations in being hostile to third possibilities. Discussing the relationship of philosophy to authority, David Rodowick suggests, 'the definitions of thought produced by specialists accord perfectly with the State's image of power and its juridical definitions of identity'.[9] He discusses what Claire Parnet has called 'the binary machine' which 'perfectly describes this technology of thought and the notions of identity it fabricates'. Dualism is, of course, inherent in nature: night/day, summer/winter, life/death, but whereas much of it had previously been without moral overlay, the influence of Christianity recast all it touched with a simplistic ethical polarisation in which the older folk gods became devils and provided a ready-made conflict-structure for all forms of drama. The Stuart masque, increasingly in the reign of Charles I a political statement, exactly illustrates Parnet's 'binary machine'. It augments moral dualism, secularised as rebellion and authority, with an aesthetic dualism that associates the former with darkness, ugliness, discord, and chaos, and the latter with light, beauty, musical harmony, and all the terpsichorean symmetry the Court's dancing masters could produce.

Antithesis operates as an organising principle throughout the drama, often as a means of compression. The *dramatis personae* of a play relates its characters in patterns. The sexes in particular are constantly presented antithetically. The French Lady in *The Four Prentices of London*, 1600, describes what a man should do if he really loves a woman:

> To sigh for her, and for her love to weep:
> As his own heart her precious favours keep:
> Never be from her, in her bosom dwell;
> To make her presence heaven, her absence hell . . .

Guy, her lover and eventual husband, replies, ''Tis pretty for some fool that could endure it.' He prefers to 'mount a steed', 'march up to the neck in snow', and 'To make my pillow of a cake of ice':

> I love to see my face besmeared with blood:
> To have a gaping wound upon my flesh,
> Whose very mouth would make a lady swound . . .

Here both genders are pushed to romantic excess, but the principle of extreme contrast holds whenever gender is in question, no doubt partly because of its technical convenience in that all the performers are male, but it lends itself thereby to the continuance of gender prejudice. In *Cymbeline* Pisanio coaches Imogen on her cross-dressing. Here the adjustments are primarily psychological:

> You must forget to be a woman; change
>   . . . fear and niceness
> (The handmaids of all women, or more truly
> Woman it pretty self) into a waggish courage . . .   (III.iv.154f.)

Femininity is thus seen as a (delightful) deficiency. In *I Tamburlaine* the hero woos the captive Zenocrate:

> *Zenocrate*, lovelier than the Love of *Jove*,
> Brighter than is the silver Rhodope.
> Fairer than the whitest snow on Scythian hils . . .
> With milk-white Hartes upon an Ivorie sled,
> Thou shalt be drawn amidst the frosen Pooles,
> And scale the ysie mountaines lofty tops:
> Which with thy beautie will be soone resolv'd.   (I.ii.87f.)

It is an image of extreme beauty, chaste and pure, to complement Tamburlaine's fiery, lusty personality, but again she is defined by what he is not. While he is active, with an appetite for self-assertion that carries him with scarcely a pause for breath through ten acts, there is really nothing much for her to do, apart from procreate. On balance, the frozen sled sounds even more incapacitating than the conventional pedestal.

The principle of duality works most frequently, however, in contrasts *between* female characters where the divide is most often between an evil, lascivious hussy and a chaste, virtuous wife or maiden, a polarisation the Elizabethans inherited from the Morality play. At one level, the unwillingness to entertain woman as an equal, as a mixture of good and bad as men are, is what the psychiatrist would call a failure of individuation, in the same way that the small child cannot reconcile the mother who punishes with the mother who nourishes, and hence the repeated topos of the former in fairy tales as witch or stepmother separate from the dead or incapacitated 'real' mother.

While many male characters also tended to polarisation, several things make the female characters more extreme in this respect. They are much fewer in number, generally subordinate in interest, and are arranged strategically at extreme points in the symbolism of the narrative. This principle of contrast is greatly intensified in the later Moralities by the process of doubling, in which the same player might undertake not only both the heroine/reward role as well as the evil seductress, but then would be called upon during the course of the action to play the *latter* pretending to be the *former*, whilst presumably keeping the relatively unsophisticated audience aware of the evil character's real identity. This, especially given the primitive conditions of touring and the short time allowed in the text for changing, would call for broad strokes rather than much by way of finesse, and would encourage the extreme polarisation of female roles, helping to establish a tradition much relished by the Elizabethans.

At its worst the antithetical pull towards extremes of impossible virtue or total lasciviousness denies a woman any kind of acceptable sexual feelings and makes her in either event someone with whom it is difficult to empathise, which is the first step in the disengagement necessary for misuse. It is interesting to note that on the rare occasions when attention is genuinely on the female characters then polarisation tends to be replaced by more subtle distinctions between the characters, as say of Rosalind and Celia, where one is bold in speech with her man, but the other more resolute in clinching a relationship.

Alterity

Such exceptions apart, the over-riding characteristic of most Elizabethan female roles is their alterity. In *1 Two Angry Women of Abingdon*, Master Barnes asks his daughter, Mall, if she would like to get married. Her answer begins with a modest preamble:

> I am a maid, and when ye ask me thus,
> I, like maid, must blush, look pale and wan,
> And then look red again; for we change colour,
> As our thoughts change. With true-fac'd passion,
> Of modest maidenhead I could adorn me,
> And to your question make a sober cour'sey,
> And with close-clipp'd civility be silent . . .
>
> (Dodsley, vol. VII, p. 293)

But then she throws caution to the winds and (though no suitor has yet been mentioned), admits that yes, she would like to get married, very much so, please. In substituting description, and of how she *might* have behaved, presumably accompanied by broad pantomime, to replace the difficulty of actually simulating these reactions, the conventional duplicity of maids is displayed, but at a distance, so that both performer and role are partly disengaged, presenting the 'pageant' of the dissembling young woman rather than identifying with her.

Where the opacity of motive is part of the dramatic technique in representing the male point of view, many roles would be spoilt by an actress trying to make sense of them, whilst others go well beyond what a woman might be expected to present with any degree of conviction, as in Mrs Goursey's admission in the same play that all women are unreasonable. A male performer would be more likely to accept lack of consistency or sympathy in a female character than an actress would. The behaviour of female characters is quite often incredible, or inconsistent. In *Promos and Cassandra*, the source of *Measure for Measure*, when Cassandra's rape is revealed and she is married at the Duke's command to Promos, she not only pleads for his life, but asks for a kiss. In arguing of female characters that their 'explanations for their actions rarely add up to the complicated declarations of interiority common to male characters by the 1590s', Sarah Eaton may be going too far in making the qualitative distinction solely a gender one – many minor male characters are no more coherent, as for instance Duke Frederick in *As You Like It*, who does not know why he hated Orlando's father – but she is surely right to highlight the tendency of dramatists at key moments to draw back from understanding their heroines' motives, so that they become, 'characters whose subjectivity can be doubted – by themselves, by male characters, by the audience'.[10] She comments, 'If given to reflection at all, female characters tend to be puzzled about why they are acting as they are', a judgement wholly consistent with male performance.

Female characters are sometimes inconsistent in ways which suggest that their purpose as constructs, either as functions of the plot or merely as vehicles for sexist comment, has overtaken any coherence of character. Bel Imperia in *The Spanish Tragedy*, for instance, takes a new lover and proceeds to intimacy not from motives of affection, she says, but merely for revenge. Young women are frequently made to couple against their apparent natures or the experiences they have undergone. The heroine of *Fair Em*, who has been entirely faithful to her noble lover Manville, punishes him at the end by marrying Valingford, towards whom she had previously indicated revulsion. Mal Berry in *The Fair Maid of the Exchange*, who had settled under pressure from her parents for the foolish Bowdler, agrees instead to marry Barnard, with whom she has previously had no interaction, merely because the Cripple persuades her she has been talking of him in her sleep. As with the main plot, this play implies that love is a fickle affliction and women in particular liable to the most arbitrary of choices. Susan, in the sub-plot of *A Woman Killed With Kindness*, is delighted to accept a proposal of marriage from her hitherto insalubrious intended despoiler. Grace in *Bartholomew Fair* seems quite willing to be the prize in a wager, apparently indifferent as to which gallant wins; just as in another of Jonson's plays, *The Alchemist*, Dame Pliant can be happily married to whatever husband is thrown up by the vicissitudes of the plot. Her name indicates not only her nature but the attitude of a whole seam of dramatists towards the young women who provide the rewards or outcomes of their plots but in whom no intrinsic interest is invested.

At a more sinister level, the cross-dressed tradition was used to suggest that women were not only different, but also unknowable, unfathomable; that you could never trust a woman because of the basic inconsistency of her sex. Isabella in *Edward II*, repeatedly spurned by her husband in favour of a male favourite, and whose behaviour we might think entirely reasonable in the circumstances, is presented as wicked when she takes a lover. Ann Frankford in *A Woman Killed with Kindness* is at once a virtuous wife and someone instantly corruptible. In *The Malcontent*, written for children but enthusiastically revived by the adults, the Duchess Aurelia elevates a suitor merely because he brings disparaging gossip of her current lover, Mendoza:

> I will love thee, be it but in despite
> Of that Mendoza. 'Witch!' Ferneze, 'witch!' –
> Ferneze, thou art the duchess' favourite;
> Be faithful, private; but 'tis dangerous . . . .
> Enjoy my favour. I will be sick instantly and take physic;
> therefore in depth of night visit –   (i.vi.43–50)

From a chronicle of individual failings, it was all too easy to pass to a generalisation that indicted the whole sex: 'Frailty', Hamlet says of Gertrude, 'thy name is woman.' And this alterity justified treating women differently, sometimes with almost casual cruelty, and often with dramaturgical indifference.

MODELS AND WARNINGS

The polarisation of female characters in Elizabethan drama was not merely a function of the theatrical needs for stereotyping. It also spoke to deep prejudices in the male psyche increasingly brought to the fore by the growing prominence of women in society and the 'Problem' this was perceived to create. Shakespeare did not enter into all aspects of the theatrical response to this manifestation of male anxiety, but he is by no means untouched by it and it helps to frame much of his work, as the following survey will show.

Containment

At the beginning of *1 Two Angry Women of Abingdon*, 1588, whilst the two couples are dining, Mistress Barnes, without evidence or logic, takes against her neighbour, Mistress Goursey, alleging that she is having an affair with Master Barnes. Her viewpoint is offered no sympathy or analysis; it is simply represented as a violent and destructive monomania which she pursues more or less to the end of the play.

After Mistress Barnes has thrown a series of insults at Mistress Goursey, Master Barnes remonstrates:

> Wife, go to, have regard to what you say;
> Let not your words pass forth the verge of reason . . .
> What will the neighbouring country vulgar say,
> When as they hear that you fell out at dinner?
> Forsooth, they'll call it a pot-quarrel straight:
> The best they'll name it is a woman's jangling.
>
> (Dodsley, vol. VII, p. 276)

When Mistress Barnes has flounced out, Mistress Goursey tries to make amends:

> 'tis but a woman's jar;
> Their tongues are weapons, words their blows of war;
> 'Twas but a while we buffeted, you saw,
> And each of us was willing to withdraw;
> There was no harm nor bloodshed . . .   (p. 278)

The female characters are thus made to discuss their own generic unreasonableness, neatly illustrating the convenience of the hermetically sealed world of Elizabethan all-male theatre.

The men cement their relationship before parting in an exchange that succinctly expresses the attitude of the play:

> MR BARNES: O Master Goursey, the mettle of our minds,
> Having the temper of true reason in them,
> Affords a better edge of argument
> For the maintain of our familiar loves
> Than the soft leaden wit of women can . . .
>
> MR GOURSEY: . . . Then here we'll part, partners of two curs'd wives.
> MR BARNES: O, where shall we find a man so bless'd that is not?   (pp. 278–9)

It is a universal misfortune. In the next scene, Barnes asks his wife her reason for hating Mistress Goursey, and she says: 'my reason equalleth my

will'. When she has gone, threatening to tell Goursey of his wife's supposed
infidelity, Master Barnes considers whether he should be angry but concludes that it will only make her worse. Instead, he will look for a remedy
by uniting the offspring of their two families, and though this is a somewhat unlikely solution in the circumstances, the rest of the play is taken up
with the fathers conspiring with their various children and servants to
neutralise by this means the destructive venom of their wives.

Musing whether his daughter will be as bad a wife as her mother, Barnes
concludes:

> If so, she'll be a plague unto her husband,
> If that he be not patient and discreet,
> For that I hold the ease of all such trouble.   (p. 290)

Wives, says the play, naturally turn into blind aggressive shrews, and man's
only recourse is to try with patience and discretion to out-manoeuvre and
not so much master as contain their fury. The secret, which to save his life
the Loathly Lady of the folk tales tells the hero, is that what women love
best, just like Chaucer's Wife of Bath, is 'sovereignty'. Hence marriage is
perceived as a constant struggle against a powerful adversary.

Misogyny is the male weapon in this battle for survival, what Tavris and
Offir call the '*Longest War*', and its commonest literary form is humour.
Although often presented as no more than an exercise for amusement, the
relentlessness of its target frequently betrays an underlying insecurity.[11]
Phyllis Rackin, suggesting that History 'is designed to construct a verbal
substitute' for the power of the mother, cites Derrida, 'the birth of writing ... was nearly everywhere and most often linked to genealogical
anxiety'.[12]

Women have occasionally replied in kind, such as Christine de Pisan,
writing from 1399, and perhaps Jane Anger, 1589 (though possibly John
Lyly), but the traditional female medium in the battle of the sexes is
scolding. Some writers are inclined to dismiss its significance. Lisa
Jardine, for instance, says, 'Women's power to disrupt is illusory: it is
only "telling tales" and "calling names".' Yet Petruchio shows just how
effective the shrew's traditional weapons are, and Jardine herself recalls the
testimony of Erasmus to the female tongue: when the husband wishes to
reverse the cure of his dumb wife, the Devil tells him that though he could
make her speak not all the devils in Hell could get her to stop.[13]

Strabo in *Locrine* offers a simple solution to scolding. Arriving home
drunk one night he finds his shrewish wife minding the baby; she advances
on him with a 'fagot stick':

Now, althogh I trembled, fearing lest she would set her ten commandements in my face, (I) ran within her, and taking her lustily by the midle, I carried her valiantly to the bed, and flinging her vpon it, flung my selfe vpon her; and there I delighted her so with the sport I made, that euer after she wold call me sweet husband, and so banisht brawling for euer . . . (IV.ii.42f.)

Servant and companion

Master Barnes does not offer his wife either carnality or violence, but relies instead on using his superior intellect to manipulate her as an ostensible equal. In this he reflects a growing dialogue in the period stimulated by Puritan discourses on the need to temper male authority in order to satisfy the newer claims of 'mutuality'. 'Wedlock', said the Protestant humanist Vives, 'was not ordained so much for generation, as for certain company of life, and continual fellowship.' The development of companionable marriage with the wife as a partner rather than a subordinate had many benefits in the increasingly complex early modern economy, but it was to be as *junior* partner: such views were held at tension with a more traditional conviction of a man's natural superiority and therefore right to rule. 'For woman is a weak creature', according to the *Homilies*, 'not endued with like strength and constancy of mind' as man. Therefore, 'to the fathers', says Hooker, 'within their private families nature hath given a supreme power'. The aim, as Simone de Beauvoir puts it, was 'to make of the wife at once a servant and a companion'. 'Mutuality' was offered as an alternative to equality, and the marriage manuals urged men to exercise their absolutism with love. As the wife was enjoined to obedience, so the husband was reminded that it was his duty to be concerned for her happiness.

Like Master Barnes, Elizabethan writers increasingly used persuasion rather than prescription to contain the wilful dangerous female, and much of the drama of this period divides its female characters between two clear models intended for the education of the female spectator, showing the benefits of one and the dangers of the other.

Bad women

One indication that these plays are part of a polemical struggle between the sexes lies in their treatment of cuckoldry. It stands to reason that for every adulteress there must be a cuckold, and yet there are very few conventional cuckolds in the adult repertory. Being a cuckold is humiliating, often a subject for public mockery, led through the streets on a wooden

rail or serenaded in *charivari*. Medieval literature is studded with jokes
at their expense, reflected in the many cuckolds in *The Canterbury
Tales* and *The Decameron*. The cuckold is exposed as less than a man.
His wife has had to look elsewhere because he has failed to give her sexual
satisfaction; such is the meaning of Nerissa's ring, the Devil coming in
the night to tell the husband where to keep his finger if he is to prevent his
wife from being unfaithful. In *Othello* and *The Winter's Tale* Shakespeare
demonstrates what the fear of cuckoldry can do to otherwise admirable
figures.

   Johan Johan, 1520, one of the earliest surviving adult plays, adapted from
the French *Farce du Paste*, gives centre stage to a traditional pitiable
cuckold, humiliated by his wife into preparing the meal, and then sent
by her to invite her paramour, the priest, to dinner. These two sit chuck-
ling, eating and drinking, whilst Johan is made to stand by the fire trying to
soften wax to mend the bucket, and consequently gets nothing to eat. His
failure to mould the wax to stop up the hole in his wife's bucket is heavily
symbolic of his condition.

   After this, however, there are few other men in the adult public theatre
mocked in the same way. The few plays which present successful cuckoldry are not surprisingly related to the City Comedy, mainly a Private
Theatre genre for the Children's troupes in which women become a
commodity in the merchant's obsession with fleecing the gallant, but
almost all adult theatre versions of this genre are subject to a sleight of
hand that prevents the husbands from becoming actual cuckolds.
Although the women are all too ready to betray their husbands, the
husbands somehow contrive to outwit them, or at any rate are saved by
events from this humiliation. In *The Family of Love*, the two husbands
have to work hard to avoid this fate. In *Bartholomew Fair*, the citizen
wives are recruited and dressed for prostitution, which is only prevented
by the turn of events. In *The Roaring Girl*, the husbands in the sub-plot
are saved by a lack of manliness amongst the gallants. In *Volpone*, the
husband Corvino is prepared to prostitute his own wife in hope of gold,
but she is saved by the intervention of the youthful Bonario. Even in this
genre, therefore, amidst its much vaunted 'realism', male pride substitutes
wish-fulfilment.

   The only exception in this group is *A Chaste Maid in Cheapside*, also
unique in both casting and venue, in which cuckoldry is humorously
pilloried and even suggested as a lower-middle-class form of livelihood;
whilst *The Devil and his Dame* takes the deliberately exaggerated position
that almost all men are cuckolds:

AEACUS: 'Tis strange what plaints are brought us every day
    Of men made miserable by marriage;
    So that, amongst a thousand, scarcely ten
    Have not some grievous actions 'gainst their wives.
                (Dodsley, vol. VIII, pp. 395–6)

And the plot demonstrates adultery as one of these. Cuckolds as minor contemptible figures in *The Duchess of Malfi* and *The White Devil* come dangerously close to justifying adultery; Julia and Vittoria can hardly be blamed for looking elsewhere for sexual satisfaction when their husbands are so clearly impotent, as the name 'Castruchio' in the latter indicates.

In the main body of plays under discussion, however, in which adulteresses are featured, the authors work hard to minimise any negative fall-out onto the husbands. If a woman takes to adultery, it is because she is a monster, and therefore her husband is hardly to blame. So both the King and audience in *Edward I* are amazed at Elinor's death-bed revelations. Matthew Shore can take no blame in *Edward IV*, being the loyal subject of a king. When at one point there is talk of Jane returning, he refuses on the grounds of *lèse majesté*. *A Woman Killed With Kindness* is at pains to stress that no inadequacy in Frankford is in any way to blame for his wife's fall:

FRANKFORD: Was it for want
    Thou play'dst the strumpet? Wast thou not supply'd
    With every pleasure, fashion, and new toy –
    Nay, even beyond my calling?
ANNE: I was.
FRANKFORD: Was it then disability in me,
    Or in thine eye seem'd he a properer man?
ANNE: O no.
FRANKFORD: Did I not lodge thee in my bosom?
    Wear thee here in my heart?
ANNE: You did.
FRANKFORD: I did indeed; witness my tears I did.   (XIII.107–15)

The crime is inexplicable, monstrous, and entirely the woman's.

Thus most adulteresses in the public theatre are seen as alien threatening creatures, lascivious, frightening, unnatural in their promiscuity, which is often augmented by some further crime. The Duchess in *The Revenger's Tragedy* is monstrous in choosing to betray her husband with her bastard stepson. Tamora in *Titus Andronicus* adds spice by cuckolding the Emperor with the black lover she brings with her. Artesia in *The Birth of Merlin*, described as 'that woman fury', failing in her attempts to woo

Uther, accuses him of attempted abduction, and finally, hurling impreca-
tions, is taken off to be walled up alive. *Lust's Dominion* begins with the
elderly Queen trying to stimulate the flagging energies of her black lover,
Eleazar, but he despairs of ever satisfying her lust:

> There's here,
> Within this hollow cistern of thy breast,
> A spring of hot blood: have not I, to cool it,
> Made an extraction to the quintessence
> Even of my soul; melted all my spirits,
> Ravish'd my youth, deflow'r'd my lovely cheeks,
> And dried this, this to an anatomy,
> Only to feed your lust?   (Dodsley, vol. XIV, p. 100)

Motive, where it exists, tends to be suppressed. A number of critics have
pointed to the way in which in Shakespeare's presentation of Goneril and
Regan he ignores his source *King Leir*, which ascribes their behaviour to
vanity and a longing for marriage, in order to make them inexplicably
evil, their motives obscure, and their actions alarming. Goneril contem-
plates murder and adultery and poisons her sister, whilst Regan is a man-
slayer.[14]

Indeed, there is an almost automatic association of adultery and murder.
Queen Argiale in *The Blind Beggar of Alexandria* has killed the hero's wife in
order to try to get him to submit to her. Aluida in *A Looking Glass for London*,
kills her husband in order to become the king's paramour. Livia, mistress of
the hero in *Sejanus*, discusses how her husband should be murdered. Lucretia
Borgia in *The Devil's Charter* does away with her third husband and pretends
to mourn him. In *Lust's Dominion* the Queen Mother strangles the Moor's
wife in order to be legally married to him.

The good woman

Models of how women ought to behave were much more frequently
represented on the adult stage than their contraries and the issue of
containment came to focus specifically on female loyalty and obedience
within marriage, replacing almost completely the emphasis traditionally
given to virginity. In *A Midsummer Night's Dream* celibacy as an alternative to paternal obedience is linked with death, which it is seen to
resemble:

> For aye to be in shady cloister mew'd,
> To live a barren sister all your life,
> Chaunting faint hymns to the cold fruitless moon   (I.i.71–3)

In Shakespeare the cloister is an acceptable choice only for older women, such as the Abbess in *The Comedy of Errors*, Thais in *Pericles*, and Hermione and Paulina in *The Winter's Tale*, but even then only as a temporary phase from which all return to marriage.

Among younger women, Margaret is regarded as fortunate to have escaped the convent in *Friar Bacon and Friar Bungay*, as Isabella appears to do at the end of *Measure for Measure*. It is quite acceptable for a girl to use entering a convent as a pretext, as the heroine is made to do in *The Merry Devil of Edmonton*, or as Portia does in *The Merchant of Venice*, and Abigail, at first, to retrieve her father's gold, in *The Jew of Malta*. Only later does she become a novitiate in earnest, and then to be the butt of lewd jokes about lecherous clergy and her likely fate therewith.

It is not unusual for women to make statements about the joys of a single life, as Lamira in *Honest Man's Fortune* (III.i):

> Command and liberty now wait upon
> My virgin state; what would I more? change all,
> And for a husband? no; these freedoms die,
> In which they live, with my virginity . . .

It is not long, however, before she is married. Similarly Emilia in *Two Noble Kinsmen* waxes lyrical about the superiority of female friendship:

> Lov'd for we did, and, like the elements,
> That know not what, nor why, yet do effect
> Rare issues by their operance, our souls
> Did so to one another . . .
> . . . the true love 'tween maid and maid may be
> More than in sex dividual   (I.iii.61–82)

Hippolyta, however, responds cynically that Emilia's 'appetite' really 'loathes then as it longs', and she is proved right when the latter has no difficulty accepting a husband at the end.

Given the Protestant unease about chastity expressed in Shakespeare's plays,[15] how far are heroines like Marina in *Pericles*, who bleat so much about their purity, expected to retain our sympathy? Certainly Olivia's retreat into ostentatious chaste seclusion in *Twelfth Night* is tinged with more than a little disingenuousness, whilst Isabella's expressed desire 'for more severe restraint' at the beginning of *Measure for Measure*, pointedly changing the more sympathetic figure of Cassandra in his source, might be said to 'place' her as a religious hysteric.

The heroines of William Rowley's *Birth of Merlin* and *A Shoemaker a Gentleman* are, therefore, extremely unusual in choosing religious chastity as an alternative to pressing marriages from quite decent suitors. Modestia in the former says of sensual pleasure:

> Great natures wisdom, who rear'd a building
> Of so much art and beauty to entertain
> A guest so far incertain, so imperfect . . .
> . . . how base
> Were life at such a rate! (I.i.121f.)

Elsewhere marriage and fruitfulness are seen as a woman's natural destiny, without which she is incomplete, becomes embittered, and ends leading apes in hell.

The Roman matron as model

The values of the Roman matron are held up for admiration in many of the plays and are closely related to the willingness of such to commit suicide to maintain their reputations. Portia in *Julius Caesar*, having stabbed herself in the side to prove her constancy, is reported taking her own life by eating hot coals. The heroine in the *Rape of Lucrece*, and again in *Bonduca*, together with her daughters, as well as Lucina in *Valentinian*, all die rather than face the shame of the violence done to them.

The playwrights, however, were also inclined to recommend to their female spectators, in line with the new emphasis on marriage and the home, the more domestic Roman virtues of a good wife. So Virgilia in *Coriolanus* will not step abroad in her husband's absence; whilst Antony is away Octavia will spend her time praying on her knees for him; and in a series of plays by Heywood, *How a Man May Choose a Good Wife from a Bad*, *1 Edward IV*, and *The Rape of Lucrece*, heroines are seen supervising households and voluntarily abasing themselves by following a narrow, restricting, huswifely code.

Shakespeare in his Argument for the poem 'The Rape of Lucrece' says that Collatine 'extolled the incomparable chastity of his wife Lucrece'. Heywood, however, using the poem as his source for this part of the play, interpreted this in a more mundane sense and has Collatine suggest:

> She of them all that we find best employed,
> Devoted, and most huswifely exercised,
> Let her be held most virtuous. (III.iii)

He adds new material in which Lucrece is seen supervising her household, spinning, rebuking her servants for unchaste speech and action, and insisting that a wife should not leave her house or accept invitations in the absence of her husband.

Prodigal-husband plays

How a Man May Choose a Good Wife from a Bad is the first in a series of plays inculcating wifely virtues concerning husbands who spurn their loving wives in favour of loose living; even plotting to kill them in order to marry prostitutes. Each is saved from justice and brought to repentance and reconciliation by the constant goodness of his wife, who puts up with any injury, even to offering her own life as a sacrifice for his.

Mistress Arthur, newly wed, is beautiful and chaste, but her husband cannot love her nor provide a reason for it except:

> My ranging pleasures love variety. (i.i)

She pleads with him to love her. She will be his slave:

> Love where you list, only but say you love me:
> I'll feed on shadows, let the substance go. (i.ii)

He responds by saying that if she wants to please him, she should die. Her father urges her to return home, but she says her husband has every right to abuse her, and she will stay and save money so that he can riot it abroad. She resists other suitors. She welcomes his whore Mistress Mary to a feast at which Arthur tries to poison her. Mistakenly he gives her a sleeping draught instead, and, unknown to him, her admirers spirit her away to safety. When she learns that he has married his whore, she says that when she dies her soul will look after him and keep him from harm. Arthur, however, makes the mistake of telling his whore he has killed his wife for her, and she reports him to the authorities. Only the miraculous return of his wife, ready to forgive, saves him.

The Fair Maid of Bristow is a crudely constructed play, much influenced by the above. Annabelle remains faithful even when her husband's whore flaunts before her.

VALLENGER: Now with a diuill what whirle wind blew you hether?
How now, minks, what makes you here.
ANNABELLE: I hard my Vallenger was all alone.
If I offend thee loue, ile straight begone,
yet I had rather stay and if you please.

FLORENCE: Vallenger, what makes your minion heere?
  What, are you iealhous huswife with a pox?
ANNABELLE: I pray you gentlewoman be not offended
  Please you my husband and all shall be mended.
VALLENGER: Gossip get home, or I shall set you packing.
FLORENCE (*ASIDE*): I haue a trick and if it fall out right,
  Shall moue her patience ere she part from hence.
ANNABELLE: Thou art to me, as bodie to the soule,
  My life is death without thy companie . . .   (lines 475–88)

Florence then demands Annabelle's rebato (collar) and gown, and Annabelle without demur promptly allows herself to be stripped of these, and continues in humiliating undress in the scenes that follow. Again, her husband plans to kill her, but is meanwhile indicted for the supposed murder of his whore's bridegroom. Annabelle, desperate to save him, dresses in breeches and offers herself for execution in his place. This is accepted, on condition that the husband will carry out the execution himself, and he repents only when handed the axe.

The London Prodigal is an even more perfunctory copy. Flowerdale, the rake–husband rejects Luce immediately after the marriage ceremony when her father is warned off him as a wastrel and withdraws his cash. Luce refuses the advice of her friends, including Sir Arthur, the man she loves, to give up Flowerdale, and her father is so vexed he disowns her. She manages to obtain some money for her husband, but he will not share it with her, threatens to slit her nose if she follows him, and suggests she should become a prostitute. This, he says, will allow of their occasional meeting. When finally the husband's crimes descend upon him, she speaks up for him, and leads him to repentance and reconciliation.

Shakespeare does not contribute directly to this altogether silly genre, but a number of his patient and abused wives, both before and after marriage, are depicted with a similar degree of idealised, selfless, and unreciprocated faithfulness, including Hermione in *The Winter's Tale*, Hero in *Much Ado*, Queen Katherine in *Henry VIII*, and Desdemona in *Othello*.

Value placed on marriage

The London Prodigal emphasises that Luce's faithfulness is not due to any intrinsic love of Flowerdale, since she has been compelled to marry him rather than her own choice, but because of her marriage vows, as she explains to her father:

> He is my husband, and hie heauen doth know,
> With what vnwillingnesse I went to Church,
> But you inforced me, you compelled me too it:
> The holy Church-man pronounced these words but now:
> I must not leaue my husband in distress
> Now I must comfort him, not goe with you. (III.iii.126–31)

In the sub-plot of Heywood's *A Woman Killed with Kindness* the ruined Charles Mountford gains his release from prison at the hands of his enemy Francis Acton, who sees this as a means of gratifying his passion for Mountford's sister, Susan. Determined to redeem what he sees as a debt of honour, and then for them both to die, Charles tricks up his sister in fine clothes, and attempts to persuade her to tender herself as a piece of flesh to Francis. Her response is typically extreme. She suggests instead that Charles should cut off her hands, rip open her breast, and send her bleeding heart to her intended despoiler. Francis, however, is so impressed by their heroism that he offers instead to marry her – at which all are delighted and the matter agreed in the mere ten final lines that conclude the scene. Susan says: 'I will yield to fate / And learn to love where I till now did hate' (xiv. 147–8). Marriage is perceived as so powerful it can redeem all else.

For the truly good wife, marriage in the plays is a moral absolute such that she can accept anything her husband does, however evil or unpleasant, even, like Eudoxia the Empress in *Valentinian*, murder in revenge when her husband's own initial crime was greater than the wrong done to him. In *Promos and Cassandra*, although Promos has apparently killed Cassandra's brother, once the King has forced him to marry her, the act of marriage forces her to plead for his life. In *James IV* Dorothea is loyal to her marriage vows and to her husband even after he has attempted to have her assassinated. When the honest Scottish lords tell her of James' infatuation with Ida (II.ii.84f.), she says that he is only testing her love, which will continue to redeem him. Even when evidence is supplied of his part in the plot on her life and she calls him the 'cruel king', she still says she loves him (III.iii.73).

Nor was this particular plot line merely a theatrical exaggeration, but was echoed in other sorts of publication. Heywood writes in one of his prose works, the *Curtain Lecture* (the curtains being those of the bedroom): 'But for a wife to bear with the weakness and imperfections of a husband, is the true Character of a wise and vertuous woman.' Such is the value placed upon marital chastity in the plays that wives are prepared to sacrifice not only their own lives, but the lives of others to avoid being dishonoured: in *George A Greene* Jane Barley her little son, and Katherine Sforza in *The Devil's Charter* her two sons; whilst in *The Death of Robert, Earl of Huntingdon* Matilda sees whole armies killed rather than yield her virtue to King John.

Wifely goodness can also be seen as a tangible thing, irrepressible, converting the most dissolute, as in Heywood's *Royal King and Loyal Subject*, and Dekker's *Match Me in London* and *If It Be Not Good, the Devil Is In It*. A regular plot in romantic comedies such as *John of Bordeaux*, *A Knack to Know an Honest Man*, and *The Weakest Goeth to the Wall* concerns wives abandoned under some compulsion, then subjected to threats and temptations but who, protected by an inner virtue, always remain true to their lost husbands, leading to a final reunion. Analogous to this is the impervious purity that protects the virgin Marina in the brothel in *Pericles* and Bess Bridges in her many predicaments in *Fair Maid of the West*.

This extreme investment in marital chastity seems to have invented a new mode of death where a woman is so consumed with shame that she dies of it, as does Lucina after her rape by the Emperor in *Valentinian*, prompted to it by her own husband:

> go, thou lily,
> Thou sweetly-drooping flower; go, silver swan,
> And sing thine own sad requiem; go, Lucina,
> And, if thou dar'st, out-live this wrong! (III.i)

'Patient Grissil'

In Dekker's version of this classic account of the obedient wife the first sixteen or so years of her marriage are one long cruel trial, which she passes with flying colours and apparently no permanent psychological damage, which distinguishes her from the normal run of venial and universally shrewish wives:

FURIO: I think, my lord, she's a true woman, for she loves her children, a rare wife, for she loves you, (I believe you'll hardly find her match), and I think she's more than a woman because she conquers all wrongs with patience.

(Bowers, p. 261)

So passive is Grissil in the face of Gwalter's cruelty and persecutions in acquiescing in her children being taken away, apparently to slaughter, that it becomes questionable whether her behaviour can really be called virtuous. It approaches the symbiosis of the kind of battered wife, as explored in *The Yorkshire Tragedy*, who makes her husband worse. Boccaccio's original story of Griselda begins by indicating that Gualtierri's treatment is cruel and inhumane, and not offered as a model for emulation:[16]

I intend to speak of a marquis; not with regard to anything noble and great, but rather monstrously vile and brutish, although it ended well at last; which, notwithstanding the event, I would yet advise nobody to imitate. (*The Decameron*, Novel x, Tenth Day)

Although Dekker provides two sub-plots, one showing a shrew and the other intended to offer a middle position that makes Grissil in some sense at the other extreme of the spectrum, nonetheless the Elizabethan version of the Patient Griselda myth as an exemplum of wifely excellence remains intact, and when at the end, Dekker's hero, Gwalter, offers to teach others how to treat a wife, no doubt is cast on the legitimacy of his behaviour or his claim to an appropriate expertise.

Patient Grissil, however, seems so to offend against common sense and real human relations that one is left wondering quite how sincere it really is, especially in the extent to which it appears to endorse royal power. When Furio comes finally to take the children away, Grissil says:

Farewell, farewell dear souls, adieu, adieu,
Your father sends and I must part from you,
Ay, must, Oh God, I must, must is for Kings,
And low obedience for low underlings. (Bowers, p. 266)

Gwalter's position is further legitimised at the denouement when Laureo, Grissil's student-brother, who has been a constant critic of Gwalter's treatment of her, finally capitulates:

Pardon me, my gracious lord, for now I see
That scholars with weak eyes, pore on their books,
But want true souls to judge on Majesty:
None else but Kings can know the hearts of Kings,
Henceforth my pride shall fly with humbler wings. (Bowers, p. 287)

In this it follows all the many plays in which kings misuse their subjects, particularly young female ones, and go unpunished. One is left wondering whether the combination of the enactment of injustice with this sort of sentiment, so supportive of the *status quo*, is not, at least covertly, if only casually, oppositional. David Kastan argues that the very representation of kings onstage weakened their authority by making them 'the subject of the author's imagining and the subject of the attention and judgement of an audience of subjects', thus subverting the absolutist's distinction between subject and sovereign.[17] Although the fictive king here is specifically not condemned by the fictive subject, the potential for, and arguably the process of, judgement is inherent in being placed to view on this particular scaffold. 'The mode of representation in the Elizabethan popular theater', says Kastan, 'refuses to privilege what is represented.' Any such political stirrings do not, however, much affect the representation of women, as Dekker's other plays confirm.

HEYWOOD'S INNOCENT ADULTERESSES

Several plays in the adult repertory have lustful adulteresses who finally repent, such as the Queen in *Lust's Dominion*, and Leuidulcia in *The Atheist's Tragedy*. Their repentance, however, is arguably out of character and can be seen as a betrayal of the resilient worldliness of the main part of the play, and as with other spirited women shown receiving the wages of sin, such as Venus in *The Cobbler's Prophecy*, burned to death, and Julia poisoned for her curiosity in *The Duchess of Malfi*, there is always a danger of their punishment or repentance being dismissed as part of the conventional conclusion, leaving the female spectator free to savour the loose woman's earlier *joie de vivre*, and thus justifying Northbrooke and other Puritan enemies of theatre when they ironically invite their readers to go to the theatre to 'Learn how' to commit the many and varied sexual crimes represented there.

Heywood's solution to this dilemma is to create adulteresses who are also sensitive moral creatures who obtain no satisfaction from their crime and suffer instead constantly for their lapse. In *1 Edward IV*, Matthew Shore is Mayor of London. King Edward visits him, becomes enamoured of his beautiful wife Jane, and returns in disguise to take her against her will as his mistress. During her elevation she continues to regret what she has been forced to do and tries to alleviate her guilt by using her new power and wealth in acts of virtue relieving others' suffering. In the second part, the King dies, and his successor, Richard III, persecutes Jane. No-one must harbour her, she is made to wear a garment of penance and walk through the streets, finally dying over the coffin of one who disobeyed the new King's commands.

Heywood had a number of accounts to work from in depicting Jane Shore: a lost play by Chettle and Day, Sir Thomas More's history of Richard III repeated in Holinshed, *The Mirror for Magistrates*, works by Drayton and Legge, and the anonymous *True Tragedy*.[18] All these show some sympathy for Jane, and stress her repentance after her fall. Only Shakespeare's treatment is hostile and dismissive. Heywood, however, is unique in having her unwilling and feeling guilty from the very beginning, and he goes much further than any of his sources in making her sympathetic. He adds a scene where she oversees her servants and tends to her sewing in the manner of the Roman matron, and the happy marriage of the Shores is entirely his invention; Thomas More says in flat contradiction:

But forasmuch as they were coupled ere she were well ripe, she not very fervently loved for whom she never longed. Which was happily the thing that the more easily made her incline unto the King's appetite.

Unlike the *True Tragedy* and Shakespeare's play, Heywood is at pains to suppress the truth about her later life. Instead of dying repentant and forgiven by her husband as Heywood paints her, the historical Jane Shore outlived her persecutor by forty-two years and went on to become mistress of Hastings, Dorset, and probably others, not dying until 1527.

Later in his career, Heywood returned to the same theme in *A Woman Killed with Kindness*. When the play opens, Anne and Frankford are at their wedding celebrations, surrounded by friends and kinsfolk. It is stressed that they are compatible in every way – intellectually, socially, and of a similar age:

SIR CHARLES: You both adorn each other, and your hands
　　　　　　　Methinks are matches. There's equality
　　　　　　　In this fair combination; you are both scholars,
　　　　　　　Both young, both being descended nobly.
　　　　　　　There's music in this sympathy, it carries
　　　　　　　Consort and expectation of much joy ...　　　　(1.65–70)

Such equality is not, of course, mirrored in their actual relationship. Sir Francis corrects himself:

　　　　　　By your leave, sister – by your husband's leave
　　　　　　I should have said ...　　　　　　　　　　　　(1.6–7)

And once she has fallen, she must wait on her husband's judgement, his absolute control.

Frankford then proceeds to introduce a third person into this happy *ménage*, Wendoll, a gentleman of small means, of whom Frankford says, 'his carriage / Hath pleas'd me much', to be his companion, and allows him horse, servant, and keeping in the house.

Wendoll fights his attraction to Anne, but, told repeatedly to treat the house as his own and be master in Frankford's absence, too many opportunities are strewn in his way, and she, after a little initial resistance, is won by his wooing. Although it is the central action of the play, no reason is given for her behaviour. Heywood offers only alterity, a vacuum where motive should be:

ANNE: What shall I say?
    My soul is wand'ring and hath lost her way.   (VI.150–1)

When Frankford is told of the liaison by his faithful servant he pretends to be summoned away on urgent business only to return that night to catch them in bed together. Heywood, unwilling to let his heroine enjoy even a moment of her adultery, has her admit, as they meet before Frankford's return, that she 'yields' to sin 'through fear', and instead of *in flagrante* he finds them: 'Close in each other's arms, and fast asleep' (XIII.43). Anne's response when confronted is to condemn herself utterly. He should kill her, she says (later her brother's view too). That Frankford does not is, of course, meant to be the play's measure of his subsequent meritorious Christian behaviour. As so often in these plays, threats to marital fidelity spark off images of sado-masochism:

                            O to redeem my honour
        I would have this hand cut off, these my breasts sear'd,
        Be rack'd, strappado'd, put to any torment ...   (XIII.134–6)

And immediately after this, she breaks into direct address, a rare intensity in these plays:

        O women, women, you that have yet kept
        Your holy matrimonial vow unstain'd,
        Make me your instance ...   (XIII.141–3)

After due delay and thought, Frankford decides on her punishment. She is to be parted from her children for ever and go to one of his other manors some distance hence and live entirely without contacting him again. Anne resolves to starve herself to death. Just before the end she has chosen she summons her husband and her family to witness her final penitence. All are moved, and Frankford forgives her and remarries her as she dies.

The double standard

After their discovery, Wendoll re-appears, grief-stricken, saying he must wander like Cain to foreign lands, and it sounds for a moment as though their punishment is to be commensurate, but then he says that when he has a smattering of other tongues he will return and find a patron at court.

The plays assume a double standard which tolerates male lust being satisfied in adulterous liaisons or in ruining girls not perceived as future wives, but withdraws sympathy from the partner in such liaisons or any girl who allows herself to be thus ruined; it being every man's natural desire to sleep with women, but every woman's duty to resist. At the end of *James IV*, as the English are advancing to revenge Dorothea's supposed death, the King, having spent most of the play wooing Ida, sensibly reconsiders his position and punishes his advisers. Dorothea re-appears, they are reconciled with the English, and James gets off scot-free, even though he had plotted her death, which Dorothea puts down to his being 'misled by youth'.

The double standard operates as a basic assumption of the 'prodigal husband' plays. *The London Prodigal* provides the most explicit contrast. Flowerdale, the rake–hero, gambles away all his money, has his whore, Mistress Apricock, who spurns him when he is down, attempts highway robbery, begging, even prostitution, but when his final reckoning comes, is redeemed by his loyal wife and disguised father, and supported in his financial embarrassment by his various friends and relations. In the depths of his fall to crime, Luce, his wife, still believes he can be redeemed:

> Imagine yet, that he is worse than naught:
> Yet one houer's time may all that ill vndo . . .
> If ere his heart doth turne, 'tis nere too late.   (IV.iii.88–9)

And her faith, of course, is justified; it takes considerably less than an hour to restore him to his place in society. The comparison is stark with the treatment of these adulteresses – hounded to their deaths for their single crime, even when committed under duress.

The double standard was recognised and often regretted by contemporaries, but there was general agreement that it was necessary to ensure the continuance of the purity of the strain and the transference of property through primogeniture. As the Marquis of Halifax explained to his daughter in 1688:

The root and excuse for this injustice is the preservation of families from any mixture which may bring a blemish to them; and whilst the point of honour continues to be so placed, it seems unavoidable to give your sex the greater share of the penalty.

Among the aristocracy, once a woman had provided an heir there was sometimes relative indifference as to how she behaved thereafter. Further down the social scale in a society without contraception a woman's part in adultery was always more serious. Bastardy was severely punished in an age when illegitimate babies fell to the immediate parish to feed.

The Wise Woman of Hogsden is perhaps the most extreme example of Heywood's tolerance of the inequalities between the sexes. Young Chartley, 'a wild-headed Gentleman', is betrothed to two girls at the same time whilst meanwhile proposing marriage to a third in order to secure her fortune. As he does so, he plans to enjoy the maidenhead of a fourth girl, the goldsmith's daughter, as an aperitif to consummating his marriage. The girl with the prior engagement eventually secures the young scapegrace when the revelation of his multiple deceptions prompts his final repentance. Fortunately there are other young men hovering by, of better faith, to marry the two runners-up. The play avoids any unpleasant outcomes for the girls but it is permissive in the extreme towards the callow, heartless young hero and treats his potentially tragic behaviour very light-heartedly, presumably secure in the resourcefulness of the Wise Woman to put things right. Boys will be boys and a young woman's lot is to suffer them whilst meanwhile trying to stay pure.

Re-evaluation of Heywood's purpose

Heywood was an influential figure. In his preface to *The English Traveller* he claims to have had 'a hand or main finger' in 220 plays. There is a surprising tendency to take him at his own estimation, and even female critics praise him for his supposedly positive representations of women. Marilyn Johnson distinguishes Heywood from Dekker as being more tolerant and optimistic. He respected women, she says, but saw them as a separate species with separate virtues whose proper place was in the home. She cites with approval the reasons he gives for his extensive prose writings on women, to provide good examples that women might 'apprehend', as he says in *Gunaikeion*, 'some one thing or other worthy imitation'. In his

Curtain Lecture he offers the character of a good wife 'according to Theophrastus' – she

must be grave abroad, gentle at home, constant in love, patient to suffer, obsequious to her neighbours, obedient to her husband. For silence and patience are the two indissoluble ties of conjugal love and piety.

It is strange that Johnson should see Heywood as benevolent rather than repressive. His real purpose in suppressing the true nature of Jane Shore's sexual career is to make normal flesh-and-blood women uncomfortable. His theme is not forgiveness but control.

The extreme nature of Heywood's treatment of adulteresses can perhaps be best seen by comparing them with Peele's treatment of the heroine in *David and Bethsabe*, 1587, who paradoxically gains a certain protected status from being venerated in the Bible, which this play closely follows. Bethsabe commits adultery, bearing a child to King David, who sends her soldier husband to the front to be killed. Vengeance quickly follows in the form of the death of the child of this adulterous union. They are filled with remorse, particularly David, who is frequently filled with remorse, but, as the sub-plot shows, very resilient with it. The story does not end there, however. After there has been sufficient remorse, Bethsabe becomes David's queen, and later in the play, now with a grown-up son, Solomon, they are presented as a venerable couple. There is something more honest about the treatment of sin in this play than is generally found in the escapist extremes of Elizabethan and especially Stuart drama.

SHAKESPEARE AND RECEIVED CHARACTER CONVENTIONS

This then is the context within which Shakespeare created his women: one of subordinated female stereotypes whose behaviour is often irrational, polarised by the joint pressures of male didacticism and dramaturgical necessity. Many of the characters Shakespeare created, to be discussed in subsequent chapters, rise above simple stereotyping and the misogynist prejudice that often goes with it, but it is not difficult to see direct evidence of the influence of the received tradition in his work. Troilus' exclamation 'This is, and is not, Cressid!' (v.ii.146) asserts female alterity, as does Cymbeline's response to news of his Queen's treachery: 'Who is't can read a woman?' (v.v.48), whilst Lady Anne and Queen Elizabeth in *Richard III* show how susceptible women are to male pressure and flattery. The early plays are full of shrews like Adriana and Kate, viragoes like La Pucelle and Eleanor of Gloucester, and there are pure Roman matrons like

Portia, Octavia, and Virgilia, and a whole range of impossibly good and long-suffering wives, as well as daughters who convert others to goodness. A brief review of the treatment of women in one of Shakespeare's finest plays gives some indication of how much the broad generality of his female characters owes to traditional stereotyping.

Female stereotypes in 'Othello'

Critics who study Shakespeare in isolation from his theatre regularly treat Desdemona as though she is a real person with a coherent, three-dimensional personality, many still echoing the views of Mrs Jameson in 1833, who says, 'I know a Desdemona in real life' and praises 'the perfect simplicity and unity of delineation', and her 'modest tenderness, and grace'. Wilson Knight sees her as 'essential woman, gentle, loving, brave'. W. H. Auden rationalises her reference to Lodovico as a 'proper man' with her incredulity about adultery:

It is as if she had suddenly realised that she had made a *mésalliance* and that the sort of man she ought to have married was someone of her own class and colour like Lodovico.

M. R. Ridley, although devoting only half a page to Desdemona, still finds time to marvel at her *offstage* behaviour, so much is she for him a real person:

Yet, by Heaven knows what wrench of resolution, she pulls herself together for a formal banquet, at which she must entertain men who have seen her publicly struck, and, judging by the subsequent farewells, she acquits herself with at least decorum.[19]

Yet any objective inspection of the play will reveal that Desdemona is quite a different person in Cyprus from the one she had been in Venice. The role is a construct made in two parts, both adapted from prevailing stereotypes. Mrs Jameson puts her earlier resolution down to 'transient energy, arising from the power of affection', but concludes, 'gentleness gives the prevailing tone of the character'. Indeed it does – but only in the later acts – where this firmly subordinated character is required to be the pure, sacrificial victim. In the earlier episodes she is an independent young woman taking the initiative to secure her own happiness, as she sees it, and her own will, in the stereotype of the Love Match: eloping with her lover, outfacing her father in open Senate, and then contradicting the Duke by insisting on going with her new husband to the battle zone of Cyprus. Only the object of her affection, an elderly black general, jars somewhat with this tradition.

N.B. Allen in 'The Two Parts of *Othello*' offers a credible hypothesis that Acts III–V were written first, closely following Cinthio, in which Othello and Desdemona were a long-established couple living in Cyprus, whilst the present Acts I and II were composed at a later date, and changed their status to newly-weds.[20] Such a theory helps to explain many problems in an apparent time-sequence in which there is scarcely a moment for Desdemona to sin, let alone for Cassio to have been absent from Bianca for a week, or indeed, as some critics doubt, for the Othellos to consummate their marriage. Allen's evidence of the double timescale makes a great deal of sense. However, time, like place, is a negotiable entity on the Elizabethan stage, as Sidney noted with some asperity, and Webster satirises:

ANTONIO: ... since you last saw her,
  She hath had two children more ...
DELIO: ... verily I should dream
  It were within this half hour.   (*Duchess of Malfi*, III.i.7–9)

In performance, however, the spectator accepts whatever timescale is offered. Notwithstanding how it comes about, part of the *donnée* of this play is that we are faced with two quite separate Desdemonas that no amount of rationalising will adequately conjoin:

BRABANTIO: Look to her, Moor, if thou hast eyes to see;
  She has deceiv'd her father, and may thee.   (I.iii.292–3)

Brabantio, like Troilus, is faced with two incompatible versions of a woman he loves; here as dutiful daughter and nubile wife; and one having developed unseen beneath the guise of the other, now revealed as a mask. Even for the erstwhile lover, and now her husband, the metamorphosis is hardly less inexplicable:

IAGO: She did deceive her father, marrying you,
  And when she seem'd to shake and fear your looks,
  She lov'd them most.
OTHELLO: And so she did.
IAGO: Why, go to then.
  She that so young could give out such a seeming
  To seel her father's eyes up, close as oak,
  He thought 'twas witchcraft –
                                              (III.iii.206–11)

The play depends on accepting as tenable the male view that women are strange and unknowable; that a man can be so uncertain of his new wife's loyalty that he can kill her when she is innocent. For the play to work we do not want to know too much about Desdemona. To have her inner workings rationalised by an actress identifying with the role, assimilating the spunkiness of the Venice scenes with her strange opaque quiescence in Cyprus into a single recognisable personality, is all from the point. A male performer can be expected to leave the inconsistencies in Shakespeare's/Othello's perception of woman unresolved. Only by this means will the play achieve its original effect.

Her function in the final scene is anticipated in the willow-song sequence in which she is prepared for bed – and death; one of a series of mannered framing sequences in the plays. Far from demonstrating any admirable purity, the final exchange of Desdemona and Emilia, in which the former protests that she cannot believe any woman would betray her husband, withdraws her from our active sympathy into Heywood's demeaning stereotype of the impossibly virtuous wife.

It is difficult to see how Stephen Orgel could possibly apply his view that 'the women of the Renaissance stage must be as much emanations of . . . self as the men are' to Desdemona. The imaginative force of Othello's anger commixed with anguish keeps him the centre of the play's attention, building a head of steam based upon a view of the humiliation of cuckoldry such that it completely destroys a man, his occupation gone, and makes Desdemona no more than the two-dimensional sacrificial victim, who, because she is so beautiful, so young, so pure – the pearl, richer than his tribe, he throws away – is of more pain – *to him*:

> you must speak
> Of one that lov'd not wisely but too well;
> Of one not easily jealous, but being wrought,
> Perplexed in the extreme . . .   (v.ii.343–6)

Unlike some of Shakespeare's other heroines, Desdemona never emerges even briefly as a recognisable human being, but remains a cipher.[21] It is perhaps significant that a contemporary testimony to the emotional effect of a (male) Desdemona concentrates on the pathos after she has been killed, when, 'she implored the pity of the spectators by her face', on her, in short, as an object.

Emilia, the shrew

If critics have difficulty accepting the artifice of Desdemona's construction, they should consider the creaking nature of Emilia's. The veniality of her misappropriation of the handkerchief, and her naivety towards Iago, 'I nothing but to please his fantasy', are both impossible to reconcile with the fiercely loyal and outspoken woman at the end. If Emilia's character had been consistent throughout with the woman who emerges in the final scene, the tragedy, hingeing so much on the circumstantial evidence of the handkerchief, would never have happened. How can a woman as street-wise as Emilia not have rumbled Iago? The truth is that, like the timescale, the subordinate characters serve the purposes of the main focus and are manipulated into a series of dramatic effects at appropriate moments in the play with little concern for consistency.[22]

Emilia is often claimed to be the 'normative' voice of the play because her views on equal sexual freedom for women in IV.iii chime in with those of the critics.[23] Carol Thomas Neely even calls her 'dramatically and symbolically the play's fulcrum'.[24] This fails to recognise, however, the significance of the stereotype of the shrew. When Emilia justifies female adultery on the grounds that women have sexual feelings too, that men set them on, and that it is no more than tit-for-tat, she represents not truth but the Devil, and is associated with what A. J. Ingram calls 'animal malevolence against God and men'. The Shrew challenged the natural order by inverting the gender hierarchy. The declension of Leontes' epithets for Paulina, the truth-telling shrew in *The Winter's Tale*, go from 'audacious lady' to 'intelligencing bawd', to 'mankind witch', and finally 'gross hag'. 'As a rebel', says Erika Gottlieb of Emilia, 'she is a proven traitor.' Her rhetoric is plausible, but her premise faulty. To the Elizabethans, men and women are not equal, especially in matters of sexual behaviour. 'Your sin', the Duke tells Juliet in *Measure for Measure*, was 'of a heavier kind than his.' One of the signs of a virtuous woman in this tradition is that she is able to withstand the corrupting and glib casuistry of just such low-caste attendants. Desdemona is not persuaded but instead confutes Emilia's arguments:

> (God) me such uses send,
> Not to pick bad from bad, but by bad mend.   (IV.iii.104–5)

Once again, Shakespeare draws back from empathy into pathos by setting the stereotype of the Shrew against that of the Good Woman.

Emilia's final function in the play is as teller of the truth, of Desdemona's virtue and Iago's infamy, but because by now, inspired by shrewish rage, she belongs to that special category of truth-tellers like the madman and the fool, so too it is a truth that can initially be disbelieved by Othello, thus lengthening out the climax of his *anagnorisis*.[25]

Shakespeare and the She-wolf

The She-wolf is a character convention that emerges in the late 1580s in the
wake of the fashion for Senecan plays and represents the male fear of
women at its most extreme. She is beautiful and womanly in appearance
but lacks the gentler qualities usually associated with her sex and instead
tends to acts of gratuitous and excessive evil:

> Thou art like the harpy
> Which to betray, dost with thine angel's face
> Seize with thine eagle's talents.   (*Pericles*, IV.iii.46–8)

Elinor of Castille in *Edward I* has the Mayoress bound to a chair, bitten by
an adder, and left to die. Regan takes part in blinding Gloucester. Margaret
of Anjou, the 'she-wolf of France', taunts the captured York, offering him a
napkin soaked in the blood of his murdered son, and mocks his pretensions
to the throne by making him wear a paper crown and stand upon a
molehill, from where he anatomises her:

> O tiger's heart wrapp'd in a woman's hide!
> How couldst thou drain the life-blood of the child,
> To bid the father wipe his eyes withal,
> And yet be seen to wear a woman's face?
> Women are soft, mild, pitiful, and flexible;
> Thou stern, obdurate, flinty, rough, remorseless . . .
> (*3 Henry VI*, I.iv.137–42)

She-wolves urge men to hurt other women, as Tamora encouraging her
sons to rape Lavinia in *Titus Andronicus*, Dionysia in *Pericles* setting on a
murderer to kill the innocent Marina, and Queen Eleanor in *Look About
You* who compasses the death of Rosamund, her husband's concubine, and
is described as:

> The tigress that hath drunk the purple blood
> Of three times twenty thousand valiant men.

They lack normal affections. Tullia in *The Rape of Lucrece* helps kill
her own father and then rides a chariot over his corpse. The wicked
daughters in *King Lear* cast out their father and drive him mad. The
She-wolf kills children, as Gwendolin intends in *Locrine*. Tamora even
wants Aaron to kill their own child, whilst Catherine de' Medici in *The
Massacre at Paris* poisons her son Charles with hypocritical relish.
Sometimes they falsely accuse men of rape in an (always doomed) attempt

at sexual conquest, as do Queen Aegiale in *The Blind Beggar of Alexandria*, Queen Elinor in *The Downfall of Robert Earl of Huntington*, Queen Aurea in *The Silver Age*, and Artesia, 'that Woman-fury', in *The Birth of Merlin*. Shakespeare adds to his portrait of Margaret taken from Hall by making her an adulteress, whilst Tamora, Regan, and her sister all conform to type as aggressive adulteresses. Universally women of power and given to employing others in their wickedness, she-wolves engage, like the viragoes before them, in acts of physical aggression, as when Regan kills the loyal servant, or Margaret beats the Duchess of Gloucester in *2 Henry VI*.

Leslie Fielder, in one of the first studies of this character convention, perceives the She-wolf as Shakespeare's own creation:

Shakespeare . . . from the start . . . calls upon his magic not to evoke what is most womanly in himself, but exorcise what is dark and female in favour of what is benign and male. One of his strategies is to invert his own desire to play the 'woman's part' and project it onto some unnatural mother, some queen who would be king . . . and then bring her to despair and suicide . . .[26]

The attractions of this sort of argument are obvious: post-Freudian psycho-analysis presented as privileging us with an insight into the creative mind, with the further bonus in finding that his genius arises from personal inadequacy. A wider perspective on the period, however, reveals instead a cluster of she-wolves around 1590. It would be foolhardy to try to deter-mine their exact sequence. Certainly the dramatists of this period are closely attuned to watching each other to see what best 'works', and Shakespeare as a relative newcomer is quick to learn from those about him, particularly Marlowe. Greene called him, 'an absolute *Iohannes fac totum* . . . beautified with our feathers'. It may well be that Margaret in the *Henry VI* plays precedes Guendolin in *Locrine* or Elinor in Peele's *Edward I*, both c.1591, but it is equally likely that she does not, and that they have anyway a common root in classical drama via the various translations of Seneca, published in an omnibus edition in 1581. In either event then, Fiedler would have to adapt his analysis to apply to a whole clutch of playwrights.

The She-wolf's pleasure is theatrical not psychological, offering a gratuitous escapist pleasure that, because of its very excesses, needs less screening through our normal moral processes to be enjoyed. Created in parallel to the Machiavel, before both were overtaken by more interest in genuine motivation, she offered a fantasy of freedom of action, lack of conscience, and skill in deception. Cymbeline is astounded at the report of his wife's confession at her death that she never loved him and abhorred his person:

> O most delicate fiend!
> Who is't can read a woman?   (v.v.47–8)

According to Thomas Andrew in *The Unmasking of a Feminine Machiavel*, such women could outdo the male original in their capacity for dissimulation, the actor's skill. Hence they provide good plot engines, tortuously clever, but also tempestuously illogical, carried by their emotions into theatrical excess; thus providing in good measure for those basic elements of the spectator's emotional configuration: surprise, anticipation, and fear.

While the male characters almost universally find her sexuality frightening, the male spectator, on the other hand, protected by the fictive context, can find in her energy, determination, and beauty a certain dark attraction. She-wolves must have been popular with women too, offering a tangle of contradictory feelings. Some show physical bravery, like Tullia and Elinor of Castille, fighting alongside their husbands; whilst Margaret fights in his place. There is a sudden access of power that comes, especially to beautiful women, when they are indifferent to moral disapproval. Here were represented upper-class, even royal, women of supreme beauty in the most fashionable and erotic of costumes, behaving as they chose, beating men at their own games, women who are not merely men's victims, and who for a time at least get their own way:

What is disturbing about a Bitch is that she is androgynous. She incorporates within herself qualities traditionally defined as 'masculine' as well as 'feminine'. A Bitch is blunt, direct, arrogant, at times egoistic. She has no liking for the indirect, subtle, mysterious ways of the 'eternal feminine'. She disdains the vicarious life deemed natural to women because she wants to live a life of her own.[27]

And perhaps beneath that, they warmed to the performers, able to present a model of triumphant femininity and still be men, offering a dangerously enticing vision of sexual equivalence, of variety, and change.

The She-wolf arguably was easier to play than the Breeches role in which the performer had to keep the sense of feminine alive through his acting in order to combat the surface appearance of being male. Here, on the other hand, the feminine is all surface and the inner personality male. Indeed, part of the chilling quality of the She-Wolf may well have been precisely this very dislocation, even capitalising as it were on the performer's limitations. If, as was suggested in chapter 1, the creation of a tradition of relatively complex major female roles being played by young adults was one in which Shakespeare had a major hand, developing the less sophisticated and less ambitious style of playing and writing he found when he started, then perhaps his She-wolves might be seen as a stepping stone in that process.

Lady Macbeth

Shakespeare used she-wolves in three phases. Tamora in *Titus Andronicus* follows Queen Margaret as a full-blooded histrionic role. He returns to the convention in his final plays with the Queen in *Cymbeline* and more briefly Dionysia in *Pericles*, both with strong echoes of fairy stories, bewitching kings and hating stepdaughters for their beauty. In his mature period Lady Macbeth closely follows on Regan and Goneril, but whereas the latter pair are unchanging, unnatural monsters, she is at once an assimilation of the convention into a more human, at times even humdrum form, and an interesting adaptation of a stereotype to encompass a whole series of other archetypal associations.

J. L. Klein notes that, 'Lady Macbeth's preparations for and cleaning up after Duncan's murder become a frightening perversion of Renaissance woman's domestic activity'.[28] As long as there is something practical to do – tidying up the daggers, smearing the faces of the grooms with blood – she gets on and does it. Her focus is immediate and thereby less moral. Despite the grandness of her famous invocation to 'you spirits / That tend on mortal thoughts, unsex me here', her purpose is only to support her husband. She wants to be filled full of cruelty and have any compassion removed, but by being 'unsexed', *not* by being made more masculine. She never becomes mannish, and remains a feminine and graceful chatelaine, ready to receive her honoured guest, to all appearances the perfect company wife. And though she takes the initiative in the murder, once Macbeth is made king he takes unquestioning command. In incorporating elements of both genders into a more human form, the role at least in its earlier scenes seems to question the simplistic dualism of the She-Wolf convention.

What makes Lady Macbeth so potent an image in *Macbeth* is her association with ancient myth. As the Witches are at once folk hags and Norns, echoing the classical Moira, so too she has elements of the Great Mother, at the intersection not only of man/woman but also nurturer/ destroyer. In his use of 'archetypal' in discussing the She-wolf, Fiedler stresses only the negative aspect, but, of course, an archetype is essentially both good *and* bad. It is the nurturing mother who destroys – hence the image of the infant with the boneless gums, to whom Lady Macbeth has given life and would now have 'dash'd the brains out' rather than break an oath. The negative aspects of the archetype are summoned up by the play's atmosphere of womb-like darkness, the pit of Acheron to which Hecate in the addition summons the witches, and their obvious association with sibyls, as at Delphi, matriarchal powers from the bowels of the earth. Lady Macbeth urges her husband: 'and you shall put / This night's great business into my despatch', and concludes, 'Leave all the rest to me.' She is as much mother to him as wife. Nowhere in Shakespeare's work are the dynamics of marriage given so much attention – the Macbeths probably spending more time on the stage together than any other married couple.

Traditionally a woman conquers by being weak, counterpoint to the male surrender through strength. Therefore for a woman to be both feminine and assertive, as Sarah Siddons conceives of Lady Macbeth, 'all the subjugating powers of intellect and all the charms and graces of personal beauty', is threatening but also exciting and seductive.[29] Some critics see *Macbeth* as a non-sexual play,[30] but that is to ignore the extent to which Lady Macbeth's taunts to her husband are all sexual, demands for his continued manhood. Dennis Biggins is right to note the sense in which the murder of Duncan is presented as an image of the sexual act, but she is also promising actual consummation if Macbeth does it.[31] Their interaction, as in I.viii, is continually viscous, anticipating his reward – supping, sucking, milking, gums, wine and wassail, drenched natures, spongy officers, bringing forth children, and finally blood. His relationship with her at this point is one of sexual bondage, demonstrating the Elizabethan view that to be besotted with a woman is a sign not of virility but of effeminisation.

Given that the earlier part of the play sets up a dynamic in which the crime of Duncan's murder is essentially a joint one, an active product of their relationship, it comes as a disappointment that her role should then be suppressed, as if, Kenneth Tynan once suggested, several of her scenes had been torn out. Her sleep-walking entry brings us up short in a variety of ways. The main *donnée* is that Macbeth ends up isolated without friends or family. Although Falstaff and particularly Mercutio suffer a similar truncation of their dramatic potential, there are some special features associated with Lady Macbeth's abrupt dismissal. Her final scene is an assertion of female alterity. It lacks any anticipation or gradation; instead it is a framed, distanced, inset-pageant of artificial, riddling madness, a youthful male-player set-piece full of his special kind of pathos, not – as the rest of the role makes clear – as an accommodation of his limitations, but a subordination of the female role (as well as being theatrically very effective). And whilst it completes a structural pattern in which Macbeth, from a faltering start, becomes an embittered criminal as she moves apparently in the other direction, though, if so, with little visible change until her end, it also serves to confirm the female stereotype: justly punished for aspiring to be what she is not, denied the She-wolf's promise of self-sufficiency, and betrayed by her male player, who even before her death is announced has already shed her costume, passed on to other things, and is probably dressing as the Young Siward.

CHAPTER 5

Dramatic empathy and moral ambiguity

Central to the Elizabethan 'problem of women' was the ambivalence in which they were held. In return for her help, the hero must marry the Loathly Lady and she gives him a choice, whether to have her fair by day and ugly by night, or vice-versa; for beauty, compliance, companionship, all are bought at a price. '*Odi et amo*', said Catullus, 'I hate and I love', and the Elizabethans too in their treatment of women ever oscillate between idealisation and denigration, illustrated so well in Mendosa's two speeches in *The Malcontent*:

Sweet women ... In body how delicate, in soul how witty ... in favours how judicious, in day how sociable, and in night how – O pleasure unutterable! (I.v.33f.)

A few moments later, however, having been rejected by the Duchess:

Women? Nay, Furies ... Damnation of mankind! ... their words are feigned, their eyes forged, their sighs dissembled, their looks counterfeit, their hair false, their given hopes deceitful, their very breath artificial (I.vi.78f.)

The Elizabethans inherited a Christian misogyny in which ever since Eve men have been seduced and betrayed into sexual activity by women. It is the early Christian writers from St Paul who most strongly urge the subordination of this dangerous helpmate. Fornication even within marriage, according to Tertullian, is shameful. Hence the tradition of literary misogyny is in essence less about women than about male sexual guilt projected onto women; not only as the instigators but also the receptacles of their shame; at once the means of their satisfaction and of their destruction.[1]

In *Locrine* the hero, against his own wishes, falls in love with the captured Estrid:

> Oh that sweete face painted with natures dye,
> Those roseall cheeks mixt with a snowy white,

That decent necke surpassing yuorie,
Those comely brests which *Venus* well might spite,
Are like to snares which wilie fowlers wrought,
Wherein my yeelding heart is prisoner cought.   (IV.i.91–6)

He is the victim of her beauty, compelled against his will, 'a cause', he says, 'to wish a speedy death'. Though courtly love held that love of women was the root of all virtue, female beauty remained something to be distrusted. 'I am of opinion', says Heywood in *Gunaikeion*, 1624, 'that beauty hath been the ruin of more cities . . . .. than the sword'; whilst the violent hero of *The Yorkshire Tragedy* observes (IV.56): 'That heaven should say we must not sin and yet made women . . .' In *The Birth of Merlin* [I.ii.71f.] the beauty of the evil Artesia at the head of an enemy delegation so bewitches the young King Aurelius he proposes marriage within minutes, and much against the advice of his counsellors. Cymbeline excuses his misjudgement of his Queen:

Mine eyes
Were not in fault, for she was beautiful;
Mine ears, that (heard) her flattery, not my heart,
That thought her like her seeming. It had been vicious
To have mistrusted her.   (V.v.62–6)

Confused by theories of the contiguity of virtue and physical attractiveness, such as Castiglione's, 'Beauty commeth of God, and is like a circle, the goodness whereof is the Centre', the Elizabethans never tire of being surprised that experience does not bear this out. 'There's no art', says Duncan in *Macbeth*, 'To find the mind's construction in the face' (I.iv.11–12).

It is this ambivalence towards woman as sexual partner which produces that strange phenomenon in Elizabethan plays of beautiful women, played of course by young men, castigating their own beauty. In the *True Tragedy of Richard III* Shore's wife blames her moral fall to concubine on her beauty: 'Ay why was I made fair that a King should favour me?' Similarly in *Patient Grissil* the heroine blames her own beauty for the hardships inflicted on the rest of her family. In *Two Noble Kinsmen* as the kinsmen and their supporters prepare to do battle for her, Emilia says her beauty is to blame:

What sins have I committed . . . that . . .
. . . the lives of lovers . . . must be the sacrifice
To my unhappy beauty?   (IV.ii.58f.)

Theseus confirms her culpability (line 149): 'You have steel'd 'em with your beauty.' In *The Faithful Friends*, III.ii, Philadelpha asks:

> Why was I born a woman? Nature, sure,
> Gave me these lineaments in mockery,
> To tempt the world, and Envy join'd with her
> To make my life a scandal to my sex.

Celia in *Volpone*, desiring mutilation or leprosy rather than dishonour, blames the 'unhappy crime of nature, which you miscall my beauty'. It is a repeated sentiment difficult to imagine in any kind of theatre other than an all-male one.

Ambivalence towards female sexuality explains both the popularity of the stage whore in Elizabethan plays and the cruel inconsistencies in their treatments, as well as providing the beginnings of a possibly more complex presentation of the opposite sex.

THE STAGE WHORE

There was a long male tradition of playing lascivious women with gusto on the one hand, and criticising the practice with equal fervour on the other. Isidore of Seville, writing in the seventh century, described '*Histriones*' as 'those men, who, dressed in female garb, mimicked the behaviour of loose women'. He is probably harking back to the end of Roman theatre in the fifth century when, said Chrysostom, concentrating his particular disapproval on cross-dressing, plays showed 'naught but fornication and adultery':

a youth, with hair combed back, who makes himself effeminate in look, in manner, in dress – aye, in everything takes on the shape and guise of a tender girl.

The Elizabethan anti-theatrical writers thus saw themselves as part of a continuing tradition from Lactantius, St Cyprian, St Augustine, Cornelius Agrippa, Dionysus Carthusianus, and other early Christian scholars, whose charges and even examples they diligently recycled. Even the terms they use to criticise contemporary theatre, as in Stephen Gosson's *Plays Confuted in five Acts*, 1582, betray their origins in antiquity, with character-types drawn from the masks of New Comedy:

The grounde work of Commedies, is loue, cosenedge, flatterie, bawderie, slye conueighance of whoredome; The persons cookes, queanes, knaues, baudes, parasites, courtezannes, lecherous olde men, amorous yong men . . .

Gosson is at pains to acknowledge this tradition: 'Our . . . play houses in London are as full of secrete adulterie as they were in Rome.' At Oxford in the 1580s and 1590s, John Rainolds at Corpus Christi is fulminating against the plays of his colleague William Gager, 'making young men come forth in whore's attire' and 'teaching them ... her wanton kiss, her impudent face, her wicked speeches and enticements', whilst John Case at St John's College, in a Latin commentary on Aristotle's *Ethics*, is defending the practice on the grounds that, 'It is not necessarily indecorum for a man to wear the dress of a harlot on the stage, if his object is to expose the vices of harlotry.' Despite their differences, both scholars give testimony to the antiquity of this practice.

The making of the Tudor whore

The prominence of the whore in early professional theatre was a result of its secularisation of the Morality. In its earliest phase, before its adaptation by the professional troupes, the Morality had dramatised the *psychomachia*, the struggle between the Virtues and Vices for the soul of Mankind. *The Castle of Perseverance*, its most elaborate manifestation, had a female Lechery but also an overplus of virtuous female characters including the Seven Virtues and the four Daughters of God, in a civic, essentially amateur, processional-pageant tradition. In the adaptation of the genre for early sixteenth-century professional companies, initially female characters disappeared completely, both good and bad, and for a time all the characters were male, as is evident in the earliest entries in the Appendix. In place of the physical battle, this second phase substituted an enduring plot motif in which the hero was misled by trickery and then redeemed to salvation or admonished before his fall. This formula no longer required the earlier armies of Sins and Virtues. Instead, the leading player became '*the* Vice', repository of all sins, and, most importantly, play-maker. His stratagems to betray *Humanum Genus* drove the plot. One of the helpers he soon began to call on to exploit the hero's fleshly weakness was Lechery, at first sometimes presented as a male character, as in *The Longer Thou Livest* and *Mary Magdalene*, but eventually, in an increasingly literal context, as a recognisable social type, the Whore.

The virtuous female, however, did not re-emerge for another sixty years and in the interim the demands of the spirit in the Tudor interlude took the form of male abstractions such as Good Counsel, Mercy, or Shrift. Only slowly in the third phase, of the Educational Morality in which Wit the hero found Wisdom the heroine and as often amateur in auspices as professional, did the chaste female re-emerge as the hero's goal and his salvation. The Whore, therefore, obtained a considerable head start.

Actor as whore

William Prynne, of course, equates all acting with whoredom. In the theatre, he says, 'the obscenity of common whores is surpassed, and men have found out how they may commit adultery before the eyes of others'. Leaving aside for the moment his characteristic conflation of reality with stage fiction, there are indeed some strong parallels between whores and actors. Neither are what they appear. The beautifully dressed whore, like the actor, is a paradox: delicate, elegant, finely dressed, winsome and yielding – and yet calculating, mercenary, deceitful, and – in control. She may protest affection, but it is only a pretence. Much of her activity is to do with wheedling money in exchange for false expectations. Thus the young male playing the role of the stage whore is exploiting the potential of theatre for multiple dissimulation, caught perhaps at its fullest in the endless dressing-up and character-playing of Doll Common in *The Alchemist*, the play itself an image of chicanery and prick-tease, each of her clients wanting to satisfy his fantasies of power and virility, but getting in return, as in the theatre, only an illusion.

An actor, like a whore, draws the eye. Dressed in other people's clothes he offers himself to be viewed on an open stage, available to satisfy the spectator's fantasies. Actors 'serve', says Michael Goldman, 'at their audience's pleasure'. Harriet Walter suggests that 'All actors are in a way female in the relationship; they have to wait to be asked, invited, they keep all they've got inside until it's required'.[2] That, however, is only half the process. The actor is also a source of power, even at his most obsequious, able to dominate and hold the spectators in his grip, a taker of the initiative, daring, frightening, unpredictable. Hence all performers cross and re-cross the conventional male/female gender barrier, alternately powerful and vulnerable, passive receptors and active promoters, attracting and repelling the spectator.

Whore as actor

From their earliest appearance in the professional plays, whores pretend virtue. Lechery in *Interlude of Youth* is angry that Riot let slip her name when she has impressed Youth as being a 'fair lady ... courteous and gentle'. Abominable Living in *Lusty Juventus* feigns modesty and has to be persuaded to stay, though she soon admits her licentiousness. Wantonness in *Wit and Wisdom* is with child by Idleness, who, charged with corrupting the hero Wit, tells her to hide her belly and call herself Modest Mirth. Later plays continue the practice. Doll, the concubine of the travelling Parson in *1 Sir John Oldcastle* passes herself off as his niece, whilst in *A Chaste Maid in Cheapside* Sir Walter Whorehound brings his cast-whore to town to marry her off disguised as a Welsh Gentlewoman. Many of the bawds pretend to be courtly, like Dildoman in *Match Me in London* or the panderess in *Valentinian*. Others use the cover of some other occupation. Mistress Drury in *A Warning for Fair Women* professes surgery and astrology, whilst Cataplasma in *The Atheist's Tragedy* is a wig-maker.

Bertram's false gloss on Diana in *All's Well* that she is a 'common gamester in the camp' indicates that virtue and modesty as well as a cover for prostitution can also be part of its titillation:

> She knew her distance, and did angle for me,
> Madding my eagerness with her restraint,
> As all impediments in fancy's course
> Are motives of more fancy, and in fine,
> Her (inf'nite cunning) with her modern grace
> Subdu'd me to her rate. (V.iii.212–17)

In *Pericles* the Bawd instructs Marina on how to be a good prostitute:

you must seem to do that fearfully which you commit willingly, despise profit where you have most gain. To weep that you live as ye do makes pity in your lovers; seldom but that pity begets you a good opinion, and that opinion a mere profit. (IV.ii.115f.)

In *The Jew of Malta* the prostitute Bellamira pretends to have fallen madly in love with Ithamore, by his own estimation a 'poor Turk of tenpence' and the slave of Barabas, whose wealth she hopes to steal. Like the earlier character convention of Lechery, she feigns modesty and gentility:

> Though womans modesty should hale me backe,
>   I can with-hold no longer; welcome sweet love. (*Kiss him*) (IV.ii.45–6)

The prodigal Spendall in *Greene's Tu Quoque* learns too late of the two-faced ingratitude of his whore, Nan Tickleman. As he parts affectionately from her, she says: 'Nay, buss [= *kiss*] first; well, / There's no adversity in the world shall part us' (Dodsley, vol. XI, p. 244). No sooner is he in the street, however, than serjeants arrest him for debt. He persuades them to return to his house to retrieve the money he has just given his whore, but she, supported by her entourage of bawd and pimp, now refuses to recognise him:

> Why, you impudent rogue, do you come to me for money?
> Or do I know you? What acquaintance, pray,
> Hath ever pass'd betwixt yourself and me?

After elaborately cursing them, Spendall is taken off to prison, but the old bawd Sweatnam sanctimoniously concludes:

Well, if men did rightly consider't, they should find that whores and bawds are profitable members in a commonwealth; for indeed, though we somewhat impair their bodies, yet we do good to their souls; for I am sure, we still bring them to repentance.

The consequences of individualisation

The early context of the stage whore in Medieval and Tudor theatre was ostensibly moral. In the traditional sequence of the Seven Deadly Sins it is the act of venery, following on from gluttony and leading to sloth, that demonstrates and confirms Mankind's fall to sin, and the wanton–whore often brought man to perdition with a relish, as do Wantonness in *Wit and Wisdom*, and Pride, Covetousness and Lechery in *The Cradle of Security*. In the Medieval *Castle of Perseverance*, when Humanum Genus succumbs to Luxuria's invitation she remarks smugly to the audience: 'I may soth singe: / "Mankind is kawt in my slinge"' (lines 1204–5). Notwithstanding her immoral purpose in the scheme of things, however, the seductive whore was often the brightest point of the play, the jam in an otherwise dull moral sandwich of interminable sermonising. Lechery in the *Interlude of Youth*, as with Abominable Living in *Lusty Juventus*, requires the representation of a lustful young woman, 'fresh and fair of hue, / And very proper of body', who willingly offers herself: 'And when it please you on me to call, / My heart is yours, body and all' (Dodsley, vol. II, p. 24). Furthermore, the theatrical representation of abstractions tends to individualise them and thereby to introduce elements, if not quite of sympathy, at least of moral ambivalence. The *Trial of Treasure*, although heavily allegorical, is in its stage representation an unusual treatment of a loose woman, almost a love story. The play has echoes of *Everyman*. Will Treasure, 'a woman finely apparelled', and her brother Pleasure stand by Lust the gallant in his adversity? God's Visitation brings Lust pain to his members, which causes Pleasure to leave, but Lady Treasure stays with him in a way not at all like the customary mercenary whore. Only Time's call ends them both, as it must end all. The lovers go out, and Time returns with a '*similitude of dust and rust*' which is all that is left of them.

The appellation 'Wantonness the Woman' given to the sole female character in *The Tide Tarrieth No Man* is a reminder perhaps of the original misogyny behind all male representations of the female, but in the event the portrait is not of a conventional strumpet but of burgeoning womanhood. Wanton the maid cannot wait to be married and thereby enjoy the power and sexual satisfactions it brings. Her mother, she reports, thinks she is too young at fourteen, but Courage the Vice urges her to ignore this and take her own pleasure, which she does. She could have walked straight out of any modern soap opera:

> Alas for griefe, my harte it will burst.
> I dayly see young women as yong as I,
> Which in whyte Caps, our dore doe go by:
> I am as able as they, with man to lye,
> Yet my mother doth still, my wedding denye.   (lines 859–63)

Her wantonness is condemned by the play's themes and structure, but in its realisation in the text there are signs of a recognition that it is also natural and inevitable. Her energy and resilience are part of the life-force that renews society and, as here, characterises the transition from maid to woman.

The stage whore and the realities of prostitution

Although, as has been shown, many of the loose women who feature in these earlier plays are called 'whores', they tend to be little more than moral abstractions, and it is only in the period after 1586 that the dynamics of prostitution begin to be reproduced in detail, and then the topic becomes extremely popular and is featured in nearly a quarter of the adult repertory. There are scenes in brothels and lodgings, with prostitutes shown dressing and making-up as well as entertaining customers. There are plain bawds, who are merely decayed prostitutes, courtly bawds, and covert part-time bawds, and there are pimps and tapsters, who display their tricks to wheedle money from customers and reveal their sometimes carnal relations with their mistresses.

Located in the suburbs in the same areas as the brothels (Prynne is at pains to match them in pairs), the new theatres, often said to be used as hunting grounds by their neighbours, were well-placed to portray prostitution from direct observation. Both Alleyn and Henslowe were brothel-owners. In his letter of 2 May to his wife Joan during the tour of 1593, Alleyn reports that he has heard that she has been, 'by my Lorde Mayor's officer made to ride in a cart, you & all your fellows', which Peter Thomson thinks indicates that Joan was punished as a prostitute, perhaps,

Gamini Salgado suggests, because she had not closed the brothel during a time of plague (though Carol Rutter suggests the reference was a joke)[3]. In either event, to the players and their customers prostitution was a daily reality.

Elizabethan dramatists are under no illusion about the capacity of prostitution to corrupt, morally and physically. When in *Greene's Tu Quoque* the whore gets drunk and falls out with the bawd, she gives a graphic description of the syphilitic condition to which all whores must come:

I pray, who feeds you, but I? who keeps thy feather-beds from the brokers, but I? 'tis not your sausage face, thick, clouted cream-rampallion at home, that snuffles in the nose like a decayed bagpipe. (Dodsley, vol. XI, p. 197)

In *Royal King and Loyal Subject* Captain Bonville returns from the war in straitened circumstances and a choric moralist on an England corrupted by money. When he visits a brothel he is shunned by the Bawd until he shows he can pay and then favoured over impecunious gentry. He tests the two Whores to see how far mercenary greed will overcome his lack of hygiene. First he says he is dirty, then lousy, and finally syphilitic, but nothing will put them off. Meanwhile, his servant the Clown, in the true tradition of dangerous innocence, takes a fancy to the Bawd:

BAWD: ... come, shall we dally together? Sit upon my knee, sweet boy, what
      money hast thou in thy purse? Wil't bestow it upon me, my sweet chick?
CLOWN: I'll see what I shall have for my money, by your favour ...

In *How a Man May Choose a Good Wife from a Bad* Mistress Splay the bawd reads a 'lecture' to Mistress Mary, now commencing her career as a prostitute, on reconciling herself to old and ugly clients who have money:

Gold can make limping Vulcan walk upright;
Make squint eyes straight, a crabbed face look smooth,
Gilds copper noses, makes them look like gold ...   (II.iii)

The whore as male fantasy

In 1596 the Earl of Northumberland wrote on the cooling of his passion, and his dissatisfaction with the time and effort demanded by courtship, which, he said, involved 'mind's disquiet, attendant servitude, flattering observance, loss of time, passion without reason' and led to 'slacking of good actions'. In doing so he points up the traditional gender differences in respect of the preliminaries to intercourse. Hence, therefore, the attractions of the whore or wanton who in contrast to the rest of her sex was represented in these plays as sharing the male's 'product-orientated' view of sexual congress, much as Leuidulcia does in *The Atheist's Tragedy* (II.iii): 'Lust is a spirit, which whosoe'er doth raise, / That next man that encounters boldly, lays.' In their use of the term 'whore' the Elizabethans deliberately confused the professional prostitute with those women who were adulterous or promiscuous or who merely, like men, made their enjoyment known. Despite its grounding in the real life around them, and whilst acknowledging her corruption, the Elizabethans used the stage whore to create an amoral vitality, celebrating a male wish-fulfilment fantasy of phallocentricity that what drives a woman to whoredom is a shared pleasure in sex. At the prospect of having to leave prostitution, Lamia in *1 Promos and Cassandra* mourns her loss of future income, the surrender of fine clothes and food, but most of all leaving the 'dalliance', for once a girl has tasted the joys of love, the play says, she will not want to forego them. Men in the plays are rarely depicted as approaching prostitutes realistically as purveyors of a commodity in the manner of Captain Bonville, but present themselves instead as being in love and expect the prostitutes to make at least a show of reciprocation. In *2 If You Know Not Me You Know Nobody* John Gresham visits a French brothel where the prostitute tells him she has tried five other nationalities but the English are the truest lovers and that she dotes on him, and the xenophobic context indicates that we are expected to believe her.

This similarity of interest did not, however, excuse the whore. She remains an unacceptable convenience.

The whore in performance

Freed from inhibition or female modesty and buoyed up by the justification that revealing the whore's immorality was a public service, the young male actor could make his wanton females more explicitly and outrageously lascivious than any woman performer, confident in the knowledge that there was no danger, as there always is for an actress, of having his own morals impugned by association. Indeed, the more outrageous the male performance, as in Luxuria's invitation to the hero in *The Castle of Perseverance* (lines 1189–90): 'Therfore, Mankind, my leve lemman, / I my cunte thou schalt crepe', the less the danger of being identified with the part. Whores are presented in the plays singing and dancing and flaunting themselves in fine clothes, as Abominable Living in *Lusty Juventus*, Clytemnestra in *Horestes*, Trial in *Trial of Treasure*, and Wantonness in *The Tide Tarrieth No Man*. Lamia sings on her first entry in *Promos and Cassandra* (I.ii):

> Al aflaunt now vaunt it, brave wenche cast away care,
> With Layes of Love chaunt it, for no cost see thou spare:
> Sith Nature hath made thee, with bewty most brave,
> Sith Fortune hath lade thee, with what thou wouldst have . . .

In *Part Two* she has her own brothel with four prostitutes in her window 'bravely apparelled' who solicit in chorus. To one observer, 'They be the *Muses*, sure.' His friend, however, is more cautious: 'Naye, *Syrens* lure' (II.ii). Aluida in *Looking Glass for London* wantonly courts the King of Cilia, singing of love and beauty and then kissing and embracing him. In Dekker's *If It Be Not Good the Devil's In It*, 1611, as part of a devilish stratagem to corrupt the Sub-Prior, '*five or six courtesans*', a '*brave set of whores*', dance accompanied by an Italian Zany, whose song, as he offers the unfortunate priest each girl in turn, is explicit in the extreme:

> Will you haue a daintie girle? here tis:
> Currall lippes, teeth of pearle: here tis:
> Cherry cheekes, softest flesh; that's shee;
> Breath like *May*, sweete and fresh; shee shee.
> Be she white, blacke, or browne,
> Pleasure your bed shall crowne,
>> Choose her then, vse her then,
>> Women are made for men.
>> Prettie, prettie wast;
>> Sweete to be embracde:
> Prettie leg, o prettie foote,
> To beauties tree the roote,
> This is she shall doo'te,
> Or she shall doo't, or she shall doo't, or she shall doo't,
>> or she shall doo't,
> Kisse, kisse, play, play, come and dally,
> Tumble, tumble, tumble, in beauties valley.   (IV.iv.17–32)

Playwright disingenuousness

Few, if any, of the later depictions of prostitutes are without some measure of ambivalence. Even Jonson, no lover of women, gives over the whole of Act II of *Catiline*, a scene of 362 lines, to Fulvia, in an ambiguous depiction of a brittle, evil, but attractive high-class courtesan, captivating in her combination of seductiveness and independence.

As her maid dresses her hair, she conducts a frank discussion of male sexual behaviour with her friend Sempronia:

FULVIA: And for the act, I can have secret fellows
    With backs worth ten of him . . .
SEMPRONIA: And those one may command.
FULVIA: 'Tis true; these lordlings,
    Your noble fauns, they are so imperious, saucy,
    Rude, and as boist'rous as centaurs, leaping
    A lady at first sight.   (lines 166–72)

When her patron enters against her commands, he proposes immediate congress:

CURIUS: Then take my gown off for th'encounter.   (lines 221)

She refuses, he eventually offers violence, and she resists:

He offers to force her, and she draws her knife.

He is about to leave, but she calls him back, and the stage direction reads:

She kisses and flatters him along still.

He thinks she is surrendering when in fact she is using her wiles to find out the details of Catiline's plot, which she subsequently reveals to Cicero.

'The Honest Whore'

Perhaps the most revealing example of the disingenuousness with which prostitution was so often presented is contained in the two parts of *The Honest Whore*. Although Dekker is clearly their main author, Henslowe also records Middleton's involvement, at least in *Part One*, and it may well be that the serious inconsistencies in the treatment of prostitution, even more obvious perhaps than in their collaboration on the *The Roaring Girl*, are due in part to their differing outlooks on the topic.

At the time of its composition Middleton was featuring prostitutes with great frequency in his plays for the Children's companies, as later in *A Chaste Maid in Cheapside* for the adult theatre. His vision is of a radically different kind to anything that has been so far discussed. In the first place, perceiving them to be ordinary people, like us, before they became trapped in their profession, he is much more inclined to offer social factors to explain their predicament. *The Roaring Girl* provides a gloss on the economic pressure and male lasciviousness that turns women to prostitution:

> Distressed needlewomen and trade-fallen wives,
> Fish that must needs bite or themselves be bitten . . .   (III.i.93–4)

Often such girls have been ruined by a single gallant for whom they retain their original love. The foolish Country Wench in *Michaelmas Term* is led into it, like the heroine of Wager's *Mary Magdalene*, by love of fine clothes.

What further distinguishes all his 'courtesans' – the term, significantly, he uses throughout – is the mutability of their condition. Unlike the eternal perdition of lost virtue that faces most whores or other fallen women in Elizabethan plays, and in the hands of his collaborator tarnishes both Moll Frith and Bellafront, Middleton's courtesans are all restored by marriage and wealth to society, even in the case of *A Mad World, My Masters* marrying the hero. Furthermore, their conversion gives them a new and superior moral status. As the Courtesan says in *A Trick to Catch the Old One*, reconciling her rich husband to his discovery of her former trade: 'She that knows sin, best knows how to hate sin.' Despite the optimistic nature of Middleton's viewpoint, however, it is cut off from reality by its clearly signalled context of wish-fulfilment fantasy. His humane concern for the social determinants of prostitution is expressed in terms of a classical literary tradition of the golden-hearted courtesan stretching back at least as far as Thais in Terence's *Eunuch*, and transmuted into the patrist Mary Magdalene of the Medieval *Golden Legend*.

It is then apparently under Middleton's influence that Bellafront is initially presented as a witty, spunky, self-confident, sprightly young woman of fifteen, small and beautiful, with her own establishment, providing a sexual magnet for the gentry and conning money from them by sending out for wine that never materialises. She first appears in undress, and completes her attire and make-up onstage. There is none of the harshness of many such representations, no bawd or venial pimp, or hints of disease, but instead the boy Roger with whom she seems at ease, talk of silk stockings, catches of popular tunes, and the good-humoured if inevitably smutty puns about 'falls' and 'pokers'.

Amongst the gallants, she is introduced to Hippolito, whose mistress, Infelice, he believes, has recently died. Steadfast in his loyalty to her memory, he does not respond to the obvious attraction both feel, but instead returns when the other gallants have gone to try to argue Bellafront out of her chosen career. That she is won over is due in main part to the love for him this augments in her, and her contrition is motivated by a desire to be faithful to a single partner – what Iago elsewhere describes as, 'the strumpet's plague / To beguile many and be beguil'd by one'.

Infelice, however, is not dead, her father the Duke is finally reconciled to their marriage, and poor Bellafront's reward for aiding this and for her reformation is to be palmed off with the man who first seduced her, Matheo. In *Part Two*, apparently written solely by Dekker, Matheo is more fully revealed as a dissipated gambler who sacrifices all to his obsession, even the gown ripped from Bellafront's back; whilst the newly married Hippolito gives reign to his passion for the reformed heroine and repeatedly opportunes her to return to her former trade. Though reduced to penury, Bellafront remains faithful to her useless, abusive husband, and, in a set-piece dialogue that exactly matches Hippolito's earlier reformation of her in *Part One*, rejects all his advances with a lengthy authorial attack upon the vices of prostitution, and with a purity so ponderous as to deny any of the wit, light-heartedness, and realism of her opening portrayal. In Dekker's hands she has become no more than a mouthpiece for political correctness.

That this is all so much humbug is revealed at the end of *Part Two* when all the characters gather for the reformation of the two well-born young men at the Milan equivalent of London's Bridewell, the punishment house for prostitutes. Here attention quickly passes from the men's contrition to a procession of whores, together with a pimp and bawd, whose severe punishments contrast uneasily with the taunts of their erstwhile clients and the tolerance shown to Matheo and Hippolito, both of whom had urged Bellafront to return to prostitution and had planned to benefit from it.

The three processional whores are all new figures in the drama, introduced in its closing moments, and in no way integral to the story. All are on their way to punishment and should, therefore, be wearing the penitential blue gowns the Beadles carry with them – but they are not. Instead, they still wear the clothes of their profession, costumes to catch the eye of client *and spectator*. Two are dressed as gentlewomen, Dorothea Target so 'brave' she looks like a bride, whilst Penelope Whorehound is got up as a citizen's wife, much perhaps in the manner so approved in *Bartholomew Fair* by Littlewit, who dresses his wife in a velvet cap and 'fine high shoes, like the Spanish lady', and later, when she is set up for prostitution, gives offence to Punk Alice as offering too much competition:

The poor common whores ha' no traffic, for the privy rich ones; your caps and hoods of velvet call away our customers and lick the fat from us. (IV.v.68–70)

The whores on their way to chastisement are presented much as the entertainment or disguising so often included in the fifth act of a play. Indeed, the Duke instructs the assembled gentlefolk not to make it look like a trial: 'Be covered all, / Fellows, now make the scene more comical' (2 *Honest Whore*, v.ii), and as the three whores present themselves, the first boldly lascivious and singing, the second plaintive, pretending gentility, and the third raucous and abusive, he observes: 'Variety is good . . .'. Whilst the conversion of Bellafront is made the vehicle for a two-part moral diatribe against female promiscuity, structurally this has the drawback of removing the object of surreptitious pleasure. New unreformed whores must be found, therefore, to maintain the visual excitement of *Part One* – spirited, lascivious, and richly dressed, to feast the eye and stimulate the senses. The raunchiness of the three whores does not so much equate with Bellafront's spirited independence as recall in its gratuitousness the devilish dancing line of Dekker's *If It Be Not Good*. Their last-minute introduction reveals the hypocrisy of Dekker's position, put so well by Charles Lamb:

A satirist is always to be suspected, who, to make vice odious, dwells upon all its acts and minutest circumstances with a sort of relish and retrospective fondness.

As a moralist Dekker is too obviously a candidate for Lear's rebuke to the beadle: 'Thou hostly lusts to use her in that kind / For which thou whip'st her' (*King Lear*, IV.vi.162–3). Dekker's hypocrisy operates by isolating the whore as a separate species, alterity being the cross-dressed convention's most immediate resource. Thus the mundane is raised to the exotic, enjoyed, and then satisfyingly punished. Whores in the corpus of plays are hanged, poisoned, burned, starved to death in the street, sent for torture, and taken off to be raped by common soldiery, but their standard punishment, relished in play after play, is to be:

> carted through the Streetes,
> According to the common shame of strumpets
> Your bodies whip'd, till with the losse of bloud
> You faint under the hand of punishment.
>
> (*The Atheist's Tragedy*, v.ii)

Shakespeare's treatment of prostitution

Mistress Horseleech in 2 *Honest Whore*, faced with being whipped until the blood flows, protests her innocence: 'I am known as a motherly, honest woman, and no bawd', and her accuser, the whore Catherina Bountinall, is made to reply:

Marry, foh, honest? burnt at fourteen, seven times whipt, five times carted, nine times ducked, searched by some hundred and fifty constables, and yet you are honest? (v.ii)

Set outside the bounds of humanity in Dekker's world by her trade, the bawd, like the whore, is fair game to be subject to any indignity.

In contrast, it comes as a surprise to realise that Mistress Quickly in *Henry IV* is also a bawd. *Part Two* begins with a good-humoured portrait of a poor widow cheated of her money by Falstaff's false promise of marriage:

Thou didst swear to me upon a parcel-gilt goblet, sitting in my Dolphin chamber, at the round table by a sea-coal fire, upon Wednesday in Wheeson week, when the Prince broke thy head for liking his father to a singing-man of Windsor, thou didst swear to me then, as I was washing thy wound, to marry me and make me my lady thy wife . . . (ii.i.86f.)

A detailed picture is built up of bourgeois pseudo-gentility, albeit amidst the taverns and stews of Eastcheap, such that Nell Quickly's very simplicity and good-heartedness seem to protect her from its corruption. Nonetheless the scene ends with her engaging to provide a whore for the evening, but the circumstantial way in which it is prepared makes it seem other than mere procurement. Fascinated by Falstaff, who owes her a hundred marks, she is manoeuvred yet again into believing that only further outlay will secure her debt and his person. This is a far cry from the uncomplicated, sordid, mercenary transactions usually ascribed to bawds. It would be wrong, however, to see the detailed presentation of Quickly as more than empathetic. For all its accuracy and insight, it is also in the tradition of cross-dressed comic parodies, and though there is a much greater effect of shock when she is carried off at the end to prison, perhaps for a punishment similar to Mistress Horseleech's, it seems not entirely inappropriate.

Shakespeare is much less inclined to introduce prostitutes into his plays than many of his contemporaries, especially the young and attractive, brittle and titillating kind favoured by Dekker and his associates[4]. There are exceptions, such as the Courtesan in the early *Comedy of Errors* 'in the habit of a light wench', and the two whores in *Timon of Athens* with their 'cherubin look' whose brief appearance is the object of considerable misogyny. The elderly (?) Doll Tearsheet in *2 Henry IV* provides much of the colour of Falstaff's debauchery, and although prostitution is not singled out for the usual overt moral disapproval, nor is it disguised. She is drunken, diseased, quarrelsome, lascivious, and appropriately punished at the end. Bianca in *Othello* is in many ways a stereotype, the whore who falls for her client, but her brief role is individualised to the extent that as the foolish, fond, part-time huswife rather than brazen whore she is the sympathetic victim, first of Cassio, and then as an instrument in Iago's plot. Unlike other treatments of the Edward IV/Richard III story, Shakespeare omits Jane Shore, and his single reference to her is scathing. The most striking contrast in his treatment of prostitution is between *Measure for Measure* and its source. In place of the luscious and spirited Lamia of Whetstone's *Promos and Cassandra*, whose career throughout its two parts counterbalances that of the heroine, Shakespeare has the much briefer role of Mistress Overdone, the bawd. Her trade is equated with disease, and when the suburb brothels are pulled down, she opens a 'bath-house'. After eleven years as a bawd, having outlived nine husbands, presumably victims of her venereal disease, she goes into the tub herself. Prostitutes, on the other hand, are conspicuous by their absence in Vienna. Kate Keepdown, whom Lucio has got with child, is mentioned (III.ii.199), and he is required to marry her at the end, but she never appears. Instead, as in *Pericles*, we are shown a bawd, a pimp, and their customers, but no whores.

Cressida

At one level Cressida is merely a girl who has fallen in love with a young man, and her uncle helps to bring them together; but his name is Pandarus, and he is the self-proclaimed founder of that profession. Although the Elizabethans might have associated Cressida with whoredom from her treatment by Henryson and others, Chaucer on the other hand dignifies the lovers, and Shakespeare's Cressida, like Bianca, wavers back and forth across the line between prostitution and mere sexual waywardness. Her widowhood is never mentioned, but she gives an aura of greater sexual experience. At her first appearance we see a highly aware, highly vulnerable, but boldly defensive young woman, coarse and knowing:

Upon my back, to defend my belly, upon my wit, to defend my wiles, upon my secrecy, to defend mine honesty, my mask, to defend my beauty, and you to defend all these . . . (I.ii.260–3)

This sounds like the catechism of a young whore. Depending upon secrecy rather than chastity is certainly not the sentiment of a good girl.

Marriage is never discussed. What Pandarus arranges is not courtship but an assignation at which sex takes place. Pandarus is obviously a social climber who makes himself agreeable by providing flesh; his kin are burrs, he says, 'they stick where they are thrown'. His visit to Helen's boudoir on the slightest of pretexts, in which he is prevailed upon after much coyness to sing a ditty in which the sounds of female orgasm are simulated, and probably male orgasm too, carries strong overtones of the brothel[5].

Rather, as with Mistress Quickly, we are in the suburbs almost without knowing it because the characters are not seen primarily as members of a despised and ostracised profession but rather as individuals whose inter-action at first seems only marginally improprietal. Troilus bewails her falseness and though his sloppy sentimentality has all the hallmarks of a strumpet's deluded customer, unlike Cassio he betrays no realisation that he is one. When Pandarus arrives in IV.ii he seems to suggest that this is Cressida's first sexual encounter:

> How now, how now, how go maidenheads?
> Here, you maid! where's my cousin Cressid? (IV.ii.23–4)

But the context and particularly the echo here of commodity-trading suggests this is no more than a pimp's business-patter, much as the courtesan's bawd-mother in *A Mad World, My Masters* tells her, 'Fifteen times thou know'st I have sold thy maidenhead' (I.i.150). The scene opens with Troilus fretting to be on his way, just like any other young man after a one-night stand, full of insincere solicitude:

TROILUS: You will catch cold and curse me.
CRESSIDA: Prithee tarry.
> You men will never tarry.
> O foolish Cressid! I might have still held off,
> And then you would have tarried. (IV.ii.14–18)

Her generalisation, 'You *men*', in the plural, as well as her anticipation that Pandarus will be mocking, suggests she has done it before, but her regret is that of a love-sick girl, not a hardened professional.

Much depends finally on Ulysses' judgement. In IV.iv, he stage-manages the pageant of Cressida's moral display. It is he who suggests (line 21) ' 'Twere better she were kissed in general', a proposal to which she is given no demur, and seems shortly after to enter into their banter. When she requires him to 'beg' his kiss, he responds by linking her behaviour with Helen's, as Pandarus had implicitly done earlier, and as she leaves, comments upon her:

> Fie, fie upon her!
> There's language in her eye, her cheek, her lip,
> Nay, her foot speaks; her wanton spirits look out
> At every joint and motive of her body.
> O, these encounterers, so glib of tongue,

That give a coasting welcome ere it comes,
And wide unclasp the table of their thoughts
To every ticklish reader! set them down
For sluttish spoils of opportunity,
And daughters of the game.   (IV.v.54–63)

It is a speech dismissing her as a prostitute in a way which challenges the judgement we have already made of the sincerity of her love for Troilus; but it also describes the wanton walk which all men find desirable.

There are two reasons why we cannot come down firmly on one side or the other. On the one hand, Shakespeare individualises her behaviour as part of the process of making the character more vivid, and Cressida's immobilising self-awareness is one of her distinguishing qualities most demanding sympathy, as in III.ii.117f. with a series of tormented speeches full of violence and contradiction. Each time she says something she becomes aware that it could be seen from some other angle in which it would be impolitic, self-indulgent, self-betraying, or disingenuously lascivious. This catches the inner workings of a mind under stress, and something of the problems a woman has in monitoring her own self-presentation of the sort that John Berger analyses so acutely.[6]

But the second reason does much to negate all of this. Cressida is not a person, she is a construct. She appears only five times, five very different snapshots, inviting yet denying the possibility of joining up the dots to make a coherent personality. The tragedy of Troilus is that he is unable to reconcile the Cressida from one snapshot, his own brief love affair, with that of another, the Cressida he sees flirting with Diomedes: 'this is and is not Cressid!' And the audience share his point of view, suffering from a similar sense of discontinuity, once again sympathising with the male dilemma. As elsewhere in his canon the apparent sympathy created by Shakespeare's empathetic exploration of her circumstance, abandoned by her father, manipulated by Pandarus, gives way finally to perhaps one of the most damning statements of female alterity.

Her appearances are always 'framed' by a male stage commentator: the smutty innuendo of Pandarus in the earlier scenes with his obvious bias towards Troilus: 'I would my heart were in her body' (I.ii.80–1); and the arguably choric Ulysses later. In addition, her final, anguished betrayal is witnessed within two such frames, an inner one of Ulysses and Troilus observing her, and beyond them Thersites observing them all. What with Chorus and Epilogue, the traditional associations of the story, and Cressid's own choric soliloquies, there is little unmediated Cressida left.

Her final scene with Diomedes is deeply disturbing. She seems unwilling to abandon Troilus and yet unable to resist the more immediate offer of Diomedes, and we can take little comfort in her final retreat into an authorial misogynist generalisation:

> Ah, poor our sex! This fault in us I find,
> The error of our eye directs our mind. (v.ii.109–10)

The scene had suggested all sorts of pressures on her, from her father's unseen tendering to the need she has for Diomed's guardianship, unacknowledged in this glib conclusion.

THE MULTI-DIMENSIONAL FEMALE CHARACTER

Elizabethan plays, as Carol Thomas Neely notes, rarely admit the existence within traditionally male preserves of female access to legal and social authority, but they do occasionally acknowledge other significant areas of female power. Perhaps inevitably, given the male perspective, they all contain some element of sexuality, but such as to question the simplistic dichotomy of quiescent virtue and diabolical cruelty, or the crude association of promiscuity with prostitution.

As has already been noted, the Elizabethans were fond of blaming women, as they make female characters castigate themselves in the plays, for the destructive power of their beauty. Over and above this obvious strategy to transfer male guilt at sexual arousal, and notwithstanding the rhetoric about the 'witchcraft' of beauty, there is a recognition that a well-proportioned woman in motion has such power to draw the eye that it makes mere legal, moral, or financial male power seem insignificant; for it speaks not merely of sexual allure but somehow of the very springs of life itself. It has already been noted of Cressida. There is something of this quality in Agrypyne's observation in *Old Fortunatus*:

And how glad is he to obey? And how proud am I to command in this Empire of affection? Over him and such spongy-livered youths, (that lie soaking in love) I triumph more with mine eye, than ever did he over a soldier with his sword. Is't not a gallant victory for me to subdue my father's enemy with a look? (III.i)

In *A Woman Killed with Kindness*, Wendoll, trying to resist his infatuation with Anne, says:

> I will arm myself
> Not to entertain a thought of love to her;

And when I come by chance into her presence,
I'll hale these balls until my eyestrings crack
From being pull'd and drawn to look that way.   (VI.12–26)

Female characters are rarely allowed to withhold their sexual favours in the plays from those with the right to receive them, no doubt because it could be seen as setting a bad example for the women in the audience. Margaret in *3 Henry VI* and Titania in *A Midsummer Night's Dream* are exceptions, and it is an important plot element in *The Woman's Prize. The Second Maid's Tragedy* shows its effectiveness. The Tyrant, having deposed Govianus with the purpose of gaining the Lady, now summons her to be his wife. She rejects him and takes Govianus instead in an opening scene which nicely contrasts the relative power of men and women and shows that however much a man may have the physical and legal power, if the woman withholds her favours, he can only huffle and snuffle without effect. Her father asks why he does not force her. No, says the Tyrant: 'It must come / Gently and kindly, like a debt of love, / Or 'tis not worth receiving' (I.i.192–4). The Tyrant then seeks to have the Lady as his mistress. She refuses, converting her father to goodness in the process. When the increasingly unhinged Tyrant sends a band of armed men to capture her, she is unsuccessful in persuading Govianus to kill her, and therefore kills herself.

The Woman's Prize, or the Tamer Tamed, in which Petruchio marries again and meets his match, is Fletcher's companion piece to *The Taming of the Shrew.* As soon as they are married, Maria announces her intention of breaking Petruchio and destroying his reputation. The play illustrates the *Realpolitik* of female power. Yes, Petruchio could force Maria to consummation, but not to reciprocity. When he threatens to relieve himself with the maid, she counters by threatening similar action with his valet, and later with his friend. She follows her refusal to have conjugal relations with the one piece of female power impossible to quell – she goes on an outrageous spending spree. Her energy is irrepressible. On one occasion she persuades everyone that Petruchio has the plague and gets him boarded up. On another she dresses as a prostitute. The play shows there really is no defence against such women and their tongues if they remain resolute, and especially if, as here, they gain support from other women. A man can spend himself in useless violence, or retreat into the fantasies of control so well expressed in Heywood's plays, but he *will* eventually be tamed.

The Devil and his Dame is perhaps the most extreme play in asserting the invulnerability of unchaste women. The devils in Hell, who seem a very moral lot, are shocked to hear from the Ghost of one Malbecco of how he was driven to suicide by the behaviour of his wife. Female unfaithfulness, it is alleged, is rampant in the World and they despatch their best-tempered devil, Belphegor, to go on earth as a man, choose a wife, and find out if it is true. Having been made a victim of the bed-trick, he eventually finds himself married to Marian, the waiting woman. The devil finds his hands very full trying to contain the immoral energy of his new wife. No sooner has he neutralised an adulterous liaison she has arranged for her mistress, than he finds Marian with a 'winking' and a 'wanton' eye lasciviously entertaining gallants in the garden with a secluded banquet and suggested intimacies. When Belphegor can stand it no longer he interrupts them, but instead of being ashamed, Marian brazens it out:

> No, sir, I'll be half mistress of myself;
> The other half is yours, if you deserve it.
>
> (Dodsley, vol. VIII, p. 441)

And for this, after further fruitless argument, Belphegor has to settle, returning to Hell with relief at the end of his year.

'Arden of Faversham' [1591]

This play serves as perhaps the sharpest critique of Heywood's fantasies of life-and-death control over a wife. Based on a historical account of a wife murdering her husband, it has the ambiguous morality of the tabloid press, ostensibly disapproving and yet fascinated by sexual transgression. Unusually for its time it concentrates on the wife, a very big role of 593 lines.

In her own eyes at least, Alice Arden acts from love:

Love is a god, and marriage is but words. (1.101)

Whatever the tenor of the subsequent moralising, once these words have been uttered they continue to have a counter-currency which challenges the received orthodoxy, and the play, therefore, is an example of the dangers of theatre for female morality. Clarke the painter calls it 'noble' to do away with Arden because enduring a loveless marriage is worse than taking whatever steps are necessary to gain the person one loves.

Alice is an extremely resolute woman, which puts her firmly in the line of later grander heroines. In the first scene, when Mosby her lover sends word that she must not visit him, her response is breathtakingly violent. She says to the landlord of the inn:

> Were he as mad as raving Hercules
> I'll see him. Ay, and were thy house of force,

> These hands of mine should raze it to the ground,
> Unless that thou wouldst bring me to my love. (1.16–19)

– and this immediately after playing the faithful little wife to Arden, who is preparing to go away on business:

> A month? Ay me! Sweet Arden, come again
> Within a day or two or else I die. (1.85–6)

She is able to alternate this surface image of a loving wife and the reality of her driving adulterous lust quite successfully throughout the play so that, as late as the scene before his murder, Arden appears to believe he is reconciling a reluctant Alice with their family friend, Mosby, whereas they are jointly preparing the final attempt upon his life.

The plot is unusual in that it begins with Arden already knowing in his heart that Alice is unfaithful. Why then does he not act? Catherine Belsey cites Holinshed's version that he feared to upset her rich and powerful friends, but there is nothing of this in the play.[7] Instead, it offers a man unable to decide between his suspicions about his wife's honesty, already condemned by the outside world, and her protestations of affection. For much of the time it is easier and more comfortable for Arden to go along with the face she offers him. This sense of a couple jointly, and to a large extent wilfully, living a lie is one of the play's felicities. In Sc.10, Alice claims to love him and he reciprocates. In Sc.13, he tells Franklin she has been more loving to him of late and they are reconciled with hope of future harmony. Alice and Mosby then meet him in a lascivious embrace designed to draw him into a quarrel, but when things go wrong and it is Mosby who gets hurt, she lies her way out of it and persuades Arden it was a jest. He, refusing his friend Franklin's more level-headed judgement, goes off with the intention of reconciling them, and Franklin is left onstage to comment that Arden is 'bewitched' by Alice.

What gives the play a further level of mordant realism is the lack of compatibility between Alice and the object of her love, Mosby. The play begins with them out of accord. There is no sense of Mosby loving Alice, except perhaps in the past. In soliloquy he proposes to kill all the accomplices and even Alice after their marriage:

> 'Tis fearful sleeping in a serpent's bed
> And I will cleanly rid my hands of her. (VIII.42–3)

Hence her behaviour does not have the traditional justification of being part of a mutual grand passion, but is merely the consequence of her inordinate lust. This may do less to justify her behaviour, but it does make it more life-like, as for instance in Sc.8, when Alice is suddenly conscience-stricken, she and Mosby mutually recriminate, and then finally, unable to sustain either hostility or piety, she promises anything for his reconciliation.

If Anne Frankford in *A Woman Killed with Kindness* did not have such a highly developed sense of guilt, derived from male strictures, she would be as free as Alice. Both characters are, of course, artificial extremes, part of the traditional polarisation of woman, but Alice is much nearer to reality, and the rarity of such portraits indicates the Elizabethan male fear that women might realise their power in this; hence the excessive importance given to matrimonial faithfulness and obedience, sanctioned and maintained by law, state, and religion. The plays suggest that it is not so much that Elizabethans felt differently about personal relations, as that male play-wrights in general chose to deal more in polemic than actuality.

'The Duchess of Malfi'

For the most part, the world of Anne Arden is not one that impinges much on Shakespeare's, and to be fair, concentrating on Alice does the play more than justice; in performance most attention tends to be on the lame failures of her hired killers, Black Will and Shagbag. Shakespeare has no taste for the dubious morality of police-court scandals, and shows instead a fond-ness for princesses and far-away lands tinged with romanticism, and there is a sharp declension throughout his canon from the well-born, whose prob-lems can be taken seriously, straight down to the plebeians, who are always comic and generally despicable. Even though some plays like *King Lear* or *Othello* are terrifying in their logic and the sacrifice of goodness this involves, one misses in the neatness of his conclusions the jagged uneven-ness and moral ambiguity of Marlowe, or Peele, or even the anonymous author of *Arden of Feversham*. It is left to his successor, Webster, to assimilate a poetic conception of noble womanhood with the raw febrile improprieties of the sixteenth-century equivalents of the police gazette.

Lisa Jardine argues that the heroine in *The Duchess of Malfi* is 'meta-morphosed . . . into lascivious whore'; William Empson on the other hand takes the more usual view that she is presented sympathetically, in line with Middleton's commendatory poem: 'For who e're saw this Duchess live and die, / That could get off under a Bleeding Eye'; whilst Elizabeth Brennan points out that Webster stresses 'her purity and her integrity'.[8] Arguably it is not a case of either/or, but of both. The impropriety of a secret, second,

and unequal marriage would have done more in Webster's day to balance
the obvious tragic pathos of her courageous death and thus leave her
ultimate moral quality ambiguous. Such a view is consonant with the
more blatant equivocation of his first heroine, Vittoria in *The White
Devil*, a play at all points a rough draft for *The Duchess of Malfi*. Is the
Duchess then, like her predecessor, an oxymoronic 'white devil', i.e. no
more than an unresolved paradox between two contrasting and polarised
stereotypes yoked provocatively together? A more positive reading of the play
would see a development towards a genuinely tragic heroine–protagonist,
like Forster's 'rounded' character capable of surprising us, perhaps one of
the first of its kind.

Enjoined by her brothers not to re-marry, the Duchess defies them,
asserting her own right to dispose of her sexuality, and takes a secret
husband:

> Why should only I,
> Of all the other princes of the world
> Be cas'd up, like a holy relic? I have youth,
> And a little beauty.   (III.ii.137–40)

Part of Webster's skill is in the juxtaposition of different styles. As well as
the omnipresent sense of evil and *grand guignol*, there are also rich touches
of verisimilitude and great attention to naturalistic observation, as in
Bosola's description of the pregnant Duchess (II.i.66f.). The play depends
upon a sophisticated and developed acting tradition that can delve into the
details of a pregnant woman's tetchiness and cravings and then present her
in labour upon the stage without a hint of farce or burlesque. Act II, Scene ii
begins with a remarkable scene of relaxed intimacy as the Duchess
attended by Cariola prepares to go to bed with Antonio. Asked by
Cariola why he leaves so early in the morning, Antonio makes gentle fun
of their love-making, saying that labouring men are glad when their labour
is over. The two creep away as a joke leaving the Duchess combing her
hair. A moment later she is interrupted by her mad brother Ferdinand
'*holding a poinard*':

DUCHESS: 'Tis welcome:
  For know, whether I am doom'd to live or die,
  I can do both like a prince.   (III.ii.69–71)

And so it proves. Throughout the long psychological torture to which
Ferdinand submits her she retains her dignity, and Webster gives her a
multiplicity of consciousness rarely seen in a female character:

Th' heaven o'er my head seems made of molten brass,
The earth of flaming sulphur, yet I am not mad.
I am acquainted with sad misery,
As the tann'd galley-slave is with his oar.
Necessity makes me suffer constantly.
And custom makes it easy. (IV.ii.26–31)

She talks of Fortune beholding her tragedy, and asks that Cariola should tell her what she looks like, thus developing the prisoner's defence against suffering – the ability to get outside the body and see the events as if happening to another. So laden with foreboding is the drama that her epitaph comes very early:

CARIOLA: Whether the spirit of greatness, or of woman
  Reign most in her, I know not, but it shows
  A fearful madness: I owe her much of pity. (I.ii.417–19)

As she faces her execution with dignity –

      Pull, and pull strongly, for your able strength
      Must pull down heaven upon me. (IV.ii.226–7)

– her courage is commingled with a motherly concern for her children:

      I pray thee look thou giv'st my little boy
      Some syrup for his cold, and let the girl
      Say her prayers, ere she sleep. (IV.ii.200–2)

Unlike other heroines who are passive victims of men's cruelty or mis-apprehensions, and albeit that she lives in a dangerous court full of unnatural lust and deceit, nonetheless the Duchess creates her own tragedy by her actions, quite wittingly, preferring to live her sexual life to the full and, knowing what they are, to risk the consequences. It is a unique portrait well in advance of its time, and one, arguably, that transcends the restrictive polarisation of women to which even Shakespeare very largely subscribes.

CHAPTER 6

Sexual violence

The frequency of violence against women

The last two chapters have been based upon an analysis of the principal ways in which women are treated in the extant plays for the adult professional theatre, considering the types of character, the events to which they are subject, and the attitudes expressed towards them by the playwrights. One of the most frequent topics to have emerged in this process is scenes in which violence, physical or psychological, is offered to the female characters.

Something of the order of seven out of every ten plays presented on the Elizabethan adult stage include at least one, and often several, such scenes. Women are kicked, struck, knocked down, incarcerated, suffer armed assault on their houses, are dragged on or off stage, and their clothes torn. As has been shown, scenes of manhandling whores were particularly popular. Often the attention is on a woman's response to anticipated violence or its results; women are threatened with torture or mutilation, shown the dead bodies of their loved ones or made to watch them being killed, they are forcibly parted from their children, or in Tamora's case in *Titus Andronicus* made to eat them. It is characteristic of the genre that characters are shown *in extremis*, but this is particularly so of female ones: brutalised, isolated, grieving, fearful for their safety, their virtue, their loved ones, and on the point of collapse.[1] Sometimes sent mad with grief, they make away with themselves in spectacular suicides, as Isabella in *The Spanish Tragedy* who '*runs lunatic*' and plunges a weapon into her breast, or Zabina in *1 Tamburlaine*, who, following the example of her husband, '*runs against the Cage and braines her selfe*'.

Women are frequently subject to set-piece violent murders or executions: Venus in *The Cobbler's Prophecy* and Semele in *The Silver Age* are both burnt alive onstage, and Rachel in *Two Lamentable Tragedies* hanged there. Women are starved to death, smothered, beheaded (offstage), walled up alive, strangled, crushed, or poisoned, in two cases with an asp. In perhaps the most bizarre execution, the saintly Winifred in *A Shoemaker a Gentleman*, a Welsh princess whose great virtue and good deeds have led to the creation of a blessed magic fountain with attendant angel, is convicted by the Romans of being a Christian, and claiming by right of birth to choose her own mode of death, elects to have a vein opened and so is bled to death onstage. The blood is then poisoned and drunk by her admirer.

So popular was such violence that in some plays it is the sole reason for the presence of female characters. *'Larum for London, or the Siege of Antwerp*, a propaganda piece on Spanish cruelty in the Netherlands, involves a total of six female cameos ranging from the Governor's wife, her jewels ripped off and her virtue threatened, to a poor ragged child slaughtered along with her blind father and the rest of her family as she clings to the legs of the butchering soldiery. In *Selimus*, Zonara sister of Mahomet, and Sulima daughter of Bajazeth, both high-born young women, are brought onstage at different points in the play to whimper for mercy, the latter being made to witness her husband's death, before being strangled. The Queen of Amasia puts up rather more resistance but her fate is the same.[2] The play is one of a number written to capitalise on the success of *Tamburlaine*, which perhaps set a fashion in such cruelty. Its Zabina is the archetype of the proud dusky Empress, ripe to be satisfyingly humiliated; whilst the full juvenile performer-resources are used for scenes of group cruelty; in *Part One* as the Virgins of Damascus shown pleading unsuccessfully with Tamburlaine to avoid slaughter, and then in *Part Two* presumably the same players appear as the Turkish Emperor's concubines, forcibly reduced to common whores by his soldiery:

TAMBURLAINE: . . . And let them equally serve all your turnes . . .
LADIES: O pity us my Lord, and save our honours.
TAMBURLAINE: Are ye not gone ye villaines with your spoiles?

[*They run away with the Ladies*] (IV.iii.73–84)

Humiliation is a popular theme in the treatment of women in Elizabethan plays. Girls who are seduced or raped are cruelly abandoned, as are wives; in the case of poor Nell, wife of the eponymous hero of *Captain Thomas Stukeley* in the nuptial bed. Others passed over in marriage are forced to officiate at the weddings of their rivals. Pregnant girls are popular for exposure and mockery, but high-born women are the most frequent targets, brought low, sometimes thrown into the streets, or made to carry out servile tasks. Queens find themselves replaced by mistresses. A particularly favourite topos is for one woman to humiliate another, taken to its ultimate silliness in *Nobody and Somebody* where two rival proud ladies repeatedly humiliate each other according to the changing fortunes of their husbands. Women are stripped onstage of their fine outer garments and jewels. Frequently, to their further shame, such women are made to wear penitential garments. Another favourite effect is to prank up a female character in some elaborate costume, especially as a bride, and then to humiliate her. Shakespeare repeats this device in *The Taming of the Shrew* and *Much Ado*, the heroine's finery, expectations, and public prominence adding to her eventual misery. Susan in *A Woman Killed with Kindness* is got up in a similar fashion by her brother to be tendered to Francis Acton, whilst Celestina in *Satiromastix* finds herself threatened at her wedding feast with *droit de seigneur*. In a *An Humorous Day's Mirth*, the maid Jacquena, dressed as Queen Fortune, and found to be with child, is mocked and despite her protestations made to finish the 'pageant of the buttery'.

Violence in performance

When in *2 Tamburlaine* the soldiers '*run away with the Ladies*', the comic possibilities of this stage direction are increased not only by the group nature of the ravishment, but also by its cross-dressed context. The cries of fear are not those of *real* women imaginatively conceived in a situation of any authenticity, but those of cross-dressed performers for whom inevitably there will be an element of male salaciousness, whichever roles they play. The infliction of violence is a serious matter, sometimes in the plays very serious indeed, but lurking not far below the surface there are traces of the Old English farcical tradition of the folk man–woman, in which mutual violence between the sexes is not only tolerated – in deliberate contradistinction to ordinary propriety – but expected. In *The Birth of Merlin* Prince Uther Pendragon meets the Clown and his sister Joan Go-too't '*great with child*' wandering in the wood, and is mistaken for the 'Gentleman' with whom she had coupled (actually the Devil):

JOAN: Do you not know me, sir?
PRINCE: Know thee! as I do thunder, hell and mischief; Witch, scullian, hag!
CLOWN: I see he will marry her; he speaks so like a husband.   (II.i.137–41)

Provoked further, the Prince beats her, despite her being near her time, and does so without any loss of status, for we all know 'Joan' is only a chap with a cushion stuffed up his frock. 'Pray God the fruit of her womb miscarry', says Mistress Quickly as the Beadle arrests Doll Tearsheet at the end of *2 Henry IV*. 'If it do', replies the Beadle, 'you shall have a dozen cushions again; you have but eleven now.' The primacy of the fable has been repeatedly stressed in this study, but before concentrating on how the stories present their violence against women and the implications it has, it is well to bear in mind the performance context. Stage violence differs from the real thing in that amongst other things it is teamwork. The prime instigator of the effect is generally the victim. Here the comic horseplay relies not on the Prince's blows, which may never land (except perhaps on the cushion), but on Joan's anguished cries. A similar dynamic operates in that popular piece of stage action, the woman being pulled about the stage by her hair. In *Alphonsus Emperor of Germany*, the Emperor treats his English-born Empress thus for at least forty lines:

EMPRESS: O pierce my heart, trail me not by my hair ...   (III.i)

Whether this is the performer's own hair, or more probably a wig, it was a carefully managed piece of business between them in which the 'victim' took the lead.

It is not being suggested that all-male performance necessarily reduced all such confrontations to comedy or bathos. Earlier discussion would suggest that the imaginative robustness gained by frank acknowledgement of the means of performance would enable much of the violence to be as terrifying in the theatre, if not more so, as it appears on the page, as here where their business with the hair contributes not to farce but to a frightening web of violent intrigue in which the Empress is the innocent victim facing the prospect of much worse cruelty:

ALPHONSUS: I'll trail thee through the kennels of the street,
                    And cut the nose from thy bewitching face,
                    And into England send thee, like a strumpet.

Rape on the Elizabethan stage

Opinions vary as to the prevalence of rape in sixteenth-century society. The traditional punishment, if brought to law by the victim, was loss of eyes and privy members. Marion Wynne-Davis notes that until 1597 educated rapists could claim 'benefit of clergy', thereby reducing their punishment to imprisonment.[3] The infrequency of rape cases is explained by Suzanne Gosset as an unwillingness on the part of the victims to report the crime, and given some credence by cases in which girls cried rape and were made to do penance.[4] In most of the cases recorded, however, what principally motivated both ravisher and litigant were property rights, and Roy Porter argues persuasively that irrespective of a woman's reluctance her male relatives would have pursued the crime, and he notes its scarcity where it might be expected: in private journals, as a target for social reformers, an excuse by pregnant girls, a punishment for witches, or as a concomitant to highway robbery.[5]

The plays too take a serious, even censorious view towards at least what they would regard as criminal rape. It figures large as a source of erotic *frisson*, and the excitement it produces is consonant with its relative absence from daily life. Women commit suicide to avoid it, or after suffering from it, or they die of shame. The consensus view in the plays is strongly against forced marriage, seen as equivalent to rape, and hence occurring as a plot motif with great frequency. Women are threatened with prostitution or concubinage, bedded with dying men, or contracted to idiot, senile, impotent, or otherwise unsuitable bridegrooms. The Queen in *Cambises* is made to commit incest, Titania couples with an ass, and Moll in *A Chaste Maid in Cheapside* is destined for an old, diseased lecher.

It would be wrong to assume, however, that other ages necessarily held the same views as we do about rape, especially in societies with little opportunity for the expression of the female point of view, and with radically different views about the relations between the sexes. Just as in the next age John Denis could explain the supposed popularity of fictive rape upon the Restoration stage amongst female spectators: 'For there the woman ... is suppos'd to remain innocent, and to be pleas'd without her Consent', so Fletcher, although one of the first playwrights to appeal specifically to the female spectator, has his choric figure in *Bonduca*, 1613, in resisting the British girls' call for vengeance against the Roman soldiery, remark: 'You should have kept your legs closed, then.' Apparently rape even in these circumstances is the woman's fault.

Rape and Greek myth

The treatment of rape in Elizabethan theatre varied sharply according to historical setting. Heywood takes the Attic equivalent of a Roman holiday from the interminable moralising of his plays in modern settings to stage by far the largest number of successful rapes and forced seductions, including those of Calisto, Deianeira, Alcmena, Proserpine, Danae, and Semele, all of which take place in his *Ages* cycle of five plays re-telling Greek myth. He presumably felt that classical sources gave Olympian sanction for such enthusiastic and salacious accounts. In *The Silver Age*, Alcemena is tricked into what she believes to be wedded consummation, Proserpina is frightened and then carried off in the infernal chariot accompanied by devils to be raped in Hell by Pluto, and Semele is seduced and then consumed in ashes, all within the same play. In *The Brazen Age* Deiandeira is heard being raped offstage by the centaur Nessus. In the first part of *The Iron Age* Oenon, robbed of her virginity, is made to plead unsuccessfully with Paris to honour her.

As well as graphic sexual encounters and the specifics of rape and forced seduction, these scenes also contain a great deal of additional violence to women, both physical and mental. In *The Brazen Age* Omphale has her head bashed in, whilst Hesione is bound to a rock to await a sea monster and, saved from this, is given away much against her will as a concubine. In the final part of *The Iron Age*, Cassandra is dragged onto the stage as a victim, whilst the matrons of Troy, after being threatened and abused, are finally all killed onstage.

Heywood also articulates an enduring masculine fantasy – so deeply grounded as to affect the whole ethos of these all-male representations – that women say 'No' when they mean 'Yes', what Shakespeare in *Richard III* calls the 'maid's part': 'still answer nay, and take it' (III.vii.51). Hence the enduring gratitude women thus forced are supposed to feel towards the rapist for introducing them to sexual pleasure; as is the case with the lasciviously aroused Danae in *The Golden Age*:

([*Re-*] *Enter Jupiter and Danae in her night-gowne*)

DANAE: Alasse, my Lord, I neuer lou'd till now,
       And will you leaue me? [Act IV p. 70]

Zenocrate similarly explains the consequence of her rape by Tamburlaine:

> Although it be digested long agoe,
> As his exceeding favours have deserv'd,
> And might content the Queene of heaven as well,
> As it hath chang'd my first conceiv'd disdaine. (III.ii.9–12)

Ultimately, therefore, it is an argument to justify the use of force in sexual encounters. Preparing his assault on his new-made stepmother, the hero of *Hoffman*, 1602, tells his audience:

> I know
> Women will like how euer they say noe;
> And since my heart is knit vnto her eyes
> If she, being sanctimonious, hate my suit,

> In loue this course ile take, if she denie;
> Force her . . .   (IV.1911–16)

I leywood further complicates matters by reducing his gods to the status of
sixteenth-century monarchs. Jupiter, for instance, is described as the 'King
of Crete', thus blurring a distinction between gods and mortals maintained
much more scrupulously in Greek myth itself where such heavenly encounters serve various ontological functions, and as Froma Zeitlin shows,
mortals in contrast receive very severe punishments. For attempting to
rape Hera, for instance, the mortal Ixion is spread-eagled on an ever-
turning wheel, whilst Tityrus, the giant who attacked Leto, is flung into
Tartarus where vultures perpetually devour his liver.[6]

Rape in contemporary setting

Attempted rape in Elizabethan plays with contemporary settings, by contrast, is almost always unsuccessful. Exceptions tend to occur either as part
of a 'given' situation, as in *The Revenger's Tragedy* where both rapes take
place before the play begins, or they lie in the grey area of the 'seduction',
still a difficult legal distinction, made especially dark in the case of kings
because as with Jane Shore in *Edward IV* the threat of coercion almost
always lies behind their blandishments. In *A Knack to Know a Knave*, 1592,
the king sends an emissary to woo the as yet unseen beauty, saying that if
she is not willing to be his concubine he can 'enforce her love' – the two
words used in a particularly unsavoury conjunction. Significantly, one
early case of actual rape was not repeated. When Shakespeare re-worked
Promos and Cassandra (1578) he was careful to substitute the 'bed-trick' for
the actual violation of the heroine. A remarkably high proportion of
unsuccessful rapists are kings, and the usual formula is that they are
persuaded to give up their lustful attempts by the manifest virtue of their
intended victim, sometimes going on to marry her. To the modern eye
their reformation often seems incongruous, as for instance that of the King
in *Satiromastix*, who, repenting his attack upon the bride Celestina, still
retains sufficient dramatic status to preside over the trial of Horace which
forms the play's focus.

It is Robert Greene perhaps who begins a tradition in which kings
are let off very lightly for the wrongs they do, as in *James IV*, where the
hero attempts the seduction of Ida as well as his Queen's murder but is
resisted by the virtue of the former and redeemed by that of the latter.
Lecherous but unsuccessful Scottish kings feature quite prominently

around 1590, forming something of a theme. James III attempts Jane a Barlay in *George a Greene*, threatening to kill her son if she resists, but when later he is captured by the English he ends good friends with Edward IV, joining him in a merry disguising amongst his subjects; whilst David II, another invading Scot, is frustrated of his designs on the Countess of Salisbury in *Edward III*, whose hero takes over the job himself with greater seriousness but no more success. Heywood in *Royal King and Loyal Subject*, Dekker in *Match Me in London* and *If It Be Not Good the Devil Is In It*, and Fletcher in *The Faithful Friends* continue the theme of lustful kings brought to repentance, one so insistent that again it raises the question of whether it contains a covert attack on the abuse of power.

Roman rape

What really stimulated Elizabethan playwrights were the tales of Roman rape. Clearly separated from contemporary mores but obviously reprehensible, they were accompanied by attractively absolute behaviour on the part of the victims that somehow helped to justify the tradition of luxuriating in the contemplation of their pain and humiliation.

Gossett identifies four plays between 1594 and 1612 containing rapes characterised by having a chaste married victim who must die as a consequence, an attacker condemned, and the victim revenged. Her purpose is to use these plays to contrast with what she identifies as a more dubious treatment of rape in the plays written between 1612 and 1624, in which the heroine survives the rape and even marries the rapist, reflecting, she says, loose Court morals and the popularity of tragi-comedy. Three of her chosen four examples tendered as more scrupulous treatments of the crime, however, are distinguished by having Roman settings: *Titus Andronicus*, Heywood's *Rape of Lucrece*, and *Valentinian*. In them 'the moral condemnation of rape', she insists, 'is constant and unambiguous'. Notwithstanding a clear difference in plot structure, the contrast in the treatment of rape is not really as significant as Gossett would wish, and in each case contains a good deal of ambivalence.

The appalling act which gives Heywood's *Rape of Lucrece* its title, for instance, jostles for attention with the story of the rapist's parents, together with comic songs, a lot of them somewhat anachronistically in Dutch. Its revenge gets caught up in the larger tale of the expulsion of the Tarquins: the evil but heroic Tullia killed by a circle of soldiers as she defends her husband dying with an arrow through his chest, together with such exciting incidents as Horatio defending the bridge, and Mutius Scevola punishing his hand by burning it off in the fire. So much, indeed, has the importance of the rape declined by the end of the play that the final great combat between Brutus the avenger and Sextus the rapist is presented as a heroic one, subject to the rules of chivalry which forbid anyone to interfere between opponents of equal stature. The combatants even begin by exchanging compliments. Brutus says that but for the crime he loves Sextus, and Sextus recognises Brutus' nobility and then says he does not regret his deed. They fight first with sword and target, then with single swords, and finally, both mortally wounded, with gauntlets, the martial delights of the Red Bull presumably predominating. Thus Sextus dies grandly in single combat, and not, as he should, as an abhorred beast. 'The moral condemnation of rape' here can hardly be regarded as either 'constant' or 'unambiguous'.

'Titus Andronicus'

It is perhaps not surprising but entirely inappropriate for modern studies to assume that Shakespeare shares our views about rape and that he wrote *Titus Andronicus* and his poem 'The Rape of Lucrece' to express them. Such studies roll together two very different artefacts with different contexts and antecedents. C. R. Stimpson, for instance, would have it that:

Shakespeare acutely shows – through Lucrece's speeches, through Lavinia's amputations – the agony a woman experiences after rape.[7]

The amputations are indeed a key issue – but as an indicator not of Shakespeare's sympathy for the victim's sufferings nor a symbol of the act of rape, but of a world of *grand guignol*, insulating audience and performers by its excesses from any serious relationship with reality; excesses not restricted to Lavinia's loss of hands and tongue, but including Titus tricked into allowing Aaron to chop off his hand and Tamora eating her own children.

DEMETRIUS: So now go tell, and if thy tongue can speak,
            Who 'twas that cut thy tongue and ravish'd thee.
CHIRON: Write down thy mind, bewray thy meaning so,
            And if thy stumps will let thee play the scribe . . .
CHIRON: And 'twere my cause, I should go hang myself.
DEMETRIUS: If thou hadst hands to help thee knit the cord.   (II.iv.1–4, 9–10)

Beyond a certain point, the more extreme the crimes and the suffering, the *less* the spectator responds with any sympathy that is not mixed with black humour. When Titus receives for the sacrifice of his hand not, as he had believed, his sons alive but only their severed heads, his brother takes off one head, but father and daughter are left onstage with two properties to be removed and but a single working hand between them by which Titus removes his son's head. Lavinia must therefore carry away her father's freshly severed hand in her mouth. We shiver, but we also chuckle.

Nor should it be forgotten, as it so often is in modern accounts, that this black humour and its attitude to rape and mutilation are the creation of an all-male ensemble. High on the list of what would be difficult to achieve convincingly in this context, were that their aim, must surely be the anticipation of rape from a female perspective. Almost any performance is going to betray gender disparity in a display of some element of male fantasies of conquest.

It is a highly selective reading of the text that can ignore the very considerable salacious pleasure that is taken in the events leading up to Lavinia's forced removal. Her own uncharacteristically uppity taunting of Tamora and her 'raven-coloured love' for their adultery, 'singled forth to try thy experiments', sets her up for humiliation. More than sixty lines separate the first suggestion of her ravishment:

DEMETRIUS: First thrash the corn, then after burn the straw . . .   (II.iii.123)

– already proposed in the previous scene – and their departure to it, during which anticipation rises as the chaste young wife, with long blonde hair (if the source is anything to go by), kneels and begs to retain her integrity before the savage, lascivious, immovable, barbarian Empress, clasping the hem of her gown in supplication, an image that incorporates both current erotic stereotypes and the rhetorical power they possess; whilst at either side, her two sons, already encouraged by Aaron to satisfy their longing for Lavinia by rape, chafe at the bit. And to prime them, Shakespeare lets slip a characteristic pun in Lavinia's final plea:

O, keep me from their worse than killing lust,
And tumble me into some loathsome pit . . .   (II.iii.176–7)

To avoid being 'tumbled' in what T. C. Onions calls the 'indelicate sense', she begs to be 'tumbled . . . into'. Whether the psychological slip is put down to author or character, it amounts to the same thing: the central interest of the exchange lies not in sympathy for the victim, or moral judgement – this pun sidesteps either – but in the horrid event itself, and this is confirmed again by the amount of stage time given over to its anticipation.

Shakespeare's 'Rape of Lucrece'

Coppélia Kahn's essay on the poem argues that Shakespeare presents Lucrece as a victim of the patriarchal concept of marriage, in which wives are hyperbolically chaste and the possessions of their husbands, so that the torment for Lucrece is the compromise of her honour, and he invites the reader, she says, to see the inadequacies of this concept. This allows Kahn to show yet again the oppressions and limitations of male domination and comfortingly to recruit Shakespeare to that end.[8] It is a construction that *can* be put upon the poem, but the sentiments that accompany the depiction of rape are of much less significance than that an artefact is made on this subject. It shares with a whole group of poems by Marlowe and others a tactile sensuousness, here to do with blotting the unblemished white purity of Lucrece, which hovers about the central question of why the outraging of virtue is such an insistently satisfying trope.

Judith Dundas tries to enlist the powers of drama to sustain what she calls the 'illusion' of the poem, contrasting the 'reality' of the presentation of Lucrece with the painting of Troy on her wall, finding the latter a perspective device like an inner play:

In *Lucrece* there is a similar irony in the contrast between the heroine's own life-and-death situation and the 'well-painted piece', which can be admired as artifact, regardless of the suffering portrayed.[9]

This is difficult to accept. The whole poem seems artificial in the extreme. Even at key moments metaphor dominates the description, the piece has an insistent stanza form that calls attention to itself, and the narrator frequently sets the figures at a distance by describing rather than repeating what they say. As Ian Donaldson observes:

There is a sense – so rare in Shakespeare's work as to be doubly remarkable – that the central moral complexities of the story are in some ways curiously evaded, while the simpler outlying issues are decoratively elaborated.[10]

Despite Dundas' objections, the real context of Shakespeare's poem is that of Renaissance art. By the time he was writing, rape had become a commonplace subject in European painting. Correggio's *Io*, for instance, painted for Charles V, is described by Norman Bryson as 'ravishment by a divine cloud which caresses every single pore of skin, and thus surpasses the limitations of the natural lover'.[11] The 'brutal myth' of Lucretia, says Donaldson, by then a popular subject for painters, had been 'ameliorated through art . . . and . . . transformed into an experience aesthetically pleasing to the beholder', or as Samuel Butler put it more crudely:

there are more bawdy pictures made of Lucrece, the Martyr of chastity, than ever were of all the common Prostitutes of all Ages and Nations in the whole world.

It is dangerous, however, to make a simple equivalence across different art forms. Painting has a distinctive agenda, arising, as might be argued of theatre, out of the formal possibilities and limitations of its own nature. Primarily in this period it was concerned with exploring and expressing the human form and its beauty; hence the attractions of a naked Lucrece, even, in contradiction to the story, in suicide; fictive context, or intellectual or moral constructions put upon it, were of much less importance. There are plenty of 'bawdy', or at least sexy, pictures of the Virgin Mary, if that is the viewer's construction, but essentially bodies are not of themselves either moral or immoral.[12]

One of the limitations of painting is that the result is static. Painters went to great lengths to try to circumvent this and make their poses excitingly momentary. They also combined more than one moment in the same painting. Titian's *Tarquin and Lucretia*, c.1570, for instance, rather than being Bryson's 'conundrum' of 'a man who rapes, and a woman who seduces', i.e. two simultaneous actions, can be read instead from left to right as a *sequence* of actions: Tarquin's threat, knife upraised, *is followed by* Lucretia's acquiescence, her left hand yielding, or even grasping, which may be an automatic response to lessen the effects of the violence threatened (lines 344–5), rather than a manifestation of desire. Hence one of the opportunities which the picture-form offers, echoed in Shakespeare's poem, where Donaldson sees it as introducing 'a fatal element of moral uncertainty', is the presentation of *both sides* of the encounter, and, precisely because it is so static and available for contemplation, of the ambiguity, the complex dynamics, inherent in any coupling.

Shakespeare's alternatives to physical rape

It is very evident that many of Shakespeare's earliest plays, partly perhaps because of his juniority in the company, are either derivative or strongly

influenced by current fashions that he later rejected as he gained not only
his own voice but also his own performance style. After the rape, mutilation, and murders of *Titus Andronicus*, he was subsequently much less
inclined than many of his contemporaries to show men offering physical
violence onstage to women; the exceptions, therefore, being the more
moving. Samuel Johnson could scarcely bring himself to read the death
of Cordelia, and the violence in *Othello* stands out as horrifying. Lady
Macduff's slaughter serves to represent the slide of a whole kingdom into
barbarism. Where there is violence, it is often by women to other women,
as Margaret to Eleanor, Goneril to Regan, or Kate to Bianca; or it is suicide:
Juliet, Ophelia, Lady Macbeth, Cleopatra and her maids, all take their
own lives.

Once again, his motivation is perhaps more technical than moral, since
violence against women – other than the straightforwardly physical –
remains an important feature of his plays, but Shakespeare finds new and
more effective ways to dramatise it. He, as it were, 'metaphoricalises'
violence, even to forced penetration, by verbal analogues and symbolic
action. This allows him better to control the passage of time as it relates to
violence – always difficult when actually presented onstage – enabling
more anticipation, and for the central event to be played as if in slow
motion. It avoids too all the inherent bathos and inadvertent humour in
trying to represent realistic sexual violence in an all-male theatre.[13]

Even before *Titus Andronicus*, he was developing this new approach.
Deep in the texture of Gloucester's wooing of Lady Anne in *Richard III*
there is an unspoken association between blood and sex. It is implied that
it is his violence that attracts her. Whilst he does not offer this directly, his
wooing is built on former violence towards her relatives to which he
continues to draw attention. His manner is aggressive and manipulative
and at the appropriate moment he does offer to let *her* commit violence
on him. This is itself a kind of violence, in forcing on her a male definition
of sexual polarities and humbling her by making her acknowledge the
vulnerable inadequacy of her own gender. Effectively he dismisses her
verbal protestations by replacing them with stage action, using the sexual
symbolism already inherent in two common theatre properties, a sword
and a ring, in which she must either respond in kind or submit to his
solicitation:

[*He lays his breast open: she offers at [it] with his sword*]

GLOUCESTER: Nay, do not pause: for I did kill King Henry –
             But 'twas thy beauty that provoked me.

Nay, now dispatch: 'twas I that stabb'd young Edward –
But 'twas thy heavenly face that set me on.
[*She falls the sword*]
Take up the sword again, or take up me.   (I.ii.179–83)

She follows decorum: a woman cannot wield the phallic sword; and in her failure lies submission, which is increasingly the undertow of her subsequent equivocation:

GLOUCESTER: Vouchsafe to wear this ring.
ANNE: To take is not to give.
GLOUCESTER: Look how my ring encompasseth thy finger,
  Even so thy breast encloseth my poor heart;   (I.ii.201–4)

Thus by a second physical action, itself an image of coitus, he effectively completes his wooing; whilst her failure, twice, to resist with physical action seals her capitulation.

Hamlet's behaviour towards Ophelia in III.ii at the performance of the 'Mousetrap' alternates intimacy, insults, and sexual suggestiveness with an undertow of violence, hinting that he might take her, without affection, at any time he chose: 'It would cost you a groaning to take off mine edge.' It is said in a publicly shaming manner, and following so soon on his violent rejection of her in the 'Nunnery' scene, keeps her ever uncertain and apprehensive as to how next – verbally or physically – he might assault her vulnerability.

The culmination of this line of treatment is undoubtedly Iachimo's proxy rape of Imogen in *Cymbeline*. It begins in I.vi with his ingratiating himself through the fulsome recommendation of Posthumus. He then praises her in a tone so tasteless as to suggest hidden menace:

Sluttery, to such neat excellence oppos'd,
Should make desire vomit emptiness,
Not so allur'd to feed.   (I.vi.44–6)

He goes on to suggest with increasing frankness that Posthumus is not valuing her matchless worth but instead 'vaulting various ramps', i.e. satisfying himself with Italian prostitutes. He suggests she should revenge herself, and when she cannot comprehend his meaning, offers to help her and demands a kiss on the lips. When she recoils in anger and threatens to tell her father the King, he pretends to have been testing her virtue. There is in his speech an overall nastiness, a gratuitous offensiveness, which constitutes in itself a kind of sexual assault. He is somehow threateningly here and there and all around her. His manner is variously suggestive, intimate, obsequious, and uneven perhaps in its delivery; almost psychotic. It is by no means clear from the text when he is addressing Imogen, when the audience, and when himself.

Finally, when she is mollified, he introduces the topic of the trunk, supposedly full of rich gifts for the Emperor, and seeks her permission to store it overnight in her bedchamber. She replies, 'Willingly; / And pawn my honour for their safety'. The irony is unlikely to have been missed. An audience comes to the theatre in all conditions, and no allusion will be taken by everyone. On the other hand, trunks, baskets, and chests were regular hiding places on the Elizabethan stage. They feature prominently in *Singing Simpkin* and in *The Merry Wives of Windsor*. There is a well-known painting by Breughel of a stage performance apparently showing the cuckolded husband returning home in a basket on someone's back. The most direct analogue is Geraldine's ruse to seduce Maria in *The Family of Love*, 1602. Hence it is likely that some of the audience at least would expect the trunk to contain Iachimo and have some suspicion of carnal intentions.

Act, II Scene ii begins with Imogen pushed on in the stage bed, dismissing her attendant, and going to sleep. All attention is on the trunk, surely downstage in the very centre of the auditorium. There is a slight movement, and the lid slowly opens to a mixed response of apprehension and amusement. Provokingly, Iachimo's first image of himself as he crosses to the bed is that of 'Our' Tarquin, a reminder of their shared nationality:

> Our Tarquin thus
> Did softly press the rushes ere he waken'd
> The chastity he wounded. (II.ii.12–4)

All is thus set for a physical assault. Instead, it takes the form of a symbolic rape, a destruction of her honour, an intrusion into her sanctuary. He removes a bracelet, and then examines her body for some intimate detail for the 'madding of her lord':

> On her left breast
> A mole cinque-spotted, like the crimson drops
> I'th'bottom of a cowslip. (II.ii.37–9)

It is a clever scene, making the most of anticipation and curiosity, erotic in his description of Imogen as some beautiful, venerated object, a partially clad young woman lying asleep in her bed, and in the lurking potential violence that might be done to her; yet requiring little of the performers and skirting well clear of impropriety or bathos.

Imogen and the attractions of vulnerability

The singular unpleasantness of Iachimo's initial wooing of Imogen is matched by Cloten's obscenities as he plans to serenade her:

> I would this music would come. I am advis'd to give
> her music a'mornings; they say it will penetrate.
> [*Enter Musicians*] Come on tune. If you can penetrate her
> with your fingering, so; we'll try with tongue too. (II.iii.11–15)

Unlike the concentration in *Richard III* on the active male protagonist, for whom the ineffectual Lady Anne is only one of a series of dupes to demonstrate his cleverness, Imogen is the passive centre of this play, to whom, desired and vulnerable, the action as well as all eyes repeatedly turn. Brought on in male attire by her admiring brothers, apparently dead, funeral rites are said over her body. Waking from her drug, she swoons with grief over the headless corpse of what she takes to be her husband, where she is found by the Roman general Lucius. In the final scene she is knocked to the ground in the crowded court, which presumably parts round her prone body as efforts are made to revive her. In this she momentarily echoes a developing tradition in Shakespeare's work in which female characters are presented as sacrificial victims, and their sleeping, dead, or comatose bodies form the focus of the action and symbol of loss: Juliet drugged in her bed on her wedding day; Ophelia in her coffin; Desdemona on her bed, murdered; and possibly the most touching moment in the canon, the lifeless body of Cordelia carried on by Lear.

On the face of it, this increased concentration on the female situation would seem to accord with Kaja Silverman's view, discussing the modern film and novel, that:

> it is always the victim – the figure who occupies the passive position – who is really the focus of attention, and whose subjugation the subject (whether male or female) experiences as pleasurable repetition of his/her own history. Indeed, I would go so far as to say that the fascination of the sadistic point of view is merely that it provides the best vantage point from which to watch the masochistic story unfold.[14]

Such a theory promises to do much to offset the dominance of the 'male gaze', but the difficulty of applying it to Shakespeare is that he resorts to particular formal techniques to present his heroines at moments of crisis all of which distance and contain female suffering: the artifice of madness, the framed pageant of sleepwalking, the poetic/retrospective 'inset' accounts of Julia and Viola, or Desdemona's Willow Song, to which the black humour of Lavinia's treatment or the choric devices around Cressida may have some analogies. Thus the viewpoint, authorially, in enactment, and in reception, remains firmly male. Even as wrongs are being done to women in Shakespeare's plays, the spectator is invited to sympathise with the husband, the father – even the perpetrator – and *his* sense of loss; so that it is Lear's agony at Cordelia's murder that is the centre of attention, and her mute body only its object. This is not to deny sympathy to the victim, but places it at one step removed, inviting pity rather than identification.

Silverman conceives of the male spectator as entering empathetically into the feelings of the victim. He 'now thinks from the place of the Other, with the language of the Other; enacts the scenario of the Other'. Transferred to the Elizabethan context, however, of lightly drawn, generally subordinated characters, Silverman's repetition of 'Other' is a reminder that putting oneself 'in the place of', is not necessarily bringing oneself 'closer to' the fictitious victim, when her very two-dimensional quality becomes more evident. Hermione in *The Winter's Tale* and Queen Katherine in *Henry VIII* are female victims whose ultimate passivity is conditioned by a noble, public, well-articulated, self-defence. When Hermione is brought to trial, she catalogues the cruelties and injustices to which she has been subject: denied Leontes' favour, her little son barred from her, her baby snatched away whilst suckling to be murdered, herself proclaimed strumpet on every post, and finally dragged from her childbed before she has recovered. She is a kind of cross-gender marvel, charming and fetching in her distress, and yet ultimately self-reliant. No woman under like conditions could have been so strong and yet so fragile. She replies to the charges against her with such cogency and rationality and yet such simplicity and lack of malice as to be nowhere more obviously a male construction; it is how *we* in our fantasies would have behaved. These characters are not so much serious examples of Kimbrough's androgynous perfection, or testimonies to some universal female pluckiness, as temporary wish-fulfilment fantasies of resilient fragility, like Imogen and Bellario, capitalising on a performance circumstance (and a particularly suitable performer). Thus neither player not spectator has ultimately any profound commitment to the female character being represented, and sympathy for the victim is aesthetic, and thereby contemplative and distanced, rather than immediate and truly heartfelt. Whatever the more general shortcomings of modern fiction and modern cinema, Silverman clearly demonstrates vistas which they offer in this regard that genuinely reflect real experience which, whilst the 'privileging' of the victim by the insistent and sympathetic concentration on Imogen might be seen to anticipate such a development, are really not available in a cross-dressed performance tradition, especially one descending into the false theatricality and contrived indulgences of tragi-comedy.

Imogen's catalogue of predicaments is the culmination of a topos in Shakespeare's work in which the situation of the comic heroine is precarious, ever threatened with violence: Silvia by rape, Hermia by her father and the law, Rosalind by Frederick, Viola at the end of the play by Orsino, Helena by death if she fails to cure the King, Isabella variously throughout, Marina with prostitution, Perdita with mutilation by Polixenes, and Miranda with rape by Stephano. Michael Shapiro links this phenomenon with Northrop Frye's 'ritual theme of the triumph of life and love over the waste land', in which the heroine undergoes threats to her chastity and loss of identity before finally winning through.[15] Imogen too wins through, but the concentration of the play is much more on her as potential victim. Repeatedly she is threatened with physical harm: incarcerated by her father; the object of a plot to be poisoned by the Queen; violently and foully propositioned, spied on, and betrayed by Iachimo; menaced with rape by Cloten; sentenced to death as a Roman by her father; and finally struck by her husband Posthumus, the only harm actually to materialise. In the tragi-comic mode such characters become less actual symbols of redemption than picaresque objects for repeated *frisson*.

The aesthetics of suffering

When Hrosvitha has the Christian-martyr heroines of her tenth-century playlets, written in the monastery at Gandersheim, suffer onstage the most horrific torments and mutilation, as in *Sapientia* in which they are scourged, their nipples cut off, themselves roasted on a gridiron – a 'sadism', Rosamond Gilder notes, 'associated with certain aspects of (monastic) repression' – they suffer all without pain because of their faith.[16] They do so in imitation of their Saviour, who looks down on them in contemporary representations alive and serene in his torment. Only later did the Renaissance concentrate on his human suffering, culminating in the dead meat of Grunewald's late Gothic depictions. Christ spread-eagled on the Cross, in the female position, naked and vulnerable, subject to the torment of thorns, pierced by the phallic spear, was given pride of place above the altar, the focus of all eyes during the ceremony of worship, creating an aesthetic of sado-masochism at the very heart of this religion; and echoed in much subsequent hagiography, especially that of St Sebastian, so popular in Italian churches that he frequently provides a visual counterpoint to the Saviour.

The Dream of the Rood is an early English testimony of the enduring Christian interest in the aesthetics of suffering. The poem empathises with the experiences of the tree which became the Cross on which the naked Christ was crucified:

Then the young Hero – He was God almighty – firm and unflinching, stripped Himself . . . I trembled when the Hero clasped me . . . As a rood was I raised up . . . They pierced me with dark nails; the wounds are still plain to view in me, gaping gashes of malice . . . They bemocked us both together. I was all bedewed with blood, shed from the Man's side . . .[17]

The final scene of *Othello* contains a beautiful description of the sacrificial victim. It recalls in its sensuousness the whole twisted tradition in Christian art of focusing on the Crucifixion, its skin tones so dexterously picked out by the Renaissance particularly in its sculpture:

> Yet I'll not shed her blood,
> Nor scar that whiter skin of hers than snow,
> And smooth as monumental alabaster.   (v.ii.3–5)

Othello kisses Desdemona before he kills her and, as he smells her fragrance, feels a moment's hesitation. Then he cannot prevent himself from kissing her again and fantasising that he will kill and then love – necrophilia, the ultimate solution to inconstancy:

> Be thus when thou art dead, and I will kill thee
> And love thee after.   (v.ii.18–9)

Certainly there are opportunities in Elizabethan theatre to indulge compensatory fantasies of revenge on uppity women and those who threaten male sexuality. What distinguishes the aesthetics of Shakespeare's treatment of female suffering, however, is that it is almost always visited upon the young, beautiful, well-born – *and virtuous*; and hence the focus is rarely on revenge or justice but on unmerited punishment, the dominant theme again of religious iconography.[18] Whilst the punishment of female sexual transgression can be enjoyed by the male spectator without any feelings of guilt, the pleasures of punishing the innocent are altogether greater and more perverse: the despoliation of female purity, the surprise of the victim, her inability to fathom the motive or extent of the enfolding punishment; the equipoise of a fragile, well-proportioned young female in bloom suddenly, deliciously, discomposed by embarrassment, fear, anticipation, and violence; the extra blush to the cheeks, perturbation of the bosom. Since there is no justification for the punishment, so too there need be no end. Hero in *Much Ado*, beautiful, innocent, and vulnerable, dressed as an emblem of purity at the altar about to be married is accused by her intended husband of monstrous immodesty with an unknown agent: 'vile encounters they have had / A thousand times in secret'. She has no defence against this false accusation, the public humiliation, and the unaccustomed harsh words which violate her purity over and over again like physical incisions: 'Her blush is guiltlessness, not modesty.' She is a 'rotten orange', an 'approved wanton', a 'common stale':

> you are more intemperate in your blood
> Than Venus, or those pamp'red animals
> That rage in savage sensuality. (IV.i.59–61)

It is one of the cruellest and most savage attacks in the canon, at once excruciating and exquisite.

We never learn what Orsino intends to do with Viola when he thinks his page has betrayed him:

Come, boy, with me, my thoughts are ripe in mischief. (V.i.29)

– but Viola has no hesitation in obeying him:

OLIVIA: Where goes Cesario?
VIOLA: After him I love
More than I love these eyes, more than my life . . . (V.i.134–5)

Why should she fear for her eyes?

Algolagnia

When in *The Winter's Tale* Polixenes finally tires of his son's obstinate determination to wed in secret and throws aside his disguise, he turns to Perdita, the simple country girl he takes to have trapped his princely son, and threatens her with mutilation: 'I'll have thy beauty scratch'd with briars and made / More homely than thy state.' People at what he takes to be her level of society have no right to be beautiful. Later in the same speech, he promises: 'a death as cruel . . . / As thou art tender to't' (IV.iv.440–1). Shakespeare thus has him posit an inverse ratio between cruelty and tenderness, and anticipates the aesthetics of the criminal in de Sade's novel *Juliette* who obtains greater brutal pleasure if the victim is innocent or virtuous and who says, 'beauty excites us more'.

By far the commonest form of assault and murder of women on the Elizabethan stage was by stabbing. It is, of course, a very effective and practical piece of stage business, especially if accompanied by appropriate responses from the player of the victim. The principal property, a retractable dagger, was readily at hand, illustrated in Reginald Scot's *Discovery of Witchcraft*, 1584, and used by the Scottish Prickers to increase their trade in witches. Strangulation was equally practical and effective, but there are only two examples in the plays under discussion compared with fifteen actual or threatened stabbings. The phallic significance of stabbing, especially on an all-male stage, needs no labouring, but its significance goes further in demonstrating what Geoffrey Gorer, in defining the term *algolagnia*, calls the 'intimate connection between sex and pain'. De Sade wrote:

Sex is to the other passions what the nervous fluid is to life; it supports them all, lends strength to them all . . . ambition, cruelty, avarice, revenge, are all founded on sex.[19]

As Christianity had drawn aesthetic pleasure from the pains of the Crucifixion and from the numerous martyrdoms that followed it, so the Elizabethan dramatists are conditioned at moments *in extremis* to equate sex and pain. A number of examples have already been noted. In *Measure for Measure*, Isabella says she would sooner die than yield her body up to Angelo, but the way in which she is made to conceive of death is itself as a lascivious act:

> were I under the terms of death,
> Th' impression of keen whips I' ld wear as rubies,
> And strip myself to death, as to a bed
> That longing have been sick for . . .   (II.iv.100f.)

This image of repressed and thereby perverted sexuality is answered in Angelo's subsequent threat to torture her brother before he kills him if she does not yield; thus his satisfaction in Claudio's pain, presumably through some sort of intrusion into his body – 'ling'ring sufferance' most usually included disembowelment – will compensate for the lost pleasures of coitus with her.

The high regard in which the Elizabethans held chastity scarcely explains the frequency with which women in the plays faced with violation or guilty of unchastity are made to beg for mutilation as an alternative punishment. Celia is still loyal to her husband and her marriage, even when he seeks to prostitute her in Volpone's bed for mercenary gain. When she resists his proposal, offering instead to take poison or eat hot coals, Corvino threatens her with terrible punishments:

> I will . . . rip up
> Thy mouth, unto thine ears; and slit thy nose
> Like a wraw rotchet . . .
> I will buy some slave,
> Whom I will kill, and bind thee to him, alive;
> And at my window, hang you forth: devising
> Some monstrous crime, which I, in capital letters
> Will eat into thy flesh, with aquafortis,
> And burning corsives, on this stubborn breast.　　　(III.vii.96–105)

When Volpone turns out to be gamesome rather than near death's door, Celia, automatically taking the blame, sues for alternatives to seduction:

> Yet feed your wrath, sir, rather than your lust . . .
> And punish that unhappy crime of nature,
> Which you miscall my beauty: flay my face,
> Or poison it, with ointments, for seducing
> Your blood to rebellion. Rub these hands,
> With what may cause an eating leprosy,
> E'en to my bones, and marrow: anything,
> That may disfavour me, save in my honour.　　　(III.vii.249–57)

In this, Celia and her husband speak the same language of mutilation – Jonson's, Roman models notwithstanding, which no amount of discussion will excuse.

CHAPTER 7

Positive representations of young women

Shakespeare, as in most things, did not invent the romantic comedy genre. Lyly with his static, decorative, Court conversation-pieces for the Children, and Greene's boisterous, good-hearted but essentially thin and under-developed romances both preceded him, but in neither case were the female roles developed much beyond simple stereotypes. In Greene's *Looking Glass for London* the women are all dusky wantons, Iphigenia in *Alphonsus King of Aragon* shows a good deal of courage, but in general his heroines, as in *James IV*, *Friar Bacon and Friar Bungay*, and *Orlando Furioso*, are simple studies in female virtue with little by way of distinguishing features. Prince Edward in *Friar Bacon* falls in love with Margaret, the Fair Maid of Fressingfield, and sends Lacy the Earl of Lincoln to woo her for him, but when she shows that her inclination is for the Earl, he confronts the couple with drawn poniard. Impressed, however, by their mutual affection he relents, and immediately remembers that there is a bride waiting for him newly arrived at Oxford, Eleanor of Castille, to whom he presses his suit with alacrity in the next scene. Lacy, having accompanied him back to Court, sends word that he too is to wed a Spanish lady, and Margaret resolves to become a nun. When, however, at the end of the play Lacy returns to reveal his letter was a test of her constancy, she has little difficulty in accepting him. The women are thus almost entirely passive, as well as interchangeable.

Shakespeare's young women in his romantic comedies by contrast are active, enabling, even redemptive, often in breeches or other disguise. They are witty and self-confident, usually well-born, always beautiful, and they bring with them a new sense of serenity and good-humour. Many of them are aristocratic young women, often unencumbered by parents, even like Olivia and Portia mistresses of their own estates, with marked social confidence in dealing with servants and lovers. Their plays tend to be set around the Mediterranean, in 'fruitful Lombardy, / The pleasant garden of great Italy', or in the stately Renaissance cities of Milan, Venice, Verona, or

Messina, with associations of sunlight, riches, art, and scholarship, or in beautiful Italian country villas like Belmont, or they belong to neighbouring countries like Illyria or France. Such associations always rub shoulders with those of contemporary England, particularly in the low-comedy characters, but, as in the Athens of *A Midsummer Night's Dream*, not so as to negate a kind of sylvan sensuousness that in reflecting the positive elements of pantheism in British alongside Renaissance culture gives the romantic characters dignity as well as eroticism.

Unlike earlier heroines such as Iphiginia, Bel-Imperia, or Dorothea, who only respond to events, this new breed of young woman is much more likely to take the initiative, and tends, as with Portia and Rosalind, to be in control of the situation, especially in matters of affection. Love had long been the ostensible topic of much comedy, but the focus had generally been on the means by which it was achieved, on the plots, stratagems, and tricks by which the older generation were manipulated and deceived; the object being to get the girl *and* the dowry. Mutual attraction in New Comedy was always taken as read, even to the extent that some plays scarcely required anything of the girl herself; indeed, in Terence's *The Girl from Andros* the eponymous heroine never appears at all. Although there are echoes of this tradition in the sub-plots of *The Merry Wives of Windsor* and *The Taming of the Shrew*, with very lightly drawn heroines at the centre of complex webs of plots to attain them, more frequently in Shakespeare's plays attention is focused on the nature of love itself, on how people fall in and out of love. Parents tend to disappear from view or are treated more sympathetically than in New Comedy, and the barriers to the successful consummation of their passion come to be found in the characters of the lovers themselves, leading eventually in the Dark Comedies to serious cases of incompatibility, as in *Troilus and Cressida* and *All's Well*.

The love which overcomes all obstacles to fulfilment is one of the strongest dramatic motifs, engaging universal sympathy in its enactment of the natural cycle, and one of the oldest. It first appears in the English adult repertory in *The Rare Triumphs of Love and Fortune*, 1582, in part showing the influence of the Italian *commedia erudita*, drawn directly from classical New Comedy, behind which stands the shadowy outline of Old Comedy and its emergence from fertility rite. The daughter always wins out because beneath her apparent virtue, modesty, and compliance, she is the facilitator of her own successful and necessary coupling with an appropriately virile mate. Thus it is that the stress on marital fidelity and obedience in the broad canon of the adult repertory is coupled, perhaps surprisingly, with a widespread tolerance of headstrong daughters and love-matches. The two love-plots of *The Shoemaker's Holiday* illustrate this. A high value is put on wifely loyalty when Jane's husband is falsely reported dead in the war; whereas the imperatives of romantic love easily outweigh the duties of a daughter in the Rose sub-plot, in which the hero Simon Eyre facilitates the outwitting of both parents, an elopement for the young lovers, and a clandestine marriage.

Contemporary Italian comedy incorporates social satire and invokes inter-generational conflict. There is rarely any sympathy for fathers, who go to great lengths to make their daughters obey. Occasionally Elizabethan plays take the same tone. In *1 Honest Whore*, the Duke has his daughter drugged, subjected to a mock burial, and then kept in seclusion at Bergamo, whilst in *The Thracian Wonder* the father sets his pregnant daughter adrift in an oarless boat; but all, of course, to no avail, the girls being eventually reunited with their lovers. More usually, especially in the plays of Shakespeare, a more equitable view is taken of the two elements in the relationship. Marriage malpractices such as buying wardships and marrying the ward, as in *The Blind Beggar of Bethnal Green*, *The Family of Love*, and *Bartholomew Fair*, auctioning the daughter to the highest bidder, as in *The Taming of the Shrew*, or ignoring her inclinations, as in *The Merry Wives of Windsor*, are generally lambasted. On the other hand, girls who flout or deceive their parents like Juliet and Desdemona are sometimes seen coming to grief.

A sensible parent chooses wisely for his daughter, taking both her wishes and her best interests into account. *Romeo and Juliet* initially demonstrates precisely that inter-relation of arranged marriage and love-match in a well-regulated family. Capulet, before his later reversion to the Pantalone stereotype, makes it clear in I.ii that his approval is dependent on Paris winning Juliet's consent. She in turn (I.iii.97f.) says she will 'look to like' (i.e. look favourably) on a recommended suitor, but will not proceed without her parents' approval; hence a well-brought up young lady chooses amongst those previously vetted as suitable by her parents. Her obedience, however, as Beatrice schools Hero in *Much Ado*, is dependent on her wishes being taken into account:

ANTONIO [*TO HERO*]: Well, niece, I trust you will be rul'd by your father.
BEATRICE: Yes, faith, it is my cousin's duty to make cur'sy and say, 'Father, as it please you.' But yet for all that, cousin, let him be a handsome fellow, or else make another cur'sy and say, 'Father, as it please me.'   (II.i.50–6)

Thus a girl like Anne Page in *The Merry Wives of Windsor*, when her parents are each fielding unsuitable matches of their own, is justified in taking matters into her own hands, as Fenton makes clear:

> You would have married her most shamefully,
> Where there was no proportion held in love ...
> Th'offense is holy that she hath committed,
> And this deceit loses the name of craft ...   (v.v.221f.)

Not only are the girls witty, self-confident, romantic and loyal, they are also practical, much more so than their lovers. In *Romeo and Juliet*, a tragedy, but sharing much of the tone and mood of these comedies, Juliet amidst all the Petrarchan love poetry, asks:

> How camest thou hither, tell me, and wherefore?
> The orchard walls are high and hard to climb ...   (II.ii.62–3)

To which the giddy Romeo replies:

> With love's light wings did I o'erperch these walls ...   (II.ii.66)

By the end of the scene she has settled that they will marry on the morrow. He merely has to send a message, 'Where and what time thou will perform the rite.' Shakespeare's young women, from *Two Gentlemen of Verona* onwards, observe their own kind of propriety but at the same time are honest to their growing sexual feelings and prepared to take action when the opportunity occurs to get what they want.

Shakespeare's heroines are frequently associated directly with Flora, the Spring, goddess of flowers, the miraculous element that turns the natural sequence of birth, death, and decay through re-birth into a cycle. Perdita in *The Winter's Tale*, 'prank'd up' as Flora for the Sheep-shearing, is, of course, the lost daughter whose recovery will redeem her parents back into the land of the living from the symbolic winter in which they are both suspended. Her mythic status is acknowledged in her welcome to the country wenches, the slight objects of an essentially self-referential disquisition on the flowers of maidenhood, that begins:

> O Proserpina,
> For the flow'rs now, that, frighted, thou let'st fall
> From Dis's waggon ...   (IV.iv.116–18)

The effect of associating his young women with classical deities is, of course, to elevate and idealise them, whilst being eulogised in terms of flowers is to emphasise both their beauty and its precious ephemerality:

ORSINO: Fair women are like roses, whose fair flow'r
  Being once displayed, doth fall that very hour.
VIOLA: And so they are; alas, that they are so.   (II.iv.238–40)

Ophelia in her second mad entrance (IV.v.155f.) carries flowers, each of
which has an appropriate association for the courtier to whom she gives it; a
kind of parody of Proserpine, but a reminder too that the latter is also
associated with death, as well as being an anticipation of Ophelia's own. At
her grave Laertes wishes that 'from her fair and unpolluted flesh / May
violets spring'.

Imogen in *Cymbeline* is continually associated with flowers. Iachimo
(II.ii.15) describes her as 'a fresh lily, / And whiter than the sheets', which is
echoed by Guiderius (IV.ii.201) of her disguise as Fidele, believing that she
is dead, 'O sweetest, fairest lily', whilst Arviragus apostrophises her supposed corpse:

> With fairest flowers
> Whilst summer lasts and I live here, Fidele,
> I'll sweeten thy sad grave. Thou shalt not lack
> The flower that's like thy face, pale primrose, nor
> The azur'd harebell, like thy veins; no, nor
> The leaf of eglantine, whom not to slander,
> Outsweet'ned not thy breath.   (IV.ii.218–24)

A flower image is likewise used by Capulet in *Romeo and Juliet* to mark
what he believes to be his own daughter's death:

> Death lies on her like an untimely frost
> Upon the sweetest flower of all the field.   (IV.v.28–9)

Flowers are repeatedly associated with a premature death that leaves
female sexuality unfulfilled. Ophelia begins her first mad scene singing
of the flowers that larded the snow-white shroud on her father's corpse
(IV.v.36f.), the snow carrying over to suggest the flowers died before they
reached the consummation of being brought to the ground by 'true-love
showers', which I take to be phallic in the Aeschylean sense,[1] and to refer
to her own uncompleted state, a theme alluded to in Gertrude's description of the garland of weeds Ophelia made before her death, which
included:

> long purples
> That liberal shepherds give a grosser name,
> But our cull-cold maids do dead men's fingers call them.
>
> (IV.viii.169–71)

Elements of objectivity and humour in their portrayal

The transitory beauty which Shakespeare sees in the young female, with all its regenerative, resilient qualities, its energy and optimism, is thus associated with sexual awakening. In *The Two Gentlemen of Verona* he treats this with a certain indulgent humour, offering Julia at a distance, 'constructing' herself in a manner not much in advance of Mal Barnes. In I.ii she prettily feigns her indifference to Proteus for the benefit of her waiting-maid Lucetta, convinced of its effectiveness:

> How angerly I taught my brow to frown,
> When inward joy enforc'd my heart to smile!   (I.ii.62–3)

She instructs Lucetta to return his love letter unread, but the latter knows her real intentions and insinuates it again so that Julia may read it before she tears it up:

> Since maids, in modesty, say 'no' to that
> Which they would have the profferer construe 'aye'.   (I.ii.55–6)

It presents in a sympathetic but essentially patronising mode the foolish but winsome hypocrisy of the well-born young female engaged in Nature's love-game, panting for love, and delightful in her transparent and self-absorbed guile.

It requires an act of will for a modern reader to disengage from the romantic associations with which the actress-tradition has imbued Shakespeare's heroines in order to recognise that the seriousness with which they treat their own feelings was not necessarily echoed by the Elizabethan performer. If the First Quarto of *Romeo and Juliet* and Malone's re-ordering of its lines is accepted as an indication of what was said in performance, as it is in most editions, then Juliet says:

> What's Montague? It is nor hand nor foot,
> Nor arm, nor face, nor any other part
> Belonging to a man.   (II.ii.40f.)

After the first four, there really are very few 'other parts' left, and 'part' of course regularly occurs in Elizabethan bawdy as a reference to genitalia. It thus qualifies her reference to Romeo's 'dear perfection' five lines later, and anticipates the undertow of awakening sexual longing which informs so much of her later dialogue, not always understood by her partner:

ROMEO: O, wilt thou leave me so unsatisfied?
JULIET: What satisfaction canst thou have tonight?
ROMEO: Th'exchange of thy love's faithful vow for mine.   (II.ii.125–7)

These are not cues for a satirical or farcical representation but grace-notes within a romantic context; the acknowledgement of the carnal requiring perhaps less jarring of Elizabethan sensibilities than of those of modern audiences. Once again, however, it points a disjunction between a young woman's ostensible maidenly modesty and her underlying appetite, a contradiction the Elizabethans very rarely omitted to note.

There seems to be an especial connection in Shakespeare's plays between the lady and the clown. It is often part of the celebration of that all too fleeting combination of young female nubility and innocence, through a collaborative performer double-act in which the heroine is threatened with, and resists, the discomposure of her virtue, analogous to the similar activities of the bawdy waiting-woman, perhaps also played sometimes for low comedy. The exchange between Isabella and Lucio in *Measure for Measure* I.iv involves a delicious unsettling of virgin complacency. The opening of the scene establishes the specious, self-centred self-abnegation of the nuns, with novice Isabella 'wishing a more strict restraint / Upon the sisterhood', into which Lucio breezes mixing an elaborate admiration for her vocation, 'I hold you as a thing enskied, and sainted', with an insistence on the earthy naturalness of Claudio and Juliet's 'crime', which in effect negates it: 'even so her plenteous womb / Expresseth his full tilth and husbandry'. At his first announcement she had flinched, fearing his praise to be mockery: 'Sir, make me not your story.' Lucio admits that this is how he normally treats virgins:

> 'tis my familiar sin
> With maids to seem the lapwing, and to jest,
> Tongue far from heart – play with all virgins so . . .   (I.iv.31–3)

Even here, as he protests he renounces mockery out of respect for Isabella, he manages to intrude further bawdy innuendo. In other lady/clown exchanges the emphasis seems more on the former withstanding the threat. Desdemona, inviting Iago as a kind of licensed fool to fill in the time whilst they wait for Othello's ship (II.i.120f.) seems remarkably resilient in the face of a catalogue of female frailty. Helena too in her dialogue with Parolles in *All's Well*, far from being discomposed, seems comfortable with the bawdy. He asks if she is meditating on virginity, and she, continuing her earlier train of thought on Bertram, asks, 'How might one do, sir, to lose it to her own liking?'

It comes as no surprise, therefore, that one of the chief topics of Shakespeare's all-female conversations is bawdy, from the Nurse's long rambling recall of her husband's remark about the baby Juliet's future carnality, to the jesting on 'bearing' and 'pricks' as the women prepare Hero for her wedding in *Much Ado*. Such exchanges take much of their particular tone from an all-male performance, supposedly revealing what women are really like when they are on their own. Clearly pleasure too is taken in showing women being bitchy to one another, feigning friendships, as the she-wolves do in *Pericles* and *Cymbeline*, and the displays of female jealousy between Helena and Hermia, Kate and Bianca, and Goneril and Regan, leading even to blows between Eleanor and Margaret in *2 Henry VI*.

More striking, however, given the performer circumstances, are the many positive relations between women in the plays. A modern reader, used to female performance, may take for granted what is really a remarkable degree of rapport in many of these all-female conversations, such that Carole McKewin can write an entire essay praising Shakespeare's feminine insight in 'Intimate Conversations between Women' without ever once considering such circumstances.[2] The plays appear to contain a genuine celebration of female friendship, harmony, and co-operation, from the bonding of the lamenting queens in *Richard III*, to the intimate, relaxed, sophisticated dialogues of *As You Like It* and *The Merry Wives of Windsor*. For such situations to have been created and enjoyed there must have been a radically different and infinitely more flexible cross-dressed tradition than anything that could be replicated today (and perhaps *some* constituency, at any rate, of female spectators).

Shakespeare and the representation of sexuality

It is a commonplace critical saw that Shakespeare talks about love more than many of his contemporaries but yet gives it less fleshly representation. The plays are filled with devices that reduce physical contact in love matches. Lovers are kept apart by vows of chastity, psychological inhibitions, their parents' interference, physical barriers, or the problems of mistaken gender.

The hindering of the progress of true love is, of course, a standard plot motif, but more surprising is the frequency with which consummation is delayed *after* marriage and forms part of the final expectations as the characters go off at the end of the play. Petruchio withholds it, not as Irene Dash rather touchingly suggests as a sign of gallantry, but as part of Kate's taming. In *The Merchant of Venice* it is delayed until after the trial. In The *Two Noble Kinsmen* the marriage rites of Theseus and Hippolyta are postponed when the Queens call for vengeance. In *Cymbeline* there is some doubt as to whether Posthumus is describing temperance or abstinence in the brief period of marriage before his banishment:

> Me of my lawful pleasure she restrained
> And pray'd me oft forbearance; did it with
> A pudency so rosy the sweet view on't
> Might well have warm'd old Saturn; that I thought her
> As chaste as unsunn'd snow.   (II.v.9f.)

However, as with *Othello*, on which critics are divided, given the other evidence above, the balance of probability is that it indicates that the marriage has *not* been consummated.[3]

There is also a stress in Shakespeare's plays on the need for continence between contract and marriage, in reality a period used in many societies to assure fruitfulness. Florizel in *The Winter's Tale* gives a voluntary commitment to continence, and later Leontes refers to it as a condition of his support for the runaway lovers (V.i.230–1). It is the crime for which Claudio is condemned to death in *Measure for Measure*. In *The Tempest* when Prospero finally decides that Ferdinand deserves Miranda, 'that for which I live', and formally gives her to him, he goes on to warn most strongly against pre-marital intercourse, putting a curse on any such union, and Ferdinand swears to obey him. As Prospero gives Ariel instructions for the marriage masque, he presumably catches sight of them kissing and embracing:

> Look thou be true; do not give dalliance
> Too much rein. The strongest oaths are straw
> To th'fire i'th'blood. Be more abstemious,
> Or else good night to your vow!   (IV.i.51–4)

The Masque which celebrates this union, from which Venus is specifically barred having tried her wiles in vain, envisions loving fruitfulness without lasciviousness.

Some critics, notably Marilyn French, would go further and accuse Shakespeare of sharing the revulsion of his characters like Hamlet and Lear towards female sexuality, but as Anne Barton points out this is to ignore his frequent positive representation of marital relations and women's active role in them.[4] Familiarity can make us forget how unique is his sympathetic depiction of Juliet's awakening sexuality. The direct nature of her carnal anticipation is expressed in a series of soliloquies as in III.ii as she waits impatiently for her secret wedding and the consummation planned for that night:

> learn me how to lose a winning match,
> Play'd for a pair of stainless maidenhoods. (lines 12–13)

> O, I have bought the mansion of a love,
> But not possess'd it, and though I am sold,
> Not yet enjoy'd ... (lines 26–8)

The originality of this presentation, the intimacy it involves with an individual consciousness, and the complexity of what was called for from the performer must not be under-estimated. Before Juliet, only whores onstage thought like this, and that rarely so frankly. Shakespeare reveals, with a blend of empathy and irony, that even the nicest girls have sexual longings.

Granville Barker asserts that 'it is Shakespeare's constant care to demand nothing of a boy-actress that might turn to unseemliness or ridicule', whilst Kenneth Muir argues that Shakespeare 'went out of his way to avoid sexual embarrassment. Physical contact between his lovers is reduced to a minimum.' He even essays to catalogue how few kisses there are in the plays: one, he says, in *The Merchant of Venice*, two in *Romeo and Juliet*, one in *All's Well*, and so on. Muir's theory breaks down, of course, when he gets to Cressida, kissed in general in the Greek camp, but, 'she is forthwith stigmatized by Ulysses as a daughter of the game'. Muir seems to have lost his thread here. He began by demonstrating Shakespeare's supposed propriety in respect of his *actors*, and ends up by applying it to his *characters*. This concept of juvenile propriety, perhaps surprisingly, still continues in certain quarters. Kinney writing in 2000, for instance, insists that 'Displays of passion (kissing particularly) were minimal, as is evident in extant dramatic texts.'[5] Such criticism somehow visualises Shakespeare working in a vacuum, and, insofar as the dynamics of performance are conceived at all, they are still seen in terms of embarrassed prep-school boys. The effectiveness of a 1930s production of *Richard II* at Sloane School, for instance, is measured in a review in the magazine *Drama* by the lack during Richard's farewell kiss to the Queen of any 'schoolboy smirk or girlish titter'. In reality, however, the physical presentation of a play is determined not simply by the text but by current stage practice, as revealed in the rest of the Lord Chamberlain's/King's Men repertory and that of their contemporaries.

The treatment of physical sexuality on the Elizabethan stage

In Act II of Heywood's *The Golden Age*, Calisto, devoted to chastity, has entered the train of Diana. Jupiter disguises himself as a nymph in order to seduce her. He corners Calisto in a forest arbour and proceeds to suggest they 'kiss and play' as women do. Calisto is not very keen – 'I do not like this kissing ... You kiss too wantonly.' To which Jupiter replies: 'Thy bosom lend, / And by thy soft paps let my hand descend' (Shepherd, p. 33). He then proceeds to grope her, still pretending to be a woman, pulling up her skirt, and inviting her to fondle him. Finally, playing on their hunting imagery, he indicates his own masculine readiness: 'Stay ere you goe, / Here stands one ready that must strike a doe.' She continues to resist, and as he carries her off, she is saying: 'To do me right, / Help fingers, feet, nailes, teeth, and all to fight.' Her next appearance is after only a twelve-line chorus indicating the passage of time:

[*A dumbe show. Enter* Diana *and all her Nimphs to bathe them: shee makes them suruey the place. They vnlace themselves and vnlose their buskins: only* Calisto *refuseth to make her ready.* Diana *sends* Atlanta *to her, who perforce vnlacing her, finds her great belly, and shewes it to* Diana, *who turnes her out of her society* ...]

Twelve lines are hardly long enough for anything more elaborate than the insertion of that long-suffering cushion, but the scene is a reminder that the contemporary stage was not as queasy about the representation of sexual activity and of all phases of the female condition as earlier generations of scholars have supposed, and further indication perhaps of the relative maturity of its performers.

Women are frequently shown preparing to go to bed with their lovers and rising from bed afterwards. In *The Maid's Tragedy* the King marries his mistress Evadne to the hero Amintor against the possibility of issue, forbidding her to have sexual contact with him. The bridal night is, therefore, something of a disappointment, but in the morning both are obliged to pretend that Amintor has taken her virginity, and to settle the matter one of her brothers demands:

DIPHILUS: Let's see you walk, Evadne.

She presumably does so, and he exclaims:

By my troth, y'are spoil'd.   (III.i.99–100)

Evidently there was considered to be a walk which indicated a pierced hymen, which was here imitated.

Conventionally female characters were removed from the stage platform for actual penetration, but playwrights went as far as they dared onstage, suggesting, as in *Catiline*, that only accident prevented congress there and then in full view of the audience. Frequently consummation is to be imagined no further than behind the curtains at the rear of the stage. It seems likely in Heywood's *Rape of Lucrece*, for instance, that rather than bearing the heroine off as the Mermaid edition tactfully suggests, Tarquin, having earlier '*discovered*' her, merely drew the curtains on his deed. In these cases stage time is often made to represent the action itself, with perhaps, as here, a brief clown scene, and then the couple are '*discovered*'. Sometimes in lieu of a more decorous interlude, attention is actually drawn to the offstage intercourse, as in the episode in *David and Bethsabe* in which Thamar is taken off to be raped by her half-brother Amnon, urged on by Jonadab, who then remains onstage to describe the rape whilst is it to be imagined taking place:

> Poor Thamar, little did thy lovely hands
> Foretell an action of such violence
> As to contend with Amnon's lusty arms
> Sinew'd with the vigour of his kindless love . . .   (lines 292–5)

And then Amnon thrusts the poor girl back onstage from the tent/arras in a paroxysm of post-coital remorse. Sometimes love-making is to be imagined on the balcony above the stage and interrupted by some action below, as Agar and Captain Gallop in *A Christian Turned Turk*, by thievish sailors who set the house on fire.

Perhaps the most explicit love scene is Jupiter's second encounter in *The Golden Age*. This time the indefatigable hero disguises himself as a pedlar to gain access to Princess Danae, who has been locked in a golden tower to avoid the predictions of an oracle. Confident she is won by his gifts, he returns in the night. Although Danae, 'naked' in her bed, protests modest surprise and token refusal, she soon acquiesces in his seduction as '*he makes unready still*' and climbs into her bed. This is then '*drawn in*'. There is a brief clown soliloquy, and the couple return, '*Danae in her night-gown*' and very grateful to her seducer. Given Heywood's prudishness in his domestic dramas, there is something distasteful in the frankness of the *Ages* plays of repeated scenes of this kind which are to a large measure gratuitous.

Kyd, on the other hand, in his seminal *Spanish Tragedy* attempts a remarkable representation of sexual congress through the formal structure of his language, which is made to serve a genuine dramatic purpose in the play, and left behind an enduring if much parodied stage image. The lovers Horatio and Bel-Imperia meet in the garden bower for their love tryst. Bel-Imperia is appropriately hesitant, expressing an undercurrent of foreboding which anticipates the tragic outcome, but Horatio overcomes her doubts with a four-line aria describing Nature's conspiracy to aid their love. She responds at similar length, and they provide a description, step by step, of their amorous encounter – the touching of the hand and foot, kisses, and then embracement. The verse form itself indicates the rhythms of foreplay: from blank verse aria, advancing to the greater urgency of rhyming couplets, leading eventually to shared couplets in stichomythia, and then a return to couplets at its imminent conclusion:

BEL-IMPERIA: If I be *Venus* thou must needs be *Mars*,
   And where *Mars* raigneth there must needs be warres.
HORATIO: Then thus begin our wars: put forth thy hand,
   That it may combat with my ruder hand.
BEL-IMPERIA: Set forth thy foot to try the push of mine
HORATIO: But first my lookes shall combat against thine.
BEL-IMPERIA: Then ward thy selfe, I dart a kisse at thee.
HORATIO: Thus I retort the dart thou threwst at me.
BEL-IMPERIA: Nay then to gaine the glory of the field,
   My twining arms shall yoake and make thee yeeld.
HORATIO: Nay then my armes are large and strong withal:
   Thus Elmes by vines are compast till they fall.   (II.iv.35–46)

As their love-play approaches its intended goal they are rudely interrupted by the arrival of Lorenzo, her Machiavellian brother, and his creatures, who tear the lovers apart and hang Horatio in the Arbour.

HORATIO: What will you murder me?
LORENZO: Ay thus, and thus, these are the fruits of love.   (lines 55–6)

He stabs him in the groin in a dark parody of the act of consummation.

Shakespeare's technical innovations

As the foregoing demonstrates, the Elizabethans had few scruples in enacting sexual relations, and in many cases the very same players who created Shakespeare's roles would have been involved in their representation. Nor are scenes indicating at least the precincts of carnality completely absent from Shakespeare's own plays. Troilus and Cressida are viewed on their way to bed and rising next day, Romeo and Juliet part from a night of love, Doll and Falstaff canoodle, Helena indicates satisfaction at her clandestine consummation, and although the specifics of stage action in *Antony and Cleopatra* are tantalisingly imprecise, it seems likely given the broader parameters of this tradition that the stage representation of the steamiest relationship in Western culture rested on more than, as conventional criticism would have it, descriptions of Cleopatra whilst she is offstage. Direct enactment of intimacy in Shakespeare's plays, however, remains the exception, and the plays are filled with devices that reduce physical contact in love matches.

So why so much chaste sexuality in Shakespeare? The exceptions above are sufficiently numerous, and the wider context of performance practice sufficiently frank, to suggest that he had some motive other than mere propriety.

The balcony scene in *Romeo and Juliet* keeps the lovers apart, straining towards each other, the woman aloft in the conventional place for the Courtly Love mistress, a successful transfer of poetry to the stage. The play does not deny the physical urge to the desired union – the lovers are later to be imagined in Juliet's bedchamber after congress – but it lengthens out the immediately preparatory stages, and it concentrates on the mental states of the lovers, providing for a longer, slower look at the process of love and loving; as Cressida says:

> Things won are done, joy's soul lies in the doing.

When Romeo sees Juliet for the first time, their mutual attraction is expressed through a combination of rich poetry and physical enactment:

> O, she doth teach the torches to burn bright!
> It seems she hangs upon the cheek of night
> As a rich jewel in an Ethiop's ear –
> Beauty too rich for use, for earth too dear! . . .   (I.v.44–7)

Oblivious to Tybalt's threats and Capulet's unease, the two lovers are absorbed in each other, their growing relationship expressed through increasing proximity. He takes her hand to kiss it, she insists they clasp or 'match' hands, he asks to kiss her on the lips, she agrees to accept it:

> Saints do not move, though grant for prayer's sake.   (I.v.105)

And he kisses her, twice. The exchange is a short one – on paper – but every word, every step in the sequence is highly charged. And it is more likely that Shakespeare's script marks only those kisses that serve a symbolic function in the stage action.

At the beginning of *Love's Labours Lost* the men vow not to see or talk with women during their three years of proposed study. Then the ladies arrive and the situation is set for a lengthy, amorous, but entirely chaste, verbally balletic interchange. The nearest they get to physical contact is kissing gloved hands, and the play ends with matters far from settled. The wit is a trifle shallow but it invites attention to style, to the appearance of the courtiers, their dress, fashion, and manners, and it catches more than most plays the essence of courtly love-in-idleness as a way of life. The play lacks the suppressed passion of some of Shakespeare's later exchanges in which the witty superficies of courtly conversation also hint at the vital issues of the right couplings. Wit, as Camille Paglia points out, has long been 'an aristocratic language of social manoeuvring and sexual display', and Shakespeare is not the first to illustrate the banter that traditionally accompanies wooing. Even as far back as 1300, there is a sprightly quality to the Maiden's initial resistance in the fragment *The Cleric and the Maiden*, perhaps the earliest recorded scene in English of an attempted seduction:

> Na kep I herbherg clerc in huse no y flore
> Bot his hers ly wit-uten dore.[6]

'Men and women', said William Harvey, 'are never more brave, sprightly, blithe, valiant, pleasing or beautiful than when about to celebrate the act.' What Shakespeare achieves is a way of verbally embodying these qualities in a witty, combative dialogue between his lovers. 'Shakespeare realised', says Stephen Greenblatt, 'that if sexual chafing could not be presented literally onstage, it could be presented figuratively.' To do so he created through the very limitations of stage levels and performance practice a style for the representation of sexual relations that best exploited his medium: male performers – talking, and interacting with properties, in various physical configurations – on a platform; but symbolically representing rather than directly simulating the physical relationships, the sexual spark so artfully recreated through the dialogue. The result, as with his similar metaphorical treatment of violence to women, was to hold reality at one stage removed, suspended in time and space, and open it out for our inspection.

There must have been a lot of bathos and perhaps unintentional humour in the direct representation of scenes of carnality in the plays of his predecessors and contemporaries, for the most part unwilling to deal with sexual relations except in terms of seduction or rape. In a sense, Shakespeare, in finding the means of representing the minutiae of sexual interaction that dignify and make meaningful that activity (hitherto left to poetry), and in giving his representations of sexual interaction a 'process' orientation, was moving towards something approaching an acknowledgement of the female point of view. It is a mark of his genius that he is able to assimilate practical and conceptual issues into the same solution.

BREECHES ROLES AND GENDER CONSTRUCTION

Rosalind, Viola, and the rest have become the unwitting targets of a great many modern critical projections bent on wresting the plays to particular polemical ends. Despite differences of emphasis, all such critics seem to agree that the breeches role has to be some sort of statement about gender. There are two main lines of argument to be examined.

The breeches role as an affirmation of gender flexibility

Until fairly recently the most popular view has been that the breeches role calls into question traditional definitions of gender and the restrictions that these have placed on women's behaviour. The breeched heroine is able, it is said, to take the initiative in determining her own life and sexual happiness. In some versions this is ascribed to the power of the garments themselves, and both Juliet Dusinberre, of Elizabethan characters, and Robert Stoller, from his modern case-histories, cite examples of women thus subject to a personality change which enabled them to do things in male dress they could not do in female.[7]

Shakespeare, on the other hand, is inclined to emphasise, as with Rosalind, that however convincing the girls may appear, they do not have a doublet and hose in their disposition. Most critics, however, in what might be called the 'positive' tradition ignore this and insist that once the heroine is in male dress, gender distinctions are seen to be false, and the girl character able more fully to express her *real* nature: 'Disguise,' says Juliet Dusinberre, 'makes a woman not a man but a more developed woman.' The characters are said to demonstrate the virtues of what might be called political or psychological androgyny (as distinct from sexual indeterminacy). Cynthia Secor describes this kind of androgyny as:

the capacity of a single person of either sex to embody the full range of human character traits, despite cultural attempts to render some exclusively feminine and some exclusively masculine.

To Marianne Novy, Shakespeare's plays:

are symbolic transformations of ambivalence about gender relations and about qualities his language sometimes calls the 'man' and 'woman' within the self.

Carolyn Heilbrun goes so far as to say, 'Shakespeare was as devoted to the androgynous ideal as anyone who has ever written', and argues that disguise for him is not always falsification but another indication of the wide spectrum of roles possible; whilst Robert Kimborough glosses what he sees as the depiction of androgyny in Shakespeare as:

the potential for achieving unity, wholeness, harmony, and perfection within the confines of the human . . .

Strictly speaking the genuine androgyne is a mythical ideal, a creature transcending sexuality, often perceived as the original state of power, the progenitor of life, and associated with sacred transvestism. It may be conceived as having the organs of both sexes, but more usually neither, 'a being', says Kimborough:

beyond a physical generative power without need for or use of sexual organs . . . of beneficence, wholeness, goodness, integrity, contentment, containment, and truth.

There is a moment in *As You Like It* when this sense of androgyny is very potent. Rosalind, who holds the destinies of all the characters in her hand and seems herself almost a shape-stealer, leads in the god Hymen to bless the weddings. As always with Shakespeare, however, there is also a more mundane explanation. Rosalind has achieved her ascendancy simply through disguise, and there may even have been some acknowledgement that the actor hitherto playing Corin, the only one of the ensemble now absent, is playing Hymen.

The only character in the canon really to approach the androgynous state is Bellario in *Philaster*, unique in having his/her sex concealed until the very end (although by 1609 the more experienced playgoer is likely to have had his suspicions). Unusually, therefore, the impersonation and its dynamics are not shared with the audience. Bellario shows the attractions of indeterminacy: so beautiful, well-proportioned, and graceful, lacking the limitations of either sex and drawing from both: male in resolution, courage and intelligence, female in sensitivity, loyalty, and beauty. He does, of course, finally turn out to be a girl in disguise, but, even more unusual, she has no ambitions to marry the hero, Philaster, and so continues to remain in an asexual limbo, vowed to chastity, as an attendant on his bride, Arethusa.

The only Shakespearean heroine to show qualities akin to the genuine androgyne is Imogen in *Cymbeline*, performed by the King's Men in the same year as *Philaster*, and almost certainly structured around the same actor. Perceiving noble virtue in the welcome of Arviragus and Guiderius, she says:

> Pardon me, gods!
> I'ld change my sex to be companion with them,
> Since Leonatus' false. (III.vi.86–8)

Like Bellario/Euphrasia, she too has an inclination to make the withdrawal from the demands of her gender into a permanent state. She is not, of course, allowed to do so, and indeed apologises to the gods for her temerity.

For the Shakespearean heroine male attire is a temporary phase, usually to allow them to travel in safety; then variously a help or hindrance in furthering their amatory affairs, and bringing with it gender expectations from others which they find intimidating or exciting. Unlike the genuine androgyne, they are not composed of equal elements of 'andro' (male) and 'gyne' (female) fused together into an integrated whole, a third sex, 'urging,' as Grace Tiffany would have it, 'an experiential sense of transexual connectedness',[8] but instead the elements are often at odds, and their concealed femininity is constantly signalled under their male exterior, as indeed it must be for practical reasons given they are played by a male performer in male attire. The breeches convention works essentially, for audience and performer, on simultaneously perceived and distinctly separate levels: a self-conscious *travestie* in an active temporary conjunction of contrasting sexual characteristics. Given that female celibacy as a state was not an acceptable choice in Protestant England and woman's natural destiny was marriage, dressing in breeches gave a temporary relief from this process, and the girls briefly take on some of the stasis of the genuine androgyne, it being not so much marriage or subordination that finally closes in on the heroine, but sexuality itself.

The dangers of ignoring the performer

The great weakness of claiming that the breeches role exposes conventional gender distinctions as false is that it either ignores the male-performer context altogether, or it assumes that the girl the Elizabethan player was able, and indeed set out to present, was a 'realistic' female, on which both as aim and achievement the foregoing has already cast some doubt. For the girl character to be able to question gender stereotypes or engage the audience in extra-dramatic confidences, stepping forward, as Peter Hyland would have it, to occupy, 'an area midway between actors and audience', 'her' own identity must be somehow 'real' and not itself subject to further layering; whereas the performance irony is, of course, not that of the female character, nor even as Catherine Belsey suggests of the female Rosalind as Ganymede, but that of the *male performer*, whose loyalty to concepts of female competence or for that matter androgyny cannot be assumed.[9]

On the face of it, as Catherine Belsey and Anne Thompson both suggest, whenever one sex is imitated by another, however orthodox the ostensible purpose, the very process is likely to call gender assumptions into question; even more so it might be imagined in breeches roles, where the layers are increased to three or even four. The practical considerations of performance, however, in which a male plays a girl character dressed in men's clothes, requires that both dramatist and actor keep 'her' *travestie* constantly before the audience. This involves emphasising her femininity, and contrasting it with her lack of masculinity, and inevitably, therefore, of using the received stereotypical indicators to do so; as Madelon Sprengnether points out, 'the representation of sexual difference by male actors . . . permits a wholly male definition of femininity'. Paradoxically, therefore, a female character in breeches is likely to be presented as *more* conventionally feminine than one in female dress. Several dramatists show this in action. In *The Four Prentices of London*, when the two heroines find themselves menaced by what they think is a predatory soldier, it is the one in skirts who takes the initiative:

[*Enter the Ladies flying, pursued by the Clown*]

FRENCH LADY: I wear a weapon that I dare not draw:
                Fie on this womanish fear, what shall I do?
BELLA FRANCE: Some of my father's spirit revives in me,
                Give me thy weapon, boy, and thou shalt see,
                I for us both will win sweet liberty.
CLOWN: I was never so over-reached; and, but for my shame, and I am a man-art-arms, I would run away, and take me to my legs. Have at thee sweet lady.

Shakespeare only once, at the very beginning of his career, allows a girl to dress in men's clothes and wield a sword effectively, and La Pucelle in

1 Henry VI is presented finally as unnatural and diabolic. Later heroines like Viola and Imogen express their femininity through their inability to rise to the occasion. Among other dramatists, Moll in *The Roaring Girl* and Bess in *The Fair Maid of the West* are also self-proclaimed exceptions, competent in the use of arms, in a tradition of contemporary London viragoes based on actual individuals, but the more typical stage-breeches heroine fails in combat, as do Perseda in *Soliman and Perseda* and Dorothea in *James IV*. Aspatia's conviction in *The Maid's Tragedy* that a breeched woman cannot successfully wield a sword even allows her to adopt male disguise and enter combat as a deliberate means of suicide.

The received dogma that, 'traditional female fashions' as Paula Berggren puts it, 'are designed to hamper movement, as traditional female roles hamper mobility', is not borne out by these plays, which are full of warrior queens going into battle in skirts. Helena in *All's Well* demonstrates that it is not necessary to dress as a man in order to take the initiative. She reverses roles in loving and pursuing one socially above her, and even appropriates the 'male-gaze':

> 'Twas pretty, though a plague,
> To see him every hour, to sit and draw
> His arched brows, his hawking eye, his curls,
> In our heart's table. (1.i.92–5)

She journeys alone to Paris in her ordinary woman's clothes and later to the war-zone in Italy, and not being subject to the passive stasis and self-indulgent temptations that afflict many cross-dressers is arguably the stronger for it.

Shakespeare's heroines are rarely as unhappy at appearing in men's clothes as Cassandra in *Promos and Cassandra*, 'Apparelled thus monstrous to my kind' to please 'lewd Promos' fleshly mind', or Phyllida in the Children's *Gallathea*, who fears she will be ashamed of her 'long hose and short coat, and so unwarily blab out something by blushing at everything' (1.iii.20f.). Indeed, despite demurrals to the contrary, Jessica in *The Merchant of Venice* (II.vi) seems quite pleased with her ambiguity. Nonetheless Rosalind, for all her high spirits and much vaunted freedom, experiences the limitations of breeches. Far from giving her that especial power of which modern critics are so fond, they hinder her in the one thing uppermost in her mind – love – so that she has to invent a proxi-Rosalind, in a symbolic, as it were, return to skirts, in order to be wooed by Orlando.

Some critics argue that if gender roles can be simulated by the opposite sex as successfully as they appear to be in these comedies, then they have no natural validity and are no more than role-playing or masquerade, and hence that these plays show that all gender-distinctions are untrue.[10] 'A woman in disguise', says Juliet Dusinberre, 'smokes out the male world, perceiving masculinity as a form of acting.' The constructional elements of Elizabethan stage femininity can all too easily be wrested to support the twentieth century concept of 'Masquerade', in which the fear a woman experiences of a loss of subjectivity through following society's dictates, especially in respect of maintaining a 'feminine' appearance, can only be assuaged, allowing her to reinstate her own sense of self, by consciously playing a part.[11] To argue thus, however, is so to empathise with the (limited) Elizabethan artefact that it becomes a real person, and what is more the person the critic wants it to be. While it is undoubtedly the case that much female behaviour in the sixteenth century was 'learnt', so also was much male behaviour, then and in all ages. Simply to appeal to plays as demonstrations that people commonly assume roles and manipulate others through them is tautological, since that is precisely what we expect actors and characters to do in plays. And whilst it is true that the breeched heroines, along with others like Cleopatra and Beatrice, as James Hill points out, are able to control situations through their role-playing, female characters do not have a monopoly in this. Tranio, Iago, and Edgar, for instance, are all consummate role-players who solve problems or destroy others through the roles they assume. Metadrama may reinforce the dramatic illusion, but ultimately it reveals the extent to which the theatre is satisfied by its own formal pleasures.

And, of course, the heroines never pretend to be *men*, only *youths*, and their assumptions, except under duress, are a disguise not an impersonation; for the young women concerned desire under their male attire to retain their femininity, as for instance Julia's refusal in *The Two Gentlemen of Verona* to cut her hair, deciding instead to knit it up in silver strings. Hence arguably the female here is conceived as less, not more adaptable than the male, who daily demonstrates *his* flexibility in the very act of cross-dressed performance.

The *persona* that breeched heroines tend to assume is a transient one like their own state, that of the fledgling adolescent. The uncertainties of puberty, when the desire to obey growing sexual urges and social imperatives is inhibited by vocal and physical limitations and fear of the consequences, can produce in their confusion another kind of temporary androgyny sometimes involving psychological regression, as in the immature homosocial tendencies already noted in Veramour in *Honest Man's Fortune*. Thus it is ambiguity and confusion that the plays explore rather than any serious assumption of opposite gender roles. A useful analogy is Vesta Tilley's studies of young men in her Edwardian musical hall vocal performances.[12] Like the Elizabethan breeches role, they involved several levels at the same time, exploiting both the gap between the performer and role – Tilley never cut her hair, for instance, and sang in her own register – and also between character and aspirations, such as to provide a gently humorous simulation of youthful uncertainty. As W. R. Titterton put it, 'all types of fledgling manhood ... are her lawful prey'. In 'By the Sad Sea Waves' a London clerk saves all through the year from his minuscule salary in order to give himself the appearance of a real 'masher' on the Brighton promenade. The society beauty he meets there turns out, of course, when he returns to London, to be a girl in a cook-shop. In the Great War, Tilley's misfits become more poignant, like the weedy youth in khaki, shortly to be cannon-fodder, who assures us: 'I joined the Army yesterday, so the Army of today's alright.' Willson Disher recalls:

She was always a very ordinary youth, but she portrayed him in an extraordinary manner. We saw him not as we saw him in real life, or as he imagined himself, but as he appeared in the eyes of a clever, critically observant woman.

Just so Goethe, visiting Rome in 1788, similarly found in an all-male production of *La Locandiera* 'a kind of self-conscious illusion', in which:

We come to understand the female sex so much the better because someone has observed and meditated on their ways, and not the process itself, but the result of the process, is presented to us.

We might not be quite so confident as to the accuracy of the result, perhaps, but Goethe is surely articulating a paradigm that underlies the practice of theatrical cross-dressing in general. Ian Buruma, for instance, suggests that in the tradition of the *onnagata* the vivid insights and startling ambiguities come from the 'sexual tension' and 'distance' between the performer's identity and that of the role he plays.[13] 'We are drawn to imitate objects', says Michael Goldman, 'towards whom intensely ambivalent emotions obtain.'

Thus it is that Shakespeare's breeches roles, like those of Vesta Tilley, assume the identities of youths who are themselves in transition between man and boy, and pretending to be what they are not, like Portia's 'bragging youth', and Rosalind's 'mannish coward'. Malvolio describes the disguised Viola:

Not yet old enough for a man, nor young enough for a boy; . . . 'Tis with him in standing water, between boy and man. He is very well-favour'd, and he speaks very shrewishly. One would think his mother's milk were scarce out of him. (I.v.156–62)

The combination of womanish appearance and masculine behaviour takes Olivia's interest, notwithstanding her earlier determination to admit no messengers from Orsino, and accords with the latter's expectation that such would be the case. He had noted the femininity of Viola's *travestie*, 'all is semblative a woman's part', but still instructed the youth to: 'Be clamorous, and leap all civil bounds' (I.iv.21). It was a combination of qualities capable of fascinating more than Olivia. Trevor Lennam, discussing the popularity of the Children of St Paul's, says of Queen Elizabeth:

Throughout her life she rarely failed to respond to the appeal of intelligent and accomplished youth, particularly to handsome, audacious and eloquent boys.[16]

There must also be a question more generally over the seriousness ascribed to the Elizabethan use of this character convention. The essential playfulness of the practice of a woman putting on men's clothes, always treated differently from male cross-dressing, becomes very apparent in the Restoration, when breeches roles of many different kinds gained even greater prominence. Some dramatists, notably Aphra Behn and 'Ariadne', continue the convention of female empowerment thereby, even dispensing with the male dramatists' caveat about being unable to wield swords and making some of them bonny fighters in their own right. Sylvia in Farquhar's sunny and good-humoured *The Recruiting Officer* even provides a serious rival for the willing Rose, object of her own lover Plume's casual attentions. The mordant Wycherley, in contrast, casts the delicate and innocent Mrs Boutell in roles that reveal the inadequacy and danger of male impersonation. When in the title role in *The Country Wife* she is dressed by her jealous husband, the decayed rake Pinchwife, as her supposed 'brother', this provides an opportunity for each of the circling gallants to kiss her in turn, whilst as Fidelia in *The Plain Dealer* once her disguise has been rumbled her male clothes provide not protection but provocation and release her attacker from the more usual gender constraints. In general, however, the convention thrived in this licentious age not because breeches concealed, but because they *revealed* the actresses' femininity, particularly in the concluding dance, which became a firm favourite. Managers and actresses ransacked the received corpus of breeches parts and then had many new ones created to exploit this. They staged all-female productions, particularly of bawdy plays like Killigrew's *Parson's Wedding*, and cast women in male roles, one of the best-known being Peg Woffington as Sir Harry Wildair in *The Constant Couple*, dressed in an especially made close-fitting suit of satin decorated with lace:

> That excellent Peg
> Who showed such a leg
> When lately she dress'd in men's clothes.[15]

Tight breeches and abbreviated coat stressed not gender similarities but their distinctions – just as they still do. Pepys noted of a performance of *The Slighted Maid*:

the play hath little good in it, being most pleased to see the little girl dance in boy's apparel, she having very fine legs, *only bends in the hams, as I perceive all women do.*[16]

And if that were not enough, the freedom from wearing stays in the adoption of male costume enabled actresses to bare their breasts at the many and necessary moments that this was required in the plots.

The spunky, non-threatening breeches heroine

The second, more recent line of interpretation of the Elizabethan breeches role takes more cognisance of the performer element, but again asserts a polemical context. Clara Park observes that 'one of the secrets of his perennial appeal' was that Shakespeare:

could create women who were spunky enough to be fun with, and still find ways to mediate their assertiveness so as to render them as non-threatening as their softer sisters . . .[17]

The breeches heroine in this reading is an attempt on the part of the patriarchy to contain and neutralise the contemporary problem of the rebellious woman by showing her self-assertion to be good-hearted, temporary, and ended by reincorporation back into society and subservience through marriage. To Martha Andresen-Thom such exceptional individuals, 'are used to justify a more general inequality'. In this view Shakespeare is no longer celebrated for his man–womanly mind but seen rather as a spokesman for a sinister all-controlling patriarchy.

It is questionable, however, whether the breeches role had very much to do with contemporary events. Attempts to relate it to the *Hic Mulier* controversy of women dressed as men raise two immediate objections. Firstly, the pamphlets concerned were not published until the 1620s, half a century after the breeches role came into vogue. Secondly, the contemporary problem that gave so much offence was not young virgins gadding about in male dress but *wives* doing so; hence marriage here was hardly synonymous with subordination. Also the power such women sought seems largely to have been erotic and not political – hence their tendency to partial *travestie* and almost always upper male garments – beaver hats, epaulettes and open doublets, as in the historical Moll Frith celebrated in *The Roaring Girl* with her male frieze jerkin and female black safeguard – retaining their skirts, but using items of male attire thereby to set off and not conceal their femininity, a stratagem also adopted in some masque and courtly cross-dressings (see figure 11).

Far more obvious promptings for the breeches convention are to be found in the theatre itself, in those raunchy, 'whiffling', cross-dressed actresses who led their Italian companies into the towns, and more particularly in the *novella* and its escapist romance tradition of female pages, sometimes imitated in real life.[18] Victor Freeburg analyses the theatre repertory to show audience familiarity with cross-dressed heroines by 1590:

Playgoers had seen the heroine apprehensive lest her male garb seem immodest; weary from travel through forests; patiently following her lover to serve him unknown, or leaving him to carry messages to a rival lady; wooed by that lady who was misled by outward appearance; wittily alluding to her real identity in veiled language; swooning like a woman, or fighting in man's harness, and dying like a soldier. The same playgoers may have heard similar events recited in ballads, or may have read of them in English novels.[19]

Such characters were commonly found in university and children's plays, and the adult repertory under consideration here includes heroines with some or all of these characteristics in *Clyomon and Clamydes*, 1570, *Promos and Cassandra*, 1578, *James IV*, 1590, and *Soliman and Perseda*, 1590, all before Shakespeare began to create them.

Contemporary evidence of female power

'The temporary nature of male disguise', says Park, 'is of course essential, since the very nature of Shakespearean comedy is to affirm that disruption is temporary, that what has turned topsy-turvy will be restored.' This argument, however, in drawing on the work of C. L. Barber and others on the carnival/festival elements in the plays,[20] conveniently separates two parts of the same issue. It focuses first on the period of confusion before the partners pair off, which cross-dressing symbolises, and then its conclusion in marriage, but ignores the main thrust of this tradition which celebrates the essential *rightness* of male–female relations expressed in the plays within the wish-fulfilment patterns of ritual comedy, as in the fertility rites which they echo, through the display of human invulnerability and sexual differentiation. Thus also Peter Erickson:

> The liberation that Rosalind experiences in the forest has built into it the conservative countermovement by which, as the play returns to the normal world, she will be reduced to the traditional woman who is subservient to men.

The plays, however, offer no support for this reading (which incidentally would demand unhappy endings for all the comedies), either in the expectations of the heroines or in what we see after their marriage. In *The Merry Wives of Windsor*, for instance, the wives are confident in their virtue and in its power to see off all men's foolish stratagems and vain aspersions, and are bested only by another woman, Anne Page, representing the natural urge to couple properly with a man of appropriate age and character. Any effective woman can put her man in the wrong, because she is in control of the things that really matter, as witnessed by a woman's unbounded energy for the inter-personal which will always be superior to a man's more diffuse energies. Mistress Ford in II.ii seems quite unperturbed by her husband's angry suspicions, when he rifles the house with a covey of friends looking for her supposed lover. His repeated failure to find Falstaff makes him the laughing stock of the town. It is quite a different vision of reality from that in so many of the plays of Shakespeare's contemporaries, and a convincing demonstration of a woman's domestic power.

There is plenty of historical evidence that real women recognised male literary and theatrical polemic for what it was and resisted it. 'From the early decades of the sixteenth century', Lisa Jardine notes, '. . . educational treatises, pamphlets on manners, spiritual tracts, sermons and literature all conspire to try to turn the wishful thinking of the male community into a propaganda reality', but it is largely, she argues, 'whistling in the dark'. It is dangerous, therefore, to take the subservience in which so many of the female characters in the plays are held, especially in the plays of Heywood and Dekker, as being an accurate reflection of the realities of contemporary gender relations.

Nor was women's actual power restricted to the domestic sphere. Kathleen McLuskie concludes from the large amount of contemporary material available, including legal depositions, that 'women had access to the courts as a means of self-defence and did not have to submit actually or symbolically to fixed images imposed on them by others' words'.[21] She cites Martin Ingram's analysis of *charivari*:

Deep in the heart of the organisers of the ridings lay the knowledge that women could never be dominated to the degree implied in the patriarchal ideal. For the ideal was only too plainly in conflict with the realities of everyday life.[22]

Keith Thomas says of Renaissance women that their 'actual independence . . . was always greater than theory allowed and that part of the evidence lies in the frequency with which that independence was denounced'.[23] Carol Thomas Neely's comparison of the constraints laid on Shakespeare's female characters with those laid on his female contemporaries in Stratford, though bedevilled by the radically different social status between the actual citizenry and the fictive princesses, is significant to the extent that it notes the relative sexual freedom of the former and the much greater part they played in marriage, inheritance, and money matters. Though Douglas Green talks much of the 'dominant male powers of Elizabethan society', Mary Beth Rose shows that, '. . . women exercised legal agency on a broad scale that contradicted their conceptual legal status, buying, selling, and bequeathing property and actively negotiating the marriages of their children, as well as planning for their education'. Margaret Ranald contrasts the realities of women's conduct with the official conduct book strictures, including widows who automatically took over their husband's businesses and estates and places in the guilds; and Karen Newman notes that though women were 'ideologically subject', nevertheless 'in the daily life of household, village, and town,' they 'often had authority over men – over servants and children, over the less wealthy or wellborn'.[24]

Companionate marriage

Shakespeare's 'Skirmishes of Wit' often involve sustained resistance to wooing, even when capitulation is inevitable, playfully putting the wooer in the wrong by tricks and deliberate misunderstandings. This is often continued after marriage, as in *The Merchant of Venice*, in order to keep the men up to the mark. A. J. C. Ingram argues that 'shrewishness' in Shakespeare is sometimes a feature of the unmarried girl as in Beatrice and Katherine, rebelling against being a daughter and a wooing object, rather than as in the Morelles' skin tradition always a bid within marriage for supremacy. The term 'shrewishness' has perhaps too many negative connotations, but the ability of his heroines to hold their own in many of the witty exchanges with men often indicates an attractive and desirable independence of mind and in asserting an equality of female intellect and status reveals the potential for a relationship of genuine reciprocity, one that ensures, as Martha Andresen-Thom puts it, 'a safer dropping of defences and a happier interdependence when trust is established'. Thus some of the relationships in his plays promise a 'companionate marriage' long before its historical occurrence in the eighteenth century as identified by Lawrence Stone. There are lots of young women in Shakespeare who would make good wives, with minds of their own as well as the conventional virtues of loyalty and compassion, capable of making genuine, equal, companionable marriages, rather than the dull, passive, subservient, unknowable creatures that Heywood and Dekker create.

Like many critics, Paula Berggren argues that the relationships the breeches heroines establish with their men are dependent on their cross-dressing so that when they 'cease to adopt men's clothes, they forgo the rewards of friendship as well, and the comic world darkens'. To put so much emphasis on the male disguise, however, is to ignore much of the evidence of the plays themselves. Beatrice and the ladies in *Love's Labours Lost*, for instance, demonstrate not only male/female friendships that promise to endure, but also ones that can be entered into whatever the heroine's costume. And as to needing breeches to take the initiative, Rosalind establishes her love-match whilst still in skirts. Critics often support their view by finding a 'reluctance' on the part of the heroine to give up her breeches, but a straw-poll suggests there is no consistency in whether or nor the heroines assume their original clothes, and it is much more likely that the issue is a practical one. For a heroine to change into breeches only involves the actor taking off his gown; Jessica in *The Merchant of Venice* (II.v–vi) has 25 lines or approximately a minute and a half to do so; the reverse would inevitably take longer.

'Dwindling into a wife'

An overview of the critical material on this topic shows a near-universal consensus that marriage is no more than a tool of patriarchy and to be condemned out of hand. To Douglas Green, 'the woman ultimately disappears from the equation into marital oblivion'. It is an orthodoxy that sweeps aside all personal considerations so that Irene Dash can thank her husband Martin in her preface and yet without any apparent awareness of contradiction go on to blame *Othello*'s tragedy not on the individuals concerned but on the institution of marriage itself. 'Marriage', says Stephen Orgel, 'is a dangerous condition in Shakespeare.' So far as tragedy is concerned, the concentration on the family is not peculiar to Shakespeare but a principle of the very form as it has been handed down. Catharsis, as Aristotle points out, is best excited, 'when suffering involves those who are near and dear to one another'.[25] One might as well counsel against sea voyages as a 'dangerous condition in Shakespeare'; failing a shipwreck, characters are almost certain to fall into the hands of pirates. But like marriage, shipwrecks serve a particular, necessary, and traditional dramatic function as the *peripeteia* (or 'reversal of fortune'), as for instance in three of the four late romances. Of course sea voyages were dangerous, but, as the Elizabethans circumnavigated the globe in search of adventure and Spanish gold, the benefits for the courageous, just as those of marriage, were worth the vicissitudes, as John Donne points out, linking them together in *Elegie XVIII*, 'Love's Progress', exploring his wife's body. 'Sailing towards her *India*' :

> Upon the Islands fortunate we fall,
> (Not faynte *Canaries*, but *Ambrosiall*)

There is tendency in modern criticism to use Congreve's phrase, 'to dwindle into a wife', in IV.i of *The Way of the World*, to describe the diminution of status a heroine is supposed to undergo in returning to her skirts, and thereby ceasing to enjoy the privileges of masculine friendship that her disguise has conferred. This is, however, to ignore the irony in Congreve's original.[26] The status of wife was seen traditionally not as a diminution, as such critics assume, but as an *enlargement* on being an unmarried daughter. As Wantonness the Woman puts it in *The Tide Tarrieth No Man*:

> Where if I were a wyfe, nothing I should misse,
> But liue like a Lady, in all ioyfull blisse.   (lines 874–5)

A married woman gains her own rights and establishment, as the Proviso dialogue in Congreve's play makes clear. Also Mirabell later asks:

Well, have I a liberty to offer conditions – that when you are dwindled into a wife, I may not be beyond measure enlarged into a husband? (lines 206–8)

Once again this is deliberately reversing the cynical expectation that whereas marriage elevates a woman, it diminishes a man by cutting off the traditional pleasures of the rake, and points it by 'beyond measure', that the irony shall not be missed.

The Proviso scene, one of many in the plays of its period, is important because it establishes an essential truth about modern marriage. The lovers are taking over the traditional bargaining function of the parents, but they too at their best want to achieve the same balance as a good father does for his daughter between ensuring a personal attraction between the partners and compatibility of rank, wealth, and outlook.

The increase of domesticity may have narrowed a woman's opportunity in the wider world of work, but it increased her scope for making family decisions. 'Everywhere men rule over women', Cato said, 'and we who govern all men are ourselves governed by women.' In essence the institution of marriage is an invention of society of mutual benefit, particularly to the young mother and child. According to Rita Freedman;

The basic primate family unit consists of a mother and her young. Human fathers are, in a sense, grafted on to that base. Paternity has been called a fragile, learned behaviour, culturally imposed on males.

With the decline of marriage and the rise of the 'feral male', Western society is now in the process of rejoining the other primates, whilst the State shoulders the paternal responsibilities.

Portia and the function of submission

The key test in respect of Park's argument that the breeches heroine is only allowed to operate in a very restricted sphere of action is Portia in *The Merchant of Venice*, a woman strong enough to enter a male world and beat a full-grown man at his own game and yet one who makes formal obeisance to her new fortune-hunting husband. She takes him she says as:

> her lord, her governor, her king.
> Myself, and what is mine, to you and yours
> Is now converted.   (III.ii.165–7)

Does she mean it, or does her subsequent conduct show her submission to be pretence? Juliet Dusinberre calls this speech, 'an act of courtesy', observing that, 'In practice, [Portia] retains total independence'.[27] Certainly Portia's response to the news of Antonio's predicament shows a freedom of action in no way diminished by her submission. Bassanio is to offer more, she says, from her fortune than the lost principle. Notice the suggestion, voiced almost as a command:

> First go with me to church and call me wife,
> And then away to Venice to your friend . . .   (III.ii.304–5)

Her performance as a lawyer is masterly, leading Shylock along until he has shown his rapacity so that his subsequent punishment and humiliation may be seen as justified. Her magisterial rebuke to Gratiano for losing Nerissa's ring and her subsequent calling of her own husband to account lead Bassanio to say:

> [*Aside*]: Why, I were best to cut my left hand off
> And swear I lost the ring defending it.   (V.i.177–8)

Inevitably critics warm to Portia's assumption of male power, but how far is it Shakespeare's intention to produce a woman who is so strong, and how far are the inconsistencies we perceive in her behaviour simply an indication of a lack of interest in the gender issue? How far is Portia simply a function of the plot, an instrument of justice? The success of her breeches performance depends on none of the men present getting an inkling of her actual sex, and hence Shakespeare uncharacteristically eschews any exploitation of the potential for gender ambiguity. Prose romances often use gender pronouns to accord with the dress rather than the gender of cross-dressed characters and the slip here is evidently an unproblematical one. The 'quality of mercy' speech might well gain in its objective, timeless, choric quality simply by being put into the mouth of a youth, separated from ordinary reality by his double disguise. Indeed, the role is strangely lacking in much by way of subtlety in its acting demands. Portia's feelings are not complex, and the ring stratagem is peculiarly bloodless in its juxtaposition of the responsibilities of love and duty. There is a *Cosi Fan Tutte* arty aimlessness about it.

It might be argued on the other hand by critics determined on a logical rationalisation of the play's ambiguities in this respect that in Portia's speech of wifely submission there is a certain unease that anything less will put Bassanio in a false position as a perceived fortune hunter and she seems anxious to erase any difference of wealth or status between them as quickly as possible. The dependence of men upon women for emotional security and the paradox that male dominance needs female recognition to validate and sustain it is frequently noted by critics.[28] Less acknowledged, however, are corresponding needs in the 'strong' woman. Joan Riviere's seminal essay 'Womanliness as Masquerade' concerns the case-study of an intellectual woman, of what Riviere calls 'intermediate' gender, who assumed:

Womanliness . . . as a mask, both to hide possession of masculinity and to avert the reprisals expected if she was found to possess it . . .

Samuel Rowley illustrates similar motives on the part of Catherine Parr in *When You See Me You Know Me*, 1604, whose life comes to depend upon being able to trivialise her own considerable disputing skills. Towards the end of the play she is indicted by the scheming clergy as a heretic for urging that Luther's views ought to be studied. At first Henry VIII encourages her to debate with the bishops, especially when she challenges their ability to be loyal to both King and Pope, but in her absence the bishops persuade the ailing paranoid that she is the focus of a treasonable league against him and they gain a warrant for her removal to the Tower. Fortunately young Prince Edward, who shares her religious views, is on hand to protect her against the hasty wrath of the King, but not before she has been obliged to dissemble simplicity and to deny her own intelligence:

> My puny schollership is helde too weake
> To maintaine proofes about religion.
> Alas I did it but to wast the time,
> Knowing as then your grace was weake and sickly . . .
>
> (lines 2668–71)[29]

Perhaps the most interesting Elizabethan case of female self-abnegation is the heroine of *The Life of Long Meg of Westminster*, 1582, a prose work. Famed for her martial deeds, when Long Meg marries, her husband is determined to test her 'manhood', but, afraid she might vanquish him, she refuses to fight:

neuer shall it be said . . . that Long *Meg* shall be her Husbands master: and therefore use me as you please.[30]

Outside marriage, in the tavern which is their livelihood, she continues to be assertive, punishing 'Huffing Dick', for instance, who has assaulted her serving-girl, by making him dress in her clothes and take her place whilst she dresses in man's apparel. Her submission to her husband, then, is in a special category; it is in order to maintain his virility for the benefit of them both.

A woman who operates successfully in a man's world is not his equal, but as Rosalind, Portia, and Moll Frith all demonstrate in their different ways, his superior. Her proficiency in male skills as well as female ones is itself a kind of threat both to equality and to reciprocity.

BRIDE: [*kneeling*]   I disdain
         The wife that is her husband's sovereign . . .

Thus says the wife of Candido, the linen draper, an incipient shrew tamed merely by being offered equivalent violence to her own. She goes on:

> If me you make your master, I shall hate you.
> The world shall judge who offers fairest play;
> You win the breeches, but I win the day.   (*2 Honest Whore*, II.iii.)

The paradox of her final line indicates an Elizabethan perception of reciprocity lying not in androgyny, psychological or political, but in complementary gender qualities.

Appendix: female characters in the adult repertory, 1500–1614

		Total lines	Total female lines	%	Speaking female roles	Largest female role
1508	Mundus et Infans	979	0	0	0	0
1513	Hickescorner	1026	0	0	0	0
1515	Magnificence	2567	0	0	0	0
1519	Pardoner and Friar	647	0	0	0	0
1520	Four PP	1236	0	0	0	0
1520	Johan Johan	678	162	24	I	162
1520	Interlude of Youth	736	18	2	I	18
1538	King John	2691	175	7	I	175
1538	Three Laws	2464	101	4	I	101
1538	Temptation of Our Lord	432	0	0	0	0
1547	Impatient Poverty	110	0	0	0	0
1550	Lusty Juventus	1167	36	3	I	36
1554	Wealth and Health	964	0	0	0	0
1558	Mary Magdalene	2035	357	17	I	357
1559	Longer Thou Livest	1988	72	4	I	72
1560	Enough is as Good as a Feast	1541	0	0	0	0
1561	Cambises	1296	149	11	6	48
1561	Pedlar's Prophesy	1592	130	17	2	74
1565	King Darius	1605	0	0	0	0
1567	Horestes	1205	107	9	4	64
1567	Trial of Treasure	1148	121	11	2	63
1568	Like Will to Like	1277	0	0	0	0
1570	Clyomon and Clamydes	2220	384	17	4	274
1571	New Custom	1076	60	6	I	60
1576	Tide Tarrieth No Man	1879	139	7	I	139
1576	Common Conditions	1894	450	24	3	267
1577	All for Money	1572	49	3	I	49
1578	1 and 2 Promos and Cassandra	2549	681	27	6	338
1579	Marriage Between Wit and Wisdom	770	149	19	6	40
1581	Three Ladies of London	1802	441	24	3	208
1582	Rare Triumphs of Love and Fortune	2016	400	20	4	161
1584	Fidele and Fortunio	1775	562	32	5	144

		Total lines	Total female lines	%	Speaking female roles	Largest female role
1586	*Famous Victories of Henry V*	2016	35	2	2	25
1587	*Alphonsus, King of Aragon*	1941	561	29	8	164
1587	*Spanish Tragedy*	2742	289	11	3	215
1587	*1 Tamburlaine*	2307	332	14	6	178
1587	*David and Bethsabe*	1920	180	9	5	96
1588	*Wounds of Civil War*	2512	114	5	2	79
1588	*2 Tamburlaine*	2367	123	5	6	82
1588	*1 Two Angry Women of Abingdon*	3584	1066	30	4	371
1588	*Three Lords and Three Ladies of London*	1802	441	24	5	208
1588	*1 and 2 King John*	2936	265	9	5	92
1589	*Friar Bacon and Friar Bungay*	1967	396	20	4	284
1589	*Jew of Malta*	2277	233	10	4	153
1589	*John a Kent and John a Cumber*	1750	163	9	3	70
1589	*Battle of Alcazar*	1591	37	2	3	17
1589	*Taming of a Shrew*	1501	191	13	3	120
1590	*James IV*	2375	441	19	4	247
1590	*George a Greene*	1328	57	4	3	27
1590	*Looking Glass for London and England*	2286	343	15	4	163
1590	*Old Wives' Tale*	914	137	15	6	51
1590	*Cobbler's Prophecy*	1696	266	16	8	110
1590	*Edward III*	2494	236	9	3	211
1590	*Fair Em*	1685	379	22	4	209
1590	*King Leir*	2664	771	29	3	289
1590	*Mucedorus*	1760	304	19	4	230
1590	*Soliman and Perseda*	2181	401	18	4	243
1591	*Orlando Furioso*	1457	123	8	2	85
1591	*Edward I*	2976	652	22	8	402
1591	*Locrine*	2116	413	20	6	117
1591	*2 Henry VI*	3156	445	14	4	313
1591	*3 Henry VI*	2904	349	12	3	278
1591	*Arden of Faversham*	2457	614	25	2	593
1591	*Jack Straw*	1056	33	3	1	33
1591	*True Tragedy of Richard III*	2223	249	11	4	135
1592	*1 Selimus*	2555	73	3	3	33
1592	*John of Bordeaux*	1770	129	7	5	96
1592	*Dr Faustus*	1931	17	1	3	8
1592	*Edward II*	2604	291	11	2	265
1592	*Comedy of Errors*	1777	468	26	5	264
1592	*1 Henry VI*	2617	337	12	3	260
1592	*Knack to Know a Knave*	1700	61	4	2	51
1592	*Woodstock*	2770	162	64	4	87
1593	*Massacre at Paris*	1266	130	11	6	94
1593	*Richard III*	3489	734	21	5	265
1593	*Two Gentlemen of Verona*	2196	542	25	3	319

		Total lines	Total female lines	%	Speaking female roles	Largest female role
1594	Two Lamentable Tragedies	2728	241	9	4	153
1594	Alphonsus, Emperor of Germany	3250	212	7	2	134
1594	Taming of the Shrew	2651	304	11	4	220
1594	Titus Andronicus	2422	336	14	3	258
1594	Knack to Know an Honest Man	1805	129	7	3	57
1595	Love's Labours Lost	2547	559	22	5	286
1595	Midsummer Night's Dream	2157	560	26	4	224
1595	Richard II	2763	267	10	4	113
1595	Romeo and Juliet	3050	918	30	4	524
1595	Sir Thomas More	2390	222	9	5	116
1595	Edmund Ironside	2061	108	5	3	74
1596	Blind Beggar of Alexandria	2050	527	26	7	178
1596	King John	2670	369	14	4	260
1596	Merchant of Venice	2673	763	29	3	571
1596	Captain Thomas Stukely	2755	230	8	4	150
1597	Humorous Day's Mirth	2300	406	18	5	216
1597	1 Henry IV	3173	114	4	3	57
1597	2 Henry IV	3423	331	10	4	187
1598	Much Ado About Nothing	2810	562	20	4	309
1598	Downfall of Robert, Earl of Huntingdon	3200	291	9	5	126
1598	Death of Robert, Earl of Huntingdon	3392	587	17	6	234
1598	Englishman for My Money	2848	391	14	3	145
1598	Every Man in his Humour	2949	116	4	3	58
1599	Old Fortunatus	2788	533	19	4	204
1599	Shoemakers Holiday	2915	390	13	4	128
1599	1 Sir John Oldcastle	2872	123	4	4	55
1599	1 Edward IV	3060	397	13	6	227
1599	2 Edward IV	3384	655	19	4	421
1599	Every Man Out of His Humour	3828	248	6	4	164
1599	As You Like It	2769	1409	40	4	736
1599	Henry V	3359	178	5	4	71
1599	Julius Caesar	2481	115	5	2	90
1599	'Larum for London	1670	75	4	6	17
1599	Look About You	3680	315	9	3	257
1599	Thracian Wonder	2262	229	12	4	150
1599	A Warning for Fair Women	1709	831	49	4	305
1600	1 Blind Beggar of Bethnal Green	2886	231	8	4	165
1600	Patient Grissil	2500	559	22	3	340
1600	Devil and His Dame	2464	501	20	4	284
1600	Four Prentices of London	3400	293	9	2	152
1600	Merry Wives of Windsor	2992	933	31	4	359
1600	Twelfth Night	2615	821	31	3	339
1600	Charlemagne	2787	249	9	4	148
1600	Lust's Dominion	2976	482	16	3	364

		Total lines	Total female lines	%	Speaking female roles	Largest female role
1600	Thomas, Lord Cromwell	1729	65	4	2	54
1600	Weakest Goeth to the Wall	2377	209	9	3	121
1601	Satiromastix	2440	256	10	7	86
1601	Hamlet	3921	303	8	2	170
1601	Trial of Chivalry	2436	304	12	3	226
1602	Hoffman	2618	355	14	2	178
1602	How a Man May Choose a Good Wife from a Bad	2848	676	24	4	425
1602	Royal King and Loyal Subject	2232	381	17	7	98
1602	Family of Love	2476	533	22	3	195
1602	All's Well That Ends Well	2961	942	32	5	448
1602	Troilus and Cressida	3470	428	12	4	348
1602	Fair Maid of the Exchange	2660	580	22	4	299
1602	Merry Devil of Edmonton	1760	147	8	4	82
1603	Woman Killed with Kindness	1992	387	19	3	230
1603	Sejanus	3266	114	3	3	75
1604	1 Honest Whore	3325	633	20	4	359
1604	Sir Thomas Wyatt	1467	196	13	4	105
1604	1 If You Know Not Me, You Know Nobody	1872	361	27	4	361
1604	Wise Women of Hogsden	2070	672	32	6	241
1604	When You See Me You Know Me	3094	210	7	6	150
1604	Measure for Measure	2783	509	18	5	390
1604	Othello	3323	604	18	3	352
1604	Fair Maid of Bristow	1225	269	22	4	137
1604	1 Jeronimo	1197	51	4	2	46
1604	London Prodigal	2210	253	11	4	128
1604	Malcontent	2278	433	19	5	198
1604	Wit of a Woman	1760	570	32	8	131
1605	Caesar and Pompey	2800	72	3	1	72
1605	2 Honest Whore	3185	566	18	7	302
1605	2 If You Know Not Me, You Know Nobody	3276	390	9	4	203
1605	King Lear	3435	452	13	3	185
1605	Nobody and Somebody	1998	324	6	4	201
1606	Whore of Babylon	2591	762	29	4	417
1606	Volpone	3111	284	9	4	206
1606	Macbeth	2156	490	23	7	255
1606	Miseries of an Enforced Marriage	3360	277	8	3	156
1606	Revenger's Tragedy	2468	324	13	3	175
1606	Yorkshire Tragedy	695	172	25	2	164
1607	Devil's Charter	3314	358	11	3	237
1607	Travels of Three English Brothers	2210	285	13	3	175
1607	Rape of Lucrece	2820	456	16	4	309
1607	Antony and Cleopatra	3114	723	23	4	591

		Total lines	Total female lines	%	Speaking female roles	Largest female role
1607	*Timon of Athens*	2374	13	1	2	9
1608	*Roaring Girl*	2812	918	33	5	558
1608	*Shoemaker of a Gentleman*	2646	784	30	5	277
1608	*Birth of Merlin*	2518	431	17	6	129
1608	*Coriolanus*	3426	385	11	4	298
1608	*Pericles*	2403	443	18	7	173
1609	*Philaster*	2594	972	36	6	343
1609	*Wit at Several Weapons*	2700	719	27	4	363
1609	*Fortune at Land and Sea*	2556	284	11	2	183
1609	*Cymbeline*	3356	697	22	4	529
1609	*Atheist's Tragedy*	2960	616	21	4	280
1610	*Maid's Tragedy*	2694	840	31	8	425
1610	*A Christian Turned Turk*	2275	264	12	3	116
1610	*1 Fair Maid of the West*	1799	588	33	2	585
1610	*Golden Age*	2628	606	23	12	129
1610	*Alchemist*	3061	219	7	2	209
1610	*Winter's Tale*	3074	632	21	8	294
1611	*A King and No King*	3333	468	14	6	258
1611	*Greene's Tu Quoque*	3392	570	17	7	194
1611	*Match Me in London*	2166	424	20	3	197
1611	*If It Be Not Good the Devil Is In It*	2582	31	1	1	31
1611	*Night Walker*	2580	934	36	8	396
1611	*Woman's Prize*	3110	1189	37	8	578
1611	*Brazen Age*	2628	687	26	10	202
1611	*Silver Age*	2808	698	25	14	150
1611	*Cataline*	3554	449	13	4	244
1611	*Chaste Maid in Cheapside*	2215	542	24	18	166
1611	*Tempest*	2040	173	8	4	102
1611	*Second Maiden's Tragedy*	2184	581	27	3	241
1612	*Valiant Welshman*	2048	190	9	6	48
1612	*Captain*	3000	1130	38	5	441
1612	*1 Iron Age*	2844	324	11	6	172
1612	*2 Iron Age*	2664	412	15	11	161
1612	*White Devil*	3021	657	21	5	333
1613	*Bonduca*	2790	324	12	3	162
1613	*Honest Man's Fortune*	3270	404	12	3	134
1613	*No Wit, No Help Like a Woman's*	2998	1088	36	5	541
1613	*Henry VIII*	2808	467	17	4	346
1613	*Two Noble Kinsmen*	2775	954	34	8	363
1613	*Valentian*	3090	626	20	7	304
1613	*Wit Without Money*	2730	844	31	3	373
1613	*Bartholomew Fair*	4054	534	13	8	171
1614	*Duchess of Malfi*	2911	775	27	4	571
1614	*Faithful Friends*	3395	410	12	3	219

Notes

PRELIMINARY: THE PERSISTENCE OF ALL-MALE THEATRE

1. R. Gilder, *Enter the Actress: The First Women in the Theatre*, Theatre Art Books, 1931, p. 86.
2. C. Radford, 'Medieval Actresses', *Theatre Notebook*, 7, 1953, 7.
3. S. P. Cerasano and Marion Wynne-Davies (eds.), *Renaissance Drama by Women*, Routledge, 1996, D. Callaghan, *Shakespeare Without Women*, Routledge, 2000, C. McManus, *Women on the Renaissance Stage*, Manchester University Press, 2002, and P. A. Brown and P. Parolin (eds.), *Women Players in England 1500–1642*, Ashgate, 2005. Noble masquing, of course, did not involve impersonation. See S. Orgel, *The Illusion of Power*, California University Press, 1975, p. 38.
4. G. Wickham, *The Medieval Theatre*, Weidenfeld and Nicholson, 1974, pp. 92–3.
5. C. T. Neely, 'Shakespeare's Women', in N. N. Holland *et al.* (eds.), *Shakespeare's Personality*, California University Press, 1989, p. 125.
6. W. Tydeman, *The Theatre in the Middle Ages*, Cambridge University Press, 1978, pp. 199–200.
7. M. Shapiro, 'The Introduction of Actresses in England', in V. Comesoli and A. Russell (eds.), *Enacting Gender on the English Renaissance Stage*, Illinois University Press, 1999, pp. 182–3.
8. J. E. Howard, 'Crossdressing', *Shakespeare Quarterly*, 39, 1988, pp. 424f.
9. M. Heinemann, *Puritanism and Theatre*, Cambridge University Press, 1980.
10. J. E. Howard, *The Stage and Social Struggle in Early Modern England*, Routledge, 1994, pp. 7 and 82f.
11. All the Shakespeare quotations are taken from G. B. Evans (ed.), *The Riverside Shakespeare*, Houghton Mifflin, 1974.
12. Quoted in T. Cole and H. K. Chinoy (eds.), *Actors on Acting*, Crown, revised edition 1970, p. 37.
13. Quoted in P. Davidson, *Popular Appeal in English Drama to 1850*, Barnes and Noble, 1982, p. 40.
14. Quoted in L. Jardine, *Still Harping on Daughters*, Harvester Wheatsheaf, 1983, p. 11.
15. T. S. Graves, 'Women on the Pre-Restoration Stage', *Studies in Philology*, 22, 1925, 193; E. Howe, *The First English Actresses*, Cambridge University Press, 1992, p. 22; and S. Orgel, *Impersonations: The Performance of Gender in Shakespeare's England*, Cambridge University Press, 1996, p. 120.

16. Gilder, *Enter the Actress*, pp. 89, 85 and 60.

17. E. A. M. Coleman, *The Dramatic Use of Bawdy in Shakespeare*, Longman, 1974, p. 208. For a dissenting view see Callaghan, *Shakespeare Without Women*, p. 71.

18. S. de Beauvoir, *The Second Sex* (1949), trans. H. M. Parshley, Pan, 1988, p. 221.

INTRODUCTION: THE SIGNIFICANCE OF THE PERFORMER

1. H. C. Goddard, *The Meaning of Shakespeare*, quoted in H. J. Oliver (ed.), *The Taming of the Shrew*, Oxford University Press, 1984, p. 56.

2. C. Kahn, *Man's Estate*, California University Press, 1981, p. 114.

3. C. Heilbrun, *Towards a Recognition of Androgyny*, Knopf, 1973, p. 57.

4. Oliver, *Taming of the Shrew*, p. 57.

5. J. C. Bean, 'Comic Structure and the Humanising of Kate in *The Taming of the Shrew*', in C. Lenz *et al.* (eds.), *The Woman's Part: Feminist Criticism of Shakespeare*, Illinois University Press, 1983, p. 66.

6. J. Dusinberre, *Shakespeare and the Nature of Women*, Macmillan, 1975; I. Dash, *Wooing, Wedding, and Power*, Columbia University Press, 1981; and M. Novy, 'Patriarchy and Play in *The Taming of the Shrew*', *English Literary Renaissance*, 9, 1979, 264–80. D. Bergeron, 'The Wife of Bath and Shakespeare's *The Taming of the Shrew*, *University Review*, 36, 1969, 279–86, argues for a process through submission to mutuality. M. West, 'Folk Background to Petruchio's Wedding Dance', *Shakespeare Studies*, 7, 1974, 63–73, sees Kate's submission as an image of the sex-act.

7. M. L. Ranald, 'The Manning of the Haggard', *Essays in Literature*, 1, 1974, 149.

8. H. M. Richmond, *Shakespeare's Sexual Comedy*, Bobbs-Merrill, 1971, p. 90.

9. Billington quoted by K. McLuskie, *Renaissance Dramatists*, Harvester Wheatsheaf, 1989, p. 7; Hobson quoted by I. Brown, *Shakespeare Memorial Theatre, 1954–56*, Max Reinhardt, 1956, p. 5.

10. M. Hamer, 'Shakespeare, Rosalind, and her Public Image', *Theatre Research International*, 11, 1986.

11. Quoted in G. Ashton, *Shakespeare's Heroines in the Nineteenth Century*, Derbyshire Museum Service, 1980, p. iv.

12. See for instance A. F. Kinney, *A Companion to Renaissance Drama*, Blackwell, 2004; and H. M. Richmond, *Shakespeare's Theatre*, Continuum, 2004.

13. H. Ellis, *Eonism*, 1923. See R. Trumbach, 'The Birth of the Queen', in M. Duberman *et al.* (eds.), *Hidden from History*, New American Library, 1989, G. Chauncey Jnr, 'Christian Brotherhood or Sexual Perversion?', in the same volume, and E. Wilson, *Adorned in Dreams*, Virago, 1985, p. 201, for evidence of homosexual cross-dressing. Studies which confirm Ellis's view include A. Woodhouse, *Fantastic Women*, Macmillan, 1989, and H. T. Buckner, 'The Transvestic Career Path', *Psychiatry*, 33, 1970, 381–9.

14. E. Cohen, 'Legislating the Norm', *South Atlantic Quarterly*, 88:1, Winter 1989, 206.

15. N. de Jongh, *Not in Front of the Audience*, Routledge, 1992, pp. 89–90.

16. Orgel, *Impersonations*, p. xiii. G. Boas' *Shakespeare and the Young Actor*, Rockcliff, 1955, indicates that there were all-male performances at Sloane School as late as 1953.
17. R. Green and J. Money, 'Stage Acting, Role-Taking, and Effeminate Impersonation During Boyhood', *Archives of General Psychiatry*, 15, 1966, 535–8. Its authors wanted to see whether there were more homosexuals in the theatre than elsewhere. Although none of the boys engaged in homosexual activities, their behaviour was categorised as sufficiently 'effeminate' for the authors to conclude that they did. They observed, 'Some leaned towards intellectual developments to offset their gross indifference to athletic pursuits.'
18. See de Jongh, *Not in Front of the Audience*, esp. pp. 49–85; and J. R. Taylor, *Anger and After*, Penguin, 1965, p. 255.
19. D. Fuss, *Essentially Speaking*, Routledge, 1989, discusses Eve Sedgwick's distinction in her *Between Men*, of 'homosexual' and 'homosocial', and the views of Luce Irigaray, *This Sex Which Is Not One*, on the '"hom(m)o-sexual monopoly" which restructures the economy around the exchange of women'.
20. A. Sinfield, 'How to Read *The Merchant of Venice* without Being Heterosexist', [1996] in K. Chedgzoy (ed.), *Shakespeare, Feminism and Gender*, Palgrave, 2001, p. 122.
21. Although the earliest critics like Kott and Fiedler were homophilic, when Jardine brought the topic into prominence in 1983 she showed little sympathy for homosexuality. Once, however, respected male scholars began not only to accept the charge but actually celebrate it, the mood changed.
22. G. Greene, 'Shakespeare's Cressida', in Lenz (ed.), *Woman's Part*, p. 137.
23. R. Smith, 'A Heart Cleft in Twain', in Lenz (ed.), *Woman's Part*, pp. 207–8.
24. P. S. Berggren, 'The Woman's Part', in Lenz (ed.), *Woman's Part*, pp. 27–8. See more recently Howard, *Stage and Social Struggle*, p. 114.
25. A. Thompson, 'Are There Any Women in *King Lear*?' in V. Wayne (ed.), *The Matter of Difference: Materialist Feminist Criticism of Shakespeare*, Harvester Wheatsheaf, 1991, p. 123. K. McLuskie, 'The Patriarchal Bard' [1985], reprinted in Chedgzoy, *Shakespeare, Feminism and Gender*, p. 40.
26. P. Gay, *As She Likes It: Shakespeare's Unruly Women*, Routledge, 1994, pp. 4 and 111.
27. C. J. Carlisle, *Shakespeare from the Greenroom*, University of North Carolina Press, 1969. For illustrations of the actors see K. Muir and P. Edwards (eds.), *Aspects of Othello*, Cambridge University Press, 1977, Plate V.
28. L. T. Fitz, 'Egyptian Queens and Male Reviewers', *Shakespeare Quarterly*, 28, (1977), 297–316.
29. Fitch, Stempel, Markels, Murry, and Alexander all quoted in Fitz, 'Egyptian Queens'; E. A. J. Honigmann, *Shakespeare: Seven Tragedies*, Macmillan, 1976, p. 163.
30. L. Jardine, ' "Girl Talk" (for Boys on the Left) or Marginalizing Feminist Critical Praxis', *Oxford Literary Review*, 9, 1986, 214.
31. For evidence of these new hegemonies see the attempt to crush Richard Levin with 24 signatories in *PMLA*, 105, 1990, 77–8, and the waspish attack by

Graham Holderness on Muriel Bradbrook's perfectly reasonable enquiry, 'Where in all this are Shakespeare's plays?', G. Holderness (ed.), *The Shakespearean Myth*, Manchester University Press, 1988, p. xiii.

32. D. Cole, *The Theatrical Event*, Wesleyan University Press, 1974, p. 157: 'The desire to give theatre a purpose is a refusal of what theatre gives – of the theatrical event itself.'

33. C. R. Baskervill, *The Elizabethan Jig* (1929), Dover, 1965, p. 6.

34. C. Kahn, 'Coming of Age in Verona', in Lenz (ed.), *Woman's Part*, p. 174. See also comments on this essay in R. Levin, 'Feminist Thematics and Shakespearean Tragedy', *PMLA*, 1988, 125–38.

35. Oliver, *The Taming of the Shrew*, p. 72.

36. Quoted in R. Karney (ed.), *Cinema Year by Year 1894–2003*, Dorling Kindersley, 2003, p. 206.

37. R. Speaight, *Shakespeare on the Stage*, Collins, 1973, pp. 177–8, and 278; R. Manvell, *Shakespeare and the Film*, A. S. Barnes, 1979, pp. 23–6; Ivor Brown, *Shakespeare Memorial Theatre 1951–53*, Theatre Art Books, 1953, pp. 16–17.

38. Quoted in J. Cook, *Women in Shakespeare*, Harrap, 1980, p. 29.

39. C. C. Rutter, *Clamorous Voices: Shakespeare's Women Today*, The Women's Press, 1988, pp. 20f. Oliver, *The Taming of the Shrew*, pp. 72f.

40. J. Elsom (ed.), *Is Shakespeare Still Our Contemporary?*, Routledge, 1989, pp. 74–5.

41. M. Gohlke, '"I Wooed Thee with my Sword"', in Lenz (ed.), *Woman's Part*, p. 159.

42. V. Woolf, *A Room of One's Own*, Harcourt Brace, Jovanovitch, 1929, p. 97.

43. A. Findlay, *A Feminist Perspective on Renaissance Drama*, Blackwell, 1999, p. 122.

44. S. Shepherd, *Marlowe and the Politics of Theatre*, Harvester, 1989, p. 179.

45. A. Thompson, 'The Warrant of Womanhood', in Holderness, *Shakespearean Myth*, p. 76.

46. E. Gottlieb, '"I Will Be Free"', in T. R. Sharma (ed.), *Essays on Shakespeare in Honour of A. Ansari*, Shalabh Book House, 1986; L. Woodbridge, *Women and the English Renaissance*, Illinois University Press, 1984, pp. 206–7; and A. Ingram, *'In the Posture of a Whore'*, Salzburg University Press, 1984, p. 84. See J. F. Danby, *Shakespeare's Doctrine of Nature*, Faber, 1961, pp. 199f. on his ultimate orthodoxy. Richard Wilson in Elsom, *Is Shakespeare Still Our Contemporary?*, argues for Shakespeare as spokesman for emerging mercantilism. A number of critics would see him tempering orthodoxy with humanity, including R. Hosely, 'Was there a "Dramatic" Epilogue to *The Taming of the Shrew?*, *Studies in English Literature*, 1, 2, 1961, 17–34; and K. Rogers, *The Troublesome Helpmate*, Washington University Press, 1966, pp. 91–2.

47. N. N. Holland, *et al.* (eds.), *Shakespeare's Personality*, California University Press, 1989, p. 10.

48. G. E. Bentley, *The Profession of Dramatist in Shakespeare's Time*, Princeton University Press, 1971, p. 77.

49. S. Callow, *Being an Actor*, Penguin, 1985, pp. 70f., describes Joint Stock's attempt to 'break the mould of the relationship between the writers and the

theatre group'. S. Craig (ed.), *Dreams and Deconstructions*, Amber Lane, 1980, pp. 105f., discussing actor-based workshops, argues that 'the fringe arose as much out of the habitual discontent of the performers as out of the wider political and social change of the sixties'. M. Wandor, *Carry On Understudies: Theatre and Sexual Politics*, Routledge and Kegan Paul, 1981, pp. 20f. discusses the politics of gender and erotic orientations in alternative theatre casting.

50. E. A. J. Honigmann, *Shakespeare the Lost Years*, Manchester University Press, 1985, advances an elaborate thesis that Shakespeare began his career amongst the Catholic gentry in Lancashire. This is resisted by S. Schoenbaum, *William Shakespeare, a Compact Documentary Life*, Oxford University Press, 1977, revised 1987, pp. 112f. A. Harbage, '*Love's Labours Lost* and the Early Shakespeare', in his *Shakespeare Without Words and Other Essays*, Harvard University Press, 1972, argues for his possible early experience of writing for a chapel choir.

51. P. Thomson, *Shakespeare's Professional Career*, Cambridge University Press, 1992, pp. 35f. outlines his aristocratic connections.

52. D. and C. Ogburn, *Shakespeare: The Man Behind the Name*, Morrow, 1962.

53. A. Gurr, *The Shakespearian Playing Companies*, Oxford University Press, 1996, pp. 70f.

54. F. E. Halliday, *A Shakespeare Companion 1564–1964*, Penguin, 1964, p. 531.

55. J. Southworth, *Shakespeare, The Player: A Life in the Theatre*, Sutton, 2000.

56. T. W. Baldwin, *The Organisation and Personnel of the Shakespearean Company*, Princeton University Press, 1927. S. Howard, 'A Re-Examination of Baldwin's Theory of Acting Lines', *Theatre Survey*, 26, 1, 1985, 1–20, reviews Baldwin's influence and shows that his 'lines' theory is not even consistent with the known assignments. P. Honan, *Shakespeare: A Life*, Oxford University Press, 1998, pp. 204–5, and n.10, cites D. W. Foster as having developed computer-assigned castings apparently based on the frequency of unusual words, reported in *Shakespeare Newsletter*, nos. 209–11, 1991.

57. Thomson, *Shakespeare's Professional Career*, p. 108. D. Klein, 'Did Shakespeare Produce his own Plays?', *Modern Language Review*, 57, 1962, 556–61, provides evidence from the plays to show that playwrights regularly assigned the parts and coached actors. S. McMillin, *The Elizabethan Theatre and 'The Book of Sir Thomas More'*, Cornell University Press, 1987, p. 61, argues that the very large roles were written specifically either for Alleyn or Burbage and in their absence were simply not attempted.

58. B. Beckerman, *Shakespeare at the Globe*, Macmillan, 1962, p. 136.

59. D. Grote, *The Best Actors in the World*, Greenwood Press, 2002.

60. D. Bevington, *From Mankind to Marlowe*, Harvard University Press, 1962, contains details of a whole series of early Tudor play texts published as 'offered for acting' which indicate the intended doubling. In *Cambises*, for instance, eight actors play thirty-nine roles between them.

61. J. K. Jerome, *On The Stage And Off* (1884), Sutton, 1991, p. 31. The Stock Company, being a hierarchy and not a series of specialisms, is a poor model for Baldwin's 'lines'. The humble 'utility man' aspired to ascend through juvenile

and heavy to leading man, and when a star visited, all would regularly descend a notch (see D. Holloway, *Playing the Empire*, Harrap, 1979, pp. 28–30).

I AGE AND STATUS

1. Several of Heywood's *Ages* plays were performed by double companies, and *Bartholomew Fair* and *A Chaste Maid in Cheapside* by Lady Elizabeth's Men, which had rather a special composition (see below), whilst the demands of *Wit of Women* and *Alphonsus, King of Aragon* raise some doubts about their auspices. The plays were selected from A. Harbage, *Annals of English Drama*, 2nd edition, revised S. Schoenbaum, Methuen, 1966, rather than from the more recent 3rd edition, because of various problems, some of which are discussed in A. Lancashire's review in *Shakespeare Quarterly*, 42, 2, 1991, 225–30. I have felt that the need for consistency over-rides the re-dating of individual texts in line with more recent scholarship.

2. Details of players are to be found in E. K. Chambers, *The Elizabethan Stage*, Oxford University Press, 1923, G. E. Bentley's, *The Jacobean and Caroline Stage*, Oxford University Press, 1941, and his *Profession of Player in Shakespeare's Time*, Princeton University Press, 1971, Gurr, *Shakespearian Playing Companies*, E. Nungezer, *A Dictionary of Actors*, repr. Greenwood Press, 1968, and D. Kathman, 'How Old Were Shakespeare's Boy Actors?', *Shakespeare Survey*, 59, 2005, 220–46. The Admiral's plats and company lists are reproduced in W. W. Greg, *Dramatic Documents from the Elizabethan Playhouses*, Oxford University Press, 1931.

3. H. Granville Barker, *Prefaces to Shakespeare*, vol. I (1930), Batsford, 1963, p. 14.

4. J. Pearson, *The Prostituted Muse*, St Martin's Press, 1988, pp. 23–4.

5. These are collected and analysed in D. A. Mann, *The Elizabethan Player*, Routledge, 1991.

6. In *Wit and Wisdom*, 1579, for instance, Player Three doubles the heroine, Wisdom, with Indulgence, and Mother Bee, whilst Player Four plays Wantonness, Fancy, and Doll.

7. S. Brown, 'The Boyhood of Shakespeare's Heroines', *Studies in English Literature*, 30, 2, 1990, 246.

8. R. David, 'Shakespeare and the Players', in P. Alexander (ed.), *Studies in Shakespeare*, Oxford University Press, 1964, p. 42; T. Lennam, *Sebastian Westcott, the Children of Paul's and 'The Marriage of Wit and Wisdom'*, Toronto University Press, 1975, p. 39.

9. R. Gair, *The Children of Paul's*, Cambridge University Press, 1982, pp. 154–5.

10. W. Robertson Davies, *Shakespeare's Boy Actors*, Dent, 1939 p. 35. M. Shapiro, *Gender in Play, on the Shakespearean Stage*, Michigan University Press, 1994 p. 245, n.15. Kathman. 'How Old Were Shakespeare's Boy Actors?, pp. 221–2.

11. W. A. Ringler, Jr, 'The Number of Actors in Shakespeare's Early Plays', in G. E. Bentley, *The Seventeenth Century Stage*, Chicago University Press, 1968, pp. 129–30.

12. The idea of slighter rather than younger performers is certainly applicable in what we know of casting in University drama, at least in the speaking roles (where facility in reciting Latin was essential). Sir Richard Cholmley at Trinity College in the 1590s though tall was 'slender and well-shaped', Samuel Fairclough, a sub-tutor, originally cast as the dwarfish Surda, the maidservant in *Ignoramus* at Queens' College, 1614/15, was 'little and low in stature' and Mr Morgan, 'a comely modest gentleman, and was supposed would well become a woman's dress' played Rosabella, the girl, in the same production. See J. Nichols, *The Progresses . . . of James I*, 1828, vol. I, p. 200 and vol. III, pp. 52–3.

13. A. Harbage, 'Elizabethan Acting', *PMLA*, 54, 1939, 702.

14. M. Jamieson, 'Shakespeare's Celibate Stage', in Bentley, *Seventeenth Century Stage*, p. 93. But see also his comment that juvenile amateur acting is 'but a shaky analogy for Elizabethan practice'.

15. R. Williams, *Drama in Performance*, Penguin, 1972, p. 171.

16. Kinney, *A Companion to Renaissance Drama*, p. 210; H. J. Oliver (ed.), *New Penguin Shakespeare: As You Like It*, 1968/1996, p. 23; J. Kott, *Shakespeare Our Contemporary*, 2nd edition, Methuen, 1967, p. 208; Richmond, *Shakespeare's Theatre*, p. 77.

17. J. Hill, ' "What Are They Children?" ', *Studies in English Literature*, 1986, Spring, 26, 2, 236. Not all critics agree on the boy actor's limitations. According to Dusinberre, *Shakespeare the Nature of Women*, p. 11, 'The presence of the boy actor . . . leads to a naturalistic portrait of the individual woman' (p. 27).

18. Criteria still being repeated by Richmond, *Shakespeare's Theatre* (2002).

19. Ringler, 'The Number of Actors in Shakespeare's Early Plays', p. 130. See also Gurr, *The Shakespearian Playing Companies*, p. 59. Davies, *Shakespeare's Boy Actors*, p. 15, on the other hand, conceives of a category of intermediate players, and assigns Regan and Goneril, Mistresses Page and Ford, Cleopatra and Lady Macbeth to 'youths'. However, like J. L. Gibson, *Squeaking Cleopatras: The Elizabethan Boy Player*, Sutton, 2002, who devotes thirty-two pages to explaining how Shakespeare catered for the boy's more limited 'breath span' but accepts boy players of seventeen, he does not let this interfere with his general treatment of the players as pre-pubescent.

20. *Independent on Sunday*, 24 November 1991. P. Hyland, 'A Kind-of-Woman', *Theatre Research International*, 12, 1, 1987, 1–8.

21. In *All for Money*, 1577, Lupton adapts his sources by keeping one female character offstage and communicating by letter, and by changing the sex of another, a petty thief, from female to male (see Bevington, *From Mankind to Marlowe*, p. 75). Incontinence, almost universally female in stage representations, is male in *The Longer Thou Livest*, as are Love and Carnal Concupiscence in *Mary Magdalene*.

22. Hypocrisy in *New Custom*, 1571, for instance, is played as an old woman, when earlier versions would have made the role male. Not all early adult female characters were presented satirically. England in Bale's *King John*, 1538, for instance, is a virtuous and oppressed widow.

23. *The Fair Maid of the Exchange*, performed about 1602, has three of the eleven actors playing female roles. Those of the two young women are not doubled. The third actor plays a combination of Ursula a serving maid, the comic Mistress Flower, together with a shop-boy, and Barnard, a male role.

24. See the playing analysis of four of the Tudor plays 'offered for acting' in Appendix D of Mann, *Elizabethan Player*.

25. J. H. Wilson, *Mr Goodman the Player*, Pittsburgh University Press, 1964, pp. 29f.

26. D. Kathman, 'Grocers, Goldsmiths, and Drapers', *Shakespeare Quarterly*, 55, 1 (Spring 2004), 1–49.

27. There are records of orphans being indentured as players by the municipal authorities at Bridgewater. See H. Berry, 'The Player's Apprentice', *Essays in Theatre*, 1, 2, 1983, 73–80.

28. See the contract of Robert Dawes in Bentley, *The Profession of Player*, p. 48.

29. Thomson, *Shakespeare's Professional Career*, p. 93, and C. C. Rutter, *Documents of the Rose Playhouse*, Manchester University Press, 1984, *passim*.

30. Rutter, *Documents of the Rose Playhouse*, p. 22, describes hired men as 'adult players whose ability and experience probably equalled the sharers' ', and who differed only in financial input and reward. D. George, 'Pre-1642 Cast Lists and a New One for *The Maid's Tragedy*', *Theatre Notebook*, 31, 3, 1977, 22–7, argues for Edward Collins as a hired man in a female role.

31. Rutter, *Documents*, pp. 124–5, takes 'bornes womones gowne' in Henslowe's *Diary* as a reference to the adult actor William Bird.

32. M. B. Rose, 'Where Are the Mothers in Shakespeare?' *Shakespeare Quarterly*, 42, 1991, 291–314, argues that there were few mothers in Shakespeare (though she lists quite a lot), because, as well as living private lives, their maternal desire was seen as potentially destabilising.

33. Harbage, *Annals of English Drama*, p. 99.

34. 'Max, Mr Archer, and Others', *Saturday Review*, 15, Oct. 1898, 498–9.

35. Bevington, *Mankind to Marlowe*, p. 68, shows that up to 1560 the average company size was four, and then occasionally up to eight. J. Wasson, 'Elizabethan and Jacobean Touring Companies', *Theatre Notebook*, 42, 2, 1988, 51–7, notes troupes of between six and twelve at Londesborough during the 1590s, substantially increasing after 1600. J. Limon, *Gentlemen of a Company*, Cambridge University Press, 1985, pp. 10–11, confirms a similar profile in English troupes visiting the Continent.

36. J. Wright, *Historica Histrionica* (1642), in W. C. Hazlitt (ed.), *Dodsley's Old English Plays*, 4th edition, 1876, vol. XV, p. 410.

37. J. Downes, *Roscius Anglicanus* (1708), edited by J. Milhouse and R. D. Hume, Society for Theatre Research, 1987, pp. 44–6.

38. Confirmed by Downes: 'being very Young made a Compleat Female Stage Beauty . . . that it has since been Disputable amongst the Judicious, whether any Woman that succeeded him so Sensibly touch'd the Audience as he' (*Roscius Anglicanus*, p. 46).

2 EROTIC AMBIENCE

1. Kott, *Shakespeare Our Contemporary*, pp. 192f.; L. Fiedler, *The Stranger in Shakespeare*, Croom Helm, 1973, p. 33.
2. Jardine, *Still Harping on Daughters*, p. 9.
3. J. Goldberg, 'Sodomy and Society', *Southwest Review*, 69, 1984, 376.
4. S. Zimmerman (ed.), *Erotic Politics: Desire on the Renaissance Stage*, Routledge, 1992, pp. 39f.
5. S. Orgel, 'Nobody's Perfect', *South Atlantic Quarterly*, 88, 1, Winter 1989, 16.
6. Shapiro, *Gender in Play*, pp. 57 and 160. See similar references on pp. 86, 120, 137, 161, and 171.
7. Callaghan, *Shakespeare Without Women*, p. 67.
8. S. Werner, *Shakespeare and Feminist Performance*, Routledge, 2001, pp. 12 and 107.
9. A. Bray, *Homosexuality in Renaissance England*, Gay Men's Press, 1982, p. 54.
10. Brown, 'The Boyhood of Shakespeare's Heroines', p. 251.
11. R. A. Small, *The Stage Quarrel between Ben Jonson and the So-called Poetasters*, 1899, J. H. Penniman, *The War of the Theatre*, Ginn, 1879, J. B. Leishman, *The Three Parnassus Plays*, Nicholson and Watson, 1949, O. J. Campbell, *Comical Satyre and Shakespeare's 'Troilus and Cressida'*, Huntington Library Publications, 1938, and Mann, *Elizabethan Player*, pp. 101–27.
12. William Ringler Snr, 'The First Phase of the Elizabethan Attack on the Stage, 1558–1579', *Huntington Library Quarterly*, 4, July 1942, 407.
13. J. W. Binns, 'Women or Transvestites on the Elizabethan Stage', *Sixteenth Century Journal*, vol. 2, Oct. 1974, 95–120.
14. F. S. Boas, *University Drama in the Tudor Age*, Oxford University Press, 1914, p. 229.
15. Nichols, *Progresses . . . of James I*, vol. IV, pp. 52–3, reports of a production of the Latin comedy *Ignoramus* at Cambridge in 1615, that one tutor, 'a rigid Puritan', objected to coaching his pupil in a female role but was over-ruled by the latter's guardians, whilst a sub-tutor declined to wear women's apparel, and when the Vice-Chancellor failed 'to laugh him out of this', his student undertook the part instead.
16. Baker cites Luther and the Jesuit, Lorinuse, both of whom except stage players from the strictures of Deuteronomy.
17. Chambers, *Elizabethan Stage*, vol. IV, pp. 223–4. Critics who interpret this as a reference to homosexuality include M. Sprengnether, 'The Boy Actor and Femininity in *Antony and Cleopatra*', in Holland (ed.), *Shakespeare's Personality*, pp. 193–4; Davies, *Shakespeare's Boy Actors*, p. 10; Howard, 'Crossdressing' p. 424; and, by implication, Brown, 'Boyhood of Shakespeare's Heroines', p. 250. L. Levine's influential article 'Men in Women's Clothing', *Criticisms*, 28, 1986, esp. pp. 134–5, builds its entire case round this supposed reference by Stubbes to homosexuality.
18. See also Orgel, *Impersonations*, p. 27.
19. Orgel, *Impersonations*, p. 48, argues that Marlowe deliberately spares his hero the poker. However, since it is in Holinshed, his source, and Marlowe includes

reference to it in the script itself, it seems most likely his audience would assume its presence in the scuffle in which Edward is killed and as the cause of the final howl his murderers fear will 'raise the town' (v.v.114).

20. S. Shepherd, 'Shakespeare's Private Drawer: Shakespeare and Homosexuality', in Holderness (ed.), *Shakespearean Myth*, pp. 96f.
21. S. Case, *Feminism and Theatre*, Methuen, 1988, pp. 22–3, quoted in C. Daileader, *Eroticism on the Renaissance Stage*, Cambridge University Press, 1998, p. 47.
22. Findlay, *Feminist Perspective*, p. 108.
23. Jamieson, 'Celibate Stage', pp. 86–7.
24. Howard, *Stage and Social Struggle*, p. 128.
25. Ibid. pp. 112–14.
26. V. Traub, *Desire and Anxiety*, Routledge, 1992, p. 93.
27. A. Rich, 'Compulsory Heterosexuality and Lesbian Existence', in A. Snitow (ed.), *Desire: The Politics of Sexuality*, Virago, 1984, p. 227. See also A. Echols, 'The New Feminism of Yin and Yang', in the same volume, p. 72: 'cultural feminists ... define lesbianism as identification and bonding with women, rather than as sexual attraction'.
28. J. Brown, 'Lesbian Sexuality in Medieval and Early Modern Europe', in Duberman, (ed.) *Hidden From History*, pp. 74 and 68.
29. L. Stone, *Family, Sex, and Marriage in England*, Harper and Row, 1977, pp. 485f.
30. J. C. Bean, 'Passion versus Friendship', *Wascana Review*, 9, 1, 1974, 231.
31. Quoted in M. A. Doane, 'Film and Masquerade', *Screen*, 23 (3/4), 1982, 78.
32. W. Knight, *The Mutual Flame*, quoted in C. Paglia, *Sexual Personae*, Penguin, 1991, p. 206. See also C. Belsey, 'Desire's Excess and the English Renaissance Theatre', in Zimmerman (ed.), *Erotic Politics*, pp. 84f., on absence as 'an emblem of desire'.
33. Trumbach, 'Birth of the Queen', p. 130.
34. J. M. Saslow, 'Homosexuality in the Renaissance', in Duberman (ed.), *Hidden From History*, p. 93.
35. G. Greene, *Lord Rochester's Monkey*, Futura, 1976.
36. M. Foucault, *The History of Sexuality*, Random House, 1978, p. 101. Stone, *Family, Sex, and Marriage*, p. 492, on the other hand, reports a strong hostility to homosexuality in England in the sixteenth century.
37. Robin Morgan is quoted in Echols, 'The New Feminism of Yin and Yang', p. 74.
38. S. Greenblatt, *Will in the World*, Jonathan Cape, 2002, p. 253.
39. J. Delumeau, *Catholicism between Luther and Voltaire*, London, 1977, pp. 170–2, quoted in C. Larner, *Enemies of God*, Blackwell, 1981, pp. 25 and 157.
40. K. McLuskie, '"Lawless Desires Well-tempered"', in Zimmerman (ed.), *Erotic Politics*, p. 105. See Stone, *Family, Sex, and Marriage*, p. 256, on the lack of privacy in this period. M. Anderson, *Approaches to the History of the Western Family 1500–1914*, Cambridge University Press, 1995, emphasises the open nature of households as reflected in the domestic architecture: 'not only was the family not a discrete group, but its members had no significant right

to privacy'. P. Laslett, *The World We Have Lost*, Methuen, 2nd edition, 1971, pp. 137–8, discusses how the Church supervised personal morality.

41. Fuss, *Essentially Speaking*, p. 3.
42. S. Greenblatt, *Shakespearean Negotiations*, Oxford University Press, 1988, p. 92. Fuss, *Essentially Speaking*, p. 110; Jane Gallop quoted in D. E. Green, 'The "Unexpressive She"', *Journal of Dramatic Theory and Criticism*, 1988, Spring, 2, 2, 42.
43. Plato, *Phaedrus*, trans. W. Hamilton, Penguin, 1973, p. 63.
44. D. English *et al.*, 'Talking Sex', *Socialist Review*, 58, 1981, 47. E. Willis, 'Feminism, Moralism, and Pornography', in Snitow (ed.), *Desire*. Echols, 'New Feminism of Yin and Yang'. W. Benjamin, *Charles Baudelaire*, New Left Books, 1973, p. 90, observes: 'The lesbian is the heroine of modernism.'
45. J. Boswell, 'Revolutions, Universals and Sexual Categories', in Duberman (ed.), *Hidden From History*, pp. 31–2.
46. Paglia, *Sexual Personae*, p. 100. Her thesis takes no account of the evidence of heterosexual love in their drama, as when Haemon sacrifices his own life over the heroine's body in *Antigone*.
47. Xenophon's *Symposium*, trans. J. Welwood, in A. D. Lindsey (ed.), *Plato and Xenophon: Socratic Dialogues*, Dent, 1954, p. 163.
48. R. Freedman, *Beauty Bound*, Columbus, 1988, p. 59.
49. W. Flugel, *The Psychology of Clothes*, Hogarth Press, 1950, p. 107; J. Laver, *Modesty in Dress*, Heinemann, 1969.
50. B. Smith, 'Making a Difference', in Zimmerman (ed.), *Erotic Politics*, p. 141.
51. George Gascoigne, *The Princely Pleasures of Kennilworth*, is discussed in M. C. Bradbrook, *The Rise of the Common Player* (1962), Cambridge University Press, 1979, pp. 247–51; *The Sudeley Entertainment* is discussed in L. Helms, 'Roaring Girls and Silent Women', in J. Redmonds (ed.), *Women in Theatre*, Cambridge University Press, 1989, p. 59, and in Gurr, *Shakespearian Playing Companies*, p. 312; the texts of the two Jonson entertainments are contained in Nichols, *Progresses . . . of James I*, pp. 431–7, 176–89.
52. P. Erickson, *Patriarchal Structures in Shakespeare's Drama*, California University Press, 1985, p. 35; Greenblatt, *Shakespearean Negotiations*, p. 47.
53. MacManus, *Women on the Renaissance Stage*, p. 130, who discusses the display of full breasts in Elizabethan miniatures, many of which, of course, are of masque costumes. See Oliver miniatures in T. J. B. Spencer and S. Wells, *A Book of Masques*, Cambridge University Press, 1967, pl. 45, and C. Winter, *Elizabethan Miniatures*, Penguin, 1943, pl. XIII.
54. Sir Dudley Carleton writes of the masque of 27 December 1604: 'One woman amongst the rest lost her honesty for which she was carried to the porter's lodge being surprised at her baseness on the top of the taras'. (Chambers, *Elizabethan Stage*, vol. I, p. 206).
55. Examples of social disapproval include: parental hostility in Plato, *The Symposium*, trans. W. Hamilton, Penguin, 1951, p. 50; and 'condemned by the ignorant multitude' p. 106; in *Phaedrus*, disapproval of 'father, mother, kindred and friends', p. 39, and of 'schoolfellows and others', p. 63; to which

might be added the generally defensive nature of the whole enterprise, e.g. *Symposium*, pp. 47–8.

56. Plato, *Laws*, trans. T. J. Saunders, Penguin, 1975, pp. 332f.
57. L. Jardine, 'Twins and Travesties: Gender, Dependency and Sexual Availability in '*Twelfth Night*', in Zimmerman (ed.), *Erotic Politics*, p. 32, makes the claim for dependent sodomy as an accepted practice; hence the service which the cross-dressed Viola owes her master Orsino, Jardine says, is anal, although during or between precisely which scenes she does not vouchsafe.
58. John Donne, 'On his Mistress'. Aretino, *Dialogue of Courtesans*, discussed in Kott, *Shakespeare Our Contemporary*, 213.
59. The Peter Stein production is reported in J. Kott, 'The Gender of Rosalind', *NTQ*, 26, 1990, p. 117. Traub, 'The (In)significance of "Lesbian" Desire in Early Modern England', in Zimmerman (ed.), *Erotic Politics*, p. 157, would extend this presumption to Helena and Hermia in *A Midsummer Night's Dream*.
60. V. O. Freeburg, *Disguise Plots in Elizabethan Drama*, Blom, 1965, p. 78. Shapiro, *Gender in Play*, p. 120, is more specific and has the French Lady submit to sodomy to maintain her disguise, albeit that Heywood, the play's author, in his *Apology for Acting*, 1612, C3R/V, specifically defends his quality against such imputations: 'nor can I imagine any man, that hath in him any taste or relish of Christianity, to be guilty of so abhored a sin'.
61. Kahn, *Man's Estate*, p. 196. Sinfield, 'How to Read *The Merchant of Venice*', p. 120, quotes Janet Adelman to the same effect: 'We do not move directly from family bonds to marriage without an intervening period in which our friendships with same sex friends help us to establish our identities.'
62. C. Bingham, 'Seventeenth-Century Attitudes to Deviant Sex', *Journal of Interdisciplinary History*, 1, 1971, 447–68.
63. T. D. Moodie, *et al.*, 'Migrancy and Male Sexuality in the South African Gold Mines', in Duberman (ed.), *Hidden From History*, give details of 'metsha', a similar practice. M. Garber, *Vested Interests*, Routledge, 1992, pp. 235f. suggests that a more elaborate stratagem of this kind enabled the French diplomat to be deceived in the real-life case that forms the subject of D. Hwang's play *M. Butterfly*, Penguin, 1986.
64. McLuskie, *Renaissance Dramatists*, p. 120. Greenblatt, *Will in the World*, p. 333, takes a similar view of James' behaviour.
65. Daileader, *Eroticism on the Renaissance Stage*, p. 28.
66. C. Bingham, *James I of England*, Weidenfeld and Nicholson, 1981, pp. 78f.; J. Goldberg, *James I and the Politics of Literature*, Johns Hopkins University Press, 1983.
67. And precisely the kind of activity indicated in the opening of Marlowe's *Dido*, written for children. Both J. G. MacDonald, 'Marlowe's Ganymede', in Comesoli and Russell (eds.), *Enacting Gender*, p. 103, and Jardine, *Still Harping on Daughters*, p. 22, assume from this exchange that Jove's relationship with Ganymede involves 'homosexuality and paedophilia', but despite

the Roman slant often given to this story, the relationship conceived in Marlowe's play may be no more than is described. Although Howard, *The Stage and Social Struggle*, p. 177, argues that when the city wives in *The Roaring Girl* say they must 'ingle with our husbands abed' to get special favours for the gallants, this must indicate that they are providing something special, i.e. anal intercourse, it may be rather that, since the husbands get so little sex, they will be happy with some kissing and cuddling.

68. D. Cressey, *Travesties and Transgressions in Tudor and Stuart England*, Oxford University Press, 2000, finds that in more than two dozen plays featuring a man disguised as a woman, 'Rather than being effeminized, the cross-dressed man is more often rendered as proactive, virile and effective.'

69. A point made long ago by C. L. Barber, *Shakespeare's Festive Comedy* (1959), Princeton University Press, 1972, p. 245: 'the disguising of a girl as a boy in *Twelfth Night* is exploited so as to renew ... our sense of difference ... it is when the normal is secure that playful aberration is benign', a view Greenblatt, *Shakespearean Negotiations*, pp. 72f., questions but does not adequately refute.

3 STAGE COSTUME AND PERFORMER ETHOS

1. P. Stallybrass, 'Transvestitism and the "Body Beneath": Speculating on the Boy Actor', in Zimmerman (ed.), *Erotic Politics*, p. 74.

2. S. Orgel and R. Strong, *Inigo Jones: The Theatre of the Stuart Court*, California University Press, 1973, catalogue no. 424. For details of Murray's career see Bentley, *Jacobean and Caroline Stage*, vol. I, pp. 60–1, vol. IV, pp. 477–8, and vol. VI, p. 58.

3. H. Prunierres, *Le Ballet de Cour en France avant Benserade et Lully*, Laurens, 1914, p. 181, suggests that at the French Court a distinction was made between genuinely nude players and those who represented nudity in 'maillots' i.e. fleshings, and that boy singers occasionally represented both genders by the former means. Buontalenti's designs for his *intermezzi* during Bargagli's *La Pellegrina* at the Florentine Court in 1589, on the other hand, show the widespread use of prosthesis to represent naked breasts (see D. Jones and P. Gerhardt, *Una Stravaganza dei Medici*, 1990, an illustrated booklet of the Channel 4 recreation).

4. S. Clark, '*Hic Mulier*', *Studies in Philology*, 82, 1985, 169.

5. Quoted in Geoffrey Bullough (ed.), *Narrative and Dramatic Sources of Shakespeare*, vol. II, Routledge and Kegan Paul, 1963, p. 203.

6. W. Hooper, 'The Tudor Sumptuary Laws', *English Historical Review*, 30, 1915, 448.

7. S. N. Garner, ' "Let Her Paint an Inch Thick" ', *Renaissance Drama*, 20, 1989, 132.

8. Wigs were obviously used in the theatre, e.g. Hamlet's 'perriwig-pated fellow' and the 'peruke' removed in *Epicoene* to reveal the real gender of Morose's wife. In v.i of *The Wise Woman of Hogsden* (1604), however, a breeched heroine

establishes her real identity when she 'scatters her hair', which rather suggests the performer's own.

9. A. Lommel, *Masks: Their Meaning and Function*, Ferndale, 1981, pp. 181 and 219.
10. E. J. Jensen, 'The Boy Actors: Plays and Playing', *Research Opportunities in Renaissance Drama*, 18, 1975, 6.
11. R. Kimborough, 'Androgyny Seen through Shakespeare's Disguise', *Shakespeare Quarterly*, 33, (1982), 17–33.
12. McLuskie, *Renaissance Dramatists*, p. 102.
13. P. Rackin, 'Shakespeare's Boy Cleopatra', *PMLA*, 87, 1972, 201; M. Sprengnether, 'The Boy Actor and Femininity in *Antony and Cleopatra*, in Holland *et al.* (eds.), *Shakespeare's Personality*, p. 202; K. Muir, 'Male as Female on the Elizabethan Stage', in Sharma (ed.), *Essays on Shakespeare*, p. 4; M. L. Novy, *Love's Argument*, North Carolina University Press, 1984, p. 189.
14. M. Shapiro, 'Boying Her Greatness', *Modern Language Review*, 77, 1982, p. 13, recalling Bethel's 'dual consciousness', says Shakespeare 'was certifying the audience's awareness of the technique of presenting Cleopatra to be a valid part of its experience of the play'.
15. L. A. Soule, 'Subversive Rosalind: Cocky Ros in the Forest of Arden', *NTQ*, 26, 1990, 126–36.
16. For players threatening spectators see particularly B2 V of *Tarlton's Jests* (1638), facsimile reprint by Edmund J. Ashbee, Kirkwall, and discussed in Mann, *Elizabethan Player*, pp. 59–62.
17. Goethe is discussing the performance of the hostess in Goldoni's *La Locandiera* at Rome in 1788, his first experience of cross-dressed performance. Quoted in A. M. Nagler, *A Sourcebook in Theatrical History*, Dover, 1952, p. 435.

4 MALE DIDACTICISM AND FEMALE STEREOTYPING

1. E.g. Greene, 'Shakespeare's Cressida', p. 145, and B. A. Mowat, 'Images of Women in Shakespeare's Plays', *Southern Humanities Review*, 11, 1977, 145. Thoughtful discussions of stereotyping include M. Andresen-Thom, 'Thinking about Women and their Prosperous Art', *Shakespeare Studies*, 11, 1978, 264, Gottlieb, " I Will Be Free", p. 110, and McLuskie, '"The Emperor of Russia Was My Father"', in W. Habicht, *et al.* (eds.), *Images of Shakespeare*, Delaware University Press, 1988, p. 176.
2. E. Burns, *Character: Acting and Being on the Pre-Modern Stage*, Macmillan, 1990, p. 32; M. Goldman, *The Actor's Freedom*, Viking, 1975, p. 50.
3. I should like to express my gratitude to the actors who took part in this interview with a group of students, and to emphasise that their comments were made off the cuff.
4. Juliet Stephenson and Fiona Shaw are quoted in Rutter (ed.), *Clamorous Voices*, pp. xxiv and xxv.
5. Quoted in C. McKewin, 'Shakespeare Liberata', *Mosaic*, 10, 3, 1977, 164. C. T. Neely, 'Men and Women in *Othello*, in Lenz (ed.), *Woman's Part*,

260   *Notes to pages 124–45*

p. 220. She explains of Desdemona: 'Her naiveté and docility in the willow scene are partly a result of her confusion and exhaustion but perhaps also a protective façade behind which she waits, as she did during courtship, whilst determining the most appropriate and fruitful reaction to Othello's rage.'

6. Ranald, 'Manning of the Haggard', p. 157; C. Heilbrun, 'The Character of Hamlet's Mother', *Shakespeare Quarterly*, 8, 1957, 201–6.

7. Gay, *As She Likes It*, pp. 120f., illustrates the modern tendency to take Isabella's silence at the Duke's proposal in *Measure for Measure* as a refusal.

8. By using the term 'acquiescence' I do not mean to imply that these are 'seductions' rather than 'rapes'. Daileader, *Eroticism on the Renaissance Stage*, pp. 27–8, is perfectly right to criticise editors for describing these encounters so, e.g. J. R. Mulryne in the Revels edition of *Women Beware Women*. See also J. Forrrester, 'Rape, Seduction and Psychoanalysis', S. Tomaselli and R. Porter (eds.) in, *Rape an Historical and Cultural Enquiry*, Blackwell, 1986.

9. D. N. Rodowick, *The Difficulty of Difference: Psychoanalysis, Sexual Difference, and Film Theory*, Routledge, 1991, pp. 1f.

10. S. Eaton, 'Defacing the Feminine in Renaissance Tragedy', in Wayne, *Matter of Difference*, p. 186.

11. C. Tavris and C. Offir, *The Longest War: Sex Differences in Perspective*, Harcourt Brace, 1977. Rogers, *Troublesome Helpmate*, R. H. Block, 'Medieval Misogyny', *Representations*, 10, 1987, Andresen-Thom, 'Thinking About Women', p. 266, and J. Kelly, 'Early Feminist Theory and the Querelle des Femmes, 1400–1789', *Signs*, 8, 1, 1982, 13.

12. P. Rackin, 'Anti-Historians: Women's Roles in Shakespeare's History Plays', *Theatre Journal*, 37, 3, 1985, 337.

13. N. Z. Davis, *Society and Culture in Early Modern France*, Stanford University Press, 1965, pp. 124f., provides testimony to the effectiveness and invulnerability of the scold by its male imitation in civil riots throughout Europe. Scolding is essentially an oral form, but examples in print include A. Dworkin, *Womenhating*, Dutton, 1974, and J. Smith, *Misogynies*, Faber, 1989.

14. C. Hoover, 'Goneril and Regan', *San Jose Studies*, 10, 3, 1984, 49–65. Ingram, 'In the Posture of a Whore', pp. 251–6.

15. I note the recent conviction amongst scholars that Shakespeare was a Catholic, c.g. Honigmann, *Shakespeare the Lost Years*, and more recently a whole raft of books from Manchester University Press too late to be included in this study, but can only point to the evidence of the plays on this particular matter.

16. Chaucer too, in the *Clerk of Oxford's Tale* in *The Canterbury Tales*, Lines 1142–6, makes it clear that if 'wyves sholde / Folwen Grisilde as in humylitee . . . it were importable'. His intention is to draw a wider moral, 'that every wight, in his degree, / Sholde be constant in adversitee'.

17. D. S. Kastan, 'Proud Majesty Made Subject', *Shakespeare Quarterly*, 37, 4, 1986, pp. 459–75. See also Howard, *Stage and Social Struggle*, p. 31, and Orgel, *Impersonations*, p. 100.

18. M. Johnson, *Images of Women in the Works of Thomas Heywood*, Salzburg University Press, 1974, p. 61.

19. A. Jamieson, *Shakespeare's Heroines: Characteristics of Women: Moral, Poetical, and Historical* (1832), 2nd edition, Bell, 1913, pp. 182 and 173. G. W. Knight, *Wheel of Fire*, Methuen, revised edition 1949, p. 111. W. H. Auden, 'The Joker in the Pack', in J. Wain (ed.), *Othello Casebook*, Macmillan, 1971, p. 220. M. R. Ridley (ed.), *Othello*, Arden Shakespeare, Methuen, 1958, p. lxv.

20. N. B. Allen, 'The Two Parts of *Othello*,' in Muir and Edwards, *Aspects of 'Othello'*.

21. McLuskie, '"The Emperor of Russia Was My Father"', p. 177: 'All of the images imposed on Desdemona – or rather that construct Desdemona, for she has no existence outside them – are drawn from custom or convention or indeed from literary tradition.' Her figure, she says, p. 179, is 'the site of meaning generated by others'.

22. Burns, *Character*, p. 186, argues that it was not until Garrick that acting was seen as 'the presentation . . . of a coherent and consistent individual'. In the period under discussion, acting had 'as its objective', Burns says, 'the rhetorical expression of common passions', and the performer would be no more than what A. J. Greimas has called an *'actant'*, 'a function in a narrative structure' (cited in Burns, *Character*, p. 226); so that male as well as female characters would lack the 'wholeness' which modern acting theory assumes.

23. Orgel, 'Nobody's Perfect', p. 9.

24. Neely, 'Men and Women in *Othello*, p. 213.

25. C. C. Rutter, *Enter the Body*, Routledge, 2001, pp. 142f. provides a very detailed account of Zoë Wanamaker's sensitive and imaginative performance of Emilia in Trevor Nunn's 1990 production of *Othello*, much of it interpreting Emilia's silences. Both are creative endeavours by clever, thoughtful, modern women who build on the original text in an entirely legitimate way, but whether they can be said to 'recuperate' it is more doubtful. To do so would be to posit layers of meaning not available to the original male performers that have lain obscured until the present day, an assumption that is perhaps unduly overweening.

26. Fiedler, *Stranger in Shakespeare*, pp. 63–4.

27. Echols, 'The New Feminism of Yin and Yang', p. 67, quoting 'Joreen's "Bitch Manifesto"'.

28. J. L. Klein, 'Lady Macbeth: Infirm of Purpose', in Lenz, *Woman's Part*, p. 245.

29. Sarah Siddons, 'Remarks on the Character of Lady Macbeth', in Cole and Chinoy, *Actors on Acting*, p. 142.

30. K. Tynan, *Tynan on Theatre*, Penguin, 1964, p. 108: 'Lady Macbeth . . . needs to be sexless . . . In fact it is probably a mistake to cast a woman at all . . .'

31. D. Biggins, 'Sexuality, Witchcraft, and Violence in *Macbeth*', *Shakespeare Studies*, 8, 1975, 255–77.

5 DRAMATIC EMPATHY AND MORAL AMBIGUITY

1. Bloch, 'Medieval Misogyny', on ambivalence; Rogers, *Troublesome Helpmate*, pp. 3f. on the misogyny of the early Church; and P. S. Berggren, 'The Woman's Part', in Lenz, *Woman's Part*, p. 26, on male transfer of guilt.

2. Harriet Walter quoted in Wandor, *Carry On Understudies*, p. 103. See also Novy, 'Patriarchy and Play', p. 19, on the cross-gender nature of acting.

3. Thomson, *Shakespeare's Professional Career*, p. 69; G. Salgado, *The Elizabethan Underworld*, Alan Sutton, 1984, pp. 51 and 58; Rutter, *Documents of the Rose Playhouse*, pp. 72–3.

4. See also 'Shakespeare as Expurgator' in A. Harbage, *Shakespeare and the Rival Traditions*, Indiana University Press, 1952, p. 351.

5. R. A. Foakes, *Shakespeare: The Dark Comedies to the Last Plays: From Satire to Celebration*, Routledge Kegan Paul, 1971, p. 53.

6. J. Berger, *Ways of Seeing*, BBC/Penguin, 1972, pp. 45–7.

7. C. Belsey, 'Alice Arden's Crime', in D. S. Kastan and P. Stalleybrass (eds.), *Staging the Renaissance*, Routledge, 1991, p. 135.

8. Jardine, *Still Harping on Daughters*, p. 77. W. Empson, 'Mine Eyes Dazzle', a review of Clifford Leech's *Webster: 'The Duchess of Malfi'*, in *Essays in Criticism*, 14, 1964. E. Brennan (ed.), New Mermaid edition of *The Duchess of Malfi*, 1967, p. xii.

6 SEXUAL VIOLENCE

1. C. C. Rutter, 'Learning Thisbe's Part', *Shakespeare Bulletin*, 22, 3, Fall, 2004, 5–30, provides a detailed account of the centrality of female suffering as subject matter in school training in Latin rhetoric.

2. The especial cruelty inflicted on Middle Eastern women in plays like *Alphonsus, King of Aragon*, *The White Devil*, *A Looking Glass for London*, and *The Blind Beggar of Alexandria* seems associated with the extreme lasciviousness ascribed to them, and often found in popular dramas exploiting quasi-factual accounts of returned adventurers, such as *A Christian Turned Turk*, *The Battle of Alcazar*, and *Captain Thomas Stukely*. For a more sympathetic account, see *The Travels of Three English Brothers*.

3. M. Wynne-Davies, '"The Swallowing Womb": Consumed and Consuming Women in *Titus Andronicus*', in Wayne, *Matter of Difference*, p. 130.

4. S. Gossett, '"Best Men Are Moulded of Faults"', *English Literary Renaissance*, 14, 3, 1984, 311–12.

5. R. Porter, 'Rape – Does it have a Historical Meaning?', in Tomaselli and Porter (eds.), *Rape*.

6. F. Zeitlin, 'Configurations of Rape in Greek Myth', in Tomaselli and Porter (eds.), *Rape*, pp. 132f., and J. Warrington, *Everyman's Classical Dictionary*, Dent, 1969, p. 512. There are further problems with rape in Greek myth as a metaphor for the fusion of cultures/peoples (see de Beauvoir, *Second Sex*, p. 106).

7. C. R. Stimpson, 'Shakespeare and the Soil of Rape', in Lenz, *Woman's Part*, p. 62, Wynne-Davies, '"The Swallowing Womb"', p. 132, and K. Cunningham, '"Scars Can Bear Witness"', in K. A. Ackley (ed.), *Women and Violence in Literature*, Garland, 1990.

8. C. Kahn, 'The Rape of Shakespeare's "Lucrece"', *Shakespeare Studies*, 9, 1976, 45–77.

9. J. Dundas, 'Mocking the Mind', *Sixteenth Century Journal*, 14, 1, 1983, 14.
10. I. Donaldson, *The Rapes of Lucrece*, Oxford University Press, 1982, p. 40.
11. See M. Jacobs, *Nude Painting*, Phaidon, 1979, p. 24, for details of Correggio's paintings. N. Bryson, 'Two Narratives of Rape in Visual Arts', in Tomaselli and Porter (eds.), *Rape*, pp. 164 and 167.
12. See for instance the *Virgin Annunciate*, c.1474, by Antonella da Messina.
13. See also T. E. Henn, *Harvest of Tragedy*, 2nd edition, Methuen, 1966, p. 53, Greenblatt, *Shakepearean Negotiations*, p. 183, and Stimpson, 'Shakespeare and the Soil of Rape', p. 61.
14. K. Silverman, 'Masochism and Subjectivity', *Framework*, 12, 1981, 5.
15. M. Shapiro, *Children of the Revels*, Columbia University Press, 1977, p. 171.
16. Gilder, *Enter the Actress*, p. 34. For a more conventional view see P. Schroeder, 'Hroswitha and the Feminisation of Drama', in J. Redmonds (ed.), *Women in Theatre*, Cambridge University Press, 1989, p. 52. *Sapientia* was one of two plays revived by M. M. Butler and reported in her study, *Hrotsvitha: The Theatricality of Her Plays*, Philosophical Library, 1960. The tortures, the reader may be relieved to note, were represented by 'stylized movement' (p. 170).
17. R. K. Gordon (trans.), *Anglo-Saxon Poetry*, Dent, 1954, p. 236.
18. B. Faust, *Women, Sex and Pornography*, Penguin, 1981, p. 79. See also K. E. Maus, 'Horns of a Dilemma: Jealousy, Gender and Spectatorship in English Renaissance Drama', *ELH*, 54, 1987, 562.
19. H. Gorer, *The Revolutionary Ideas of the Marquis de Sade*, Wishart, 1934, p. 202.

7 POSITIVE REPRESENTATIONS OF YOUNG WOMEN

1. 'The clear pure Heaven yearns to wound the Earth / and yearning seizes the Earth to wed the Heaven – / rain comes down from the throbbing skies / and pierces the Earth ... and from that drenching marriage-rite the woods, / the spring bursts forth in bloom' – an Aeschylean fragment quoted in R. Fagles (trans.), *Aeschylus, 'The Oresteia'*, Penguin, 1977, p. 41. For a very different view see Ann Thompson, 'Feminist Theory and the Editing of Shakespeare' (1997), in Chedgzoy, *Shakespeare, Feminism and Gender*, p. 55.
2. C. McKewin, 'Counsels of Gall and Grace', in Lenz, *Woman's Part*.
3. Dash, *Wooing, Wedding, and Power*, p. 37. Neely, 'Men and Women in *Othello*, p. 233. Maus, 'Horns of a Dilemma', p. 575. V. Traub, 'Jewels, Statues, and Corpses', *Shakespeare Studies*, 20, 1988, 223, and E. A. Snow, 'Sexual Anxiety and the Male Order of Things in *Othello*, *English Literary Renaissance*, 10, 1980, 390, argue that the strawberries symbolise hymeneal blood.
4. M. French, *Shakespeare's Division of Experience*, Jonathan Cape, 1982, p. 325, and *passim*; A. Barton, 'Was Shakespeare a Chauvinist?' *New York Review of Books*, 11 June 1981.
5. Barker, *Prefaces to Shakespeare*, p. 15; Muir, 'Male as Female', p. 2. See Durband, *Shakespeare Made Easy: 'Macbeth'*, Stanley Thornes, 1984, and more recently Kinney, *Companion to Renaissance Drama*, 2004, p. 210.

6. B. Dickins and R. M. Wilson (eds.), *Early Middle English Texts*, Bowes and Bowes, 1951, pp. 132–5.

7. Dusinberre, *Shakespeare and the Nature of Women*, p. 232. R. Stoller, *Observing the Erotic Imagination*, Yale University Press, 1985, p. 135.

8. G. Tiffany, *Erotic Beasts and Social Monsters*, Delaware University Press, 1995, p. 68.

9. P. Hyland, 'Shakespeare's Heroines', *Ariel*, 9, 1978, 18. C. Belsey, 'Disrupting Sexual Differences: Meaning and Gender in the Comedies', in J. Drakakis (ed.), *Alternative Shakespeares*, Methuen, 1985, p. 180.

10. Howard, 'Crossdressing', p. 435. Novy, 'Patriarchy and Play ', p. 191, and P. Rackin, 'Androgyny, Mimesis, and the Marriage of the Boy Heroine on the English Renaissance Stage', *PMLA*, 102, 1987, 29.

11. J. Riviere, 'Womanliness as Masquerade', *International Journal of Psychoanalysis*, vol. 10, 1929, 303–13 (see below).

12. W. R. Titterton, *From Theatre to Music Hall*, Swift, 1912, pp. 145–51, W. Disher, *Winkles and Champagne*, Collins, 1938, p. 76. See also S. Maitland, *Vesta Tilley*, Virago Press, 1986.

13. I. Buruma, *Behind the Mask*, Pantheon, 1984, p. 116.

14. Lennam, *Sebastian Westcott*, p. 36.

15. J. Dunbar, *Peg Woffington and her World*, Heinemann, 1968, p. 39.

16. Pepys, *Diaries*, 23 February 1662–3.

17. C. C. Park, 'As We Like It: How a Girl Can be Smart and Still Popular', *American Scholar*, 42, 1973, 265.

18. See W. Smith, *The Commedia dell'arte*, Lancaster Press, 1912, p. 49, on whiffling actresses.

19. Freeburg, *Disguise Plots*, pp. 67–8. See J. Anson, 'Female Monks: the Transvestite Motif in Early Christian Literature', *Viator*, 5, 1974, on the genesis of the breeched heroine in early monastic literature.

20. Barber, *Shakespeare's Festive Comedy*. See also N. Frye, *A Natural Perspective*, Columbia University Press, 1965.

21. McLuskie, '"The Emperor of Russia Was My Father"', p. 186.

22. McLuskie, *Renaissance Dramatists*, p. 49.

23. Thomas quoted in Woodbridge, *Women and the English Renaissance*, p. 135.

24. Orgel, *Impersonations*, p. 117.

25. Aristotle, *Poetics*, trans. T. S. Dorsch, Penguin, 1965, chapter 14: 'Fear and Pity', p. 50.

26. E.g. Belsey, 'Disrupting Sexual Differences', p. 187, and Shapiro, *Gender in Play*, pp. 84 and 112.

27. Dusinberre, *Shakespeare and the Nature of Women*, p. 95. C. Leventon, 'Patrimony and Patriarchy in *The Merchant of Venice*', in Wayne (ed.), *Matter of Difference*, on the other hand, argues that the play reinforces the values of the patriarchy by showing that obedient daughters fare better than unruly ones.

28. See Kahn, *Man's Estate*, p. 12, and Andresen-Thom, 'Thinking About Women', p. 274.

29. Notice Jonson's persistent campaign to brand the female intellectual as monstrous; e.g. Lady Would-Be in *Volpone*, the collegiate ladies in *Epicoene*, and Doll Common's impersonation of the 'rare' female scholar in *The Alchemist*, 'gone mad with studying Broughton's works'. Chapman, however, describes Cornelia in *Caesar and Pompey* as 'most loving and learned', and even Heywood's presentation of Anne Frankford as a 'scholar' is meant to be positive.
30. F. D. Waage, 'Meg and Moll: Two Renaissance London Heroines', *Journal of Popular Culture*, 20, 1, 1986, 105–17, p. 112.

Bibliography

Aldington, R., *A Book of Characters*, George Routledge.

Allen, N. B., 'The Two Parts of *Othello*', in Muir and Edwards (eds.), *Aspects of Othello*.

Anderson, M., *Approaches to the History of the Western Family 1500–1914*, Cambridge University Press, 1995.

Andresen-Thom, M., 'Thinking about Women and their Prosperous Art: a Reply to Juliet Dusinberre's "Shakespeare and the Nature of Women"', *Shakespeare Studies*, 11, 1978.

Anson, J., 'Female Monks: the Transvestite Motif in Early Christian Literature', *Viator*, 5, 1974.

Aristotle, *Poetics*, trans. T. S. Dorsch, Penguin, 1965.

Asp, C., 'In Defence of Cressida', *Studies in Philology*, 74, 1977.

Ashton, G., *Shakespeare's Heroines in the Nineteenth Century*, Derbyshire Museum Service, 1980.

Auden, W. H., 'The Joker in the Pack', in J. Wain (ed.), *Othello Casebook*, Macmillan, 1971.

Baldwin, T. W., *The Organisation and Personnel of the Shakespearean Company*, Princeton University Press, 1927.

Barber, C. L., *Shakespeare's Festive Comedy* (1959), Princeton University Press, 1972.

Barish, J., *Anti-Theatrical Prejudice*, California University Press, 1981.

Barker, H. Granville, *Prefaces to Shakespeare*, Vol. I, (1930), Batsford, 1963.

Barton, A., 'Was Shakespeare a Chauvinist?', *New York Review of Books*, 11 June 1981.

Baskervill, C. R., *The Elizabethan Jig and Related Song Drama* (1929), Dover, 1965.

Bate, J., *The Genius of Shakespeare*, Picador, 1997.

Bean, J. C., 'Passion versus Friendship in Tudor Matrimonial Handbooks and some Shakespearean Implications', *Wascana Review*, 9, 1, 1974.

   'Comic Structure and the Humanising of Kate in *The Taming of the Shrew*', in Lenz *et al.* (eds.), *The Woman's Part*.

Beckerman, B., *Shakespeare at the Globe*, Macmillan, 1962.

Belsey, C., 'Disrupting Sexual Differences: Meaning and Gender in the Comedies', in J. Drakakis (ed.), *Alternative Shakespeares*, Methuen, 1985.

   'Alice Arden's Crime', in Kastan and Stalleybrass (eds.), *Staging the Renaisance*.

'Desire's Excess and the English Renaissance Theatre.', in Zimmerman (ed.), *Erotic Politics*.

Benjamin, W., *Charles Baudelaire: A Lyric Poet in the Era of High Capitalism*, New Left Books, 1973.

Bentley, G. E., *The Jacobean and Caroline Stage*, Oxford University Press, 1941.
The Profession of Player in Shakespeare's Time, Princeton University Press, 1971.
The Profession of Dramatist in Shakespeare's Time, Princeton University Press, 1971.

Bentley, G. E., (ed.), *The Seventeenth Century Stage*, Chicago University Press, 1968.

Berger, J., *Ways of Seeing*, BBC/Penguin, 1972.

Bergeron, D., 'The Wife of Bath and Shakespeare's *The Taming of the Shrew*', *University Review*, 36, 1969.

Berggren, P. S., 'The Woman's Part: Female Sexuality as Power in Shakespeare's Plays', in Lenz (ed.), *Woman's Part*.

Berry, F., *The Shakespeare Inset*, Southern Illinois University Press, 1971.

Berry, H., 'The Player's Apprentice', *Essays in Theatre*, 1, 2, 1983.

Bethel, S. L., 'Shakespeare's Actors', *Review of English Studies*, New Series, 1, 1950.

Bevington, D., *From Mankind to Marlowe*, Harvard University Press, 1962.

Biggins, D., 'Sexuality, Witchcraft, and Violence in *Macbeth*', *Shakespeare Studies*, 8, 1975.

Bingham, C., 'Seventeenth-Century Attitudes to Deviant Sex', *Journal of Interdisciplinary History*, 1, 1971.
James I of England, Weidenfeld & Nicholson, 1981.

Binns, J. W., 'Women or Transvestites on the Elizabethan Stage: an Oxford Controversy', *Sixteenth Century Journal*, vol. 2, October 1974.

Block, R. H., 'Medieval Misogyny', *Representations*, 10, 1987.

Boas, F. S., *University Drama in the Tudor Age*, Oxford University Press, 1914.

Boas, G., *Shakespeare and the Young Actor*, Rockcliff, 1955.

Boswell, J., 'Revolutions, Universals and Sexual Categories', in Duberman *et al.* (eds.), *Hidden From History*.

Bradbrook, M. C., *The Rise of the Common Player* (1962), Cambridge University Press, 1979.

Bray, A., *Homosexuality in Renaissance England*, Gay Men's Press, 1982.

Brown, I., *Shakespeare Memorial Theatre 1951–53*, Theatre Art Books, 1953.

Brown, J., 'Lesbian Sexuality in Medieval and Early Modern Europe', in Duberman *et al.* (eds.), *Hidden From History*.

Brown, P.A., and P. Parolin (eds.), *Women Players in England 1500–1642*, Ashgate, 2005.

Brown, S., 'The Boyhood of Shakespeare's Heroines: Notes on Gender Ambiguity in the Sixteenth Century', *Studies in English Literature*, 30, 2, 1990.
Shakespeare Memorial Theatre, 1954–56, Max Reinhardt, 1956.

Bryson, N., 'Two Narratives of Rape in Visual Arts: Lucretia and the Sabine Women', in Tomaselli and Porter (eds.), *Rape*.

Buckner, H. T., 'The Transvestic Career Path', *Psychiatry*, 33, 1970.

Burns, E., *Character: Acting and Being on the Pre-Modern Stage*, Macmillan, 1990.

Buruma, I., *Behind the Mask*, Pantheon, 1984.

Butler, M. M., *Hrotsvitha: The Theatricality of Her Plays*, Philosophical Library, 1960.

Callaghan, D., *Shakespeare Without Women: Representing Gender and Race on the Renaissance Stage*, Routledge, 2000.

Callow, S., *Being an Actor*, Penguin, 1985.

Campbell, O. J., *Comical Satyre and Shakespeare's 'Troilus and Cressida'*, Huntington Library Publications, 1938.

Carlisle, C. J., *Shakespeare from the Greenroom*, University of North Carolina Press, 1969.

Cerasano, S. P., and Marion Wynne-Davies (eds.), *Renaissance Drama by Women*, Routledge, 1996.

Chambers, E. K., *The Elizabethan Stage*, Oxford University Press, 1923.

Chauncey Jnr, G., 'Christian Brotherhood or Sexual Perversion? Homosexual Identities and the Construction of Sexual Boundaries in World War I', in Duberman *et al.* (eds.), *Hidden From History*.

Chedgzoy, K., (ed.), *Shakespeare, Feminism and Gender*, Palgrave, 2001.

Cibber, C., *An Apology for the Life of Mr Colley Cibber* (1793), Whittaker, Treacher & Arnott, 1830.

Clark, A., *Working Life of Women in the Seventeenth Century* (1919), Frank Cass, 1968.

Clark, S., *'Hic Mulier, Haec Vir* and the Controversy over Masculine Women', *Studies in Philology*, 82, 1985.

Cohen, E., 'Legislating the Norm: from Sodomy to Gross Indecency', *South Atlantic Quarterly*, 88 1, Winter 1989.

Cole, D., *The Theatrical Event: A Mythos, a Vocabulary, a Perspective*, Wesleyan University Press, 1974.

Cole, T., and H. K. Chinoy (eds.), *Actors on Acting*, Crown, revised edition 1970.

Coleman, E. A. M., *The Dramatic Use of Bawdy in Shakespeare*, Longman, 1974.

Comesoli, V., and A. Russell (eds.), *Enacting Gender on the English Renaissance Stage*, Illinois University Press, 1999.

Cook, A., *The Privileged Playgoers of Shakespeare's London*, Princeton University Press, 1981.

Cook, J., *Women in Shakespeare*, Harrap, 1980.

Craig, S., (ed.), *Dreams and Deconstructions*, Amber Lane, 1980.

Cressey, D., *Travesties and Transgressions in Tudor and Stuart England*, Oxford University Press, 2000.

Cunningham, K., ' "Scars Can Bear Witness": Trial by Ordeal and Lavinia's Body in *Titus Andronicus*', in K. A. Ackley (ed.), *Women and Violence in Literature*, Garland, 1990.

Daileader, C., *Eroticism on the Renaissance Stage: Transcendence, Desire, and the Limits of the Visible*, Cambridge University Press, 1998.

Danby, J. F., *Shakespeare's Doctrine of Nature*, Faber, 1961.

Dash, I., *Wooing, Wedding, and Power: Women in Shakespeare's Plays*, Columbia University Press, 1981.

David, R., 'Shakespeare and the Players', in P. Alexander (ed.), *Studies in Shakespeare*, Oxford University Press, 1964.

Davidson, P., *Popular Appeal in English Drama to 1850*, Barnes & Noble, 1982.

Davies, W. Robertson, *Shakespeare's Boy Actors*, Dent, 1939.

Davis, N. Z., *Society and Culture in Early Modern France*, Stanford University Press, 1965.

de Beauvoir, S., *The Second Sex* (1949), trans. H. M. Parshley, Pan, 1988.

de Jongh, N., *Not in Front of the Audience*, Routledge, 1992.

de Marly, D., *Fashion for Men*, Batsford, 1985.

Dickins, B., and Wilson, R. M. (eds.), *Early Middle English Texts*, Bowes and Bowes, 1951.

Diehl, H., 'The Iconography of Violence in English Renaissance Tragedy', *Renaissance Drama*, New Series, 2, 1980.

Disher, W., *Winkles and Champagne*, Collins, 1938.

Doane, M. A., 'Film and Masquerade: Theorising the Female Spectator', *Screen*, 23 (3/4),1982.

Donaldson, I., *The Rapes of Lucrece: A Myth and its Transformations*, Oxford University Press, 1982.

Downes, J., *Roscius Anglicanus (1708)*, edited by J. Milhouse and R. D. Hume, Society for Theatre Research, 1987.

Duberman, M., *et al.*, *Hidden from History*, New American Library, 1989.

Dunbar, J., *Peg Woffington and her World*, Heinemann, 1968.

Dundas, J., 'Mocking the Mind: the Role of Art in Shakespeare's *Rape of Lucrece*', *Sixteenth Century Journal*, 14, 1, 1983.

Durband, A., *Shakespeare Made Easy: 'Macbeth'*, Stanley Thornes, 1984.

Dusinberre, J., *Shakespeare and the Nature of Women*, Macmillan, 1975.

Dworkin, A., *Womenhating*, Dutton, 1974.

Eaton, S., 'Defacing the Feminine in Renaissance Tragedy', in Wayne (ed.), *The Matter of Difference*.

Ellis, H., *Eonism*, 1923.

Echols, A., 'The New Feminism of Yin and Yang', in Snitow (ed.), *Desire*.

Elsom, J. (ed.), *Is Shakespeare Still Our Contemporary?*, Routledge, 1989.

Elyot, Sir Thomas, *The Book Named the Governor* (1531), S. E. Lehmberg (ed.), Everyman, 1962.

Empson, W., 'Mine Eyes Dazzle', a review of Clifford Leech's *Webster: 'The Duchess of Malfi'*, in *Essays in Criticism*, 14, 1964.

English, D., *et al.*, 'Talking Sex: a Conversation on Sexuality and Feminism', *Socialist Review*, 58, 1981.

Erickson, P., *Patriarchal Structures in Shakespeare's Drama*, California University Press, 1985.

Esslin, M., *Theatre of the Absurd*, Penguin, revised edition, 1968.

Evans, G. B. (ed.), *The Riverside Shakespeare*, Houghton Mifflin, 1974.

Evans, H. A., *English Masques* (1897), Books for Libraries Press, 1971.

Fagles, R., (trans.), *Aeschylus, 'The Oresteia'*, Penguin, 1977.

Faust, B., *Women, Sex and Pornography*, Penguin, 1981.

Fiedler, L., *The Stranger in Shakespeare*, Croom Helm, 1973.

Findlay, A., *A Feminist Perspective on Renaissance Drama*, Blackwell, 1999.

Fitz, L. T., 'Egyptian Queens and Male Reviewers: Sexist Attitudes in *Antony and Cleopatra* Criticism', *Shakespeare Quarterly*, 28, 1977.

Flugel, W., *The Psychology of Clothes*, Hogarth Press, 1950.

Foakes, R. A., *Shakespeare: The Dark Comedies to the Last Plays: From Satire to Celebration*, Routledge Kegan Paul, 1971.

    Illustrations of the English Stage 1580–1642, Scholars Press, 1985.

Forrester, J., 'Rape, Seduction and Psychoanalysis', in Tomaselli and Porter, (eds.), *Rape*.

Foucault, M., *The History of Sexuality*, Random House, 1978.

Frye, N., *A Natural Perspective*, Columbia University Press, 1965.

Freeburg, V. O., *Disguise Plots in Elizabethan Drama: A Study in Stage Tradition*, Blom, 1965.

Freedman, R., *Beauty Bound*, Columbus, 1988.

French, M., *Shakespeare's Division of Experience*, Jonathan Cape, 1982.

Freud, S., *The Standard Edition*, edited by J. Strachey, Hogarth Press, 1953–74.

Fuss, D., *Essentially Speaking: Feminism, Nature and Difference*, Routledge, 1989.

Gair, R., *The Children of Paul's*, Cambridge University Press, 1982.

Gamman, L., and M. Marshmen (eds.), *The Female Gaze*, The Women's Press, 1988.

Garber, M., 'The Logic of the Transvestite', in Kastan and Stalleybrass (eds.), *Staging the Renaissance*.

    Vested Interests, Routledge, 1992.

Garner, S. N., '"Let Her Paint an Inch Thick": Painted Ladies in Renaissance Drama and Society', *Renaissance Drama*, 20, 1989.

Gay, P., *As She Likes It: Shakespeare's Unruly Women*, Routledge, 1994.

George, D., 'Pre-1642 Cast Lists and a New One for *The Maid's Tragedy*', *Theatre Notebook*, 31, 3, 1977.

Gibson, J. L., *Squeaking Cleopatras: The Elizabethan Boy Player*, Sutton, 2002.

Gilder, R., *Enter the Actress: The First Women in the Theatre*, Theatre Art Books, 1931.

Gohlke, M., '"I Wooed Thee with my Sword": Shakespeare's Tragic Paradigms', in Lenz (ed.), *Woman's Part*.

Goldberg, J., *James I and the Politics of Literature*, Johns Hopkins University Press, 1983.

    'Sodomy and Society: the Case of Christopher Marlowe', *Southwest Review*, 69, 1984.

Goldman, M., *The Actor's Freedom*, Viking, 1975.

Goodlad, J. S. R., *A Sociology of Popular Drama*, Heinemann, 1971.

Goodman, L., 'Women's Alternative Shakespeares and Women's Alternatives to Shakespeare in Contemporary British Theatre' (1993), in Chedgzoy (ed.), *Shakespeare, Feminism and Gender*.

Gordon, R. K. (trans.), *Anglo-Saxon Poetry*, Dent, 1954.

Gorer, H., *The Revolutionary Ideas of the Marquis de Sade*, Wishart, 1934.

Gossett, S., ' "Best Men Are Moulded of Faults": Marrying the Rapist in Jacobean Drama', *English Literary Renaissance*, 14, 3, 1984.

Gottlieb, E., ' "I Will Be Free": Shakespeare's Ambivalence to Katherina's Challenge to the Great Chain of Being', in Sharma (ed.), *Essays on Shakespeare*.

Graves, T. S., 'Women on the Pre-Restoration Stage', *Studies in Philology*, 22, 1925.

Green, D. E., 'The "Unexpressive She": Is there really a Rosalind?', *Journal of Dramatic Theory and Criticism*, 1988, Spring, 2, 2.

Green, R., and J. Money, 'Stage Acting, Role-Taking, and Effeminate Impersonation During Boyhood', *Archives of general Psychiatry*, 15, 1966.

Greenblatt, S., *Shakespearean Negotiations: The Circulation of Social Energy in Renaissance England*, Oxford University Press, 1988.

Will in the World, Jonathan Cape, 2002.

Greene, G., 'Shakespeare's Cressida: "a Kind of Self" ', in Lenz (ed.), *Woman's Part*.

Lord Rochester's Monkey, Futura, 1976.

Greg, W. W., *Dramatic Documents from the Elizabethan Playhouses*, Oxford University Press, 1931.

Grote, D., *The Best Actors in the World: Shakespeare and his Acting Company*, Greenwood Press, 2002.

Grotowski, J., *Towards a Poor Theatre*, Methuen, 1969.

Gurr, A., *Playgoing in Shakespeare's London*, Cambridge University Press, 3rd edition, 2004.

The Shakespearian Playing Companies, Oxford University Press, 1996.

Halliday, F. E., *A Shakespeare Companion 1564–1964*, Penguin, 1964.

Hamer, M., 'Shakespeare, Rosalind, and her Public Image', *Theatre Research International*, 11, 1986.

Harbage, A., 'Elizabethan Acting', *PMLA*, 54, 1939.

Shakespeare and the Rival Traditions, Indiana University Press, 1952.

Annals of English Drama, 2nd edition, revised S. Schoenbaum, Methuen, 1966.

'Love's Labours Lost and the Early Shakespeare', in his *Shakespeare Without Words and Other Essays*, Harvard University Press, 1972.

Hartnoll, P., *A Concise History of Theatre*, Thames & Hudson, 1968.

Hawkes, T., *Meaning by Shakespeare*, Routledge, 1992.

Heilbrun, C., 'The Character of Hamlet's Mother', *Shakespeare Quarterly*, 8, 1957.

Towards a Recognition of Androgyny, Knopf, 1973.

Heinemann, M., *Puritanism and Theatre: Thomas Middleton and Opposition Drama under the Early Stuarts*, Cambridge University Press, 1980.

Helms, L., 'Roaring Girls and Silent Women: the Politics of Androgyny on the Elizabethan Stage', in Redmonds (ed.), *Women in Theatre*.

Review of C. Rutter (ed.), *Clamorous Voices: Shakespeare's Women Today*, in *Shakespeare Quarterly*, 1990, pp. 115–6.

Henn, T. E., *Harvest of Tragedy*, 2nd edition, Methuen, 1966.

Heywood, T., *Apology for Acting*, 1612.

Hill, J., '"What Are They Children?": Shakespeare's Tragic Women and the Boy Actors', *Studies in English Literature*, 1986, Spring, 26, 2.

Holderness, G. (ed.), *The Shakespearean Myth*, Manchester University Press, 1988.

Holland, N. N., *et al.* (eds.), *Shakespeare's Personality*, California University Press, 1989.

Holloway, D., *Playing the Empire*, Harrap, 1979.

Honan, P., *Shakespeare: A Life*, Oxford University Press, 1998.

Honigmann, E. A. J., *Shakespeare: Seven Tragedies*, Macmillan, 1976.
Shakespeare the Lost Years, Manchester University Press, 1985.

Hooper, W., 'The Tudor Sumptuary Laws', *English Historical Review*, 30, 1915.

Hoover, C., 'Goneril and Regan: "So horrid as in Woman"', *San Jose Studies*, 10, 3, 1984.

Hosely, R., 'Was there a "Dramatic" Epilogue to *The Taming of the Shrew?*, *Studies in English Literature*, i 1, 2, 1961.

Howard, J. E., 'Crossdressing, the Theatre, and Gender Struggle in Early Modern England', *Shakespeare Quarterly*, 39, 1988.
The Stage and Social Struggle in Early Modern England, Routledge, 1994.

Howard, S., 'A Re-Examination of Baldwin's Theory of Acting Lines', *Theatre Survey*, 26, 1, 1985.

Howe, E., *The First English Actresses*, Cambridge University Press, 1992.

Hwang, D., *M. Butterfly*, Penguin, 1986.

Hyland, P., 'Shakespeare's Heroines: Disguise in the Romantic Comedies', *Ariel*, 9, 1978.
'A Kind-of-Woman: the Elizabethan Boy-Actor and the Kabuki Onnagata', *Theatre Research International*, 12, 1, 1987.

Ingram, A., *'In the Posture of a Whore': Changing Attitudes to 'Bad' Women in Elizabethan and Jacobean Drama*, Salzburg University Press, 1984.

Jacobs, M., *Nude Painting*, Phaidon, 1979.

Jamieson, A., *Shakespeare's Heroines: Characteristics of Women: Moral, Poetical, and Historical* (1832), 2nd edition, Bell, 1913.

Jamieson, M., 'Shakespeare's Celibate Stage', in Bentley (ed.), *Seventeenth Century Stage*.

Jardine, L., *Still Harping on Daughters: Women and Drama in the Age of Shakespeare*, Harvester Wheatsheaf, 1983.
'"Girl Talk" (for Boys on the Left) or Marginalizing Feminist Critical Praxis', *Oxford Literary Review*, 9, 1986.
'Twins and Travesties: Gender, Dependency and Sexual Availability in *Twelfth Night*', in Zimmerman (ed.), *Erotic Politics*.

Jensen, E. J., 'The Boy Actors: Plays and Playing', *Research Opportunities in Renaissance Drama*, 18, 1975.

Jerome, J. K., *On Stage and Off (1884)*, Sutton, 1991.

Johnson, E. and E., *The Dickens Theatrical Reader*, Victor Gollancz, 1964.

Johnson, M., *Images of Women in the Works of Thomas Heywood*, Salzburg University Press, 1974.

Jones, D., and P. Gerhardt, *Una Stravaganza dei Medici*, 1990.

Kahn, C., 'The Rape of Shakespeare's "Lucrece"', *Shakespeare Studies*, 9, 1976.
Man's Estate: Masculine Identity in Shakespeare, California University Press, 1981.
'Coming of Age in Verona', in Lenz (ed.), *Woman's Part*.
Kaplan, E. A., 'Is the Gaze Male?', in Snitow (ed.), *Desire*.
Karney, R. (ed.), *Cinema Year by Year 1894–2003*, Dorling Kindersley, 2003.
Kastan, D. S., 'Proud Majesty Made Subject: Shakespeare and the Spectacle of Rule', *Shakespeare Quarterly*, 37, 4, 1986.
Kastan, D. S., and P. Stalleybrass (eds.), *Staging the Renaissance*, Routledge, 1991.
Kathman, D., 'Grocers, Goldsmiths, and Drapers: Freemen and Apprentices in the Elizabethan Theatre', *Shakespeare Quarterly*, 55, 1 2004.
'How Old Were Shakespeare's Boy Actors?', *Shakespeare Survey 59*, 2005.
Kelly, J., 'Early Feminist Theory and the Querelle des Femmes, 1400–1789', *Signs*, 8, 1, 1982.
Kernodle, G. R., 'The Mannerist Stage of Comic Detachment', in F. Galloway (ed.), *The Elizabethan Theatre III*, Macmillan, 1973.
Kimbrough, R., 'Androgyny Seen Through Shakespeare's Disguise', *Shakespeare Quarterly*, 33, 1982.
Kinney, A. F., *A Companion to Renaissance Drama*, Blackwell (2002), 2004.
Klein, D., 'Did Shakespeare Produce his own Plays?', *Modern Language Review*, 57, 1962.
Klein, J. L., ' "Lady Macbeth: Infirm of Purpose" ', in Lenz (ed.), *Woman's Part*.
Knight, G. W., *Wheel of Fire*, Methuen, revised edition 1949.
Kott, J., *Shakespeare Our Contemporary*, 2nd edition, Methuen, 1967.
'The Gender of Rosalind', *New Theatre Quarterly*, 26, 1990.
Lancashire, A., review of S. S. Waggonheim, third edition of the *Annals of English Drama*, in *Shakespeare Quarterly*, 42, 2, 1991.
Larner, C., *Enemies of God: The Witch-hunt in Scotland*, Blackwell, 1981.
Laslett, P., *The World We Have Lost*, Methuen, 2nd edition, 1971.
Laver, J., *Modesty in Dress*, Heinemann, 1969.
Leishman, J. B., *The Three Parnassus Plays*, Nicholson and Watson, 1949.
Lennam, T., *Sebastian Westcott, the Children of Paul's and 'The Marriage of Wit and Wisdom'*, Toronto University Press, 1975.
Lenz, C., *et al.* (eds.), *The Woman's Part: Feminist Criticism of Shakespeare*, Illinois University Press, 1983.
Leventon C., 'Patrimony and Patriarchy in *The Merchant of Venice*', in Wayne (ed.), *Matter of Difference*.
Levin, R., *New Readings vs. Old Plays*, Chicago University Press, 1979.
'The New Refutation of Shakespeare', *Modern Philology*, 83, 2, 1985.
'Feminist Thematics and Shakespearean Tragedy', *PMLA*, 1988.
'Women in the Renaissance Theatre Audience', *Shakespeare Quarterly*, 40, 1989.
'The Poetics of Bardicide', *PMLA*, 105, 1990.
Levin, R. (ed.), *Michaelmas Term*, Arnold, 1966.
Levine, L., 'Men in Women's Clothing: Anti-theatricality and Effeminisation from 1597 to 1642', *Criticisms*, 28, 1986.
Limon, J., *Gentlemen of a Company*, Cambridge University Press, 1985.

Lloyd-Evans, G.,'Shakespeare, Seneca, and the Kingdom of Violence', in Dudley and Dorey (eds.), *Roman Drama*, London, 1965.

Lommel, A., *Masks: Their Meaning and Function*, Ferndale, 1981.

MacDonald, J. G., 'Marlowe's Ganymede', in Comesoli and Russell (eds.), *Enacting Gender*.

McKewin, C., 'Shakespeare Liberata: *Shakespeare and the Nature of Women* and the New Feminist Criticism', *Mosaic*, 10, 3, 1977.

'Counsels of Gall and Grace: Intimate Conversations between Women in Shakespeare's Plays', in Lenz (ed.), *Woman's Part*.

McLuskie, K., 'The Patriarchal Bard: Feminist Criticism and Shakespeare: *King Lear* and *Measure for Measure*' (1985), reprinted in Chedgzoy (ed.), *Shakespeare, Feminism and Gender*.

'The Act, the Role, and the Actor: Boy Actresses on the Elizabethan Stage', *New Theatre Quarterly*, 3, 1987.

'"The Emperor of Russia Was My Father": Gender and Theatrical Power', in W. Habicht, *et al.* (eds.), *Images of Shakespeare*, Delaware University Press, 1988.

Renaissance Dramatists, Harvester Wheatsheaf, 1989.

'"Lawless Desires Well-tempered"', in Zimmerman (ed.), *Erotic Politics*.

McManus, C., *Women on the Renaissance Stage: Anna of Denmark and Female Masquing in the Stuart Court 1590–1619*, Manchester University Press, 2002.

McMillin, S., *The Elizabethan Theatre and 'The Book of Sir Thomas More'*, Cornell University Press, 1987.

Maitland, S., *Vesta Tilley*, Virago Press, 1986.

Mann, D. A., *The Elizabethan Player: Contemporary Stage Representations*, Routledge, 1991.

'The Roman Mime and Medieval Theatre', *Theatre Notebook*, 46, 1992.

Manvell, R., *Shakespeare and the Film*, A. S. Barnes, 1979.

Masters, W., and V. E. Johnson, *Sex and Human Loving*, Little, Brown, 1986.

Maus, K. E., 'Horns of a Dilemma: Jealousy, Gender and Spectatorship in English Renaissance Drama', *ELH*, 54, 1987.

Mayer, D., 'Towards a Definition of Popular Theatre', in D. Mayer and K. Richards (eds.), *Western Popular Theatre*, Methuen, 1977.

Miller, G., *Odd Jobs: The World of Deviant Work*, Prentice Hall, 1978.

Moodie, T. D. *et al.*, 'Migrancy and Male Sexuality in the South African Gold Mines', in Duberman (ed.), *Hidden From History*.

Mowat, B. A., 'Images of Women in Shakespeare's Plays', *Southern Humanities Review*, 11, 1977.

Muir, K., 'Male as Female on the Elizabethan Stage', in Sharma (ed.), *Essays on Shakespeare*.

Muir, K., and P. Edwards (eds.), *Aspects of Othello*, Cambridge University Press, 1977.

Mulvey, L., 'Visual Pleasures and the Narrative Cinema', *Screen*, Autumn 1975, 16, 3.

Nagler, A. M., *A Sourcebook in Theatrical History*, Dover, 1952.

Neely, C. T., 'Men and Women in *Othello*: "What Should a Fool/ Do with so Good a Woman?",' in Lenz (ed.), *Woman's Part*.

'Shakespeare's Women: Historical Facts and Dramatic Representations', in Holland *et al.* (eds.), *Shakespeare's Personality*.

Nichols, J., *The Progresses, Processions, and Magnificent Festivities of James I*, 1828.

Novy, M., 'Patriarchy and Play in *The Taming of the Shrew*', *English Literary Renaissance*, 9, 1979.

Novy, M. L., *Love's Argument: Gender Relations in Shakespeare*, North Carolina University Press, 1984.

Nungezer, E., *A Dictionary of Actors*, repr. Greenwood Press, 1968.

Ogburn, D. and C., *Shakespeare: The Man Behind the Name*, Morrow, 1962.

Oliver, H. J. (ed.) *The Taming of the Shrew*, Oxford University Press, 1984.

Onions, C. T., *A Shakespeare Glossary*, Oxford University Press, 2nd edition, 1958.

Opland, J., *Anglo-Saxon Oral Poetry: A Study of Traditions*, Yale University Press, 1980.

Orgel, S., *The Illusion of Power*, California University Press, 1975.

'Nobody's Perfect: or Why Did the English Stage Take Boys for Women?', *South Atlantic Quarterly*, 88, 1, Winter 1989.

Impersonations: The Performance of Gender in Shakespeare's England, Cambridge University Press, 1996.

Orgel, S., and R. Strong, *Inigo Jones: The Theatre of the Stuart Court*, California University Press, 1973.

Paglia, C., *Sexual Personae: Art and Decadence from Nefertiti to Emily Dickinson*, Penguin, 1991.

Park, C. C., 'As We Like It: How a Girl Can be Smart and Still Popular', *American Scholar*, 42, 1973.

Pearson, J., *The Prostituted Muse: Images of Women Dramatists 1642–1737*, St Martin's Press, 1988.

Penniman, J. H., *The War of the Theatre*, Ginn, 1879.

Plato, *The Symposium*, trans. W. Hamilton, Penguin, 1951.

Phaedrus, trans. W. Hamilton, Penguin, 1973.

Laws, trans. T. J. Saunders, Penguin, 1975.

Porter, R., 'Rape – Does it have a Historical Meaning?', in Tomaselli and Porter (eds.), *Rape*.

Prunierres, H., *Le Ballet de Cour en France avant Benserade et Lully*, Laurens, 1914.

Rackin, P., 'Shakespeare's Boy Cleopatra, the Decorum of Nature, and the Golden World of Poetry', *PMLA*, 87, 1972.

'Anti-Historians: Women's Roles in Shakespeare's History Plays', *Theatre Journal*, 37, 3, 1985.

'Androgyny, Mimesis, and the Marriage of the Boy Heroine on the English Renaissance Stage', *PMLA*, 102, 1987.

Radford, C., 'Medieval Actresses', *Theatre Notebook*, 7, 1953.

Raleigh, W., (ed.), *Johnson on Shakespeare*, Oxford University Press, 1925.

Ranald, M. L., 'The Manning of the Haggard: or *The Taming of the Shrew*', *Essays in Literature*, 1, 1974.

Redmonds, J. (ed.), *Women in Theatre*, Cambridge University Press, 1989.

Rich, A., 'Compulsory Heterosexuality and Lesbian Existence', in Snitow (ed.), *Desire.*

Richmond, H. M., *Shakespeare's Sexual Comedy*, Bobbs-Merrill, 1971.

Shakespeare's Theatre, Continuum (2002), 2004.

Ridley, M. R. (ed.), *Othello*, Arden Shakespeare, Methuen, 1958.

Ringler Snr, W., 'The First Phase of the Elizabethan Attack on the Stage, 1558–1579', *Huntington Library Quarterly*, 4, July 1942.

Ringler, Jr, W. A., 'The Number of Actors in Shakespeare's Early Plays', in Bentley (ed.), *Seventeenth Century Stage.*

Riviere, J., 'Womanliness as Masquerade', *International Journal of Psychoanalysis*, vol. 10, 1929.

Rodowick, D. N., *The Difficulty of Difference: Psychoanalysis, Sexual Difference, and Film Theory*, Routledge, 1991.

Rogers, K., *The Troublesome Helpmate: A History of Misogyny in Literature*, Washington University Press, 1966.

Rose, M. B., 'Where Are the Mothers in Shakespeare? Options for Gender Representation in the English Renaissance', *Shakespeare Quarterly*, 42, 1991.

Rosenberg, M., 'Elizabethan Actors: Men or Marionettes?' in Bentley (ed.), *Seventeenth Century Stage.*

Rubin, P., *Everything You Need to Know About Shakespeare*, David and Charles, 2004.

Rutter, C. C., *Documents of the Rose Playhouse*, Manchester University Press, 1984.

Enter the Body: Women and Representation on the Shakespearian Stage, Routledge, 2001.

'Learning Thisbe's Part – or – what's Hecuba to him?', *Shakespeare Bulletin*, 22, 3, Fall, 2004.

Rutter, C. C., (ed.), *Clamorous Voices: Shakespeare's Women Today*, The Women's Press, 1988.

Saslow, J. M., 'Homosexuality in the Renaissance: Behaviour, Identity, and Artistic Expression', in Duberman (ed.), *Hidden From History.*

Salgado, G., *The Elizabethan Underworld*, Alan Sutton, 1984.

Salgado, G. (ed.), *Eyewitnesses of Shakespeare*, Sussex University Press, 1975.

San Francisco Lesbian and Gay History Project, reported in '"She Even Chewed Tobacco": A Pictorial Narrative of Passing Women in America' in Duberman (ed.), *Hidden From History.*

Schoenbaum, S., *William Shakespeare, a Compact Documentary Life*, Oxford University Press, 1977, revised 1987.

Shakespeare's Lives, Oxford University Press, revised edition 1993.

Schroeder, P., 'Hroswitha and the Feminisation of Drama', in Redmonds (ed.), *Women in Theatre.*

Shakespeare, W., *As You Like It*, ed. H. Oliver (New Penguin Shakespeare, 1968), Penguin, 1996.

Shapiro, M., *Children of the Revels*, Columbia University Press, 1977.

'Boying Her Greatness: Shakespeare's Use of Coterie Drama in *Antony and Cleopatra*', *Modern Language Review*, 77, 1982.

Gender in Play on the Shakespearean Stage: Boy Heroines and Female Pages, Michigan UP, 1994.

'The Introduction of Actresses in England: Delay or Defensiveness', in Comesoli and Russell (eds.), *Enacting Gender*.

Sharma, T. R. (ed.), *Essays on Shakespeare in Honour of A. A. Ansari*, Shalabh Book House, 1986.

Shepherd, S., *Marlowe and the Politics of Theatre*, Harvester, 1989.

Silverman, K., 'Masochism and Subjectivity', *Framework*, 12, 1981.

Simonson, L., *The Stage is Set*, Theatre Arts Books, 1963.

Sinfield, A., 'How to Read *The Merchant of Venice* without Being Heterosexist' (1996) in Chedgzoy (ed.), *Shakespeare, Feminism and Gender*.

Small, R. A., *The Stage Quarrel between Ben Jonson and the So-called Poetasters*, 1899.

Smith, J., *Misogynies*, Faber, 1989.

Smith, R., 'A Heart Cleft in Twain: the Dilemma of Shakespeare's Gertrude', in Lenz (ed.), *Woman's Part*.

Smith, S. R., 'The London Apprentices as Seventeenth Century Adolescents', *Past and Present*, 61, 1973.

Smith, W., *The Commedia dell' arte*, Lancaster Press, 1912.

Snitow, A. (ed.), *Desire: The Politics of Sexuality*, Virago, 1984.

Snow, E. A., 'Sexual Anxiety and the Male Order of Things in *Othello*', *English Literary Renaissance*, 10, 1980.

Soule, L. A., 'Subversive Rosalind: Cocky Ros in the Forest of Arden', *New Theatre Quarterly*, 26, 1990.

Southworth, J., *Shakespeare, The Player: A Life in the Theatre*, Sutton, 2000.

Speaight, R., *Shakespeare on the Stage*, Collins, 1973.

Spencer, T. J. B., and S. Wells (eds.) *A Book of Masques*, Cambridge University Press, 1967.

Sprengnether, M., 'The Boy Actor and Femininity in *Antony and Cleopatra*', in Holland *et al.* (eds.), *Shakespeare's Personality*.

Stalleybrass, P., 'Transvestitism and the "Body Beneath": Speculating on the Boy Actor', in Zimmerman (ed.), *Erotic Politics*.

Sternfeld, T. W., *Music in Shakespeare's Tragedies*, Routledge (1963), 2005.

Stimpson, C. R., 'Shakespeare and the Soil of Rape', in Lenz (ed.), *Woman's Part*.

Stoller, R., *Observing the Erotic Imagination*, Yale University Press, 1985.

Stone, L., *Family, Sex, and Marriage in England*, Harper and Row, 1977.

Styan, J. K., 'Changeable Taffeta: Shakespeare's Characters in Performance', in P. C. McGuire and D. A. Samuelson (eds.), *Shakespeare: The Theatrical Dimension*, AMS, 1979.

Tavris, C., and C. Offir, *The Longest War: Sex Differences in Perspective*, Harcourt Brace, 1977.

Taylor, G., *Reinventing Shakespeare: A Cultural History from the Restoration to the Present*, Hogarth Press, 1989.

Taylor, J. R., *Anger and After*, Penguin, 1965.

Thompson, A., Review of C. Novy, *Love's Argument*, '"Who Is't Can Read a Woman?"', *English*, Autumn, 1985.

'The Warrant of Womanhood: Shakespeare and Feminist Criticism', in Holderness (ed.), *Shakespearean Myth*.

'Are there any Women in *King Lear?*', in Wayne (ed.), *Matter of Difference*.

'Feminist Theory and the Editing of Shakepeare: *The Taming of the Shrew* Revisited' 1997 in Chedgzoy (ed.), *Shakespeare, Feminism and Gender*.

Thomson, P., *Shakespeare's Professional Career*, Cambridge University Press, 1992.

Tiffany, G., *Erotic Beasts and Social Monsters: Shakespeare, Jonson, and Comic Androgyny*, Delaware University Press, 1995.

Titterton, W. R., *From Theatre to Music Hall*, Swift, 1912.

Tomaselli, S., and R. Porter (eds.), *Rape, an Historical and Cultural Enquiry*, Blackwell, 1986.

Traub, V., 'Jewels, Statues, and Corpses: Containment of Female Erotic Power', *Shakespeare Studies*, 20, 1988.

Desire and Anxiety: Circulations of Sexuality in Shakespearean Drama, Routledge, 1992.

'The (In)significance of "Lesbian" Desire in early Modern England', in Zimmerman (ed.), *Erotic Politics*.

Trumbach, R., 'The Birth of the Queen: Sodomy and the Emergence of Gender Equality in Modern Culture, 1660–1750', in Duberman *et al.*, (eds.), *Hidden From History*.

Tydeman, W., *The Theatre in the Middle Ages*, Cambridge University Press, 1978.

Tynan, K., *Tynan on Theatre*, Penguin, 1964.

Waage, F. D., 'Meg and Moll: Two Renaissance London Heroines', *Journal of Popular Culture*, 20, 1, 1986.

Wandor, M., *Carry On Understudies: Theatre and Sexual Politics*, Routledge Kegan Paul, 1981.

Warrington, J., *Everyman's Classical Dictionary*, Dent, 1969.

Wasson, J., 'Elizabethan and Jacobean Touring Companies', *Theatre Notebook*, 42, 2, 1988.

Wayne, V., *The Matter of Difference: Materialist Feminist Criticism of Shakespeare*, Harvester Wheatsheaf, 1991.

Webster, J., *The Duchess of Malfi*, ed. E. Brennan (New Mermaids), A. and C. Black, 1967.

Weimann, R., *Shakespeare and the Popular Tradition*, Johns Hopkins University Press, 1978.

Werner, S., *Shakespeare and Feminist Performance: Ideology on Stage*, Routledge, 2001.

West, M., 'Folk Background to Petruchio's Wedding Dance', *Shakespeare Studies*, 7, 1974.

Wickham, G., *The Medieval Theatre*, Weidenfeld and Nicholson, 1974.

Wiles, D., *Shakespeare's Clowns*, Cambridge University Press, 1987.

Williams, R., *Drama in Performance*, Penguin, 1972.

Willis, E., 'Feminism, Moralism, and Pornography', in Snitow (ed.), *Desire*.

Wilson, E., *Adorned in Dreams*, Virago, 1985.

Wilson, J. H., *Mr Goodman the Player*, Pittsburgh University Press, 1964.

Winter, C., *Elizabethan Miniatures, Penguin*, 1943.

Woodbridge, L., *Women and the English Renaissance: Literature and the Nature of Womankind, 1540–1610*, Illinois University Press, 1984.

Woodhouse, A., *Fantastic Women: Sex, Gender, and Transvestitism*, Macmillan, 1989.

Woolf, V., *A Room of One's Own*, Harcourt Brace, Jovanovitch, 1929.
Books and Portraits, 1977.

Wright, J., *Historica Histrionica* (1642), in W. C. Hazlitt (ed.), *Dodsley's Old English Plays*, 4th edn, 1876, vol. XV.

Wynne-Davies, M., '"The Swallowing Womb": Consumed and Consuming Women in *Titus Andronicus*', in Wayne (ed.), *Matter of Difference*.

Xenophon's *Symposium*, trans. J. Welwood, in A. D. Lindsey (ed.), in *Plato and Xenophon: Socratic Dialogues*, Dent, 1954.

Zeitlin, F., 'Configurations of Rape in Greek Myth', in Tomaselli and Porter (eds.), *Rape*.

Zimmerman, S. (ed.), *Erotic Politics: Desire on the Renaissance Stage*, Routledge, 1992.

Index of adult repertory

Alchemist, The, 1610, Jonson (S. Musgrove (ed.), Oliver and Boyd, 1968), 87, 130, 164, 245, 265 n. 29

All for Money, 1577, Thomas Lupton (E. Vogel (ed.), *Jahrbuch de deutschen Shakespeare Gesellschaft,* XL, 129–86, 1904), 41, 241

All's Well that Ends Well, 1602, Shakespeare (Evans), 50, 125, 165, 209, 214, 221, 227, 244

Alphonsus, Emperor of Germany, 1594, George Peele? (Parrot), 31, 94, 189, 242

Alphonsus, King of Arragon, Robert Greene, 1587 (Collins), 208, 242, 262 n. 2

Antony and Cleopatra, 1607, Shakespeare (Evans), 6, 14, 17–18, 69, 74, 91, 102, 110, 118, 122, 123, 138, 221, 244

Arden of Faversham, Anon. 1591 (K. Sturgess (ed.), *Three Elizabethan Domestic Tragedies,* Penguin, 1969), 94, 181–3, 242

As You Like It, 1599, Shakespeare (Evans), 13, 16, 23, 24, 53, 54, 55, 69–72, 92, 93, 94, 117, 119–20, 123, 128, 129, 215, 224, 227, 235, 243

Atheist's Tragedy, The, 1609, Cyril Tourneur (J. C. Collins (ed.), Books for Libraries Press, 1878), 67, 144, 165, 169, 174, 245

Bartholomew Fair, 1614, Jonson (G. R. Hibbard (ed.), Benn, 1977), 43, 55, 129, 134, 173, 210, 245

Battle of Alcazar, 1589, Peele (Malone), 242, 262 n. 2

Birth of Merlin, The, 1608, William Rowley (Brooke), 135, 137, 155, 161, 188, 244

Blind Beggar of Alexandria, The, 1596, Chapman (Malone), 136, 155, 243, 262 n. 2

Blind Beggar of Bethnal Green, 1600, Henry Chettle and others (Bang), 100, 210

Bonduca, 1613, John Fletcher (Dyce), 138, 190, 245

Brazen Age, The, 1611, T. Heywood (Shepherd), 7–8, 53, 103, 160, 191, 245

Caesar and Pompey, 1605, Chapman (Parrot), 244, 265 n. 29

Cambises, 1561, Thomas Preston (T. W. Craik (ed.), *Minor Elizabethan Tragedies,* Dent, 1974), 7, 40, 42, 103, 122, 160, 190, 241

Captain, The, 1612, Fletcher (Dyce), 245

Captain Thomas Stukeley, 1596, Anon. (Shepherd), 187, 243, 262 n. 2

Catiline, 1611, Jonson (W. F. Bolton and J. F. Gardner (eds.), Arnold), 53, 170–1, 219, 245

Charlemagne, 1600, Anon. (Malone), 243

Chaste Maid in Cheapside, A, 1611, Middleton (A. Brissenden (ed.), Benn, 1968), 42–3, 109, 125, 134, 165, 171, 190, 245

Christian Turned Turk, A, 1610, Robert Daborne, (A. E. H. Swaen (ed.), *Anglia,* (1898–9), 219, 245, 262 n. 2

Clyomon and Clamydes, 1570, Anon. (Malone), 94, 232, 241

Cobbler's Prophecy, The, 1590, Robert Wilson (Malone), 144, 149, 186, 242

Comedy of Errors, The, 1592, Shakespeare (Evans), 21, 22, 44, 125, 137, 175, 242

Common Conditions, 1576, Anon. (C. F. T. Brooke (ed.), Yale Elizabethan Club Reprints, 1915), 241

Coriolanus, 1608, Shakespeare (Evans), 16, 46–7, 138, 244

Cymbeline, 1608, Shakespeare (Evans), 5, 8, 35–6, 73, 93–4, 100, 127, 144, 149, 157, 160, 199–203, 212, 215, 216, 225, 227, 244

David and Bethsabe, 1587, Peele (A. Thorndike (ed.), *Pre-Shakespearean Tragedies,* Dent, 1910), 50, 144, 149, 219, 242

Death of Robert Earl of Huntington, The, 1598, Henry Chettle and Antony Munday, (Dodsley), 142, 243

Devil and his Dame, The, 1600, William Haughton (Dodsley), 134–5, 180–1, 243

Devil's Charter, The, 1607, Barnaby Barnes (Bang), 67–8, 103, 136, 142, 244

General Index